BATTLEGROUND UKRAINE

BATTLEGROUND UKRAINE

From Independence to the War with Russia

ADRIAN KARATNYCKY

Yale
UNIVERSITY PRESS
New Haven and London

Yale University Press books may be purchased in quantity for educational, business, or promotional use. For information, please e-mail sales.press@yale.edu (U.S. office) or sales@yaleup.co.uk (U.K. office).

Set in Janson type by Integrated Publishing Solutions.
Printed in Great Britain by TJ Books Limited, Padstow, Cornwall

Library of Congress Control Number: 2023949848
ISBN 978-0-300-26946-8 (hardcover : alk. paper)

A catalogue record for this book is available from the British Library.

10 9 8 7 6 5 4 3 2 1

To Natalia, her daughters, and brother, and to all families who have built an independent Ukraine

Contents

Preface

A National Rebirth

Nations travel different trajectories to their consolidation. And the pathways to a fully formed nation take centuries. The journey of Ukraine and Ukrainians is therefore not unique. But modernity—with its widely accessible media, universal education, and ability to mobilize vast financial resources—can quickly reach all classes, ethnicities, regions, and localities, speeding up—or undoing—processes that in the past took centuries to congeal.

The trajectory taken by Ukraine and Ukrainians is of much greater importance than an academic discussion of the construction of nations. Today, amid Russia's brutal—indeed, genocidal—war, the emergence of a cohesive Ukrainian nation is a matter of life and death. It is a matter of a living history, which in the last three decades has seen the rapid revival of deeply rooted cultural, linguistic, and political processes historically disrupted by war and colonial rule. Ukraine's history since 1991 is a chronicle of how an ethnopolitically conscious nation, in concert with its emerging democratic state, revived and reconstructed its cultural, linguistic, and national unity after centuries of assimilation under the rule of the Russian Empire and the Soviet Union.

Ukraine, the modern-day state of a formerly stateless people, has been in existence for a little over three decades. The social, political, geopolitical, and cultural processes that led to a unified Ukrainian state and nation are today demonstrating their culmination in the resilience of a people under brutal attack by an enemy state four times their size. The personalities, processes, and forces that have shaped a people today displaying deep courage and endurance are the subject of this short history of the independent Ukrainian state that emerged in 1991.

When the USSR collapsed, most of Ukraine had been under Soviet totalitarian rule for seven decades. Western Ukraine—absorbed into the Soviet Union in stages between 1939 and 1945—remained under uninterrupted Soviet or Nazi totalitarian rule for over five decades. This terrible legacy of repression and enforced conformism was accompanied by the obliteration of much of Ukraine's culture, language, and history. This process created deep divisions within the Ukrainian nation, which was split between those who (often at the risk of their freedom) quietly but stubbornly preserved their culture, traditions, and memory, and those who succumbed to the pressures of Russification and Sovietization, losing their sense of national identity. When independence came in 1991, these fissures set off complex political, cultural, and social processes that over time led to the gradual emergence of a dominant Ukrainian civic and national identity. It is therefore hardly surprising that Ukrainians who had traditionally resisted a Russified cultural identity were also more likely to embrace a European course and the post-Communist values of democracy.

The attainment of statehood by Ukraine amid the dismantling of the Soviet Union endowed Ukrainians with a powerful instrument to undo the effects of centuries of colonial and imperial rule. But Ukraine's path to national unity did not occur in a straight line. Powerful forces—inside both Ukraine and Russia—were inimical to the shaping of a fully sovereign state based on a distinctly Ukrainian cultural and linguistic identity.

A unified Ukrainian people and a stable and ultimately capable state emerged from the interplay of powerful polarities. The first was the geopolitical and cultural pull between the democratic West and an increasingly authoritarian Russia. The second polarity was between civil society and an emerging entrepreneurial class on the one hand and a powerful array of rent-seeking oligarchs with significant lobbies inside the state on the other. These opposites stymied the pace of reform and national consolidation even as they ensured that the country preserved a high degree of pluralism, personal liberty, and political freedom. As important, Ukrainian unity was also the result of three decades of battle waged between Russia's cultural, economic, political, and military power and the Ukrainian state and its ethnically conscious population over the hearts and minds of Russian-speaking Ukrainian citizens who possessed a vague sense of their national identity.

This book's chapters focus on the six presidencies (with a discussion of an "acting president" in 2014) since Ukraine's independence. There is one chapter for each president, with two devoted to Volodymyr Zelensky's presidency—the first under hybrid, low-intensity Russian attack; the second during Russia's full-scale war. An eighth chapter looks at the future of Ukraine. This organizing principle is well justified as Ukraine's presidents have exerted deep influence over the state and often represented the social trends of their time. Ukraine's presidents have wielded significant influence through substantial constitutional powers and frequent success in shaping ruling majorities. In office, they have been a powerful—if not always dominant—force shaping domestic and foreign policy.

Modern Ukraine has never been an ordered top-down polity—an autocracy in which a small elite holds power. Nor has Ukraine's fate been driven primarily by the public square, despite a rich tradition of mass mobilizations. Instead, Ukraine is what sociologists call a heterarchy, a society in which no institution or force has predominant influence and in which there is no set hierarchy of power. Rather, power ebbs and flows among stakeholders in a complex interplay between various ethnic, economic, social, and political groupings and forces.

This permanent competition among domestic and external forces has prevented the consolidation of authoritarian power and preserve democratic pluralism. The resulting freedoms are one key reason Ukrainians have fought so committedly against the onslaught from authoritarian Russia.

In the pages that follow, readers will encounter a diverse array of reputable and disreputable political, civic, business, and external actors whose contestation and cooperation have shaped a democratic Ukrainian state and led to the emergence of a unified nation. Ukraine's internal freedoms and its ethno-national identity are the two factors that have anchored Ukraine in a fight for its very existence—a struggle many Ukrainians see as their War of Independence. To be sure, until Russia's all-out war, Ukraine's version of the "founding fathers" measured up miserably to their American counterparts. Most of Ukraine's early leaders lacked the public-spiritedness and high purpose necessary for building a new state. Ukraine's early leaders were bland bureaucrats, "red directors," and ex-Communist officials. And yet, Ukraine's own founding has seen several figures whom history will judge kindly and around whom legends will form. These leaders will most certainly include Vyacheslav Chornovil, the head of the civic movement for independence; Crimean Tatar leader Mustafa Dzhemilev; and, more recently, General Valeriy Zaluzhny, who leads Ukraine's armed forces in the war with Russia; and President Volodymyr Zelensky, who has grown in stature as a wartime leader. A place, accompanied by caveats, also belongs to Viktor Yushchenko, whose trailblazing championing of Ukrainian culture, arts, and history had an important impact in developing a new generation of patriots; and Petro Poroshenko, who, despite many mistakes, ably represented Ukraine on the global state and built a capable military that evolved into the impressive fighting force of 2022–23.

After independence, Ukraine was largely on the back burner of world media attention. Most Western newspapers and news channels relied on stringers for information, and did not have full-fledged offices in the country, parachuting in only amid crisis. Coverage swelled around three pivotal events: the Orange Revolution of 2004, whose months-long winter protests demonstrated the commitment of Ukrainians to democracy; the Maidan Revolution of 2014, which unseated an authoritarian president; and Russia's military attacks on Ukraine in 2014, which led to thirteen thousand deaths in the Donbas and were a precursor to the far more deadly war that began on February 24, 2022.

In the main, however, international media paid little attention to Ukraine's internal development. Instead, corruption, political crises, oligarchs, the trope of a deep ethnic divide between a "Ukrainian" west and a "Russian" east, and an obsessive focus on fringe far-right political movements were the fodder of intermittent and superficial reporting—often by Moscow-based reporters and journalists who occasionally swept in to cover the latest crisis. As a result, Ukraine's emergence from Communist statism, the rise of a dynamic entrepreneurial sector, achievements in high technology, Ukraine's culture of ethnic and religious tolerance, its increasingly sophisticated civil society, the strengthening of Ukraine's national identity, and Ukrainians' persistent attachment to democracy were given short shrift.

Academic scholarship is the one arena in which Ukraine has consistently received detailed and informed attention. Political and social scientists as well as historians have been drawn to Ukraine because its politics are transparent, its officials frequently leak information, its media are diverse, its investigative reporters are relentless, and its libraries and archives are user-friendly—including Soviet-era archives that are off-limits in most post-Soviet states.

Despite the important work of scholars, in the wider Western public imagination, Ukraine has remained a stereotype: a den of corruption and a failing, if not failed, state riven by poverty and dominated by oligarchs. Its language is misunderstood to be a close relative of Russian (in fact, Ukrainian is closer to Polish and Belarusian). It is widely believed that Ukraine's history and culture were shaped primarily by association with Russia. There is little knowledge of Europe's influence on the country: much of Ukraine spent centuries as part of the Lithuanian Commonwealth, Poland, and Austro-Hungary. In the first years of independence, the belief that Ukraine was part of Russia was something diasporic Ukrainians as well as Ukrainian visitors heard frequently in the United States and Europe. If anything, Ukraine was seen by many as an accidental nation, created mainly because the USSR had fractured along the boundaries of its republics.

The persistence of these misapprehensions led to surprise at Ukraine's courageous, effective, and unified resistance to an invasion by a country believed to be a military superpower. Ukraine's story is marked by the remarkable rise of a cohesive and resilient state whose society is determined to fight to preserve its nation, culture, and sovereign democracy.

Battleground Ukraine is the product of my thirty-five-year relationship with Ukraine and its wide array of political, business, civic, and cultural leaders. That engagement has led me cumulatively to spend years visiting and living in that country and observing at close hand most of the pivotal events described and analyzed herein. This book is the fruit of interactions over the decades with the women and men who have played a key role in the evolution of the modern Ukrainian state and society.

Over the period 1989 until the present day, I have cumulatively spent more than four years of my life in Kyiv or traveling within Ukraine. My direct observations, augmented by reliable news sources, eyewitness accounts, interviews, and readings, have given me what I hope readers will find are helpful insights into the processes and forces that shaped contemporary Ukraine, a nation that has emerged as a united force at a time of great peril issuing from Russia's invasion.

In the 1970s and 1980s, I worked with Ukrainian and other political prisoners through the Committee for the Defense of Soviet Political Prisoners. This led me into a close association with such leading Ukrainian and Russian human rights defenders as General Petro Hryhorenko, Leonid Plyushch, Vladimir Bukovsky, Ludmilla Alexeyeva, Elena Bonner, and the family of Andrei Sakharov. In the 1980s, working at the U.S. labor federation, the AFL-CIO, I was engaged in providing material assistance to Poland's Solidarity movement and later to its underground structures after martial law was imposed. My trade union work also connected me to the freedom movements in Hungary, Czechoslovakia, Romania, Bulgaria, and the miners' movement of the disintegrating USSR.

With my then wife, the late Nadia Diuk, who played an important role in supporting democratic forces in Ukraine as vice president of the National Endowment for Democracy, I coauthored two books. One, *The Hidden Nations: The People Challenge the Soviet Union* (1990), told the story of the rise of national movements throughout the USSR and their struggle for ethno-political rights and independence. The other, *New Nations Rising* (1993) took the story through the disintegration of the Soviet Union to the emergence of fifteen independent post-Soviet states.

While writing these books, I traveled throughout Ukraine as dissidents and cultural activists organized small gatherings and protests that involved thousands in what would become a mass movement pressing for national sovereignty that eventually engaged millions of citizens. I observed the founding conferences of the People's Movement of Ukraine (Rukh), on which I reported for the *New Re-*

public and about which I wrote, if a trifle too optimistically, for *Foreign Affairs*. At that time, my work led me to meet most of Ukraine's leading democratic and cultural activists and student leaders as they pressed for state independence. Among them was Ihor Hryniv, who became lifelong friend and one of Ukraine's leading campaign strategists, helping to elect Presidents Viktor Yushchenko and Petro Poroshenko, and nearly succeeding in electing Yulia Tymoshenko. Hryniv's clarity of thought and keen analytic skills grounded in sociological data have been important to my understanding of Ukraine's politics and society.

My encounters with Ukraine deepened as part of efforts to support an emerging miners' and free trade union movement in the late 1980s. On my frequent trips to Ukraine, I developed a friendship with Rukh leader Vyacheslav Chornovil, who emerged as the most important political leader of the country's independence movement. I met a broad range of remarkable moral leaders and visionaries, including former political prisoner Mykola Horyn, the writers Yevhen Sverstyuk and Ihor and Iryna Kalynets, theater director Les Tanyuk and his actress wife Nelli Kornienko, and a new generation of independent journalists, including Oleksandr Kryvenko, Serhiy Naboka, and Vitaliy Portnykov.

Leaving the AFL-CIO in 1994, I spent over a decade as president of Freedom House, an international monitor of political rights and civil liberties, where I supervised a portfolio of programs supporting and financing civil society in Ukraine. This work led me to engage with Ukraine's first post-Communist think tanks, the most important of which were the Ukrainian Center for Independent Political Research and the Democratic Initiatives Foundation, headed by Ilko Kucheriv, which, with our initial assistance, pioneered independent polling after the fall of Communism.

Work at Freedom House offered opportunities to frequently visit Ukraine as well as to host many of Ukraine's civic, political, and government officials on their U.S. visits. Under my tenure Freedom House became a venue for discussions with Ukrainian civil society leaders, journalists, and politicians. My offices in New York City and Washington, DC, were also visited by many of Ukraine's top officials, including then presidential hopeful Leonid Kuchma, future prime minister Yevhen Marchuk, the notorious former prime minister Pavlo Lazarenko, and former prime minister Yulia Tymoshenko.

At Freedom House and the Atlantic Council, I had the opportunity to organize meetings with Ukraine's presidents, including Leonid Kuchma (before the Gongadze murder), Viktor Yushchenko, Viktor Yanukovych, and Petro Poroshenko. I cultivated relationships with many of the chiefs of staff of Ukraine's chief executives, seeing in them important sources of information about the country's inner workings and priorities as well as with countless prime ministers, ministers, and national security and intelligence officials.

After Freedom House, my engagement with Ukraine intensified when I launched the Orange Circle, an international network of friends of Ukraine that sought to build support for Ukraine in the aftermath of the Orange Revolution. Early in the Yushchenko presidency, well before our effort could gain serious traction, it became clear to me that the country's democratic forces were riven by internal rivalries, dissension, and blind ambition, which crippled reform and opened the door to revanchism.

In 2007 I proposed to Fred Kempe, the new CEO of the Atlantic Council, that the think tank launch a Ukraine program. With the support and encouragement of Fran Burwell and Fred, the initiative would grow into the largest Ukraine think tank program in North America. With Ambassador John Herbst at the helm, the Ukraine program today has a robust budget, a core team of in-house experts, and more than a dozen nonresident fellows. It publishes an important daily analytic overview of developments in Ukraine, organizes conferences and panels, issues in-depth research reports, hosts Ukrainian and world leaders to discuss the challenges facing the country, and is a beacon of clearheaded thinking about Ukraine and Russia. In early 2021, I took an eighteen-month leave from the Atlantic Council to serve as an advisor to Ukraine's state company Naftogaz as part of an effort to stop the Nordstream 2 pipeline, returning to the council in the early stages of Russia's war.

In the mid-2000s, along with several Jewish and Ukrainian diaspora leaders, I joined in founding the Ukrainian Jewish Encounter (UJE), a Canada-based organization devoted to dialogue between the two communities. The UJE supports research, publishes books, organizes cultural events and conferences, and promotes research and discussions on the Shoah in Ukraine and on Ukraine-Israeli relations. Work on this project has deepened my understanding of minority and religious rights in Ukraine.

All these assignations have given me firsthand perspectives on Ukraine's evolution and have helped me build a wide network of relationships and sources invaluable in the preparation of this book. For the first twenty-five years after independence, my time spent in Ukraine consisted of multiple annual visits, most lasting ten to fourteen days. In 2016 I took up part-time residence in Ukraine, spending months at a time there. Eventually, I remarried and became part of a Ukrainian family with roots in the defense and preservation of Ukrainian culture and language during the Soviet period. Through my wife, Natalia, her daughters, and her late mother I became more deeply connected to Kyiv and Ukraine, a connection that became all the more intense as Russian aggression targeted Ukrainian civilians, including my family. On the morning of February 24, my stepdaughters fled Kyiv for Western Ukraine, then on to temporary asylum in Poland, and still later to the United States. My brother-in-law, a concert violinist, age fifty, volunteered for military service that would take him to the front.

This book, then, is a chronicle of the coalescing of the state and of the Ukrainian political nation. It is based on readings, news reports, books, and other secondary sources, including Ukrainian broadcast media. But it is enriched by my three and a half decades of personal interactions with Ukrainian civic, business, religious, cultural, governmental, and political actors who have given me an insider's view and have enabled me to be an eyewitness to many of the pivotal events in the young nation's remarkable and tumultuous history—a journey that remains unresolved amid a brutal war of aggression.

BATTLEGROUND UKRAINE

CHAPTER ONE

A New State

The Presidency of Leonid Kravchuk

The collapse of the Soviet Union represented the disintegration of the largest multi-ethnic state in human history. Its rapid breakdown created fifteen new countries, several of them with legacies of independent statehood. With the exception of the USSR's successor state Russia, none would prove more consequential than Ukraine.

While many factors contributed to the Soviet Union's disintegration, there is no question that the superpower state would not have survived if not for the actions of Ukraine's citizens and elites. In truth, Russia—whose leaders, elites, and public were inclined to support a degree of decentralization within a federal or confederal state—would not have relented and acquiesced to the dismantling of the USSR had not Ukraine, the second most populous republic, asserted its firm determination to dissolve the bonds of the unitary Soviet state.

The march toward the breakup of the USSR coincided with the breakdown of Communist regimes in Central and Eastern Europe. Ukrainians and citizens of other non-Russian republics who had been protesting in large numbers since 1987 watched the political and civic ferment in Poland, Hungary, Czechoslovakia, East Germany, and Romania that had led to the fall of the Berlin Wall and the emergence of democratic post-Communist governments unshackled from Soviet influence. Under the rule of Mikhail Gorbachev's policies of *perestroika* (reform) and *glasnost* (openness) enunciated in 1987, civic actors in the USSR began to challenge the monopoly of the Communist Party and the permanence of one-party rule, censorship, and political repression. This ferment was especially strong in many of the non-Russian republics, where a desire for greater freedom was reinforced by the power of nationalism and the desire for self-determination after decades—or in most cases centuries—of stifling imperial rule from Moscow and St. Petersburg.

Civic Ferment

Nonviolent civic ferment in Ukraine began at a modest clip after Gorbachev's accession to power in the mid-1980s and accelerated throughout the rest of the decade. Indeed, Ukraine was regarded as among the most conservative backwaters of the Soviet Empire. In the pivotal year of 1989, as Central Europe made its dash toward freedom, flying the blue and yellow Ukrainian flag—an illegal act in the Soviet state punishable by long terms of imprisonment—became common in much of the country. The flag—a unifying symbol of the desire for statehood—became omnipresent at marches, protest demonstrations, and mass meetings that swept through most of Ukraine.

The blue and yellow flag flew in the west Ukrainian cities of Lviv, Chernivtsi, Ivano-Frankivsk, and Ternopil and in the central Ukrainian capital, Kyiv. In April 1989, after nationalists and former political prisoners scored stunning electoral triumphs in city and regional council elections, the flag was raised at the top of the city hall of Lviv, a metropolis of nearly 1 million inhabitants. On September 24, 1989, at the Chervona Ruta music festival in Chernivtsi, tens of thousands in attendance joined in the boisterously defiant singing of the long-banned Ukrainian national anthem, "Shche ne vmerla Ukrayina" (Ukraine has not yet perished). The singing of the anthem occurred despite the presence of a militia heavily armed and menacingly displaying batons.

Patriotic and separatist sentiment went far beyond the charged atmosphere of mass demonstrations, which eventually numbered as many as several hundred thousand participants. Parallel to growing mobilization was the rise of organized civic life, self-organization, and a de facto end to the Communist Party's monopoly on institutional life. Often such self-organization originated under the cover of support for Gorbachev's reform of the Soviet state. Within months, these civic initiatives progressed toward independent action and opposition to the Communist Party.

Such was the case with the Rukh, initially the People's Movement (Rukh) of Ukraine to Support Perestroika. I attended the organization's founding congress in Kyiv. The atmosphere at the September 1989 gathering was electric. Ukraine's intellectual, artistic, and scholarly leaders gathered, joined by a large swath of former political prisoners and human rights activists such as lawyer Levko Lukyanenko, who had spent twenty-seven years in Soviet jails, and journalist Vyacheslav Chornovil, who had endured nearly a decade of prisons and forced labor.

Support and encouragement came from the leaders of the Belarusian People's Front as well as leaders of Poland's Solidarity movement, including Bogdan Borusewicz, a Gdansk Solidarity labor leader who would become the marshal of the Polish Senate. *Gazeta Wyborcza*'s chief editor, the Polish dissident Adam Michnik, struck one of the most radical notes at this assembly, declaring: "You, as Ukrainians, and we, as Poles, know the face of great Russian chauvinism. We know how much harm it has brought to Russians themselves. No nation can be happy if it degrades and oppresses other nations. Poland is with you! Solidarity is with you! Long live a democratic and free Ukraine!" His oration was met with a thunderous standing ovation.

While numerous establishment-friendly Ukrainian writers, educators, and cultural figures were present, the movement had a distinctly oppositionist cast, which underscored the anomaly of the presence of Communist Party ideological chief Leonid Kravchuk, who would soon emerge as a key advocate of an independent Ukrainian state. Out of 1,100 delegates at the congress, 238 were members of the Communist Party, and the rhetoric, though firmly patriotic, did not in the main openly advance the idea of the dissolution of the Soviet Union.

The ultimate aim of state independence was not explicitly spelled out in official documents. Instead, expansive plans for the restructuring of Soviet Ukraine were drawn up. These included the reassertion of the primacy of the Ukrainian language; strong ecological planks to tame polluting industries and promote nuclear safety in a country that had suffered from the Chernobyl accident; and an economic program to decouple Ukraine from the centralized planned economy. Behind these aims stood a sophisticated leadership that made clear the movement would be a force to be reckoned with.

In the ensuing months, the Rukh grew to more than seven hundred thousand members and by 1990 had become the most popular voluntary organization in the country.

As the Rukh emerged, industrial action challenged the core of the Leninist canon—that the party acted in the interests of the working class. An independent workers' movement emerged, anchored by coal miners in the Donbas in Ukraine's east and the Lviv region in the west. Its leaders quickly established links with the Rukh and other reformers inside and outside the Communist Party. Over time, this solidarity would erode as the heavily Russified east and south differed over ethno-politics.

On January 21, 1990, hundreds of thousands of citizens linked arms, connecting Western Ukraine to Kyiv in a human chain spanning over four hundred miles. And by March 1990, in elections for the formerly rubber-stamped Supreme Soviet of the Ukrainian SSR, non-Communist activists joined Communist reformers in an umbrella coalition called the Democratic Bloc and challenged the Communist Party list. This was an important marker in the formerly totalitarian state—the first contested election in Soviet Ukraine's history. The Democratic Bloc included Communist renegades and non-Communist civic groups such as the Shevchenko Ukrainian Language Society, environmental organizations and parties, human rights groups such as the Ukrainian Helsinki Union, and Rukh.

The slate also won majorities in local legislatures in Western Ukraine and made strong showings in most major cities around the country. Public scorn for the Communist Party led to the defeat of many powerful local party secretaries. Such honchos lost their campaigns in high proportions not only in the more nationally conscious west Ukrainian ridings, but also in the eastern city of Donetsk and in Crimea. At the national level, despite sparse access to broadcast

Citizens in the west Ukrainian city of Lviv join in the Unity of Ukraine human chain, January 21, 1990. (Radio Free Europe / Radio Liberty)

and print media, the Democratic Bloc captured 111 out of 450 seats in the new Rada and constituted itself as the People's Council, the Narodna Rada, under the leadership of physicist Ihor Yukhnovsky.

In the ensuing months, Ukraine's Parliament underwent a radicalization that mirrored evolving public demands and expectations. By July 1990, ninety-two Communists had left their party, becoming independents closely aligned with the Narodna Rada and leaving a weakened core majority of Communists dubbed the Group of 239. Even this establishmentarian group was subject to the ferment in society and inside the Communist Party. On July 16, 1991, a week after Communist Party boss Volodymyr Ivashko resigned as speaker of the Parliament, the body voted 355–4 in favor of a declaration of national sovereignty. The document fell short of a call for outright independence, but it represented a major step toward the dissolution of the USSR.

The sovereignty declaration asserted the primacy of Ukraine's laws over those of the Soviet Union and announced that the Ukrainian SSR would maintain its own army. Ukraine was to become "a neutral state that does not affiliate with military blocs." Per the declaration, the new state would not "accept, nor produce, nor purchase nuclear weapons," leaving unclear the disposition of the hundreds of nuclear warheads then in Ukraine. Other provisions called for national self-determination, the right to separate Ukrainian citizenship, Ukraine's sovereign conduct of international relations, and economic independence, including control over trade relations, customs and taxation, and a national bank with the power to introduce a currency. In short, the sovereignty declaration carried the attributes of statehood without declaring a formal break with the USSR.

Two days after the vote, Leonid Kravchuk, the Ukrainian Communists' ideology secretary, was elected speaker of the Ukrainian SSR's Parliament and soon would emerge as the leader of his country's march toward statehood. In his first year in power, Kravchuk would rely on the support of Communists and ex-Communists in Parliament, balancing the interests of the Communist establishment and the increasingly radical demands of the public square.

Ukraine's sovereignty declaration and steps toward its realization did not quell—but accelerated—civic ferment. In October 1990, after a nationwide general strike, students built a tent city and conducted a hunger strike in what was then known as October Revolution Square (later Independence Square—Maidan Nezalezhnosti) demanding the government's ouster. After two weeks of protests in Kyiv and other localities, including a demonstration of 100,000 in the capital, hardline prime minister Vitaly Masol tendered his resignation on October 17. The Granite Revolution, named for the stone square where demonstrators assembled, became an iconic part of young Ukraine's modern-day history and inspired a new civic confidence that contributed to an upsurge of self-organization.

Rukh itself was undergoing a transformation. A year before, it had been a supporter of reform. By the time of its second congress, held in Kyiv October 25–28, 1990, Ukraine's movement for perestroika had morphed in a pro-independence, anti-Communist opposition. Gone were references to cooperation with the Communist Party, and the word *perestroika* (*perebudova* in Ukrainian) was demonstrably dropped from the organization's name. It now became the People's Movement (Rukh) of Ukraine *tout court*.

As separatist ferment grew in Ukraine and elsewhere, the Communist leadership in Moscow grew increasingly nervous. To stave off

A student tent city rises in central Kyiv during the Granite Revolution, a mass event that toppled an unpopular prime minister in October 1990. (From Oles Donii, ed., *Students' Revolution on the Granite* [Smoloskyp, 1995])

hard-liners and slow centrifugal forces, Party Secretary Gorbachev approved a wave of repression by Soviet troops in the Baltic states, resulting in the loss of twenty lives and hundreds wounded in early 1991. In Ukraine, prominent opposition leaders became victims of KGB operations to discredit and intimidate them. Some were arrested and others beaten. Pro-democracy and pro-independence movements found it increasingly difficult to print and circulate literature. A wide-ranging propaganda campaign portrayed Ukraine's pro-democracy leaders as extremist, far-right radicals.

In the spring and summer of 1991, tensions mounted between the Communist state and the public in most Soviet republics. Gorbachev's limited attacks on freedom movements had proved ineffective and were denounced as weak by much of the central party leadership. These hard-liners staged a coup on August 19. Ukraine's opposition leaders quickly mobilized protests denouncing the hard-line usurpers. Establishment leaders like Leonid Kravchuk disappeared or remained on the sidelines. The focus of the dramatic events was Moscow, as Kyiv and major Ukrainian cities saw little sign of military activity or an unusual police presence, confirmation that the coup was the action of a narrow group with little backing or advance planning. The unraveling of the coup days later—and Gorbachev's return from detention in the Crimean resort of Foros—left Ukraine's Communist Party in disarray. Implicated in collaborating with the rump State Committee on the State of Emergency, the party was outlawed as a criminal organization by a Ukrainian Parliament that consisted primarily of Communists.

Soviet Collapse and the Drive to Independence

After the coup collapsed, Ukrainian Communist stalwarts saw their salvation in the embrace of the radical public mood. On August 24, two days after the arrest of the coup plotters in Moscow, by a vote of 346–1, the Ukrainian Parliament proclaimed the country a sovereign and independent state, subject to confirmation by a December 1, 1991, referendum. Events had moved at a lightning pace. Just weeks before, on August 1, President George H. W. Bush had traveled to Kyiv to address to Ukraine's leaders. In what was dubbed the "Chicken Kiev" speech, the U.S. president lectured Ukrainians about the dangers of "ethnic hatred," "local despotism," and "suicidal nationalism" while sounding the praises of Gorbachev. His remarks invoked the straw man of a backward, xenophobic nationalism far removed from the liberal democratic values predominant in the leadership of Ukraine's Rukh. The speech was seen as a betrayal by pro-independence leaders, whom the U.S. president demonstratively refused to meet.

The collapse of the coup delivered a fatal blow to the USSR. And that blow came from Ukraine. As Zbigniew Brzezinski had observed, "Without Ukraine, Russia ceases to be an empire . . . and a great power." So, too, it would be with the USSR. Without Ukraine, the union could no longer hold. Brzezinski's accurate assessment also was well understood by the proponents of empire in Moscow, who remained influential inside Russia's ruling elite. The loss of Ukraine stirred anger and resentment and would remain an unresolved issue in Russian political discourse over the coming decades.

On December 1, Kravchuk easily defeated the civic leader of Ukraine's path to independence, Vyacheslav Chornovil, receiving nearly 62 percent compared to Chornovil's 23.3 percent amid a voter turnout of 84 percent. Some 31.6 million Ukrainians voted in the first direct election of a head of state and the first referendum in their history. Chornovil was a journalist who had been jailed for his dissident and patriotic views. As the recently elected governor of the Lviv region, he was the de facto leader of the mass Rukh movement. Kravchuk, by contrast, had the former Communist apparat behind him and enjoyed the significant advantage of support from the dominant state-owned radio, television, and print media as well as support from national and local government officials. The vote, moreover, reflected the still significant hold of Soviet rule over the population.

Four days after his election and after 90.32 percent of Ukrainians had voted "yes" on the country's independence, Kravchuk took the oath of office as president of a new country. Placing his hand on two documents: Ukraine's rudimentary constitution (an amended version of the basic document of the Ukrainian SSR) and the Act of Declaration of the Independence of Ukraine, he intoned: "I solemnly swear to the people of Ukraine to realize my authority as president, to strictly adhere to the Constitution and laws of Ukraine, to respect and protect the rights and liberties of people and citizens, to defend the sovereignty of Ukraine and to conscientiously fulfill my obligations." Above the podium of the Parliament, a giant statue of Lenin was replaced by the blue and yellow national flag. This was more than symbolism. Not only was Ukraine moving toward statehood, it was firmly on a post-Communist path.

With the public's backing, Ukraine insisted on a complete break with the unitary Soviet state and triggered the negotiated, peaceful disintegration of the USSR. Ukraine insisted on state independence at Belovezhskaya Pushcha, a government *dacha* in the Belarus forest. There Russia's leader Boris Yeltsin, Belarus's parliamentary speaker

Stanislav Shushkevich, and Kravchuk met to settle their relations. The representatives of the USSR's three Slavic republics had differing ideas about sovereignty and confederation. But Ukraine's firm demand for statehood carried the day. Kravchuk's leadership and negotiating skills proved essential assets in the Belarus forest. A calm negotiator, he steered the temperamental and mercurial Yeltsin purposefully toward the inevitable.

Yeltsin and most of his inner circle advocated the transformation of the USSR into a union of sovereign states under a coordinating body. Such a mechanism would permit the removal of Gorbachev, who was fighting a last-ditch battle to preserve the USSR in some form. As Harvard historian Serhiy Plokhy documents in *The Last Empire: The Final Days of the Soviet Union*, having failed to convince Kravchuk to accept a new confederation, Yeltsin opted for the creation of a loose Commonwealth of Independent States (CIS), which the Russian elite saw as the means for the eventual restoration of a unitary state. Russia's leadership viewed the divorce agreed at Belovezhskaya Pushcha as temporary and the CIS as interstate "couples therapy." Ukraine's leaders, emboldened by overwhelming public support, saw the CIS as a mechanism for a civilized political divorce that could preempt a bitter fight over marital assets.

The Belovezhskaya Forest agreement among Russia, Belarus, and Ukraine was signed on December 8 without the participation of the USSR. The signatories represented nearly two-thirds of the USSR's population. In the ensuing days, the agreement was endorsed by the leaders of the other republics and by the Supreme Soviet—the USSR's legislature. On December 26, the Council of the Republics, the upper—then the sole—functioning Soviet legislative chamber, voted to dissolve the Union of Soviet Socialist Republics, creating twelve new states, which joined the already independent Baltic republics. President Gorbachev was out of a job and the superpower he headed was no more.

Before December 26 only Hungary, Bulgaria, and Lithuania had extended diplomatic recognition to Ukraine. In the days that followed, international capitals rushed to recognize Kyiv. The United States extended recognition on January 3, 1992. Russia came on board only on February 6. Within two months, fifty-one states had recognized independent Ukraine.

Boris Yeltsin (*left*) and Leonid Kravchuk were the two leaders most responsible for the peaceful dissolution of the USSR. Here, during Yeltsin's visit to Kyiv on November 20, 1990, the two leaders signed a treaty on the mutual recognition of the sovereignty of the respective Soviet Socialist Republics: a precursor to the Belovezhskaya Forest agreement that led to the end of the Soviet Union. (Valeriy Solovyov / UNIAN)

Conservative Revolutionaries

Kravchuk, the man who had formally sparked this history-shattering event, did not fit the bill of a revolutionary. He was no George Washington or Thomas Jefferson. Ukraine's president had been a loyal cog in the ossified Soviet system—a leader of Ukraine's branch of the Communist Party. But Kravchuk and Ukraine's other Communist leaders understood that the embrace of state independence not only preserved their present power, it offered them vastly more than under the Soviet system.

There was another important factor that animated Kravchuk's historic role. He came from Volyn, a west Ukrainian region where the Ukrainian language and nationalism had deep roots. Kravchuk's father had links to the Ukrainian nationalist underground during the period of Polish, Nazi, and Soviet dominion. This legacy made Kravchuk different from other ex-Communist leaders, giving him deeper insights into the motivations of patriotic advocates of Ukraine's independence and, likely, real sympathy for the aim of statehood.

Though he played his political hand skillfully on the march to independence, Kravchuk was ill equipped for the job of running, much less shaping, a modern new state. Creating a state nearly *ex nihilo* would be a daunting challenge for any leader. But Kravchuk's lack of real-world administrative experience, his ignorance of economic matters, and his totalitarian past were great disadvantages. Not surprisingly, in the sphere of political reform Ukraine's new president was a study in contradictions. While partially opening Ukrainian media and reducing the ferocity of the state security apparatus, he made no changes in traditionally intrusive surveillance activities. Political opponents, Western aid workers, and civil society were objects of intense interest and extensive monitoring. Virtually all his appointed ministers and advisors, even those from the democratic camp, were former Communists. After Parliament granted Kravchuk sweeping powers in March 1992, three-quarters of his appointments were former apparatchiks, including numerous regional and local party secretaries. These leaders, many of whom spoke only rudimentary Ukrainian, knew little about Ukraine's culture and history. As with many Ukrainians under imperial Soviet rule, Ukrainian culture was understood as something quaint and charming: a one-dimensional peasant culture of folk arts and music frozen in time. Ukrainian history and the great exemplars of Ukrainian literature and the arts, its realist and modernist traditions, could hardly be taught without redaction, as in the main they had advocated Ukrainian autonomy and statehood. The former Communists who became the country's first leaders had little knowledge of Ukraine's history or its cultural and linguistic identity. They had even less of an understanding that these values and traditions needed to be revived.

The democratic civic forces that had pressed for independence were well aware of the educational and cultural tasks of nation-building. They knew they had to press Kravchuk and the leaders he brought to power if there was to be a comprehensive process of nation-building. And they worried that the hidebound ex-Communists were intent on preserving power by slowing the pace of change and paralyzing local legislatures and governments now in the hands of elected Ukrainian patriots. These trepidations proved right. Under the aegis of the apparatchiks, cultural and educational reforms stalled and privatization was delayed. Numerous state assets were leased for a pittance or illegally seized by private interests even as the state deficit skyrocketed, feeding hyperinflation. When limited economic reform came shortly after Kravchuk left office, privatization lacked transparency and brought scant revenues to the state budget.

Ukraine's first prime minister, Vitold Fokin, reflected Kravchuk's conservative approach to governing. Fokin had been a mining technician and coal-mining engineer before moving up the ranks in the Communist Party. At the time Kravchuk and Fokin took the helm of state and government, Ukraine was seen by Western economists as a country with great potential. A widely cited study published in 1990 by Deutsche Bank predicted Ukraine would become the fastest-growing post-Soviet republic. With its rich agricultural and industrial base, abundant raw materials, the former USSR's rocket technologies, significant machine building and heavy metallurgy, as well as high human capital generated by strong scientific and educational institutions, Ukraine was viewed as poised for success.

Such rosy predictions ignored several important factors. Unlike Russia, which was refashioning a developed state and state institutions, Ukraine was building most of these from scratch. Moreover, many of Ukraine's most talented managers and scientists traditionally moved to Moscow and Leningrad (St. Petersburg), where they served in key bureaucratic, economic, and scientific institutions. Coaxing this talent pool home in the absence of adequate resources for compensation proved a challenge. Additionally, in these first years, Ukraine was denied the full complement of the economic and technical assistance that other ex-Soviet republics received as Western aid was held back to press the country to surrender its nuclear arsenal. Ukraine also inherited a disproportionately high percentage of the military industrial sector. With the USSR's disintegration, further state orders collapsed, given the huge existing arsenal of weapons. Ukraine now needed to convert many of these facilities to peaceful commercial ends, but it lacked the resources amid a growing budget deficit, a collapsing currency, and in the absence of developed markets and trade relationships.

Under Communist rule, Poland, Hungary, and Czechoslovakia had experienced significant business interchange with the West. With the exception of mainly fringe Western Communist movements, the Soviet Union had treated contact with the West with suspicion, blocking almost all such interaction for its intelligentsia and managerial elites. This isolation was even more extreme in Ukraine and other non-Russian republics, which were viewed as potentially disloyal by the central Soviet apparat. Ukraine, therefore, lacked knowledge of markets.

Western companies had been more significantly engaged in the economies of Central Europe through trade and investment than the USSR. Central European scholars, lawyers, and economists had traveled to the West to take part in seminars, had won fellowships and grants, and had enjoyed other higher educational opportunities. As a result, Central European reformers had an idea of how market economies and free societies worked and what structural reforms were required. And they had a network of established contacts to advise them on the liberalization of their economies. Ukraine was starting from scratch.

President Kravchuk, the Fokin government, and the holdover 1990 Parliament almost immediately had to grapple with more than the institutional consequences of building a new state. They faced currency collapse, mounting inflation, the disintegration of the planned economy, and the emergence of powerful organized crime groups that planted roots in the new economy.

In 1992 President Kravchuk attempted to strengthen the authority of the central government by establishing his own regional representatives. However, the appearance of these "viceroys" created a spate of new conflicts with local authorities who sought to preserve their prerogatives. By the middle of 1992, the collapse of the economy sparked growing discontent among the regional elites and the "red directors" who dominated industry. They forced Kravchuk to jettison his ally Fokin and replace him with a new prime minister—Leonid Kuchma.

The choice would prove fateful. In responding to pressure from discontented regional elites and seeking to add balance to his leadership team, Kravchuk's nomination of Kuchma was a logical choice. Soon, however, personal rivalries and disputes over policy between president and prime minister intensified—a pattern in Ukrainian politics that would often be repeated in the coming decades.

Economic Decline

Ukraine's economy declined by 8.4 percent in 1991, by 9.7 percent in 1992, by 14.2 percent in 1993, and in the last year of Kravchuk's presidency (in July 1994), output would drop by a further 22.4 percent. Economic links among the former Soviet republics had been disrupted and were in disarray. The collapse of the ruble and the rise of weak national currencies plagued virtually all the independent republics. Ukraine also faced a price spiral that reached hyperinflationary levels in 1993, topping 10,000 percent and creating havoc for producers, investors, and consumers. To cope with the inflationary disarray, an unstable currency, and the absence of investment capital and credits, businesses often resorted to a barter system that operated outside the tax structure, denying the state revenues while creating a major spurt in corruption. Energy-trading middlemen sold domestic Ukrainian goods on a barter basis to Russia, Kazakhstan, and Turkmenistan in return for the delivery of oil and gas. But who was to value the actual goods that were sold? Were they sold at their market value or were they marked down and compensated with untaxed cash payments or payments to offshore accounts? In the absence of established export controls, poorly paid employees of the customs service and tax administration were corrupted and bent to the will of exporters who were politically connected.

Without credit and capital markets, early Ukrainian capital formation found other pathways. Criminality was rampant; extortion and protection rackets reigned. The fight for property was often deadly as corporate raids and armed takeovers spiraled, often abetted by the dubious rulings of corrupt judges. Outside the dominant state sector, private enterprise operated in a gray zone of semi-legality. Impossibly high tax rates made tax evasion common. Widespread barter arrangements, moreover, made the actual profits from transactions difficult for the state to tax and value, while corrupt tax officials often looked the other way. The stripping of industrial assets in fire sales depleted the infrastructure for production that was built in the Soviet period. Great fortunes were created through trade, barter, and corporate raids. Criminal control of major open-air public markets generated income that financed the establishment or purchase of small banks. These, in turn, became cash cows that financed the purchase of state enterprises. This was the means by which Ukraine's oligarchs gradually emerged.

Operating in the black market, often in the shadow of organized crime, Ukraine's first entrepreneurs faced violent and predatory attacks from rivals. Criminal gangs operated in the space created by weakened or corrupted state institutions. The perilous state of property rights was exacerbated by what would become a culture of corruption among prosecutors and judges. As respected investigative journalist Katya Gorchinskaya detailed in an analysis published in the *Kyiv Post* in May 2020, "It wasn't until relatively late in Kravchuk's tenure that he mounted a governmental effort to address burgeoning corruption." In November 1993 his presidential decree established the Coordinating Committee for Fighting Corruption and Organized Crime. "By then, however, it was too little, too late," Gorchinskaya concluded. Her verdict reflected the general tenor of the fight against corruption that would persist for decades. As she summarized: "The general lack of government oversight meant that anti-corruption measures were toothless. Money-making schemes of dubious legality kept mushrooming."

The delay of privatization did not mean property relations remained frozen. Business interests initiated de facto privatizations, often orchestrated by the red directors. Small fortunes made in the private sector and through criminal activity created the seed capital that enabled the acquisition of vast state assets for a pittance. Amid a state sector in crisis and with incomes in steep decline, the foundations of massive fortunes were established. Many with a head start had originated in black market or gray market activities. Some had come from local government or worked in state companies and ventured into commerce through the barter of goods and commodities. Others were talented and ambitious members of the Komsomol who in the last years of the USSR had won the right to engage in small-scale commercial activities. On this basis they established modest entertainment, commercial, and trading enterprises, accumulating start-up capital for ambitious acquisitions in a chaotic environment.

For pensioners and ordinary workers, the story was far different. Their modest purchasing power, pensions, and cash savings were wiped out by hyperinflation. To be fair, there were no easy answers for those in power. But the decisions taken or deferred by Kravchuk and his prime ministers exacerbated a downward economic spiral. In addition, inflation, an unreliable currency, and problems in the Russian and Central Asian economies meant gas and oil shortages regularly plagued the country, disrupting transportation, the delivery of goods, agriculture, and industrial production.

The economic devastation of those years took its toll on the state and on public perceptions of the state, which was deeply distrusted. I recall a meeting in the winter of 1993 in the offices of the deputy prime minister for economic matters, Viktor Pynzenyk, a market liberal who was losing his battle to introduce some budget discipline into the dysfunctional economy. When I arrived at his cavernous, unlit office, he was wearing a heavy winter coat as there was no heating in the building that was the seat of government. In such circumstances, there was an immediacy to our discussion of the obstacles he faced in his efforts to speed up privatization and tame inflation.

Independent Ukraine's first national cash exchange mechanism was the *karbovanets* (*kupon*) introduced on January 1, 1992. By that summer, it had replaced the ruble entirely as a currency. The Ukrainian kupon was conceived as a transitional mechanism before the conversion to a national currency, the *hryvnia*. However, in the context of economic uncertainty and hyperinflation, this temporary currency remained in use through the end of 1995. In 1992 the currency was priced at 200 to the dollar; by the fall of 1996, a 500,000 note was worth $4 or 125,000 to the dollar—a devaluation of over six thousand times.

Ukraine faced its massive economic crisis in the absence of market reform know-how, as it was denied meaningful Western technical assistance and financial aid as a means of pressing the country to surrender its nuclear arsenal. Western assistance in the reform of Russia and other republics was flawed and did not preclude the emergence of oligarchs. However, the denial of such aid and the absence of Western advisors proved to be devastating for Ukraine as the economic crisis unfolded.

While dragging out the process of denuclearization in the hopes of extracting security assurances and serious financial aid, Kravchuk was nevertheless eager to win the West's approval. At the West's behest, he consented to the rapid shipment of tactical nuclear weapons to Russia. In April 1992 Parliament confirmed Ukraine's intention to be a neutral, nonnuclear state. Actual denuclearization of Ukraine's strategic arsenal nonetheless had many starts and stops as Ukraine insisted on control over all nuclear weapons on its soil. Although nuclear warheads remained under the jurisdiction of an awkward joint CIS command (effectively involving Russia), Ukraine's own control over the delivery systems was officially asserted to ensure their "non-use."

Renouncing Nuclear Weapons

In mid-March 1992, with more than half of its tactical nuclear warheads already removed from its territory, Ukraine excited international alarm by suspending further weapons transfers to Russia. At issue, Ukrainian leaders asserted, were inadequate controls over the timely destruction of the warheads by the Russian side. The Ukrainian decision was further influenced by the emergence of ominous rhetoric from Russian leaders concerning the revision of borders and tension with Russia over the disposition of the Black Sea Fleet.

Ukraine eventually received sufficient evidence that the tactical warheads it was sending to its neighbor were indeed being destroyed, and Kyiv resumed transferring warheads "for destruction under international supervision." Still, Ukrainian anxiety over Russia's intentions contributed to delays in the denuclearization process. President Kravchuk demonstrated the depth of Ukrainian concern about Russian hegemonic intentions in April 1992 when he announced the republic's intention to seek Western security guarantees in exchange for scrapping Ukrainian nuclear arms.

Nearly two hundred strategic intercontinental ballistic missiles with more than sixteen hundred nuclear warheads remained on Ukrainian soil as Presidents Kravchuk and Bush met in Washington in early May 1992 and agreed Ukraine would be free of all strategic nuclear weapons by the end of 1994. Importantly, Kyiv remained true to its commitment that all four thousand tactical nuclear warheads would be removed by July 1992. With the exception of those that remained with the Black Sea Fleet, which Ukraine did not fully control, that commitment was met.

Still, Ukraine's leaders were reluctant to shed remaining nuclear weapons in the absence of security assurances by the world's nuclear powers. Only in December 1994 did negotiations over security guarantees result in a modest set of security assurances for Ukraine. These were incorporated into the Budapest Memorandum, an interstate document endorsed by Russia, China, the UK, France, and the United States that was not a full-fledged treaty with absolute security guarantees but a declaration of obligations and intentions. The signing of the memorandum was meager compensation for the transfer of Ukraine's nuclear arsenal. Ukraine's failure to extract more in the security sphere was matched by its failure to negotiate a generous financial aid and technical assistance package. Having damaged itself by dragging out negotiations, Ukraine capitulated to intense international pressure with little to show for its concession.

Some experts argue that Ukraine had little bargaining power as it lacked control over its strategic arsenal. That may have been true, but most of the complex components of the strategic nuclear arsenal were produced in Ukraine's Pivdenmash factory, and the mechanisms for missile guidance and control were made in Kharkiv. Even if control over the strategic arsenal was beyond the ability of Ukraine's technicians, it was a very different matter when it came to tactical nuclear weapons. Ukraine had the potential to establish control over these weapons and it had the skilled scientists and engineers to initiate its own nuclear weapons program.

Not everyone agreed it was in Ukraine's interest to abandon its nuclear arms. University of Chicago professor John Mearsheimer, three decades later a controversial critic of Ukraine's and the West's approach to Russia, famously argued that Ukraine should retain its nuclear arsenal as a deterrent. But he was, as he remains to this day, an outlier in the foreign policy community.

The denial of financial aid and technical assistance was intended to compel Ukraine to surrender its nuclear weapons. But the consequences for economic reform were dire. Along with a paucity of programs for training Ukrainian government officials, civil servants, and parliamentarians in market economics, Ukraine was denied a cadre of Western technical advisors to assist in the transition process. USAID and European Union spending on Ukraine was *de minimus*, focused primarily on democracy building and election monitoring.

Financial assistance also was held back, as was technical support for privatization, which occurred without well-established bidding systems and in the absence of civic and independent media monitoring. Surrounded by old-school Soviet-era apparatchiks and in the absence of Western advice on market reform, President Kravchuk decided Ukraine could not endure the radical shock therapy tried in Poland. "We have to learn from the experience of other East European states," he said. "Ukraine will take its own path."

Even Ukraine's military and security structures were initially given meager support, ensuring that there was little outside technical assistance for the essential goal of creating a full-fledged military, rationalizing existing weapons and their supply chains, and building a professional internal security and police structure.

In retrospect, the West's hard line was excessive. Ukraine had declared it would be a non-nuclear power, and at any rate there was no good reason why the aim of denuclearization should be linked to the denial of reform assistance. Indeed, while Ukraine was being squeezed on assistance, Russia received generous support, even as imperialists and revanchists gained influence inside Yeltsin's circle and predominated in the mainstream opposition.

The country ended up without ironclad security assurances or even a major aid and assistance package to match that offered Russia. Under President Bush, the United States had offered an aid program with specific assistance to Russia for currency stabilization but none for Ukraine's own monetary unit. Likewise, the IMF's capital quota for Russia was nearly 60 percent greater per capita than Ukraine's. Even the West's decision to provide direct food assistance to Russia worked to Ukraine's disadvantage by making Russia less dependent on Ukrainian food and reducing revenues to Ukraine's economy. No similar effort was made to reduce Ukraine's dependence on Russian exports. A balanced Western aid package would have provided assistance to make Ukraine more energy efficient and less dependent on imported Russian fuel. Such an aid package did not come in the crucial early years of independence, nor did the United States or the West in general ensure equity in levels of aid and loan assistance. Parsimonious financial support and technical expertise to a young state creating institutions ex nihilo was highly damaging.

The Presidential Administration: A New Power Center

In 1991 Kravchuk established the Office of the Administration of the President, which settled in the offices of the former Ukrainian Communist Party on Kyiv's Bankova Street. Bankova, as the building is known, is imposing, stifling, and forbidding: a vast complex built in the empire style, with elements of classicism merged with Soviet monumentalism and brutalism. The building, dramatically expanded in the 1930s, came to serve as the headquarters of the Kyiv Special Military District and was later home to the Central Committee of the Communist Party, where Kravchuk had spent much of his political life. It was no wonder he repurposed it for his presidential office.

The Presidential Administration soon became a large bureaucratic structure, employing hundreds of staff, including legion policy experts and presidential advisors. Many of the functions of the administration paralleled government structures, giving the chief executive influence well beyond his constitutional prerogatives in the presidential-parliamentary system. Thirty years after its creation, Kravchuk's administration is still around in the form of the Office of the President, with a staff now numbering nearly one thousand and augmented by the State Affairs Administration. State Affairs controls a vast network of real estate assets—including until 2020 a sprawling hotel in central Kyiv, supplies and equipment, presidential vehicles, and numerous villas.

As head of the administration, Kravchuk installed Mykola Khomenko, a former Communist functionary who served in the upper ranks of the staff of the Supreme Soviet of the Ukrainian SSR. Khomenko shared Kravchuk's long-standing relationships with the former Communist elite and was well schooled in matters bureaucratic, including paper flow—a prodigious feature of the Soviet and now Ukrainian state.

Kravchuk's main political strategist was Mykola Mykhalchenko, a sociologist who in the Soviet era had studied the role of ideology and propaganda in the shaping of public consciousness. Throughout Kravchuk's presidency he was the key advisor who shaped policy, interacted with state-run and state-influenced media, maintained outreach to the intelligentsia, and designed electoral strategies. Mykhalchenko exhibited little sympathy for the democratic West, advocating a "unique" Ukrainian path to reform and a middle ground between Russia and the West, which became a fundamental state tenet in the first decade of independence.

Mykhalchenko stayed out of the public light, developing the reputation of a gray cardinal. His interlocutors reported he was suspicious of outside influences on the country and facilitated the expansion of an extensive culture of surveillance inside the nascent Ukrainian state. Agents of influence from the state infiltrated civic and opposition groups to report on and destabilize these forces.

After the USSR collapsed, Russia's highly centralized security services were disoriented and temporarily weakened. In Ukraine an opposite process was underway: the shaping of a security system for the new state and the empowering of an institution formerly ruled from Moscow. The new grandees of Ukraine's state security, military intelligence, and external intelligence services were wooed, coddled, incentivized, and resourced by a post-Communist elite that feared internal instability, was suspicious of civil society, and had concerns about the influence of Russia and the West.

Ukraine's newly autonomous security services were unleashed to listen, follow, monitor, and—if necessary—intimidate independent domestic and foreign actors in the country. These services closely monitored members of the Ukrainian diaspora and expatriates who had flocked to Ukraine to pursue business, educational, and social projects. In particular, intelligence operatives closely monitored the small expat community whose members had come as volunteers or as staff for modest programs aimed at building new, transparent institutions. I experienced several instances of attempts to discredit my work with civic organizations and think tanks via interrogations by the authorities and the creation of fake documents alleging massive transfers of funds to democracy advocates.

To prove their value, the security services often exaggerated threats posed by extremist far-right and far-left groups. Such radical structures in fact were thoroughly infiltrated and controlled by agents of the intelligence services, who used them in operations against mistrusted Westerners and domestic actors. President Kravchuk and his top advisors not only enabled this phenomenon, their action or inaction established precedents that became a worrying factor in Ukraine's early years.

The first years of independence saw displays of occasional public joy and celebrations around important milestones for the new country. In the main, however, Kyiv and other major cities were bleak and forbidding. At nighttime streets were dark and menacing, with a smattering of new coffee shops, restaurants, bars, and dodgy nightclubs, many associated with organized crime. There were few visible signs in the first years of independence to indicate market dynamism. In Kyiv only a few new shops and businesses had opened—a posh liquor and wine shop opened by the Seagram's brand, a garish Italian restaurant decorated like a bordello, a handful of pubs, and a few grocery stores and supermarkets that catered to the small stream of Western diplomats, the diaspora, and foreign-aid contractors. To those who had struggled for independence, these first years were full of disappointment about the lost opportunity for rapid reform.

President Kravchuk and his cohorts largely shunned the intelligentsia and civic activists who had led the march to freedom, keeping them at arm's length from power. Ministries were dominated by the old Communist establishment. This, too, was the case in the Parliament, where Kravchuk's political partner, Speaker Ivan Plyushch, shared a Communist pedigree, having been a member of the Party *nomenklatura* and the former director of a collective farm.

An Emerging Economic Elite

In October 1992, Leonid Kuchma, the general director of the Southern Machine-Building (Pivdenmash) complex in the Dnipropetrovsk (now Dnipro), was voted in as prime minister. Pivdenmash was the USSR's primary manufacturer of intercontinental ballistic missiles (120 per year at peak capacity) and other rocketry, including orders for the Soviet space program. After the dissolution of the USSR, the complex diversified and was by 1992 a major producer of trolley buses for the Ukrainian and post-Soviet market. A "red director" and member of the Communist nomenklatura par excellence, Kuchma was an engineer by training and the former head of the space rocket production program at Pivdenmash. The appointment of someone regarded as an effective manager was welcomed by the industrial lobby, which was reeling from the collapse of state orders and the decline in cross-border trade with other ex-Soviet republics.

In the middle of 1992, Ukraine left the ruble zone and introduced a temporary coupon currency. The introduction of the hryvnia as a full-fledged currency was delayed because of a wave of inflation that morphed into hyperinflation. The collapse of the ruble additionally hurt Ukraine's half-realized currency market. Natural gas prices climbed one-hundred-fold and more.

In this environment, the first generation of gas and oil importers and exporters made fortunes, as the economy ground to a halt for most Ukrainians. While a small cohort of sharp operatives grew rich, the vast majority of Ukrainian workers and pensioners suffered from the industrial and financial collapse. Kuchma assumed the prime minister's office in October 1992, with the economy in deep crisis and industrial strikes erupting sporadically. Though Kuchma was little known to much of the Kyiv establishment, his experience in the real economy was deeper than the expertise of his predecessor Vitold Fokin, who had drafted plans, timetables, and goals in a planned economy.

On November 18, 1992, a ministerial team in place, Kuchma made a dramatic address to the Parliament, painting a dire picture of the economic state of affairs. In the following weeks, Ukrainian legislators were urged by Kuchma to act. On January 20, 1993, Kuchma brought an even more dire message to the nation. Under his predecessor, he reported, the state budget deficit amounted to 33 percent of Ukraine's GDP. "Having had a year that was both full of celebration and full of misery," Kuchma declared, "we have to start from scratch. . . . We have reached a dead end. We have to take steps backward, and only then will we be able to move forward." Kuchma's speech revealed hard truths to the public. He spoke of Ukraine's absolute dependence on the Russian market and underscored that the first year of independence had been squandered: new markets had not been opened, there were no sources of credit, and there was little development aid. In essence, Kuchma's remarks were a comprehensive indictment of Kravchuk's leadership, setting the stage for an eventual challenge to the incumbent president.

In 1992, as inflation raged and enterprises idled or operated at low capacity, the government decreed a massive privatization. Over twelve thousand state enterprises were to get private owners. In reality, privatization lagged far behind the shiny reformist rhetoric. In the absence of supervision from the top of the state—and sometimes with its collusion—enterprise directors became autonomous actors of great wealth and privilege. When privatization began in earnest in 1994 in somewhat egalitarian fashion, with workers holding shares in their enterprise through vouchers, red directors, local officials, and organized crime groups awash with ill-gotten cash were in the strongest position to buy vouchers from economically distressed workers. Privatization was implemented without civic monitoring, open media scrutiny, and the rule of law, creating vast wealth for a narrow group of insiders. The voucher privatization was implemented only after Kravchuk left office. Had it occurred in 1992, before dark money had proliferated, privatization would not have seen the widespread phenomenon of *skupki*—the purchase of workers' vouchers by a small wealthy elite. Instead of becoming stakeholders in the new private sector, workers in dire economic conditions mostly sold their shares in public assets at far below their real value, often under the pressure of a cynical management. Over time, this process created great antipathy for Ukraine's new rich.

The Inflationary Spiral

In 1993, Leonid Kuchma's only full year as prime minister, the Ukrainian economy performed dreadfully. Hyperinflation raged at 10,155 percent. To cope with rising prices, Ukrainians relied on growing their own vegetables. More and more city dwellers grew their own produce on government-allocated plots. In June 1993, coal miners launched a strike in response to the collapse of production in many mines, arrears in wages, and the erosion of earning power. The strike wave spread to other industries, threatening the nascent state's stability. Pressure from discontented workers continued throughout the summer, forcing President Kravchuk and Ukraine's Parliament into a number of concessions, including the decision to mandate new elections to the legislature in March 1994 and for president in June 1994.

As prime minister, Kuchma proved unable to turn the economy around. But the prime minister had one advantage over Kravchuk. As a new arrival, he could blame the president and his circle for the economic disasters as discontent over Ukraine's dire economic performance fell squarely on Kravchuk. In addition to a still powerful, partly reconstituted Communist Party, opposition to the president was on the rise in the Parliament, among regional leaders, and with enterprise directors from the heavily industrialized south and east.

Kuchma's influence was suddenly on the rise. On June 17, the Ukrainian Parliament voted a motion of no confidence in Kravchuk that was to trigger a referendum on his tenure in office in September 1993. On September 22, just four days before the referendum, Kuchma left his post as prime minister, declaring his intention to seek the presidency. He then assumed leadership of the Union of Industrialists and Entrepreneurs, a powerful body linking the Red Directors, a sinecure from which he could mobilize financing for his campaign.

The election of a new Parliament came in two rounds, in March and April 1994, and resulted in a steep decline in Kravchuk's power. His supporters won only 87 seats out of 450, compared to the 239 backers he had had at the outset of independence. The election witnessed the resurgence of the retrograde Communists, who had reconstituted themselves after they were banned in 1991. They ended up with 83 seats. Democratic patriotic forces linked to the Rukh movement and other reformers won 54 seats. Backers of former prime minister Kuchma captured 26 seats, with 25 going to the Socialist Party, made up of idealist leftists and disaffected young Communists. Significantly, 118 independent and nonaligned legislators reflected the rising power of local economic interests and politicians. An interim government headed by Yukhym Zvyahilsky, a mine director from Donetsk, functioned until presidential elections could be held. At the time, Zvyahilsky was viewed as an ally of President Kravchuk, but he did little to help his cause. Accusations of corruption eventually led to Zvyahilsky's departure to Israel.

Instead of an initial plan for a referendum on Kravchuk's tenure, elections had been sped up to June 26. The campaign was on. Kuchma's case for election as president was succinct. He promised to restore severed economic links with Russia and to proceed with serious market reforms to replace an increasingly criminalized system dominated by the black market, barter, and tax evasion. He argued that he had tried to change things, but Kravchuk's ruling group had stymied his reform efforts. Quickly, Kuchma recognized that in addition to his economic and managerial credentials, he would need to shore up his command of foreign policy issues and introduce himself to the international foreign policy and business communities.

In the early spring of 1994 Kuchma visited Washington, DC, on a confidence-building mission to introduce him to U.S. leaders, analysts, media, and the business community. The visit intended to show that, while Kuchma represented the interests of Ukraine's east, he was pro-Western in orientation and far from Moscow's man. I organized a meeting for Kuchma with key foreign policy and national security actors in Washington, including members of the Freedom House Board, where I was CEO. Those gathered included Zbigniew Brzezinski; Ambassador Mark Palmer, an investor in post-Communist Germany, Hungary, Poland, and Ukraine; Ken Adelman, who had been an arms control official in the Reagan administration; and Jeane J. Kirkpatrick, scholar and former UN ambassador. I greeted Kuchma in Russian, having heard him speak publicly only in that language. To my surprise, Kuchma responded in Ukrainian and in our meeting and throughout his U.S. visit took scrupulous pains to speak in the state language. It was clear he was seriously preparing to win power.

Kuchma's entourage included Oleksandr Volkov, a Kyiv businessman; Dmytro Tabachnyk, then a young scholar best known for research on Stalin's repression of Ukraine's intelligentsia who later fled to Moscow to support Putin's war on Ukraine; and a young journalist, Oleksandr Tkachenko, who videotaped the meetings and later became an important media executive and, in 2020, Ukraine's minister of culture.

Kuchma projected the image of a U.S.-friendly political moderate determined to address the weaknesses in Ukraine's economy. Given Kravchuk's economic failures and the slow pace of political reform, I concluded that Kuchma was the better of two imperfect choices for Ukraine.

Building Institutions

With the exception of—mainly fringe—Western Communist movements, the Soviet Union had treated contact with the West with suspicion, blocking its intelligentsia and managerial elites from almost all such interaction. This isolation was even more extreme in Ukraine and other non-Russian republics, which were viewed by the central Soviet apparat as potentially disloyal.

Independence meant establishing the armed forces; dividing the assets of the former USSR; negotiating the division of the former Soviet fleet, much of which was anchored in the Ukrainian port of Sevastopol in Crimea; establishing a chain of command between national, regional, and local governments; turning around industries in dire financial straits because of Soviet-era decrepitude and disrupted international and inter-republic trade patterns; overseeing privatization of state assets; establishing the rudiments of a national justice system; setting up diplomatic missions; and structuring ministries that either had not existed or were pale facsimiles of the real thing.

Ukraine had only one diplomatic institution in place: its ambassadorial mission to the United Nations and its representations to various UN agencies. With independence, it needed to establish diplomatic missions in major capitals. In this regard, the country had one important advantage: Kyiv's Shevchenko University had one of the strongest international affairs faculties and international law specializations in the USSR. Kyiv had trained generations of top diplomats to serve Soviet foreign policy. Now Ukraine had a potential reserve of young diplomats in training who could be asked to populate the country's diplomatic service.

Because the Foreign Affairs Ministry was being created ex nihilo, some of Ukraine's diplomats came into its service through the radical act of leaving the diplomatic service of the new Russian state, which had inherited the personnel, traditions, and organizational structure of the Soviet Ministry of Foreign Affairs. This cohort consisted of strong, well-motivated supporters of the country's independence and sovereignty. To them were added numerous young diplomats who had completed their training in the more open atmosphere of glasnost and perestroika. With this pedigree, the Foreign Ministry developed the reputation of being one of the most capable, least corrupt, and most patriotic institutions inside the Ukrainian state—a status it enjoys to this day.

The effort to structure Ukraine's armed forces also was an important early success. That effort began quietly, soon after Ukraine's declaration of sovereignty in July 1990. Formally, Ukraine had inherited the world's third-largest nuclear arsenal, after that of the United States and Russia. It possessed a large air force with fifteen hundred military aircraft, a naval force that would eventually be subdivided with Russia, some sixty-five hundred tanks, seven thousand armored personnel carriers, and sixteen hundred nuclear warheads. The total force on Ukrainian territory stood at over three-quarters of a million troops. Significantly, because the USSR had forward-positioned its more well-armed and effective forces closer to the borders of NATO, Ukraine wound up with some of the more advanced weaponry and technology of the Soviet arsenal. But a military is far more than weaponry and resources; its effectiveness above all is rooted in patriotism and esprit de corps.

The transfer of the armed forces and weapons reserves on Ukrainian soil to direct Ukrainian control gained momentum in the days after the Parliament's declaration of independence. After the Soviet hard-liners' coup collapsed on August 24, 1991, Ukraine's Parliament had passed legislation "placing all armed forces on the territory of Ukraine under the Supreme Soviet of Ukraine, creating a Ministry of Defense of Ukraine, and instructing the government of Ukraine to proceed with the creation of the Armed forces of Ukraine."

Although Ukraine's independence referendum was held in December 1991, a defense ministry was already operating in October. At the time, many experts in the West refused to acknowledge what was happening in Kyiv, regarding the prospect of separate Ukrainian armed forces with skepticism even after Konstantin Morozov, a forty-eight-year-old colonel general in the Soviet Air Force, resigned his commission to become defense minister. He moved rapidly to "Ukrainianize" the military, assembling a staff of military professionals and advisors, and engaged the help of the Union of Ukrainian Officers, which had been launched with the assistance of the Rukh. By 1992 the union, one of Ukraine's first civil society organizations, had grown to seventy thousand active-duty and reserve soldiers and officers. It provided Morozov with a cohort of patriotic experts. The union, moreover, represented an informal network inside official military structures that assisted in securing the military's loyalty to the emerging state.

The tasks of transforming troops into loyal forces, elaborating new missions and threat assessments, preparing for defense conversion, and orchestrating a substantial demobilization would be daunting for any defense establishment. This was especially true for a newly sovereign military unsure of precisely how many troops were on its soil. Although the most reliable estimate put Ukrainian troop strength at 750,000, that number was actually far higher, as the estimate did not include border troops and the National Guard.

Although passions ran high, there were enough level heads in charge. Kyiv quickly declared its intention to scale back forces to between two hundred thousand and three hundred thousand over the next five years. That level was well within the range accepted by most European powers and was a reassuring signal to the West that Ukraine did not seek to be a major military power. Ukrainian officials hoped, perhaps naïvely, that their reductions would be compensated by technological improvements, yielding a military whose firepower would match that of the existing force levels. However, a mounting economic crisis meant the country's defense production ground to a near-total halt.

Russia and Ukraine: Ambivalence and Hostility

Amid the daunting challenges of building *de novo* state institutions and structuring a market-based post-Soviet economy, Ukraine's most important issue was its relationship with Russia. From the inception of Ukraine statehood, Russia's elite and public maintained a troubling ambivalence—in some cases outright hostility—regarding the emergence of the Ukrainian state. This was especially the case inside Russia's security services and military structures, where imperialist ideas and the desire for the restoration of a unitary state predominated. Crimea, a part of Ukraine since 1954, with a majority ethnic-Russian population, quickly became the key source of interstate tensions, revealing that all was not settled in Russian-Ukrainian relations.

On May 5, 1992, the Crimean Parliament heightened tensions by adopting a declaration of independence, an action the Ukrainian Parliament quickly annulled. Within a day, the Crimean Parliament appeared to back away from its earlier decision by inserting into its legislation a declaration that Crimea was part of Ukraine. However, on May 21 the Russian Parliament, albeit reaffirming Ukraine's current borders, added to the turmoil by voiding the 1954 transfer of Crimea and calling for negotiations over the peninsula's future. Ominously, tensions with Crimea were accompanied by the activization of Russian nationalist groups on the peninsula—groups that Ukrainian officials believed were financed and inspired by Russia. These groups allied with local elites, including criminal organizations, to create momentum toward autonomy.

In an effort to reduce the appeal of separatists and dampen tensions with the peninsula, in June 1992, Kyiv granted Crimea the status of an "autonomous republic" within Ukraine. Over the next six years, the elaboration of the details of this autonomy would involve a back-and-forth between the legislatures and leaders of Crimea and Ukraine. It was only in January 1999, when a new Crimean Constitution came into effect, that the region's rights were settled within the jurisdiction of the Ukrainian state. Still, the concessions made to pro-Russian, separatist, and opportunist forces in Crimea would impede efforts to fully integrate Crimea into the Ukrainian state and strengthen the Ukrainian cultural and political identity of Crimeans. Autonomy ensured that pro-Ukrainian patriotic sentiment never predominated but was confined to the peninsula's ethnically Ukrainian and Crimean Tatar minorities. The bulk of the Russian and Russian-speaking majority (which represented over 60 percent of the population) remained ambivalent, if not hostile, to Kyiv and the Ukrainian state.

Nevertheless, the local Crimean elite was not interested in shifting its allegiances to Moscow, which would have placed it under the control of another state; instead it sought to extract maximum autonomy. In a territory with deep-sea ports, such autonomy offered the local elite vast opportunities for collecting duties on imports, falsifying bills of lading on exports, importing and exporting contraband, and evading taxes and tariffs.

I visited Crimea several times in Ukraine's early years to meet with local leaders. One was Anushavan Danelyan, an ethnic Armenian businessman who helped create the Party for the Economic Rebirth of Crimea. In 1993 he headed a committee of the Crimean Parliament but by 1995 he would become vice chairman of the autonomous republic's Parliament. In our discussions, he focused on the plight of small and midsize business and offered barbs against Kyiv's "incompetent" leadership. In 1996 Danelyan fled Crimea after he was implicated in a series of corruption scandals. In 1997 he resurfaced as prime minister of the majority Armenian Nagorno-Karabakh Republic, another autonomous entity which, after a bitter war and ongoing conflict, had broken free of Azerbaijan, offering the local political and business elite an opportunity to operate in an economic no-man's-land similar to autonomous Crimea.

While parts of Russia's establishment were fanning tensions in Crimea, Ukrainian officials understood that Russian president Boris Yeltsin was as good a partner as one could expect in Moscow. Yeltsin never questioned Ukraine's 1991 borders. Yeltsin aides had told me in 1992 that the Russian president was committed to honoring a 1990 treaty confirming existing frontiers he had signed with Ukraine as then head of the Russian SFSR. Ukrainian officials, however, were also wary of an increasingly revanchist opposition to Yeltsin's external policies in Russia, including within the security services. Despite welcoming his acceptance of statehood, Ukraine's leaders worried about the durability of Yeltsin and his policies. These anxieties would soon be confirmed.

Yeltsin made clear that a major component of Russia's democratic and Western-oriented foreign policy was a turn away from empire and from the use of force. Yeltsin told the Congress of People's Deputies on April 7, 1992, that Russia "was parting with the remnants of ideologized thought and messianic ideas." He added that "work to strengthen Russia's international position . . . by no means amounts to an attempt to usurp the role of a superpower." Russia, Yeltsin assured them, would pursue "radical change" that sees a "relative decline in the role played by military power." For Ukraine, the period of Yeltsin's liberal rule would prove too short. Nevertheless, his presidency afforded the country nearly a decade to consolidate its state, its military, and its post-Soviet identity largely unimpeded by Russian intervention.

Amid occasional flare-ups in tensions with Russia and a rising tide of Russian hard-line voices calling for the restoration of a unitary state, Ukraine began to seek closer relations with the West. Ukraine's central foreign policy preoccupation remained Russia, but Kyiv moved quickly to develop the contours of a broader foreign policy that expressed Ukraine's desire to secure full-fledged membership in democratic Europe, making clear that the Ukrainians, like their Central European neighbors, sought eventual entry into the structures of the European Community. As an early step toward that aim, Ukraine lobbied for membership as the fourth partner in the Visegrad process, through which Poland, Hungary, and then Czechoslovakia were seeking to coordinate their own passage into Europe.

The new state was emerging as an important presence in Central and Eastern Europe, sharing borders with Poland, Hungary, Czechoslovakia (later Slovakia), Romania, Russia, Belarus, and Moldova as well as the Black Sea coastline with Turkey, Bulgaria, Romania, Russia, and Georgia. In this environment, Ukraine clearly and prudently renounced irredentist claims on ethno-Ukrainian territories and sought reciprocal actions from bordering states. Relations with Poland and Hungary in the early years of independence were especially strong. Poland was first to recognize Ukraine's independence, and activists from the Solidarity movement had offered technical and material assistance to Rukh as it pressed for independence. Hungarian president Arpád Göncz, a liberal writer, visited Kyiv, and the two states signed a military cooperation agreement.

But while the state was making important strides in consolidating its authority and shaping its new institutions and ministries, public opinions on foreign policy and national identity were far from fully united.

Polls showed that despite independence and the fall of Communism, the effects of decades of Soviet propaganda retained a deep influence on attitudes and beliefs. Ukrainians opposed NATO membership by large margins and were ambivalent about Europe. Moreover, a poll by the Kyiv International Institute of Sociology found in 1992 that just 45.6 percent of Ukrainians identified as citizens of Ukraine, with the balance identifying primarily with their regions or expressing nostalgia for the former USSR. Ukrainian national or civic identity during Kravchuk's presidency was strong in Western and Central Ukraine, but a majority of Ukrainians in the south and east showed no similar association with the Ukrainian state. The economic hardships endured in the early years of independence deepened these tendencies, eventually opening the door for revanchist and pro-Russian politicians to build beachheads inside the country. Indeed, given the fragmented state of Ukrainian identity, the military apart, it is remarkable how little Kravchuk's team did to instill a sense of patriotism. The absence of such a policy would continue for the next decade, despite the best efforts of a patriotic cohort of politically, culturally, and socially active citizens.

Kravchuk's Legacies

Prime Minister Kuchma, who lacerated Kravchuk for resisting change and promoted himself as an economic reformer, was elected on July 10, 1994, in a second-round runoff, capturing 52 percent to 45 percent for the incumbent president. Ukraine had experienced a rotation of power, demonstrating that the public will mattered in the young state.

In retrospect, despite his many flaws, President Kravchuk had set the tone in the young independent Ukrainian state's development. Whatever can be said of his economically disastrous and culturally dormant presidency, he staunchly and deftly maneuvered to ensure Ukraine's state independence. From the moment the Soviet coup collapsed, he was unwavering in his support for Ukrainian statehood and when it was clear that he had lost an election, he quietly accepted the people's verdict.

During Kravchuk's two and a half years of rule, powerful forces and trends emerged that would go on to influence politics, the economy, and national security in the first three decades of Ukraine's statehood.

First, the failure to launch a serious privatization effort set in motion a murky process that over time would usher in an economy dominated by oligarchs.

Second, delays in the implementation of privatization and structural reforms augmented by irresponsible fiscal policies had long-term impacts that put Ukraine far behind all of its Central European and most of its post-Soviet neighbors. The rampant poverty experienced by average Ukrainians even as former and current public servants gradually accumulated vast wealth made the people deeply resentful and suspicious of the state.

Third, the failure to intelligently manage institutional reform of criminal justice meant Ukraine failed to address extensive grand and petty corruption and criminality in the economic sphere. The omnipresence of a powerful, if by contrast with Russia, largely benign, security establishment saw its origins in these early years.

Fourth, the judicial system proved unable to shed its Soviet legacy of "telephone justice" and assert independence. As a result, the fight against corruption was politicized and Ukrainian courts were weaponized: those controlling political power tended to use the judicial system to try to reinforce their positions and punish competitors who wielded economic and political influence.

Fifth, the absence of a dynamic reform of education and the lack of a strong policy of support for Ukrainian language and culture contributed to a weak sense of national identity within the population and among the elites of the new state. In these first years of independence, fissures between Russophone and Ukrainophone segments of the population were not yet fully present. However, local politicians soon found the mobilizing value of divergent local attitudes to culture and language as a means of winning or holding power.

Sixth, compromises made by Kravchuk to mollify regional elites weakened the authority of the central state. Power gradually began to shift to regional leaders, who exploited and mobilized popular discontent for a greater share of influence and power in Kyiv. These regional elites were heavily influenced by, if not intertwined with, local economic interest groups. These elites quickly understood the importance of influence over local government and lobbies that would advance their interests in Kyiv. As a result, the first Parliament of independent Ukraine was dominated by these interest groups and retrograde Communists and ex-Communists.

Seventh, while post-Soviet Russia was weakened during the Yeltsin presidency, there were troubling signals that revanchist ideas had great currency within the Russian elite and that the Kremlin was eager to press Ukraine into a close economic and political embrace.

And eighth, in the vacuum created by Russian weakness, the West was emerging as a major new force that would help significantly shape Ukraine's polity, society, and economy.

At its birth, modern independent Ukraine showed signs it was susceptible to cleavages between the Russophone east and the Ukrainophone west, cleavages rooted in centuries of Russification and imperial propaganda. But the new country also had begun its march toward consolidating statehood and sovereignty with a strong civil society that had demonstrated a high degree of self-organization and mass activism. In these first years, Ukraine also witnessed the rudiments of an emerging oligarchic elite, partly born of criminal origins. As important, the fragile new state was subject to the significant external influences of the West, which much of the country aspired to join, and Russia, whose intentions many Ukrainian leaders feared but to whose economy Ukraine was closely bound.

These characteristics would establish the contours of the main forces—positive and negative—that would further shape Ukraine's evolution. In their interplay, these oft-competing forces not only contributed to political stalemate and slow progress on reforms but, paradoxically, ensured the country's pluralism, its successful preservation of democratically contested politics, and its significant civic freedoms.

CHAPTER TWO

Money and Power

Kuchma and the Rise of the Oligarchs

On election night, July 10, 1994, President Leonid Kravchuk received unwelcome news: the early tabulated returns showed him trailing badly. Early on the morning of July 11, the initial trends were confirmed. Kravchuk was told he had lost the presidency. To his credit, Ukraine's first president resisted the temptation to buy time and try to cook the results. His decision set a precedent that in the main was to serve Ukraine well. Unlike Russia, its neighbor to the north and east, Ukraine would be governed by the outcome of competitive democratic politics and the frequent rotation of power.

This result—the first rotation of power in a non-Baltic post-Soviet state—should not have been surprising. From its first years, Ukraine experienced the development of a highly differentiated, pluralistic system of competing interests. These included an active nongovernmental sector, a range of small and midsize private business enterprises, a rent-seeking big-business elite, and a growing diversity of interests defined by locality. These local interests were to prove an obstacle to rapid national consolidation and the emergence of a widely shared sense of identity, and they also impeded efforts to consolidate absolute state power.

By 1993–94 the populous industrial regions of the Donbas and

Dnipropetrovsk were beginning to flex their economic and political muscles. It was these industrial regions that had pressed President Kravchuk to name Leonid Kuchma as prime minister, a position that became a launching pad for his presidential bid. And after Kravchuk had led round one by 38-31 percent, the eastern and industrial interests consolidated around Kuchma, allowing him to prevail by 52-45 percent. The industrial heartland of Ukraine, its mainly Russian-speaking regions, had delivered decisive votes against the incumbent and secured overwhelming support for Kuchma, the red director from the east. Kuchma's election, then, was an indication of the emerging influence of power centers in Donetsk and Dnipropetrovsk, which had made common cause with a segment of the elite in Kyiv and the port city of Odesa. Their merger of interests was driven by discontent at the poor performance of Ukraine's economy under Kravchuk.

A Power Shift

Kuchma brought with him a team of allies from Dnipropetrovsk. Included in the cohort were two contrasting personalities who, like the president, had worked at Pivdenmash: one fiercely loyal and willing to carry out unquestioningly all the president's orders, the other a sage advisor who often challenged Kuchma and tried to steer the president toward his better self. The first was Leonid Derkach, a career Dnipropetrovsk security services official, whom Kuchma installed as head of the powerful, revenue-rich, and notoriously corrupt State Customs Committee. Derkach would soon after serve as first deputy head (1994–98) and later (1998–2001) as Kuchma's head of the security service of Ukraine (SBU). The second was Kuchma's national security advisor, the erudite Volodymyr Horbulin who, like Derkach, had worked alongside Kuchma at Pivdenhmash in the mid-1970s and intersected with him when Kuchma headed the party cell at the sprawling factory. A brilliant strategic thinker, Horbulin was to become a major influence on Kuchma and several subsequent presidents. Horbulin was Kuchma's guide in the development of a multi-vector policy that sought strong relations with the West while maintaining close relations with Russia. So long as Russia cooperated with the United States, multi-vectorism was sustainable. As the Kremlin's relations with the United States deteriorated, Russia's se-

One of the grand strategists of Ukraine, Volodymyr Horbulin, in June 2023. Horbulin, as advisor to several presidents, was an early voice warning of Russia's rising threat to Ukraine. (Myroslava Luzina)

curity services increased their influence on Ukraine's politics. In this context, Horbulin became wary of the Russian elite's efforts to undermine Ukraine's sovereignty and began to advocate for integration into Western security and economic institutions.

Rounding out the initial inner circle were Dmytro Tabachnyk, a young intellectual from Kyiv who became Kuchma's first chief of staff, and Oleksandr Volkov, a beefy businessman and parliamentarian from Kyiv who had headed Kuchma's campaign and became a key advisor in Kuchma's relations with business world and the Kyiv elite. Soon they would be joined by a longtime acquaintance of Kuchma's from Dnipropetrovsk, Leonid Derkach, who in rapid succession became first deputy head of Ukraine's security service, head of customs, and then head of the security service. Derkach's son would be charged in 2022 with being an agent of Russian military intelligence. Upon assuming office, it was expected that Kuchma would pursue a foreign policy tilting toward Russia. This was favored by business interests in Ukraine's east, whose requirements for cheap energy and high levels of trade with Russia depended on good interstate relations. Moscow also saw Kuchma as the preferred choice, and Russian television, widely watched in Eastern and Southern Ukraine, had given highly favorable coverage to Kuchma's presidential quest.

Surprisingly, due to the influence of Horbulin, Kuchma's early appointments reflected geopolitical balancing rather than a tilt toward Moscow. Although there were bows in the direction of the Kremlin, the key foreign policy and national security appointees were mainly professionals deeply suspicious of Moscow. Kuchma's first foreign minister was Hennadiy Udovenko, an establishmentarian figure who later would lead the conservative patriotic movement Rukh. Udovenko pushed Ukraine toward closer cooperation with the West to offset Russia's influence.

Kuchma's second foreign minister was the veteran diplomat Borys Tarasyuk, who served from April 1998 until he was forced from his post in September 2000 by pro-Russian forces. As we walked toward the imposing home of the Foreign Ministry one year into his tenure as Kuchma's foreign minister, Tarasyuk told me: "This may look like a foreign ministry. But it is as much the Ministry of Russian Relations. The majority of our diplomacy is focused on Russia and the challenges it presents . . . abroad." Russia's policy toward the young Ukrainian state was never entirely friendly. Yeltsin had welcomed the disintegration of the USSR as it gave him a legitimate means for shifting power from Soviet president Gorbachev. Initially, there were signs of the emergence of an inward-looking Russian patriotism nourished by politicians and intellectuals like parliamentarian and ethnographer Galina Starovoytova (assassinated in 1998), top Yeltsin presidential aide Yevgeny Burbulis, Orthodox priest Gleb Yakunin, and Oleg Rumyanstev, a young politician who wrote the constitution of the emerging state.

Even as some Russians awakened to the potential of a Russian state shed of imperial ambitions, most retained their attraction to the imperial project that had been at the heart of Russian and Soviet rule. The views of Ukraine's leaders, both from the east and the west, were often quite different about their Russian neighbor. However, whether they were proponents of Western integration or of a close working relationship with Russia, the Ukrainian elite—Russian agents of influence apart—saw independence as irrevocable and borders as inviolable. Kuchma, in turn, saw in the balancing of relations between West and East, between Washington/Brussels and Moscow, the key to maximizing sovereignty. Over time, especially after his second term was rocked by scandal, this balancing act would prove harder to sustain.

Resistance to Reform

Kuchma's highest priority was to eradicate Ukraine's multiple domestic social and economic crises, including hyperinflation, currency devaluation, a deep recession, and plummeting industrial production. However, his initial domestic team did not appear to have a predisposition to reform. He retained as prime minister Vitaly Masol, who in 1990 had been driven from power by the Granite Revolution. In his last days in office, President Kravchuk had appointed Masol to bolster support among former Communist apparatchiks and government bureaucrats. Kuchma's decision to leave Masol in place surprised the international community, as the latter had openly opposed the new president's promised reform agenda. The Masol interregnum would be brief—a little over a half year.

Masol's successor, Yevhen Marchuk, came into office in March 1995. Marchuk had worked in the Soviet KGB and its Ukrainian successor, the security service of Ukraine, which he headed from late 1991. At the time of his appointment, Marchuk was first deputy prime minister responsible for the security bloc and had no economic credentials. The selection signaled that the young state faced serious geostrategic and national security challenges. Marchuk understood his own strengths and weaknesses, and with Kuchma's concurrence, took on as his first deputy the well-regarded liberal economist Viktor Pynzenyk, whose tenure included impressive efforts to promote reform and whose accomplishments included the introduction of the hryvnia as the national currency, the taming of inflation, and a measure of budgetary discipline that enabled the economy to reverse its freefall. Working in tandem with the young head of the National Bank of Ukraine, Viktor Yushchenko, Pynzenyk pushed through important market reforms at a time when Ukraine's budget deficit was a gaping 44 percent of gross domestic product and the country was suffering from hyperinflation. Their joint efforts tamed the inflation spiral.

Further reform progress, however, was soon stifled by an uncooperative government team and by opposition from powerful corporate lobbies, some of which saw their subsidies reduced by Pynzenyk's budget balancing. Despite numerous accomplishments, Pynzenyk was let go after a mere eleven months. His replacement was the governor of Dnipropetrovsk oblast, Pavlo Lazarenko. Despite his image as a tough, effective administrator, Lazarenko was the first Ukrainian government leader who recognized the full potential state power presents for the accumulation of vast personal wealth. Soon he would become the poster child for massive corruption.

Prime Minister Marchuk proved to be a man of grand political ambitions, and Kuchma quickly began to see in him a direct rival for the presidency. The Marchuk appointment, too, was short-lived, just fifteen months, ending on May 27, 1996. Kuchma's next prime minister, the third of eight who would serve during his ten-year tenure, was a disastrous mistake. In late May 1996, the Rada voted in Pavlo Lazarenko to head the government. In nominating Lazarenko, Kuchma, perhaps unknowingly, was bringing the country's most corrupt politician to the pinnacle of the governmental pyramid.

Within months, Kuchma was receiving reports of the scale of Lazarenko's corruption and about his ambitions to build an independent political base. Both the *New York Times* and Canadian media published detailed accounts documenting Lazarenko's misdeeds. Behind the scenes, Western diplomats quietly expressed to Kuchma their disapproval of Lazarenko. As important as the Western pressure was, Kuchma himself soon concluded that what initially appeared to be the appointment of a supportive governor from his home base, Dnipropetrovsk, was in fact the empowerment of a sophisticated and determined criminal mastermind. As important, this criminal was quietly building a vast fortune in collusion with local business leaders—including a young and ambitious gas trader, Yulia Tymoshenko—and was financing his own political movement. Consequently Lazarenko was dismissed at the beginning of July 1997, having served thirteen months as head of the government.

A few months after his dismissal, Lazarenko visited me in my office on Wall Street, in my capacity as CEO of Freedom House, a democracy-monitoring organization. He spun a tale in which he depicted himself as a reformer facing political repression, for opposing President Kuchma's corruption. Lazarenko also outlined plans to make his nascent political party, Hromada, an engine of reform. Above all, he sought to convince me that he was facing persecution because he dared to challenge Kuchma. The discussion was cordial, but I was well aware that Lazarenko was engaged in a con aimed at establishing a narrative of political persecution that he would try to rely upon in the event of his flight from Ukraine.

On February 17, 1999, Ukraine's Verkhovna Rada lifted Lazarenko's parliamentary immunity. The move came too late. The former prime minister fled to the United States via Greece. Upon his escape, Hromada leaders Yulia Tymoshenko and Oleksandr Turchynov left Lazarenko's party and established their own project, Fatherland, which soon became an important force in Ukrainian politics and would remain so for two decades.

Upon requesting political asylum, Lazarenko was detained at New York's Kennedy Airport on February 20, 1999, on suspicion of illegal entry and presentation of false documents. He subsequently was convicted in U.S. courts of money laundering and served eight years in federal prisons. His punishment included the confiscation of tens of millions of dollars of ill-gotten wealth on U.S. soils, including the seizure of an eighteen-thousand-square-foot mansion, the largest in Marin County, that had been rented by comedian and film actor Eddie Murphy. What U.S. authorities recovered was but a small portion of the hundreds of millions he is said to have stolen over the course of more than a decade in key government posts.

Amid an array of dodgy prime ministers, political opposition to market reforms, and privatization of state-owned industries came a parliamentary majority of former and current Communists, rent-seeking oligarchs, and energy traders. With this conglomeration of powerful interests, it was hardly surprising that Ukraine was slow to reform as the economy declined. In 1995, Kuchma's first full year in office, the GDP dropped a disastrous 12.2 percent, though this decline was half that of the previous year. In 1996 the GDP would fall a further 10 percent. The following years showed a turnaround, mainly due to the reform efforts of Pynzenyk and Yushchenko. Still, there was no sign of dramatic improvement. The economy had ended its freefall but still declined 3 percent in 1997, 1.9 percent in 1998, and 0.2 percent in 1999, the year Kuchma faced the electorate for a second time.

On June 28, 1996, Kuchma set in motion the political dynamics of the next decades of Ukraine's governance when the country adopted its post-Communist constitution, the last of the former Soviet republics to do so. Before that, Ukraine had operated on the basis of a modified version of the Soviet Ukrainian Constitution and on an informal set of understandings among the ruling post-Communist elite. The new Constitution strengthened presidential powers and formally created a presidential-parliamentary system in which the president nominated the prime minister, held the reins of foreign and defense policy and the security services, significantly influenced the appointments of justices to high courts, and exercised veto power. In creating a relatively strong but not all-powerful presidency, the Constitution set in motion future tensions between Parliament, government, and president with heterarchic power shifts that were exacerbated by the reluctance of the high courts to intercede. This tension would characterize Ukraine's governance for decades to come.

After the loud dismissal of Lazarenko, Kuchma's appointment of Valery Pustovoitenko as prime minister was viewed as a step forward. Then age fifty, Pustovoitenko was an engineer and government administrator who, like so many Kuchma appointments, came from his home base of Dnipropetrovsk (now Dnipro). Like Kuchma, Pustovoitenko had worked in the real economy as manager of a state construction company and had experience as a regional government manager. His service as minister of the Cabinet of Ministers, the de facto chief of staff for prime ministers Marchuk and Lazarenko, gave him a good handle on the state bureaucracy.

Pustovoitenko was no market reformer. His hybrid government included old-school statists as well as young market-oriented technocrats with some experience of the private sector, among them bankers Ihor Mityukov, the finance minister, and Serhiy Tihipko, the deputy prime minister for economic affairs. Pustovoitenko's two and a half years as head of the government improved income tax, value added tax, and tariff collections; introduced budgetary discipline; and led to increased exports to the former Soviet republics.

Kuchma's Rivals

As his first term in office approached an end in the fall of 1999, Kuchma's prospects for reelection were threatened by Ukraine's poor economic performance. His team rightly worried that, like Kravchuk, Kuchma could be voted out of office. To ensure victory, the election campaign employed dirty tricks and the use of administrative resources, while state media attacks on potential challengers intensified.

In early 1999, Kuchma's main threat to power came from Vyacheslav Chornovil, the journalist, former political prisoner, Rukh leader, member of Parliament, and former chairman of the Lviv Regional Council. Notwithstanding his significant national popularity, in February 1999, Chornovil was ousted from the leadership of Rukh's faction in the Parliament in a vote led by Yuri Kostenko, who had served as environment minister in the Pustovoitenko government. Kostenko then mounted a challenge to Chornovil for the leadership of the entire Rukh movement. Chornovil withstood that challenge, but the battles inside Rukh sapped energy from preparations for the election year. For this reason, Chornovil and his allies suspected Kuchma's involvement in encouraging the internal dissension.

On March 25, 1999, two weeks after retaining his leadership of the Rukh movement and just one day after he declared his candidacy for president, Chornovil was returning home to Kyiv from a campaign trip to Kirovohrad (since renamed Kropyvnytskyi) . On a road near Boryspil airport, the Toyota Corolla carrying Chornovil struck a Kamaz truck that had blocked the highway. The large rig had allegedly stalled at a bend. Chornovil's car plowed into the rig at full speed, killing the Rukh leader and his driver. A key advisor, Dmytro Palamarchuk, was seriously injured but survived. The driver of the lorry was sentenced on charges of recklessness but later amnestied. Chornovil's son, Taras, a political activist, believes his father had been assassinated. In 2005, after Kuchma had left the political scene, Ukrainian authorities reopened the Chornovil case, investigating it as a possible political killing, but no charges were forthcoming.

With the death of his main rival, Kuchma faced one last threat to reelection: a unified front of his left, center-left, and centrist opponents. On August 24, Ukrainian Independence Day, four powerful

Vyacheslav Chornovil, modern-day Ukraine's most important civic leader, on the campaign trail in February 1998. In March 1999 he would die when his automobile crashed into a truck in an incident his family and associates believe was an assassination. (Oleksandr Klymenko / POOL / UNIAN)

politicians pledged to unite around a single candidate from among them based on who was shown in public opinion polling to have the best chance to win. The quadrumvirate, known as the Kaniv Four (so named for the city in which they allied), consisted of former prime minister Marchuk, Socialist Party leader Oleksandr Moroz, speaker of the Parliament Oleksandr Tkachenko, and the mayor of Cherkasy Volodymyr Oliynyk. The Kuchma team made widespread use of dirty tricks during the campaign. A transparently fake assassination attempt against leftist presidential candidate Natalia Vitrenko appeared designed to boost her standing to draw votes from this group, advantaging Kuchma.

Amid a stagnating economy, Kuchma's team believed the president's best chance for reelection was to face the retrograde Communist leader Petro Symonenko in the second round. The Kuchma campaign team concentrated its efforts to ensure just such an outcome. Fortuitously for Kuchma, just a few weeks before the presidential election, the opposition quadrumvirate splintered, with two of the candidates—Moroz and Marchuk—running separately and Tkachenko shifting allegiances to the Communist Symonenko.

The splintering, it turned out, may not have been a naturally occurring event but the consequence of manipulations by Kuchma operatives. I was told by a Kuchma intimate and political consultant that several months prior to the election, Kuchma operatives began to sow discord inside the opposition electoral quadrumvirate. According to my informant, members of the Kuchma team learned their campaign had been infiltrated by a Marchuk loyalist. They arranged for this infiltrator to gain access to a fake poll that showed Marchuk enjoying far greater support than other members of the quadrumvirate and thus with the strongest chance to unseat Kuchma. Real polling, in fact, showed Socialist Party leader Moroz with the highest support. Marchuk, however, was convinced by the tainted data and demanded he be the standard-bearer. Amid disagreement, the coalition splintered weeks before the first-round vote.

Inasmuch as the main non-Communist opposition had splintered, the first round of elections on October 31 gave Kuchma what he wanted: a 38 percent victory, with the unelectable Communist Symonenko second with 23 percent. Moroz, the Socialist Party standard-bearer, received 11.8 percent, while Marchuk gained 8.5 percent.

With Symonenko as his runoff opponent, Kuchma waged a campaign that stoked fears of Communist revanche, which played especially well among voters in Western and Central Ukraine. As his advisors had anticipated, Kuchma won the second round handily on November 14, winning nearly 59 percent of the vote compared to 39 percent for Symonenko. With Eastern Ukraine and Crimea tilting toward Symonenko, Kuchma's second-term victory was the product of support from the Ukrainophone, patriotic west and center of the country rather than the Russophone regions that had been his bedrock in 1994.

A Government of Reforms

Mandate in hand, Kuchma was pressed by the West to adopt serious reforms in exchange for financial support from the International Monetary Fund and the World Bank, whose loans had been held up as a result of the Pustovoitenko government's inconsistent economic policies. U.S. vice president Albert Gore, Kuchma's counterpart on the bilateral Kuchma-Gore Commission, made it known that the United States believed the strongest candidate for prime minister was the head of the National Bank of Ukraine, Viktor Yushchenko, who successfully helped tame Ukraine's hyperinflation.

On December 22, 1999, Yushchenko became prime minister with the backing of 296 deputies in the Rada. His government was populated with several holdovers from the Pustovoitenko team, but included several important new ministers. Yushchenko prevailed in pressing the appointment of Yuri Yekhanurov, a well-regarded manager, as his first deputy prime minister and Yulia Tymoshenko as deputy prime minister for the Fuel and Energy complex. Tymoshenko's nomination was part of a bid to increase state energy revenues and clean up the notoriously corrupt energy sector, relying on her firsthand knowledge as a former gas trader. Yushchenko's appointments of Mykola Zhulynsky as deputy prime minister for Humanitarian Issues and celebrated actor Bohdan Stupka as culture minister added strong advocates of Ukrainization to positions of influence. The Foreign Ministry remained in the hands of Borys Tarasyuk, an ardent advocate of Ukraine's European integration. These appointments strengthened support for Yushchenko among Ukrainian patriots and nationalists.

The former gas trader Tymoshenko understood the operations of the opaque energy sector and knew most of its key players. In short measure, she bolstered state coffers with electricity sector revenues and reduced graft and corruption in the gas sector. This earned Tymoshenko very powerful enemies within the oligarchy, while her success with reforms, charisma, and strong political instincts planted the seeds for long-standing political popularity.

Yushchenko's appointment was welcomed by the West. He took patriotic positions, supported deeper cooperation with Europe and North America, was Ukrainophone, and was a strong proponent of market mechanisms. The taming of inflation during his tenure as head of Ukraine's National Bank won Yushchenko admirers from the international financial institutions. His marriage to Kateryna Chumachenko, a former official in the George H. W. Bush White House who worked on economic reform in Ukraine, gave him an important partner and sounding board in his efforts to reform the economy and in his relations with Washington.

Because of his Ukrainian patriotism and marriage to an American, Yushchenko was regarded with suspicion within the nascent Putin administration and among pro-Russian politicians in Ukraine. Nor was Yushchenko accepted into Kuchma's inner circle or welcomed by the increasingly influential oligarchs, who saw him as a threat to their state capture. His engagement of Tymoshenko to attack entrenched economic interests did not help. In her post, Tymoshenko had made bitter enemies of many energy traders who exerted significant influence inside the Kuchma team. One such enemy was Ihor Bakai, the head of the state oil and gas company, Naftogaz. Between 1994 and 1996, Bakai had run companies that played a lucrative intermediary role in Ukraine's gas trade with Russia. By 1997 the role of main intermediary had passed to Yulia Tymoshenko and a Russian company, Itera. A Western Ukrainian, Bakai developed a strong personal relationship with Kuchma, to whom he served as an advisor and who served in his role as head of Naftogaz as a counterweight to Tymoshenko. Intermediary companies and schemes had cost the Ukrainian treasury billions of dollars. Yet such schemes could not have been possible without the collusion of the Russian state company, Gazprom. Clearly, the Kremlin and its loyal corporate underlings saw in Ukraine's gas traders a means by which to win influence in Ukraine's politics and gain leverage within its corrupt corporate elite. These practices would be central to Russia's long-term effort to maintain a powerful fifth column in Ukraine.

Under Yushchenko and Tymoshenko, revenue collections from the energy sector significantly increased through the elimination of barter arrangements—by which Tymoshenko herself had built a large fortune. With pressure on companies to make proper payments for energy use and with cash transfers replacing barter arrangements, the scope for massive tax evasion, underpayments, and corruption was reduced significantly. Several billion dollars in new revenues came into the state budget over several years, contributing to budgetary equilibrium and strengthening Ukraine's currency. This, in turn, meant that Yushchenko's government could benefit from the disbursal of most of the IMF's $2.6 billion loan facility for Ukraine. Together, these factors opened the door to GDP growth of 6.1 percent in 2000 and 3.3 percent in 2001.

Despite the weight of the Soviet past and the early years of misrule, the rudiments of a market economy took root. Competitive politics, a diverse array of media (albeit mainly under oligarchic control), and civic engagement also began to regain pace. Ukraine had begun to right itself. A fragile center-right parliamentary majority had emerged, composed of free market liberals, conservative nationalists, parties with ties to oligarchic clans, and Kuchma loyalists. This coalition successfully pushed for economic reforms, including the stepped-up privatization of state-owned industries. President Kuchma drew praise from the West for dismantling Ukraine's Soviet-era nuclear arsenal, managing tensions between the ethnic Ukrainian majority and its Russian minority, and appointing a reasonably effective government under Yushchenko. Ukraine's economy also appeared to have taken off. In January 2001, GDP was significantly up from the year before and industrial production increased 19.5 percent. At the same time, the government projected an inflation rate of just 13.5 percent for the year, a huge turnaround from the hyperinflation that had devastated the country only a few years earlier. Wage and pension arrears also were eliminated for most Ukrainian workers and retirees. All this was achieved even as the country, which then imported most of its energy, was coping with skyrocketing oil and gas prices. But Ukraine's policy successes in the months after Kuchma's reelection came to a crashing halt as the country found itself in the throes of a major crisis featuring a headless corpse, secret audio tapes, and alleged intrigues by Ukrainian and foreign intelligence and security services.

Ukraine's only two-term president, Leonid Kuchma (*fourth from the right in the front row*), attempted to manage the rise of oligarchs. Here he meets the president of Poland, Aleksandr Kwaśniewski (*third from the right in the front row*), at the Pivdenmash aerospace factory on June 4, 2001. Kuchma had been CEO of Pivdenmash from 1986 to 1992. (Courtesy of Leonid Kuchma's Ukraine Presidential Foundation [Президентський Фонд Леоніда Кучми "Україна"])

Heorhiy Gongadze and the "Kuchmagate" Crisis

The crisis began with the disappearance of a trailblazing investigative journalist and thorn in Kuchma's side. The case would quickly morph into a lurid scandal at the top echelons of Ukraine's government, deeply destabilize the country, weaken the hand of reformers in government, and damage cooperation with the West.

On September 16, 2000, Heorhiy Gongadze—an investigative journalist who used the nascent internet to report on corruption—was abducted on a Kyiv street. Two months after Gongadze's disappearance, a headless and badly decomposed body was found outside the town of Tarascha, near Kyiv. Gongadze's friends were told of the find, and a preliminary autopsy by a local investigator suggested the body was his. Within hours of his friends' arrival on the scene, the body was surreptitiously removed from a morgue. Several days later, the corpse resurfaced in Kyiv. However, the prosecutor-general's office declared the body had been dead for far longer than two months, and government investigators said it was too badly decomposed to be identified. Officials also announced that Gongadze had been seen outside the country and issued a missing-person alert through Interpol. Eventually DNA testing, long delayed by the authorities, confirmed the identity of the corpse.

The disappearance of a journalist largely unknown to the broader public might have been written off as a minor matter, despite the fact that Gongadze's family and colleagues launched a publicity campaign and lawsuits to press for a thorough investigation. But the disappearance assumed major proportions on November 28, when Oleksandr Moroz, the Socialist rival to Kuchma in the recent presidential campaign, revealed to a stunned Parliament audio tapes of conversations among Kuchma, his chief of staff, the head of state security, and the interior minister suggesting their complicity in the journalist's disappearance.

Widespread protests erupted throughout Ukraine, drawing tens of thousands of militants, who regularly clashed with militia. Most significantly, the crisis alienated Ukraine's Western supporters, causing Kuchma to move toward Russia's nonjudgmental embrace. This shift endangered Kuchma's multi-vector foreign policy that sought balanced relations between East and West and weakened him as he faced an increasingly tense relationship with an assertive Russia and President Vladimir Putin, who came into office in December 1999.

While the motives of those who had made the recordings may have been related to efforts to isolate Ukraine from the West, this did not invalidate the evidence, nor did it mean that Kuchma was innocent of illegal activities. The existence of hundreds of hours of recordings undermines the idea that they had all been doctored. If the tapes are genuine, they offer a rare glimpse into the nature of the Kuchma regime. They reveal a Kuchma who consistently sought retribution against his political enemies and critics. The taped conversations are laced with obscenities, crude humor, and antisemitism. In them, Kuchma appears obsessed with details of what was being said about him by insiders as well as critics. The tapes connect Kuchma and his closest aides to the surveillance of parliamentarians, the suborning of judges, interference in criminal investigations, massive graft, falsification of election results, and physical attacks on opponents—including, most dramatically, the disappearance and murder of Gongadze.

In the recordings, Kuchma regularly complains about numerous publications critical of the administration and listens to detailed reports from the security services about their harassment and intimidation of media critics. In one excerpt, Interior Minister Kravchenko describes an elite unit engaged in the harassment of opponents. "This unit, their methods, they're without morals, they don't have any principles," he boasted. "My group is beginning to stifle [Gongadze]. And with your permission I will also talk with [the head of the tax service]"—a request for permission to harass Gongadze through tax inspections. The interior minister also brags about an act of arson against a distributor of anti-presidential newspapers.

The tapes include conversations in which a regional governor seems to offer Kuchma's family a 25 percent share in a factory soon to be privatized. The tapes further document the president and his security and law enforcement ministers making plans to intimidate judges, shut down Radio Liberty and the BBC, and interfere in criminal investigations. One conversation features the head of the state tax administration telling Kuchma how he was covering up the multimillion-dollar tax fraud of a friendly oligarch. In other discussions, local officials are openly ordered to deliver votes for Kuchma in the 1999 presidential election.

While there is no evidence Kuchma gave an explicit instruction to kill anyone, including journalist Gongadze, the actions he sanctioned and his loyalists' patterns of behavior are appalling. Kuchma does appear to have overtly instructed his underlings to beat, punish, and scare the journalist. At one point in the recordings, a voice resembling Kuchma's speaks of deporting Gongadze to Georgia (where earlier he had fought alongside freedom fighters) and alternatively suggests kidnapping and handing him over to the Chechens. "Grab him, strip him, leave him without his pants, let him sit there," Kuchma's voice urges interior minister and confidant Kravchenko. Years later, in 2005, Kravchenko would be found dead from a gunshot wound after the Orange Revolution toppled Kuchma's anointed successor, Viktor Yanukovych.

The abduction and murder of investigative journalist Heorhiy Gongadze in the summer of 2000 set off a chain of events that rocked the Kuchma presidency and reenergized a broad-based civic movement that would culminate in the Orange Revolution of 2004. (UNIAN)

On January 29, 2013, a Ukrainian court would find that Oleksiy Pukach, ex-head of the Interior Ministry's surveillance department, had murdered Gongadze on Kravchenko's instruction.

As the scandal unfolded, Kuchma denied the accuracy of the tapes, claiming they were all skillful montages. His son-in-law Viktor Pinchuk supported an outside investigation by the Kroll detective agency that focused on the authenticity of the tapes. Nevertheless, many of the discussions on the tapes were corroborated by real-world events, and many of the actions in which the tapes implicated Kuchma were criminal. It is, thus, plausible to conclude that Kuchma relied on thuggery to gain retribution against critics. Moreover, the preponderance of evidence suggests that while Ukraine's president likely was not directly or legally responsible for Gongadze's murder, at the least, Kuchma bears moral responsibility for the journalist's death and for conspiracy to commit a kidnapping that went very wrong.

Even more damaging for Ukraine's national security was evidence on the tapes of a scandal with international implications. In a conversation with the director of the Ukrspetsexport state arms-trading company, Kuchma is heard approving the sale of Ukraine's Kolchuga anti-aircraft system to Saddam Hussein's Iraq. It was agreed that the sale and transfer of the radar system would be handled by a trusted Kuchma associate, Leonid Derkach, then chief of the Ukrainian security service, the SBU.

With tensions rising between the United States and Iraq, such a secret operation was foolhardy, and evidence of Kuchma's mendacity and of the deeply cynical nature of Ukraine's leaders evoked intense anger among U.S. officials, including President George W. Bush. The Kolchuga system identified, detected, and locked anti-aircraft missiles onto aerial targets at a range of 500 miles and detected ground targets at a distance of over 350 miles. Significantly, the radar system was capable of overriding U.S. "stealth" technology.

The United States remained silent about the Kolchuga tapes for months, but on September 24, 2002, State Department spokesman Richard Boucher confirmed that the government had determined that the tape discussions were authentic. "This recording's authentication has led us to reexamine our policy towards Ukraine, in particular towards President Kuchma," Boucher asserted. "We've initiated a temporary pause in new obligations of Freedom Support Act assistance that goes to the central government of Ukraine."

By the time the recordings had been authenticated, the United States had fought a war against Saddam Hussein's Iraq, and the view of the U.S. administration was that Kuchma had colluded—or tried to collude—with an enemy of the United States. After the war ended, U.S. and allied forces looked for but did not find any trace of the Kolchuga system in Iraq. Nevertheless, officials concluded that at a minimum Kuchma had intended to sell the system and so they distrusted the Ukrainian president for the remainder of his tenure.

Because the tapes were digital recordings, their authenticity could be disputed, and some Western technical experts cautioned that the conversations could have been altered. But the U.S. government's confirmation of the authenticity of the Kolchuga conversation and the sheer volume of recorded data suggest that the conversations were real. Kuchma admitted that the voice and the crude conversational style were his, although he claimed that the tapes were doctored to suggest incriminating actions. Despite denials, sources in the Parliament confirmed they had been told by the president's representative to Parliament that Kuchma, like Richard Nixon, routinely taped meetings as a means of record-keeping.

Major Mykola Melnychenko, a member of Kuchma's security detail who emerged as the source who had leaked the tapes, could well have recorded the conversations. More likely, he copied the tapes from the presidential archives and was shielding colleagues from accusations of negligence. This would explain the dismissal in February 2001 of State Security Chief Leonid Derkach, whose responsibilities were believed to have included setting up the recording system and who was implicated as the middleman in the planned anti-aircraft radar sale to Iraq.

Whatever the origin of the tapes, the defensive behavior of the president's inner circle and numerous connections between the conversations and actual criminal events reinforced the Ukrainian public's belief that the recordings were authentic, contributing to the rise of a strong and increasingly consolidated opposition movement.

Public opprobrium mounted as more of the tapes' contents began to filter into Ukraine through U.S.-funded Radio Liberty and Ukrainian coverage of stories from Western newspapers. Protests mounted, and polls taken in 2000–2001 suggested Kuchma was losing the battle for the hearts and minds of his citizens. By February 2001, fewer than one in eight Ukrainians believed the president's claim that the tapes were fabricated, whereas one in four thought they were authentic. By a 5–1 margin, the public said it had absolutely no trust in Kuchma, while 95 percent were dissatisfied with the country's state of affairs.

In the nine years following independence, Ukrainian foreign

policy was directed westward, aiming at eventual integration into European political and economic institutions. Months after Gongadze's disappearance, this vector was in danger; there were the first signs of an eastward shift after the pro-Western foreign minister Borys Tarasyuk was replaced by Anatoly Zlenko, a genial Soviet-era diplomat without an anti-Russia pedigree.

"Kuchmagate" reinforced and hastened the tilt to the east as Western governments, media, and public opinion quickly began to make clear that they disapproved of close cooperation with Kuchma's repressive and corrupt regime. Western investors shied away from a country with so much political uncertainty. In response, Kuchma began to articulate the need for an improvement in the state of relations with Moscow, a trend reinforced by Ukrainian industry's heavy dependence on Russian energy.

At a February 2001 summit between Kuchma and Vladimir Putin, the new closeness in their relationship was much in evidence. Meeting in Kuchma's former home base of Dnipropetrovsk—not Kyiv, for fear of mass protests—the two leaders agreed to deeper economic and technological cooperation, largely through joint aerospace, military, and industrial production. Putin and Kuchma also agreed to reconnect Ukraine to Russia's energy grid, a step that increased Ukraine's already marked dependence on Russia. The agreements also included several secret protocols, reinforcing the view that the two countries were moving ever closer together.

Momentum toward closer cooperation with Russia was further bolstered by a sudden surge in Russian capital investment in Ukraine. In 2000 and 2001 Russian companies went on a shopping spree, picking up Ukrainian enterprises in privatization auctions as the West, wary of Ukraine's instability, held back. Russian businesses acquired oil refineries, aluminum plants, dairies, banks, and Ukrainian broadcast media. These investments brought much-needed capital to Ukraine and spurred short-term growth. Some analysts asserted, however, that Russian investment would threaten Ukraine's sovereignty if it was not balanced by Western investment.

After ten years of state independence, Ukraine's public and Ukraine's elites, including an emerging cohort of oligarchs, had become accustomed to and protective of the great advantages for personal gain offered by state sovereignty. Pro-Russian sentiments in

Ukraine, moreover, were far weaker than in neighboring Belarus. As a result, Kuchma's tilt toward Russia stirred concern within the indigenous business community.

Growing Russian Influence

Signs of growing Russian influence and the opening of Ukraine's economy to a potential Russian takeover began to face resistance from large segments of the Ukrainian public, and from many business leaders and regional officials. The country's economic turnaround and its haphazard privatizations had empowered a broad range of economic actors who understood that Ukraine's prosperity required access to Western as well as Eastern markets. Ukrainian businesspeople also understood that the additional foreign loans needed to maintain the stability of the Ukrainian currency could come in sufficient scale only from Western sources. Thus, many of Ukraine's powerful oligarchs strongly criticized the country's isolation from the West.

The impact of Kuchmagate on Ukraine's geopolitical orientation was a sign that the entire affair could well have been a Russian security service operation. Given the United States' determination, some two decades later, that Leonid Derkach's son was a Russian agent, Kuchma's security service chief could also have been linked to Russian intelligence. There was also the dubious conduct of the main source for the tape data, Major Melnychenko. Melnychenko, a decorated and highly trusted official, claimed he had used a digital recorder to record around one thousand hours of the president's conversations over a year and a half.

I met several times with Major Melnychenko after his escape from Ukraine. On one occasion, in my Manhattan apartment, he confirmed that he had visited Moscow several times while in exile. This admission, made blithely, raised a number of questions. If Moscow and Kyiv were working together closely, how was he not held and extradited to Ukraine? Melnychenko, while residing in the Czech Republic and in the United States, had employed significant efforts to mask his whereabouts, living in secret locations. Yet he seemed unconcerned about visiting a country that enjoyed warming relations with Ukraine; nor was he fearful of Russian pressure to surrender his Kuchma archive, which he claimed was a treasure trove of further revelations.

The events and personalities linked to the tape scandal—at the least—raise the question of a Russian hand in Kuchmagate. Clearly, Russia benefited. Kuchma was deeply weakened and wounded by the crisis. His former constructive and cooperative relationship with the United States was sundered. In an effort to bolster his wobbly regime, he became far more reliant on the pro-Russia lobby in his inner circle as well as on the oligarchs from Eastern Ukraine and, at least temporarily, on Putin himself. In short, the scandal ostracized him from the West and turned him full circle toward a renewed dependency on the more Russia-friendly forces in Eastern and Southern Ukraine. The ostracism and alienation from Western backers weakened the pro-reform and pro-Western voices inside the Kuchma administration. Russian pressure had already forced the dismissal of the pro-Western foreign minister Borys Tarasyuk.

Over time, the crisis came to have great impact on the configuration of the Kuchma government team. Prime Minister Yushchenko began to be seen by Kuchma as a liability because of his pro-Western positions and relationships. Another early victim of Kuchma's ire was Deputy Prime Minister Yulia Tymoshenko, who had earned Western plaudits for her reforms in the energy sector. She and her husband had made many enemies in regard to power issues, and she could not withstand the campaign waged against her by her former competitors in the gas lobby. In August 2000, while she was still a minister, Tymoshenko's husband was arrested for allegedly corrupt business transactions related to their gas-trading company, United Energy Systems of Ukraine.

In early 2001 Kuchma ordered Tymoshenko's dismissal from office, followed by her arrest on criminal charges on February 13, days after she announced the rebranding of her political movement as the Yulia Tymoshenko Bloc (BYuT). All this occurred in the context of rising mass protests under the banner of the "Ukraine without Kuchma" movement. Tymoshenko remained jailed for six weeks in the winter of 2001 on the charge of smuggling. She was never brought to trial and would continue to play a major role in Ukrainian politics into the 2020s.

The charismatic Tymoshenko's arrest fed the already vigorous anti-Kuchma protest movement. The protests, at times brutally suppressed by the state, now focused on support for Tymoshenko as well as on Kuchma's ouster, solidifying a hard-core base of followers. The Gongadze case and increased political repression deeply alienated Kyiv's journalists, civic activists, and the intelligentsia and for the first time drove many into radical opposition.

Initially, Tymoshenko's dismissal relieved pressure on Prime Minister Yushchenko. Yet as civic unrest grew, Kuchma needed a fully loyal prime minister, and Yushchenko was dismissed in May 2001. His replacement, Anatoliy Kinakh, a bland creature of the industrial lobby, was a caretaker closely linked to both the fading generation of state company managers and the emergent oligarch power brokers. Under his watch, international financial institutions froze financing of Ukraine's debt, and the economic growth generated by Yushchenko began to slow.

Important changes occurred inside the offices of the Presidential Administration. There, presidential aide Anatoliy Orel saw his influence on the ascendant, eclipsing that of the pro-Western Volodymyr Horbulin. As deputy head of the administration, Orel assumed a key role in shaping Ukraine's foreign policy, pushing for close cooperation with Russia and against the impulses of the patriotic, pro-Western Foreign Ministry, most of whose professionals were highly suspicious of Russian intentions.

The appointment of Viktor Medvedchuk, another pro-Kremlin voice, as head of the Presidential Administration in June 2002 further signaled Kuchma's geopolitical pivot. Medvedchuk served in his post until Kuchma left office in January 2005. He had extensive Kremlin links that only deepened during his tenure with Kuchma. While still in his twenties, Medvedchuk had worked as a lawyer appointed by the Soviet state to represent politically sensitive defendants, many of them political dissidents, and had built long-standing associations with the security services.

Medvedchuk's collaboration with the Soviet security services is confirmed by the testimony of prominent dissidents he was assigned to defend. They uniformly saw him as an advocate of the Soviet state who discouraged defendants from challenging state charges and assisted them in admitting their guilt. Vasyl Stus, a dissident and one of modern Ukraine's greatest poets, sought to dismiss Medvedchuk as his attorney during his 1980 trial, believing he was colluding with the prosecution. Stus died in a forced-labor camp in 1985 while serving a ten-year sentence.

In the 1990s, Medvedchuk already showed his appetite for power, playing a key role in the creation of the Social Democratic Party (United). By 2000 he was deputy chairman of the Ukrainian Parliament, only to be voted out months later for intrigues and procedural manipulations. His partisan political efforts showing little success, Medvedchuk linked his further advancement to backing from the Kremlin. In his new post as Kuchma's top aide, Medvedchuk's influence grew as a result of both his ruthless effectiveness and his well-cultivated network of Moscow contacts. By 2004 his relations with Vladimir Putin had become so close that the Russian president became godfather to Medvedchuk's youngest child—daughter Darya.

As head of the Presidential Administration, Medvedchuk steered Kuchma toward more authoritarian policies. The emergence of powerful political challengers to Kuchma—most notably Tymoshenko and Yushchenko—led Medvedchuk to develop for Kuchma a sophisticated system of media manipulation and direct control of media content. At its center were *temnyky* (thematic directives) for the major broadcast media. The directives were developed in a nondescript office near the Monastery of the Caves, one of Ukraine's most important Orthodox Christian shrines. There, political technologists such as Mykhaylo Pohrebinsky and television news director Vyacheslav Pikhovshek, who became notorious as a staunch apologist for voter fraud in the 2004 presidential elections, were joined by administration representatives and news directors to shape a daily plan of what was to appear on the major news programs. The team also determined which politicians and what issues were to be highlighted, ignored, or censored. As Pikhovshek told me, temnyky were produced in the midafternoon and distributed to the highest-rated TV channels for the evening's broadcasts.

In addition to taking inspiration from Russia's state dominance over the media, Medvedchuk admired the authoritarian presidential system Putin was consolidating. Russia's turn toward authoritarian rule was made possible by the concentration of power in the executive branch. Amid rising mass protests and the complete loss of public trust (by March 2001, just 7 percent of public trusted the presidency), Kuchma, too, was increasingly tempted by the promise of a stronger presidency. The restructuring of Ukraine's polity had an added advantage. Such changes would be introduced through a new constitution, opening the door to extending Kuchma's presidency beyond its second term.

For an increasingly antagonistic civil society and a significant parliamentary opposition, a powerful executive represented a threat to democracy. For the oligarchs, a powerful president would mean that rent-seeking required complete loyalty to the chief executive, reducing the role of the legislature and thus the influence big business exercised via elected surrogates.

From early in his second term, President Kuchma pursued a two-track policy. He first tried to pass constitutional changes that would transform Ukraine into a presidential system and open the door to extending his time in office. When this maneuver failed, Kuchma pivoted and quietly began searching for a successor who would protect him from legal jeopardy. Kuchma's inner circle was divided on the best path forward. Billionaire Viktor Pinchuk, the president's son-in-law, lobbied for Serhiy Tihipko, a competent manager with a record of accomplishment as a businessman, minister, and head of the Central Bank. But Kuchma believed Tihipko lacked the necessary electoral base to guarantee election. Pro-Russian voices in the inner circle lobbied for a more reliably Russia-friendly candidate. Such a candidate, these insiders believed, should come from the populous Donbas region, which represented over 15 percent of the national vote and whose loyalty could be secured through administrative and oligarchic financial and media resources.

An Alliance with the Donbas Clan

Kuchma opted to cement his alliance with the increasingly influential Donbas clan of oligarchs and politicians; Prime Minister Kinakh was replaced on November 21, 2002, with the governor of the Donetsk region, Viktor Yanukovych, Kuchma's anointed successor. That Yanukovych was viewed with favor by Moscow was an added advantage for Kuchma, whose relationship with the West was now at its lowest point in his presidency.

Parliament voted in Yanukovych with 234 votes, only 8 above

the minimum required. His government team had no pro-Western voices or economic reformers. Kuchma loyalists dominated. These included officials linked to former prime minister Pustovoitenko's Popular Democratic Party and allies of Chief of Staff Medvedchuk, as well as a new partner, the Donbas elite. As these three interest groups shared in running the government, Yanukovych began to embellish his public image as an "effective administrator" and "skilled manager" and to enhance his name recognition through a highly visible set of tours through the regions, all favorably covered in the oligarch and state media.

To seal the political marriage with the Donbas clan, in June 2004, less than half a year before presidential elections, Kuchma ensured that his son-in-law Pinchuk and the Donbas oligarch Rinat Akhmetov, Ukraine's richest man, entered into a partnership that successfully won a noncompetitive tender for the privatization of Kryvorizhstal, a massive steel complex in Central Ukraine. Their winning bid came in at $800 million. A year later, an open tender conducted under the presidency of Viktor Yushchenko would realize the price of $4.84 billion, six times more than the rigged bid of the year before. Indeed, the net income realized by Kryvorizhstal in 2006 alone was nearly $700 million, nearly the amount of the purchase price of the entire asset under the rigged bidding.

U.S. and European Union officials worried about the political rise of Yanukovych, pointing to his criminal past (he was a twice-convicted felon) and corrupt practices. U.S. government analysts also believed there was a high likelihood that Yanukovych had been recruited by the Soviet security services, and could well be a Russian asset. There was no other way to explain how a twice-convicted felon without high-level Communist Party relations would have been allowed to travel to Europe at the height of the Brezhnev regime.

Yanukovych's entry into national politics signaled the growing political and economic power of the Donbas, Ukraine's heavily industrial and coal-mining region. At the same time, it was clear that Kuchma continued to control the main levers of power when it came to foreign and security policy. Having survived the crisis around the murder of Heorhiy Gongadze and the Kuchmagate tape revelations, Ukraine's president sought to repair relations with the West. In 2003 Kyiv revived cooperation with NATO and, to make amends for the

Kolchuga scandal and bolster U.S. confidence, Ukraine deployed troops as peacekeepers in post-Saddam Iraq.

Amid political turmoil that strengthened the cohort of increasingly sophisticated civic activists and NGOs, the Kuchma years also saw the rise of a new generation of industrialists, steel barons, energy traders, landowners, real estate developers, and media moguls. Vast suburban settlements with lavish mansions surrounded the capital. The national airport was crowded with private jets. And the streets of Kyiv were populated by large numbers of Maybachs, Bentleys, and Mercedes. In addition to oligarch billionaires, a new generation of millionaires and entrepreneurs began to plant roots. Some of their fortunes were rooted in corruption, but many reflected honest initiative and creativity. As an upper middle class slowly began to emerge, Kyiv and other major cities began to bustle. An increasingly sophisticated international food culture developed, featuring excellent restaurants, and an energetic, sophisticated nightlife blossomed. New construction and renovations began to change drab Kyiv, Kharkiv, and Lviv into a palette of lively colors. Major hotel chains like Hyatt and Radisson began to make inroads into the country.

The new rich were beginning to feel their growing power in economic and political life. The business elite of red directors who had helped elect Kuchma in his first run for office was fading from the scene. The influence of the new generation of oligarchs was first fully manifest in the second round of voting in the 1999 election, when big business and its media coalesced in a major effort on behalf of Kuchma.

The Rise of the Oligarchs

The new oligarchs of the Kuchma years often traced their origins to careers as middle managers, commodity traders, and young entrepreneurial former Komsomol leaders; but some also had originated in criminal groups. These were the first economic actors to accumulate millions of dollars in the early 1990s, positioning them to be multimillionaires and billionaires by the end of that decade and early in the next. Most would remain major pillars in Ukraine's life for decades.

Ukraine's young business elite had emerged by taking advantage of an unstable, high-risk economic environment foreign investors were loath to enter. In the absence of wealthy domestic competitors, these forces acquired major industrial assets on the cheap, wresting control of underperforming or bankrupt state assets for pennies on the dollar. Some new investors were canny enough to build their own small, rapidly growing banks that in turn would finance their acquisitions. These rudimentary post-Communist capitalists quickly supplanted hidebound red directors who failed to cope with the creative destruction of market forces emerging in post-Soviet Ukraine. The future oligarchs understood their assets could not grow optimally if trade was confined to the post-Soviet space. But they also understood they could take advantage of cheap energy available in the early post-Soviet years to generate big profits on sales to advanced industrial economies and the third world.

This young, ambitious, and ruthless generation of twenty- and thirty-somethings was rapidly pivoting to the legitimate acquisition—and the occasional forcible takeover—of industrial assets and resources formerly controlled by the Soviet state. These new oligarchs also understood that the protection of their assets required major engagement in the politics and governance of their young country.

In the Donbas two powerful groups emerged: the Industrial Union of the Donbas and a conglomerate that would eventually become System Capital Management (SCM) and grow into Ukraine's largest private economic power. System Capital Management was created in 2000 to systematize the Donbas-based industrial empire of Rinat Akhmetov, who was in his late twenties when President Kuchma came to power. Akhmetov, a Muslim son of a coalminer from Tatarstan, studied economics at Donetsk State University. Details of Akhmetov's early years in business are sketchy. There are videos of him partying alongside Akhat Bragin, an alleged kingpin in the Donetsk criminal underworld. Akhmetov has denied he inherited Bragin's empire after the latter's assassination in October 1995. But after Bragin's death in an explosion at the Donetsk Shakhtar football stadium, Akhmetov acquired the team, succeeded Bragin as president, and financed a mosque in his memory.

I first encountered Akhmetov, already a major force in Ukraine politics, in January 2005, when I interviewed him for the *Wall Street Journal.* We met in his gaudy Donbass Palace Hotel, expropriated in

2017 by the Russian-controlled Donetsk People's Republic. In a wide-ranging conversation, we spoke about the origins of his economic empire. In Akhmetov's telling, in the early 1990s, he established an association of Donetsk open-air markets, which had proliferated after the collapse of the planned Soviet economy. Revenues from these bazaars and markets allowed him to invest "his first million" in the Dongorbank, encouraging sellers from the market to place their savings into his fledgling financial institution.

Through the resources and revenues of Dongorbank, an acronym for Donetsk City Bank (today operating as the First Ukrainian International Bank), Akhmetov financed the acquisition of large industrial holdings in the steel and coal sector at a pittance. As he told me, these assets attracted little foreign interest as Ukraine was emerging from hyperinflation and economic instability and few Ukrainian competitors had investment capital.

Beginning in the 1990s, Akhmetov acquired, restructured, and modernized major coal and steel assets, which he merged in 2000 into his holding company—System Capital Management. Assets included numerous coal mines and iron ore fields in the Donbas; steel mills in Avdiyivka, Mariupol, and Yenakiyeve; and coke and chemical plants. Later, with the profits from these industrial assets, Akhmetov moved into power generation, investing in solar and wind renewables, mineral extraction, and domestic oil and gas extraction mainly through the DTEK energy company, the largest power generator in Ukraine. He diversified into marine and rail transportation while transforming his Donetsk Shakhtar club into a top-ranked European football power that fielded world-class players from Ukraine, Brazil, and the Balkans. His media assets included Segodnya, a newspaper group with one of Ukraine's top-five online news sites, TRK Ukraina—one of Ukraine's highest-rated TV stations—as well as several sports channels and an all-news channel. He later expanded his empire by acquiring Ukrtelecom (a major phone carrier) and added assets in wireless telephony, banking, insurance, hotels, agricultural holdings, and real estate ventures.

Over time SCM was to become one of the more transparent conglomerates in Ukraine—and its holdings Ukraine's largest taxpayers. At times the conglomerate employed as many as three hundred thousand Ukrainians, and its output represented as much as 6 percent of the country's GDP. SCM's companies produced transparent audits with credible profit and loss data, allowing them to access Western credit markets. Despite a reputation of being "pro-Russian," Akhmetov eschewed the Russian market, focusing most of his investments on Ukraine and venturing modestly into Italy and the United States.

In the early years of Kuchma's presidency, Akhmetov was uncomfortable with media attention. He focused on deepening relationships with the Donetsk political elite and supported its ambitious, and ultimately larcenous, governor—Viktor Yanukovych. By the mid-2000s, Akhmetov was a major player in Ukraine's politics, exerting major influence over the Donbas-dominated Party of Regions, which emerged as a national political force.

In mid-1990s Donetsk, another industrial group began its economic ascent—the Industrial Union of the Donbas, created by Serhiy Taruta, an engineer and trader at Azovstal, one of Ukraine's largest steel plants. Taruta saw opportunity in the steel and iron trade, the source of his earliest earnings. He allied with Vitaly Haiduk, another engineer who in 1994 was the deputy head of the Donetsk regional legislature. Haiduk became, in effect, the political partner of the more business-focused Taruta. Over the years, Haiduk would weave in and out of government, serving as deputy governor of Donetsk (1996), then as energy minister (2001–2) and deputy prime minister (2002–3) in the first Yanukovych government, and finally as secretary of Ukraine's National Security and Defense Council. In time, the economic power of the Industrial Union would wane and its main assets eventually were acquired by Russian investors. But Taruta retained important wealth that enabled him to remain a player in Ukraine's politics into the early 2020s.

In New York City in 2006, Serhiy Taruta told me of the battle over assets in Donetsk in the late 1990s. In between business meetings and a visit to his daughter, then a student, Taruta explained that in the early stages, ownership of various assets among his partners was vague. "At one point we divided our assets cleanly and symmetrically," Taruta said. Then he added, with a touch of irony: "We received ninety percent of the bad assets and ten of the good. Akhmetov received ninety percent of the good assets and ten of the bad."

Indeed, Azovstal, where Taruta launched his career, would eventually become a key part of Metinvest, a part of Akhmetov's System Capital Management.

While some of the mergers and acquisitions of the early 1990s were peaceful and amicable, in much of the Donbas, Crimea, and in parts of Western Ukraine, as rivals carved up assets, violence, armed corporate raids, and assassinations were part of the lawless environment that took the lives of Donbas politicians, including members of the Industrial Union of the Donbas.

By contrast, the early business environment of Dnipropetrovsk, while competitive, was less cutthroat than in the Donbas. Dnipropetrovsk was home to what U.S. scholar Sergei Zhuk called the "disco mafia" and "Komsomol capitalism"—a kinder, gentler form of post-Communist wealth creation and privatization. In his essay "The Disco Mafia and Komsomol Capitalism in Soviet Ukraine," Zhuk described life under perestroika and the business subculture that emerged in Dnipropetrovsk. Many of the magnates who influenced and shaped Ukraine made their first money in business activities under the umbrella of the Komsomol, the Young Communist League, often in the cultural and entertainment spheres.

Before becoming the "gas princess" of Ukraine, Komsomol activist Yulia Tymoshenko was one such entrepreneur who took advantage of opportunities under Mikhail Gorbachev's reforms that permitted limited profit-making activities. Her small business screened films from the United States and Europe and rented videos to a public starved for access to the outside world. The experience of accumulating modest working capital awakened her entrepreneurial fervor and positioned her for the fiercely competitive business environment that emerged with the collapse of Communism.

Dnipropetrovsk yielded three of Ukraine's most important industrialists: Viktor Pinchuk, who became a major force in building a network of Ukraine's influential international supporters, and the controversial tandem of Ihor Kolomoysky and his co-equal business partner Gennadiy Bogolyubov. Kolomoysky was the public face of the business. In 1992, initially working together with thirty-two-year-old Serhiy Tihipko, Kolomoysky, age twenty-nine, and Bogolyubov, thirty, launched PrivatBank. The bank would grow into Ukraine's largest, two decades later holding over 50 percent of Ukrainians' individual savings and issuing and managing over 50 percent of the country's credit cards. Employing a formula at the root of other major fortunes, Kolomoysky and Bogolyubov used Privat to finance the expansion of an empire that would include ferrous metals plants, airlines, oil extraction and refining, real estate, and important media holdings, including print, internet, and TV, most notably Ukraine's frequent audience ratings leader, 1+1.

Kolomoysky presented the combative public image of the company, using the nickname Benya and casting himself as a bad boy, the modern-day counterpart of a fictional gangster, Benya Krik, the antihero of Isaac Babel's short stories. Tough-talking Benya Kolomoysky was often linked to corporate raids of dubious legality. He and Bogolyubov also earned a reputation as the most litigious of the oligarchs. Initially, the partners were not directly engaged in electoral politics, but in time, the group would support a series of major political figures and parties, mainly with the help of their influential national media assets.

In the early 1990s Viktor Pinchuk was a lesser player on the Dnipropetrovsk scene. But he quickly advanced to the oligarchic first division. He was a metallurgical engineer and entrepreneur who in 1990 established a small engineering research group, Interpipe. By the end of the 1990s, Pinchuk's empire has expanded significantly as Interpipe evolved into a major industrial brand that produced pipes for the oil and gas systems of the former USSR and wheels for the railways.

Pinchuk's rise to power was significantly enhanced by his marriage to Olena Franchuk, the daughter of President Kuchma. Multimillionaire Viktor Pinchuk soon became a billionaire, regularly listed in the top ranks of Ukraine's richest. By 2006 he would sell his prospering Ukrsotsbank, whose assets and profits spiked dramatically during the Kuchma years, to Italy's Bank Intesa for $1.16 billion. By 2000 Pinchuk, like other oligarchs, had launched a media empire that within a decade would include national TV channels ICTV, STB, and Novyy Kanal and music channels M1 and M2. The cumulative ratings of his TV assets ranged between an audience share of 20 and 35 percent of Ukrainian viewers, enabling him, along with several super-rich counterparts, to play an important role in shaping public attitudes.

Pinchuk became an innovative trailblazer in the policy world as a major donor to humanitarian and educational causes at home and abroad. He became a leading promoter of Ukraine on the international stage, advocating Ukraine's European path through the Yalta European Strategy, an annual autumnal conference that brings together hundreds of the world's leading thinkers, statesmen, and journalists to discuss Ukraine's place in the global system and the state of its reforms and institutions. He engaged the world's celebrity A-list in the cause of Ukraine: from Paul McCartney to Elton John, from Hillary Clinton to Donald Trump, from Tony Blair to Boris Johnson, from Ashton Kutcher and Mila Kunis to Robin Wright, from Jeff Koons to Anselm Kiefer.

For a time, Pinchuk engaged directly in politics, and even served in Parliament. Later he removed himself from direct partisan engagement, asserting he wasn't an oligarch because, unlike most super-rich contemporaries, he didn't support or control a political party or parliamentary group. The demurral notwithstanding, Pinchuk found alternate ways of projecting political influence, in part by supporting the development of emerging political leaders, many of whom became credible reformers.

Yulia Tymoshenko was another significant member of the Dnipropetrvosk oligarchic elite. In the 1990s, she was Ukraine's most important gas trader, abetted by her then political protector, Pavlo Lazarenko, who served as governor of the region before his brief ascent to the post of prime minister. Tymoshenko's company, United Energy Systems of Ukraine (UESU), purchased natural gas through the barter of commodities and machinery in a largely unsupervised environment. By 1996–97 UESU controlled as much as 80 percent of Ukraine's gas trade with Russia.

Initially, President Kuchma had tolerated the Tymoshenko/Lazarenko business interests. But Lazarenko represented a darker and more ominous side of Dnipropetrovsk life than the members of the "disco mafia." In July 1996, he survived an assassination attempt when a car bomb exploded near his armed cortege on the way to Kyiv's Boryspil airport. The media speculated that the attempt had been ordered by Yevhen Shcherban, a Donetsk parliamentarian who wanted a piece of the gas trade. Shcherban himself was assassinated on the tarmac of Donetsk airport in November of that year in what some speculate was a reply from the Lazarenko camp. Whatever the truth about his links to violence and murders, President Kuchma described his appointment of Lazarenko as among his greatest mistakes.

Control of the gas business eventually passed to members of President Kuchma's team of advisors and to the government-owned Naftogaz stock company, which today is the major state gas and oil monopoly and was for several years Ukraine's most profitable enterprise. One of President Kuchma's trusted advisors, Ihor Bakai, was appointed head of Naftogaz. A businessman in the food services industry, Bakai became a major force in the energy sector until he fled to Russia in 2005, ostensibly to escape potential criminal charges related to his gas-sector activity. Under Bakai, the state gas trade expanded, and with it the role of important new middlemen who would make great fortunes simply for brokering the transit of Turkmen and later Russian gas to Ukraine. The most prominent gas trader would soon became Ukraine's most notorious oligarch. He was Dmytro Firtash, and he would play a key role in the country's politics and economy for over a decade.

In Kyiv, another group of powerful business interests emerged. Its leaders were active in gas trading, petroleum, hotels, utilities, construction, and real estate. In addition to Bakai, the group included the Surkis brothers and Viktor Medvedchuk. Several of these players were integrally linked to and partnered with Russian business interests and the Russian state. Another Kyiv-based entrepreneur turned politician was Petro Poroshenko, a future president of Ukraine. He developed the country's dominant confectionary business, expanded a major bus and auto manufacturing business, and held key news media assets that would play a crucial role in support of civic movements and civic revolutions in the early 2000s.

Powerful agricultural lobbies also emerged in the Kuchma years and by the early 2000s would grow into economic powerhouses. In the period 1995 to 2005, much of the moneymaking in the farming sector was organized through state trading institutions rather than private sector players. There was money to be made by well-connected rent-seekers and, in rarer cases, risk-raking entrepreneurs. In time, the capital they acquired from trading would allow them to enter the agricultural and political marketplace as independent forces. The best exemplar of this path to wealth was Yuriy Kosyuk, who established MHP, which would grow from a small trading and farming business into Europe's second-largest poultry producer with a global clientele.

There was an additional area for rapid oligarchic enrichment in a state that had control over most natural wealth: licenses for the exploitation of major natural resources. From gas fields to iron ore deposits, coal mines, titanium mines, and the like, control of Ukraine's mineral and industrial riches became points of fierce contestation. Privileged access to these sources of wealth required—indeed, necessitated—political clout and investment in media resources. In this fashion, the emerging oligarchic elite was joined at the hip with the country's nascent political movements and politicians, creating a basis for pluralism, but also for dependency and corruption. This meant that during the Kuchma years, Ukraine's super-rich were different from their counterparts in Russia. Unlike in Russia, where oligarchs were quickly tamed by the increasingly authoritarian police state of Vladimir Putin, Ukraine's oligarchs remained politically independent, and their competing interests and individual rivalries created a high degree of political and media pluralism inside the country. At the same time, direct oligarchic engagement in politics often yielded political parties that were prisoners to the whims of their main financial backers.

Kuchma's Balancing Act

One can criticize the inconsistent Kuchma's domestic policies and his role in advancing the economic interests of his inner circle, but Ukraine's second president also carefully and cannily sought to balance among the various competing oligarchic groups, at times stepping in to adjudicate, at other times empowering new players to create a more diverse playing field.

Kuchma clearly sought to harness business interests to support his political projects and policies. At times he greenlighted the persecution of his opponents and sanctioned political dirty tricks, and he worked unsuccessfully to cement a loyal party majority, but he never sought to consolidate an absolute dictatorship, which never took shape. Under Kuchma, Ukraine, one of Europe's poorest countries, was developing an inordinate share of billionaires. And its super-rich accumulated disproportionally more of their home country's wealth than their Western counterparts. Nevertheless, not all Ukraine's super-rich attained wealth through state capture or corruption. Many entered the ranks of the oligarchy through individual entrepreneurship, intelligent management, and innovation.

When the term *oligarch* is invoked in modern-day Ukraine, it reflects a phenomenon with both positive and negative impacts on the country's economic and political development. Whatever one thinks of Ukraine's super-rich, Ukraine's oligarchs (even the worst of them) differed fundamentally from their Russian counterparts. In Russia, oligarchs all marched to the beat of Vladimir Putin's drum (especially after he destroyed the fortune of uppity oligarch Mikhail Khodorkovsky, imprisoning him for over a decade). Russian billionaires were cogs in the authoritarian state, required to work in lockstep with Vladimir Putin and the ruling security service elite. By contrast, while Ukraine's oligarchs often acted in tandem with those in power, just as often they acted independently, pursuing political and personal interests at odds with the president and government. Sometimes they backed the party in power, at other times they and their media supported the opposition. Ukraine's oligarchs, moreover, jostled among themselves for rents, tariffs, subsidies, and tax incentives, often canceling out each other's influence. This competition—as much as Ukraine's active civil society—contributed to the fact that since 1991, Ukraine has retained a high degree of political pluralism amid a competitive electoral environment. Ukraine's confluence of rival economic powers, their lobbies in various parties and in Parliament, and their media holdings were both a key reason why progress in overcoming rent-seeking and corruption proved so difficult and why, paradoxically, Ukraine also preserved its pluralism and democracy.

During the Kuchma years, many of Ukraine's newly rich worked systematically to penetrate Ukraine's national legislature and local government by backing and even creating their own political parties as well as running their own candidates in district elections under Ukraine's mixed electoral system, in which 50 percent of candidates derive from party preferences and 50 percent from individual districts in a first-past-the-post system. This latter cohort of locally elected legislators became the most important mechanism for big-business influence. Business interests also worked to both corrupt and win the loyalty of members of party caucuses within the Verkhovna Rada. Legislators elected through party lists often switched allegiances, joining parliamentarians elected in regional districts as what came to be known as *tushky*—the Ukrainian equivalent of "road kill"—that is, inanimate carcasses rather than live politicians with views and consciences. The distribution of factions two years into a parliamentary convocation often little resembled the convocation at the start. To prevent this practice and lock the Rada into a configuration that voters had originally intended, civil society and some parties successfully campaigned to implement an electoral law requiring a proportional, party-list-based system with an "imperative mandate" by which legislators would lose their seats if they switched to a different faction. The fifth and the sixth convocations of the Rada (2006–7 and 2007–12) were constituted according to this principle, but the system turned out to be far less democratic than civil society had hoped, as it gave party leaders near-absolute control over their factions. A further amendment of the electoral law of 2011 reintroduced the proportional-majoritarian system, which survived until reforms in 2019.

Significantly, in the Kuchma years and beyond, wealthy interests often didn't pour their resources into a single party but spread their financing and so obtained influence over deputies in several factions. In single-mandate elections, the wealthy advanced their interests through political manipulation. This often meant backing several minor local candidates, seeking to ensure a proliferation of choices at the ballot box, which could mushroom to as many as several dozen, thus dispersing the vote and allowing a single well-funded candidate—one who often dispensed gifts and food packets to impoverished voters—to win office with as little as 15 percent or 20 percent support in the crowded field.

In addition to electing their own agents to office, oligarchs and their surrogates engaged in trading favors and providing favorable media support in exchange for influence over the appointment of government decision makers. At times such transactions involved under-the-table cash payments. There was, too, the deeper problem of outright corruption that resulted from oligarchic-backed internal lobbies; corrupt influence over the police, prosecutors, and courts;

and compensated access to inside intelligence about government policies.

Under Vladimir Putin, Russia systematically sought to establish economic footholds in Ukraine and to entice some Ukrainian billionaires and power holders with the promise of easy money through corrupt transactions. Such machinations created pockets of support for Russia in Ukraine. However, the Kremlin's best efforts notwithstanding, the vast majority of Ukraine's oligarchs sought to limit the penetration of Russian, as well as Western, capital into their country, seeing such as a threat to their privileged interests.

Kuchma's domestic policies oscillated between market-based and statist approaches. Over time government policies increasingly began to reflect the influence of the oligarchs. By contrast, Kuchma's foreign policy remained remarkably consistent from 1994 through 2005. Although the Kuchmagate scandal of 2000–2001 disrupted relations with the United States and Europe and led to the short-term rise of Russian influence in Ukrainian affairs, Kuchma rapidly looked for ways of repairing the damage his conduct had created, with the aim of maximizing Ukraine's sovereignty.

In some sense, Kuchma's foreign policy can be seen as a mirror image of his approach to domestic affairs: constant balancing among influential forces as a means of ensuring stability. He and his team deepened relations with the West, at the same time seeking fraternal relations with Russia and the countries of the post-Soviet Commonwealth of Independent States. Such a balance between a relatively supportive and benign West and an increasingly imperialist and malign Russia made this policy increasingly untenable.

Russia: Imperial Aspirations on the Ascent

During the Yeltsin presidency, Russia's policies toward Ukraine were relatively benign. As the Russian president's health deteriorated and the influence of Russia's oligarchs and security services grew, Moscow's external actions acquired more aggressive colorations. This shift in policy surfaced late in the Yeltsin presidency and escalated with the ascendancy of Vladimir Putin. Putin held the office of acting president of Russia from December 31, 1999, before he was elected president in May 2000. He quickly revived Russia's ambitions to ingather the republics of the former USSR into a new commonwealth that would share the Russian imperial narrative. In particular, influenced in part by Russian Nobel laureate Aleksandr Solzhenitsyn, Putin believed Ukraine was an artificial construct; instead, the country was an integral part of the larger *Russkiy narod* (Russian nation).

Even before the full handover of power from the Yeltsin clan to Putin and the de facto dominance of the security services and military, the *siloviki*, Russian intelligence, was using its Soviet-era relationships and networks to infiltrate, influence, and disrupt Ukrainian policymaking and policy. Ukraine's intelligence services became a point of contestation for the Russian intelligence services. Ukraine's main point of vulnerability was its own security service, which was populated by personnel from the Soviet-era KGB. By contrast, the younger Ukrainian military intelligence service, which was greatly enhanced and created virtually de novo after Ukraine's declaration of independence, proved more difficult for Russia to penetrate.

In January 1994 the CIA published a national intelligence estimate written by analyst George Kolt that predicted Ukraine's fragmentation along an east-west axis and pointed to separatist trends in Crimea. The dark prognosis suggested that Russia was making strides in its reforms and growth while Ukraine was suffering a deep economic crisis, experiencing worsening living standards that would tear at the country's fabric.

The separation of Ukraine's east and south, in fact, had little backing within the public and the elite. However, Kolt's assessment reflected U.S. intelligence that showed growing efforts by Russia to penetrate into Ukraine's life and correctly assessed that Russia would test the fragility of the unity of the Russian-speaking and Ukrainophone parts of the young country. Nowhere was that fragility greater than in Crimea.

During Kuchma's presidency Russian efforts to exert pressure on Ukraine focused on Crimea; on the Kerch Strait near the Sea of Azov, an important transportation route for Ukraine's exports; and on internal efforts to build intelligence sources and lobbies inside Ukraine's business and political elites. In contrast to overwhelming support in most of Ukraine, Crimeans had narrowly (54 percent) supported Ukrainian independence in the December 1991 referendum.

As a result, from the first months of statehood, Ukraine was fending off Russian meddling in Crimea. During the Kravchuk presidency, with the encouragement of some Russian officials, on May 5, 1992, the Crimean Parliament had declared its independence from Ukraine, precipitating a crisis that accelerated by the next day, when the peninsula's legislature voted for a constitution establishing Crimea's independence and providing for Russian dual citizenship for the Crimean population. As part of this process, the Crimean Parliament passed a resolution calling for a referendum on secession from Ukraine. In response, Kyiv threatened direct presidential rule. Sober minds compromised quickly. However, a new constitution granting Crimea significant autonomy was agreed, establishing a separate constitution for the Crimean Autonomous Republic of Ukraine.

This episode confirmed that Russia viewed Crimea as a pressure point against Ukraine, one that could be used to force concessions from Kyiv. Such concessions included the Partition Treaty of 1997, in which Kuchma agreed to a formal division of the former Soviet Black Sea Fleet. Most of the weaponry in Crimea was transferred from Ukraine to Russia. The Soviet Black Sea Fleet was divided in Russia's favor 81.7 to 18.3 percent, with Sevastopol becoming a de facto Russian naval base for twenty years. In addition to the fleet, the agreement allowed a massive Russian military presence on Crimean territory. In all, Russia deployed twenty-five thousand troops, twenty-two armed aircraft, and twenty-four artillery systems on Ukraine's peninsula. The agreement proved a fateful mistake by the Ukrainian elite of that time—undertaken on the seemingly sound logic that it eliminated the threat of Russian military confrontation in the event of no agreement. In return, a cash-strapped Ukraine received over half a billion U.S. dollars and nearly $100 million more in cash for the lease of a naval base in Sevastopol.

In securing special status for the peninsula and perpetuating a major Russian naval and military presence on the peninsula where there was a majority Russian ethnic population, the Kremlin—together with its allies in Crimea—successfully eroded the influence of Ukrainian central authorities. Crimea would be illegally annexed by Russia in 2014. But the foundations for that takeover were laid by Russian actions taken in the first years of the newly independent Ukraine's history.

In 2003 a new Russo-Ukrainian crisis erupted around the Kerch. It came as Kuchma was making progress in repairing his damaged relationship with the West. The standoff over control of the Kerch passage between the Azov Sea and the Black Sea led to heightened military tensions between Russia and Ukraine. In September Russia precipitated the crisis by building a land passage in the form of a dam to the small island of Tuzla, an action that had the potential of extending Russian territorial claims. This aggressive Russian action led to the deployment in the area of armed forces by both countries. After a standoff lasting a few months, Ukraine deescalated the crisis by signing an agreement giving Russia significant rights in the Kerch Strait and establishing joint administration over the Kerch transit point with Russia in return for Russia's cessation of the effort to extend a dam and land passage to Tuzla.

The Kuchma Record

It is clear from this narrative that the legacy of Leonid Kuchma's ten-year tenure was decidedly mixed. His management of Ukraine's complex system of rents, spoils, and oligarchic power and his efforts to steer a foreign policy between East and West were impressive balancing acts. His political instincts allowed him to be the only two-term president thus far in Ukraine's history. Yet the compromises he made domestically and internationally eroded his influence and weakened the capacity of Ukraine to reform and integrate with Europe. As new business and regional elites asserted themselves, Kuchma continued his geopolitical vacillations and the public remained divided along an east-west axis. This retarded the emergence of a stable Ukrainian political nation and contributed to Ukraine's failure to reform amid mounting corruption.

For the better part of his ten years in power, Kuchma was largely successful in balancing the interests of Ukraine's increasingly powerful regional and financial elites. The persistence of these diverse forces and interests reinforced Ukraine's pluralism and together with civic activism kept Kuchma in check, despite his inchoate authoritarian impulses. To balance the interests of major business groups, Kuchma and his allies directly interfered in judicial and administrative processes, entrenched a massive system of corruption, and undermined the rule of law, establishing a foundation for long-standing problems that would distort the country's development for decades.

Under Kuchma's predecessor Kravchuk, Ukraine had been governed mainly by former Communist ideologues, primarily from Northern, Central, and Western Ukraine. They had focused on state-building, creating a military and security service, and restructuring a monetary system and an economy that had previously been administered by the central authorities in Moscow and was beset by hyperinflation. Kuchma inherited this young Ukraine in which a wild and uncontrolled privatization was occurring, spitting out powerful new economic and political players, and sought to balance their interests.

Like his ex-Communist predecessors, Kuchma had grown up with limited knowledge of Ukraine's largely suppressed culture and history. He had been the quintessential "Soviet man," spending most of his adult life speaking Russian and surrounded by Russian speakers, first at the technology and physics faculty of Dnipropetrovsk State University and later at the massive Pivdenmash missile production enterprise. Only after he won the presidency did Kuchma begin to consider the nature of his own and his country's identity and the challenges of shaping independent Ukraine's raison d'être and state ideology.

He found answers in the evocation of Ukraine's centuries-long struggle for autonomy and independence, in a foundation of political competition and openness inside the country, in the country's atmosphere of pluralism, and in the ability of Ukrainians to reach compromise and consensus among seemingly bitterly opposed factions and interests. Kuchma defined these traits and differences in his book *Ukraine Is Not Russia*, which sought to define his legacy and spelled out his vision for the young country.

The book was published in 2003 in the seventh year of his presidency, after Kuchma had survived the greatest threat to his presidency in the tape scandal and after experiencing years of growing pressure from Russia on Ukraine's sovereignty. The volume revealed the underlying assumptions that governed Kuchma's actions as president. In a very personal manner and in his own plainspoken voice, the book addressed a Ukrainian audience, in particular the Ukrainian state and business elites, in an effort to impart a short lesson in Ukrainian identity and history. The book also addressed the Russian public, in particular the Russian state elite, to awaken them to the reality of both the permanence of Ukrainian statehood and the separate and distinct linguistic and national identity of the country.

In the book, Kuchma reached into his childhood in the small village of Chaikino in North Central Ukraine to find the sources of the deep differences between Ukrainians and Russians. He sought to anchor Ukraine's independence in the efforts to create an autonomous and sovereign state between 1917 and 1920 as well as in the aspirations for autonomy of the Cossack hetmans and their seventeenth-century proto-state, the Zaporizhian Sich. The book made clear that Kuchma saw his own effort at nation-building as rooted in economic and geopolitical pragmatism, including the acknowledgment that Ukraine and Russia were deeply interrelated. But he equally understood that Ukraine and Russia consisted of fundamentally different peoples and states. The book showed he was well attuned to the historical and contemporary Russian intentions to deny Ukrainians their state and their identity as a separate nation. His book was a warning to Russians not to underestimate the force of Ukrainian patriotism, nor the depth of most Ukrainians' attachment to their independence. It was in the end his valediction as well as an expression of the political consensus of the country's major political forces and elites.

The views Kuchma put forth were already widely shared by the citizens of Ukraine's Western and Central regions, who had no doubt about their national identity. But the book also carried a strong message aimed at consolidating the citizens living in Ukraine's south and east, where national identity was vague and fluid and where Soviet legacies were still deeply entrenched.

Yet despite occasional public expressions of a sense of Ukrainian identity, President Kuchma was largely indifferent to cultural and educational matters. He was inconsistent and inconstant in using the state, media, and educational system to reinforce a coherent Ukrainian identity or to strengthen the Ukrainian language. This inconsistency may have been a part of Kuchma's balancing act, but it arrested the consolidation of the Ukrainian public around a patriotic shared identity.

To be sure, Kuchma's sometime alliances with Ukrainian patriots raised concerns within the Eastern Ukrainian elite—which depended on the Russian market and its cheap energy sources. Kuchma understood the significance of Eastern Ukraine's powerful new economic and political elite, to integrate it into the workings of the state, and to incorporate its population into the national narrative. The Eastern business elite did not fully understand or accept the patriotic narrative that had emerged in the young Ukrainian state. They lacked, moreover, a specifically Ukrainian identity and were focused instead on a specific Donbas identity that highlighted pride in the region's contributions to the economy and manipulated resentment at the alleged exploitation of the workers of the Donbas by the Kyiv elites. But this also meant that they did not have a specific Russian national identity. Instead, they became a cultural field of contestation between a Ukrainian national narrative and one promoted by Russia's influential media, whose audience in Ukraine was often larger than that of domestic media. This state of affairs opened new opportunities for Russian state influence. In response, President Kuchma began to address the east's discontents; to serve as an arbiter who preserved a complex balance among competing regional interests; and to give East Ukrainian leaders a place in the upper reaches of power.

Rhetorically, Kuchma was a cheerleader for closer integration with the European Union, even voicing his support for a free trade agreement with the EU. But he always explained this support as a component in Ukraine's larger effort to advance the integration of the entire "Euro-Asian cultural and economic space" into a broader Europe. Such language was the quintessential expression of his multivector foreign policy. In truth, however, it was a form of dissimulation, employed to stave off pressure from Russia to integrate into the Commonwealth of Independent States. Increasingly, Ukraine excepted, the Euro-Asian space was moving toward the consolidation of one-party or dominant-party authoritarian rule. As importantly, Russia was increasingly pressing the former Soviet republics to reintegrate into a common economic, political, and security space. Kuchma sought to maneuver in this complex environment.

Even as Kuchma vacillated on integration into NATO structures and obfuscated Ukraine's geopolitical future, he strongly backed his defense ministers in serious efforts to align Ukraine's military reforms with NATO standards, and largely encouraged the efforts of Ukraine's patriotic and pro-Western Foreign Ministry to deepen support for the country within the Euro-Atlantic community, especially in Brussels and Washington. At the same time, he and his inner circle bristled at the West's numerous lectures about human rights and problems of corruption.

His presidency confronted the challenge posed by the Russian news media and their predominance in Eastern and Southern Ukraine and by the presence of powerful political lobbies and fifth columns in the country, oftentimes nurtured by access to lucrative business deals and trade preferences. As important was Russia's gigantic cultural presence in the country, often realized through Russian pop culture, including TV programs celebrating and heroizing Russia's military and security services.

Despite Russian pressures to integrate into its security and economic spheres, and despite Kuchma's occasional vacillations, Ukraine edged toward deeper and more systematic security cooperation with the United States and NATO as a counterweight to Russia. This fed Russia's interest in driving a wedge between Kuchma and the Western world, an effort that achieved a temporary success in the aftermath of the Kuchmagate scandal. Significantly, despite domestic vulnerability and international isolation, Kuchma never crossed the line into outright authoritarianism and widespread repression, nor did he tilt decisively toward Russia, understanding the threat it posed to the country's independence.

Despite significant Russian soft power and Kuchma's inconsistent domestic public education and information policies, Russia's influence on Ukraine's public and elite gradually diminished as a sense of a civic Ukrainian identity began to take root in the young state, making modest inroads in the south and east of the country. Amid this battle for Ukrainian hearts and minds, the influence of the Communist Party declined steeply, especially after the defeat of its presidential standard-bearer Petro Symonenko in 1999. With the party's demise there was no major domestic voice invoking nostalgia about the Soviet era. That role was assumed by Russian propaganda and cultural products.

Leonid Danylovych Kuchma served as president of the new country of Ukraine from its fourth to its fifteenth year. By way of comparison, in the early history of the United States, these were the years of the presidencies of George Washington and Thomas Jefferson. The chasm between these great American statesmen and the compromised, wheeling-dealing president of Ukraine says a great deal about why, from its very founding, Ukraine was held back from realizing much of its economic and creative potential.

CHAPTER THREE

Yushchenko

The Dreamer as President

In Ukraine's first fourteen years of independence, the country was rudderless. Despite the best efforts of patriots, civic activists, and young reformers, it veered from hyperinflation and budgetary profligacy to short periods of budgetary discipline and slow growth. Corruption and state capture were endemic. The country's national identity pulled in three directions—between those who still clung to Soviet nostalgia and had remained loyal Communist voters; those who had shed their socialist allegiances but had no true national identity, spoke Russian rather than Ukrainian, knew little of Ukrainian history and culture, and saw Russia as a natural ally; and those who explicitly wished to create a Ukraine rooted in the Ukrainian language and national identity. It would fall to a banker to become the bearer of the hopes and aspirations of this latter group, the national democratic current.

That banker was Viktor Yushchenko, fifty years old, in 2004. He had served as prime minister under President Kuchma before losing the post because Ukraine's corrupt ruling elite saw him as an unreliable partner, a real believer in reform. In his years as the country's central banker, Yushchenko had tamed hyperinflation and as prime minister had earned a reputation for integrity and a commitment to fiscal responsibility, which resulted in restoring significant revenues that had formerly been stolen from the gas and energy sectors.

That record earned him the respect of Western diplomats and international financial institutions. Yushchenko also had a following among those in Europe and North America who saw Ukraine as a pivotal state in the architecture of post-Communist East-Central Europe (the "keystone in the arch," as political scientist Sherman Garnett put it). For many Ukrainians, however, Yushchenko represented far more than the promise of cleaner government and integration with Europe and the world beyond the former USSR. For them the banker would become the unlikely embodiment of a Ukraine deeply rooted in its language, traditions, history, and aspiration for sovereignty and independence.

In his youth, Yushchenko had been a nominal member of the Communist Party. However, he retained a strong Ukrainian identity and was a traditionalist and conservative who proudly traced his own family history to the Cossack Hetmanate. Yushchenko's early years were spent in the Sumy region in a Ukrainophone household, surrounded by Ukrainian songs and traditions. This made him different from many in the independent Ukraine's political establishment, who had grown up in the Russified Ukrainian urban centers and had emerged from leadership positions in the Communist Party and Komsomol. As important, Yushchenko's second marriage in 1998 to Kateryna Chumachenko, a Ukrainian American business and banking consultant with an MBA from the University of Chicago who had served as a staffer in the Reagan and George H. W. Bush administrations, gave him a political confidante and linked him to Western networks and to the influences of the North American Ukrainian diaspora, where patriotic and nationalist narratives predominated.

Ukraine's Eastern and Western Elites

Despite his patriotic views and a track record of reforms, Yushchenko had also been part of the bureaucratic and political establishment, serving from 1993 to 2001 as head of the central bank and as President Kuchma's prime minister. Yushchenko's decision to break ranks with the governing establishment came only after a failed effort by some of his allies to shape a compromise that would have established elite consensus among a broad range of interest groups that included patriotic reformers. In early 2001 a number of political parties and leaders from a wide geographic spectrum held preliminary discussions regarding the creation of a broad-based establishmentarian party. Enlisted in the effort were Yushchenko's representatives and allies, including Petro Poroshenko, and leaders of the Party of Regions, including Mykola Azarov.

Had this political negotiation been successful, it might well have contributed to national unity and might have changed the course of contemporary Ukraine's tumultuous history by uniting Ukraine's centrist patriots with the powerful political bloc of the Donbas. This is likely why it was fiercely resisted by President Kuchma's chief of staff Viktor Medvedchuk, the main ally of President Putin inside Ukraine's political establishment.

Medvedchuk's vigorous internal lobbying scuppered the unity effort. Had it succeeded, Ukraine might well have moved along a less tumultuous path. In a sense, Ukraine would have replicated the tacit coalition between Ukrainian patriotic and dissident forces and the former Communist establishment, whose temporary alignment reestablished the Ukrainian state in 1990–91. At the least, an alliance between the patriots and the Russophone Eastern establishment offered the tantalizing possibility of a process of national consolidation.

The nation-building views of the Central and Western Ukraine elites had consolidated in the first decade of independence around a pro-Ukrainian historical and cultural narrative that stressed the country's centuries-long struggle for independence. By contrast, the country's Eastern elite had no true narrative to explain its support for an independent Ukraine. For them state independence was largely an accident of history that had created an opportunity for personal enrichment. For this reason, the publics and elites to the east and south continued to oscillate between the idea of reintegrating with Russia and the tantalizing possibility of drawing closer to the wealthier rules-based Western economies and their lucrative markets.

Had the doomed merger of the two elites succeeded, the country's patriotic national identity could have consolidated more quickly in Russophone Ukraine. This in turn could have opened the door to politics based on socioeconomic programs and ideologies rather than on linguistic and cultural wars. While such a merger might have slowed the prospects for reform in the short term, Ukraine could well have been spared some of the tumult that would characterize the next fifteen years of its history.

Russian leaders understood the potential implications of such a merger, and they and their agents in Ukraine waged a fierce behind-the-scenes campaign to derail the effort at unity. For the Kremlin, a unified Ukrainian elite reduced its ability to destabilize the Ukrainian state or to press it into a closer economic and geopolitical embrace.

Yushchenko: A Challenge to Entrenched Power

After the unity talks between the reform patriots and the Eastern oligarchic establishment broke down, the die was cast. And on July 16, 2001, during a climb of Ukraine's highest mountain, Hoverla, Yushchenko announced to accompanying reporters his intention to go it alone and create the opposition bloc "Our Ukraine." Yushchenko's coalition united traditionally moderate nationalist parties such as the People's Movement of Ukraine (Rukh), the Liberal Party, a small Christian Democratic Party, and the free market Reform and Order Party, as well as Solidarity, the political movement of Petro Poroshenko—one of the leaders who had explored a merger with the Donbas establishment.

Our Ukraine quickly attracted support from entrepreneurs, small businesses, and the middle class, who felt abandoned by the state and angered at widespread corruption. These market-oriented interest groups also were deeply unhappy with the power of the oligarchic elite. And they chafed at impossibly high payroll and income taxes that forced law-abiding businesses into the gray and black markets. Moreover, they resented the endless violations of property rights and rule of law by criminal economic actors in collusion with local officials and courts, which resulted in broken contracts, criminal corporate raids, and shakedowns of businesses. Ukraine's rising generation of entrepreneurs bristled at the massive grand corruption that was eroding the capacity of the state to meet elementary social needs. Together with these new-generation business leaders and their economic reform agenda, Our Ukraine mobilized around a patriotic agenda that supported European integration, Ukrainianizing the state, ameliorating centuries of Russification, and reducing Russian influence.

In legislative elections in 2002, Our Ukraine demonstrated its widespread appeal, winning 23.9 percent of the vote and emerging as the country's single most popular political force—far ahead of parties allied with President Kuchma. But the party was shut out of power, in large measure because among the 50 percent of legislators elected in local constituencies, the winners often represented rent-seeking business interests that sided with the Kuchma coalition.

The emergence of Our Ukraine and Yushchenko's decision to seek the presidency unleashed bitter contests: the entrepreneurial millionaires versus the entrenched oligarchic billionaires, the emerging upper-middle class that was building businesses from the bottom up versus the super-rich, many of whom had taken over former state assets and most of whom lobbied or used corrupt means to secure rents or privileged access to the country's natural resources.

In the face of the emerging Yushchenko challenge and with presidential elections approaching in the fall of 2004, Kuchma allied with the Donbas oligarchs to support his new prime minister Viktor Yanukovych for the top post, setting the stage for what would be the dirtiest, most polarized election in Ukraine's history.

Prelude to the Orange Revolution

"Razom nas bahato! Nas ne podolaty!" The rhythmic chant spread through the crowd of hundreds of thousands that filled Kyiv's Independence Square on the evening of November 22, 2004. "Together, we are many! We cannot be defeated!" Emerging from a sea of orange, the mantra signaled the rise of a powerful civic movement, a skilled political opposition group, and a determined middle class that had come together to stop the ruling elite from falsifying an election and hijacking Ukraine's presidency.

Over the next seventeen days, through harsh cold and sleet, millions of Ukrainians staged nationwide nonviolent protests that came to be known as the Orange Revolution. The entire world watched, riveted by this outpouring of the people's will in a country whose international image had been warped by its corrupt rulers. By the time victory was announced—in the form of opposition leader Viktor Yushchenko's electoral triumph—the civic protests had set a major new landmark in the post-Communist history of Eastern Europe: what seemed a seismic shift westward in the geopolitics of the region. Ukraine's revolution became part of a series of victories for "people power"—in Poland, Hungary, and Czechoslovakia in the late 1980s and in Serbia and Georgia in 1990.

The spark that ignited the popular fire in Ukraine's case was the apogee of all the deficiencies of the Kuchma presidency—election fraud. Nonpartisan exit polls during the November 21 presidential runoff election had given Yushchenko a commanding lead, with 52 percent of the votes, compared to Prime Minister Viktor Yanukovych's 43 percent. Yet when the official results came in, Yanukovych, the favorite of Ukraine's corrupt elite, had supposedly beaten the challenger by 2.5 percent.

This tally was instantly challenged. After polling stations had first closed, the Central Election Commission (CEC) reported that voter turnout in Ukraine's Russian-speaking eastern districts was consistent with the nationwide average of 78 to 80 percent. Four hours later, after prolonged silence, the election commission radically increased the east's turnout figures. The Donetsk region—Yanukovych's home base—went from a voter turnout of 78 percent to 96.2 percent overnight, with support for Yanukovych at around 97 percent. In neighboring Luhansk, turnout magically climbed from 80 percent at the time the polls closed to 89.5 percent the next morning, with Yanukovych winning 92 percent or more of the votes. Indeed, in several eastern districts, turnout was as much as 40 percent greater than during the first round of the presidential election three weeks before. This "miraculous" last-minute upsurge was responsible for approximately 1.2 million new votes—well over 90 percent of which went to the regime's favorite, giving him enough for a comfortable eight-hundred-thousand-vote margin of victory.

The effort to steal the election for Yanukovych had started much earlier, however. The oligarchs owned or controlled their own national broadcast media and local and national newspapers, from which Yanukovych benefited. Each injected massive funding into the political campaign. For six months, major national television channels subjected Yushchenko to a steady torrent of negative press and distortions while refusing him the opportunity to speak for himself. Russia also injected itself into the campaign. Vladimir Putin was popular with Ukraine's southern and eastern electorate as he was seen as someone who had revived the Russian economy—in stark contrast to Ukraine's moribund economic indicators. He lent his personal support to Yanukovych, with whom he met several times. Kremlin political technologists—including Gleb Pavlovsky (who years later would turn away from Putin), head of the Foundation for Effective Politics; Marat Gelman, former vice chair of Russia's ORT TV channel; and businessman Maksim Kurochkin planted themselves inside government offices and played an important role in designing Yanukovych's campaign, which was replete with anti-NATO and anti-American tropes focused in part on Yushchenko's American wife Kateryna (she was derisively called "Ket-reen" to emphasize the Anglicized version of her name).

Yushchenko's campaign faced major impediments. Sometimes his plane was denied landing rights minutes before major rallies. Road barriers slowed his travel, and once a truck tried to force his car off the road in an episode reminiscent of the likely assassination of Vyacheslav Chornovil. At the moment rallies were scheduled to begin, electricity was turned off. In one incident, Yushchenko's private security detail discovered he was being followed by state security operatives, one of whom was caught with false identity papers, multiple license plates, and eavesdropping equipment.

On September 6, 2014, Yushchenko became gravely ill. His mysterious sickness forced him from the campaign trail for nearly a month, and left his body weakened and his face badly scarred. Tests revealed he was suffering from dioxin poisoning. The poisoning would later become an important factor in the fate of Ukraine's future president, as a debilitated Yushchenko was weakened in the exercise of power during his first crucial months in office.

Yushchenko was not the only one to face harassment—such techniques extended to campaign workers, some of whom were arrested on false charges. Students living in university housing were told by university officials that if their districts voted for the challenger, they would be evicted from their dorms in the middle of winter. When Election Day came, monitors discovered that at polling sites in several areas where support for Yushchenko was high, pens had been filled with disappearing ink, so that ballots would appear blank after they were cast.

Nongovernmental groups were quick to complain. The nonpartisan Committee of Voters of Ukraine, which deployed more than ten thousand monitors to observe the runoff, declared the vote "the biggest election fraud in Ukraine's history." According to the group, eighty-five thousand local government officials helped perpetrate the fraud, and at least 2.8 million ballots were rigged in favor of Yanukovych. Claims of massive voter fraud were bolstered by an unlikely source: Ukraine's security service (SBU). In the days before and after the runoff vote, a high-ranking SBU official had kept in regular contact with Oleh Rybachuk, Yushchenko's chief of staff. Some SBU operatives had been cooperating with the Yushchenko camp since the first round of elections, regularly reporting on possible security threats and dirty tricks. SBU wiretaps provided crucial evidence of the government's chicanery, including late-night manipulation of data in the CEC's computer server.

Why did Ukraine's ruling elite resort to brazen fraud to preserve its power? The answer is great wealth and corruption, which had become systemic during the Kuchma presidency. This had been revealed in the Kuchmagate scandal's clandestine recordings, which demonstrated a system of dispensing favors, a culture of massive kickbacks, and a deployment of conspiracies to suppress political opponents—making it clear that the president had tolerated the emergence of a sprawling criminal arrangement symbiotically linking the state and big business.

With the Constitution limiting Kuchma to two terms as president, elites had chosen Prime Minister Viktor Yanukovych as their standard-bearer. He had been prime minister since November 2002, and with Russia's significant backing had become the presidential favorite of the ruling class. But the elite's optimism over his likely election was short-lived. As the 2004 presidential elections drew near, his backers grew nervous. Despite unrelentingly favorable television coverage and a bill doubling retiree pensions, his criminal record (three and a half years in jail on assault and robbery convictions) and the strong personal backing of President Putin raised deep doubts among many voters.

Two days before the November 21 runoff election, Yulia Tymoshenko, a former deputy prime minister in Yushchenko's government and a charismatic opposition leader, declared: "They are going to steal the election." She was nervous about the civic response. "There will be several days of protest, and then they will crack down. . . . We are not adequately prepared for this," she told me in one of our regular meetings in Kyiv. Indeed, few opposition leaders could have anticipated the scale and persistence of the coming protests. Although Kyiv was an "orange town," the omnipresent color of Yushchenko's insurgent campaign, no one knew that orange would soon become a symbol of the public's determination to defend its democracy.

Mass Protests and Civic Activism

On the morning after the second-round runoff vote, Kyiv was buzzing with excitement. Cars, trucks, and buses adorned with orange banners drove down the boulevards and avenues, honking three short bursts: Yush-chen-ko! Responding to Yushchenko's appeal, hundreds of thousands of Kyiv residents, most of them wearing orange, walked with a steely determination toward Independence Square. Over the years, Ukraine had gradually acquired an international reputation as a seamy state led by a criminal elite ruling over a passive populace. Under Kuchma's presidency, the authorities had cynically proclaimed the virtues of the people's democratic choice while doing everything possible to thwart it.

The Orange Revolution was the outcome of a series of processes. Ukraine had benefited from more than a decade of civil society development, a good deal of it nurtured by donor support from the United States, European governments, the National Endowment for Democracy, and private philanthropists such as George Soros. Although such sponsorship was nonpartisan, it reinforced democratic values and deepened the public's understanding of free and fair electoral procedures. Authentic democratic values were also reinforced by a new generation that had initially grown up under glasnost and later attained an awareness of democratic practices around the world.

New economic forces—millionaires and a rising middle class of entrepreneurs—resented the latticework of corruption, politically motivated multiple tax audits, and shakedowns by officials connected to business clans. These new business interests were quick to back

The Orange Revolution: presidential candidate Viktor Yushchenko addresses a mass rally in Kyiv's Maidan Nezalezhnosti (Independence Square) protesting the rigging of the election, November 22, 2004. (Oleksandr Synytsia / UNIAN)

the civic and political opposition financially, albeit often discreetly to avoid state retaliation.

The ruling elite's corruption also energized the dynamic civic sector. In a society in which the police and courts failed to defend people's elementary rights, civic self-organization was a matter of survival for small businesses and local communities seeking to stave off illegal property seizures and unregulated construction. These phenomena contributed to the development of a highly engaged civic sector that cooperated to protect fundamental rights in an atmosphere of impunity and government indifference.

The country's emerging internet news sites—which had widely disseminated the damning Kuchma tapes—were another part of this civic empowerment and awakening. By November 2004, Ukraine, with a population of 48 million people, boasted some 6 million distinct users accessing the internet—a number that was to rise exponentially in the coming decade, and although it was small by today's Ukrainian standards, it put a massive dent in the elite's ability to control the flow of information. By 2004 the lion's share of internet access was represented by residents of Kyiv and other major cities—where protests and civic action were the most widespread.

Old media played a modest role. Despite the government's huge influence on the political content of national television and notwithstanding significant pressure on independent media, a wide array of objective newspapers, journals, and local radio and television stations continued to function. One opposition nationwide television station—Channel 5—was confined to cable broadcasting and had a national audience of only around 3 percent, but it was highly popular in Kyiv and other major cities.

In the days before the Orange Revolution, journalists, bristling at government control and censorship, launched strikes and public protests, demanding the right to tell voters the truth. At 1+1, a major national television channel, the entire news team of producers, reporters, and editors walked out, forcing the station's news director and government loyalist Vyacheslav Pikhovshek to hold multi-hour talk marathons by himself. He soon became the butt of jokes such as "Question: What does 1+1 stand for? Answer: Pikhovshek and a cameraman."

By banishing Yushchenko from the airwaves, the authorities forced him to run a grassroots campaign. In July, August, and early September, Yushchenko and his surrogates had crisscrossed the country at a blistering rate of five or six meetings per day. Yushchenko gathered crowds in the thousands and tens of thousands in cities and towns across Eastern and Central Ukraine. These meetings fed the growth of networks of civic and party activists who would prove crucial in organizing the mass protests.

A final factor in the Orange Revolution's success was its experienced leadership. In 2000–2001, after the murder of Heorhiy Gongadze, a significant anti-Kuchma movement had flourished in Ukraine. Although these mass protests eventually dissipated, they represented a dry run for the next revolution. Many of the leaders of the Orange Revolution protests had cut their organizational teeth four years before in the "Ukraine without Kuchma" protests.

With the massive criminal voter fraud well documented in the runoff election, Yushchenko and his advisors opted for a two-track strategy: one revolutionary and the other constitutional and institutional, revolving around efforts to appeal to both the Parliament and the Supreme Court.

Engaging a revolutionary strategy, Yushchenko declared himself president and took the oath of office in an abbreviated session of the Parliament on November 22—the first day of the nationwide protests. As "president," he called for a nationwide general strike, urged the militia and the military to stand with the people, and called on local governments to transfer their allegiance to him. In the hours that followed the "swearing-in" ceremony, a palpable nervousness was in the air. Would the authorities respond with force? Fortunately, the answer was no. Yushchenko's risky tactics paid off, creating confusion within the security forces' rank and file. Ukraine suddenly had three presidents: the outgoing but still incumbent Kuchma; the "official" winner of the runoff, Yanukovych; and Yushchenko, whose own swearing in had been covered by the increasingly rebellious national media.

As C. J. Chivers of the *New York Times* reported on January 17, 2005, Ukraine's military and security services began to fragment as the protests gained strength. Although Yanukovych and other hardliners demanded that force be used to disperse the protestors, the authorities dared not intervene, given divisions inside the military and the SBU. According to Chivers, after the Interior Ministry unilaterally marshaled troops to attack the demonstrators, some SBU leaders made clear that they would use force to protect the protestors. The cooperation of segments of the SBU with the Yushchenko camp appears to have been a crucial element in preserving the peace.

But Yushchenko's inner circle also understood that a successful civic coup could set a precedent for street-driven politics and remain a long-term source of institutional instability. The actions of the protestors therefore needed to be reinforced by constitutional bodies. Popular demand and coordinated pressure from the international community pushed forward the institutional approach. Soon deputies from the government majority began to turn to Yushchenko, as Kuchma's power waned and the scale of the fraud became incontrovertible. On November 27, after days of mass protests and the siege of the cabinet of ministers, the Presidential Administration, and Kuchma's residence, Parliament met and by a clear majority voted to declare the poll invalid. Six days later, Ukraine's Supreme Court annulled the results of the runoff, accepting Yushchenko's legal team's evidence of massive fraud. The court ordered a fresh rerunning of the second-round elections.

Poland's president Aleksandr Kwasniewski, Lithuania's president Valdas Adamkus, and European Union foreign affairs commissioner Javier Solana worked in Kyiv to negotiate the contours of a democratic solution among the rival interests. President Kuchma, who was reluctant to resort to mass repression and state violence, agreed to a comprehensive agreement. It featured significant new protections in the election law to reduce the potential for voter fraud.

The agreement also extracted a major opposition concession, as it called for amending the Constitution to reduce the powers of the president, which had grown considerably under Kuchma. As a result, by the end of 2005 Ukraine was to become a parliamentary-presidential republic, with the president responsible for foreign policy, national defense, and security and holding veto power over the legislature. The appointment of the government would be the purview of the legislature, which faced election only in March 2006 and until then would be dominated by the Kuchma majority. Yushchenko accepted these changes with reluctance. Nevertheless, he and most key aides believed that the one-year window of strong presidential power would give him sufficient time to deal with the legacies of corruption and to shape a broad future parliamentary majority. They would be proved wrong.

Yushchenko's Victory

On December 26 Ukrainians went to the polls for the third time to vote for president (formally a rerun of the second round) in an election that attracted the largest contingent of international observers in the country's history: more than twelve thousand monitors from Europe, North America, Russia, and Asia took part. The result was predictable but not dramatically different from what exit polls had registered in the annulled second round: Yanukovych received 44 percent of the votes and Yushchenko 52 percent, with a winning margin of 2.2 million votes out of 28 million cast. The results showed significant regional variations: Yushchenko carried seventeen regions in the western, central, and northeastern parts of the country, and Yanukovych retained dominant majorities in Ukraine's ten southern and eastern regions. In essence, despite evidence of massive fraud by Yanukovych, his regional base of support had hardly budged.

As president, Yushchenko immediately faced serious domestic and international challenges. Many of Yushchenko's newly appointed ministers had served in high government posts and had been dismissed only when they challenged the corrupt elite. His team knew how to run bureaucracies and understood the fierce resistance that true reform would face. Yushchenko reluctantly nominated Yulia Tymoshenko to the post of prime minister, cognizant of her popularity. His appointees represented a broad base of the Ukrainian establishment. Some were longtime members of the opposition to Kuchma, while others had made common cause with oligarchic parties just a few years before. Some were members of the nouveau riche, while others were civic activists deeply suspicious of "new oligarchs." Some belonged to the social democratic left, others were conservative nationalists, while still others were free market liberals and secular libertarians. In the absence of an immediate legislative election Yushchenko shaped a majority coalition that included politicians who had backed his opponent. This diversity became the source of deep-seated internal divisions and rivalries.

Yushchenko's Our Ukraine took its place as part of the European People's Party, a centrist amalgamation of political forces, many of them in power. His social policies included a robust safety net for Ukraine's elderly, but he was an equally strong proponent of fiscal discipline. The various currents in his coalition and his desire to balance them initially contributed to his centrism and broad-based appeal. In the end, however, his very broad coalition would become an obstacle in moving forward boldly and decisively toward structural reforms. An additional challenge was how to take on the corrupt, criminal culture that had strengthened significantly during the Kuchma years. Yushchenko also faced Ukraine's perennial cultural-political differences, which were underscored by Eastern and Southern Ukraine's overwhelming support for Yanukovych, a divide that persisted even in the honest rerun of the presidential vote.

On the surface, Yushchenko's project to Ukrainianize education, media, and culture had strong potential for success. By the early 2000s, ethnic Ukrainians made up three-quarters of Ukraine's population, while Russians constituted only 21 percent. However, deep differences in identity between the regions persisted. In the east, the local press and omnipresent Russian TV had fanned the flames of regional discontent and painted Yushchenko and his team as ultranationalists and CIA agents. Eastern Ukrainians were unlikely to move beyond such stereotypes unless they gained consistent long-term access to balanced information that put them in direct contact with their new leaders. Neutralizing the negative impact of the Russian media and oligarchic media, which exerted a predominant influence in the Crimea and Eastern Ukraine, became a further challenge for the Yushchenko team.

Another challenge involved media reform. State television had long been a wasteland of bland and propagandistic programming. Oligarch media frequently engaged in character assassination and distortions in the interests of their owners, often in return for favors from the government. Although broadcast and print content improved in the aftermath of Yushchenko's victory, there remained the challenge of diversifying ownership of privately owned media, largely controlled by Yushchenko's oligarchic opponents.

In the economic sphere, Yushchenko confronted a rising budget deficit and an economic slowdown. His aides hoped to cover the growing debt by revisiting several insider privatizations that cheated the treasury. One such case was the June 2004 privatization of the lucrative Kryvorizhstal steel plant, bought by oligarch insiders for $800 million, less than the offer from a consortium of investors that included U.S. Steel. In addition, the Yushchenko team hoped to reassert control over the notoriously corrupt energy sector, and committed to eliminating Ukraine's preferential "special economic zones," which primarily benefited the oligarchic elite. With such measures, they believed, there would be no need to reduce public benefits or raise taxes.

The Russia Challenge

Ukraine's most pressing international challenge was—as it had been since independence—its relationship with Russia. For Yushchenko this challenge was further complicated as President Putin had strongly and openly backed his rival Yanukovych. Putin had spent four days in the week before the first-round vote promoting Yanukovych in lengthy press interviews and public meetings. Kremlin image makers had played a crucial role in advising and directing the Yanukovych campaign, and the Yushchenko camp believed Russia had spent several hundred million dollars in the effort to help Yanukovych prevail. Yushchenko's victory was thus a humiliating defeat for Putin and a setback for Russia's hegemonic aspirations.

Notwithstanding, Yushchenko and his advisors earnestly sought stable and pragmatic relations with Russia. As prime minister, Yushchenko had worked to resolve Ukraine's payment arrears for Russian energy, and Russian investment in Ukraine had reached its highest levels since independence. One day after his inauguration, Yushchenko traveled to Moscow on his first official international visit, before trips to Warsaw, Brussels, and Washington. During that visit, Yushchenko told me years later, he informed Putin of his intention to press ahead with Ukraine's aspirations to join the European Union and NATO. But he also proposed to Putin the idea of a treaty that would assure that no NATO troops would have bases or a permanent presence on Ukrainian soil. "There was no reaction. Putin simply ignored my comments. He didn't engage and we moved on to other topics," Yushchenko recalled.

Yushchenko's effort to improve relations with Putin did not yield results—quite the contrary. According to a study by Volodymyr Horbulin, after the political rise of Yushchenko, Russia dramatically expanded the activity of its security services on Ukrainian soil. "In 2004," Horbulin noted, "Russia and its agents for the first time played the card of 'Eastern Ukrainian separatism.'" On November 26, 2004, amid the Orange Revolution protests, the Luhansk regional council voted for the creation of a "South-Eastern Republic." On November 28 in Severodonetsk, Luhansk region, a congress of deputies of all state levels from seventeen of Ukraine's twenty-five regions convened. Encouraged by Russia and its political technologists, these local, regional, and national legislators sought to exert pressure against the Maidan protestors, who were demanding the rejection of Yanukovych's falsified election. At the same time, their action was fomenting regional separatism. The Russia-driven exercise in brinksmanship yielded nothing at that time, but during the Yushchenko presidency Russia continued to deepen relations with extremist groups in the south and east. It was a harbinger of Russia's future efforts to partition Ukraine.

A Tilt to the West

Yushchenko's main domestic goals were consolidating Ukraine's democracy, unifying the country around a common national identity, and creating a market economy based on the rule of law through EU integration. The latter aim had previously seemed remote, but the Orange Revolution had changed that by generating weeks of positive international publicity for Ukraine, branding it as a society committed to democratic norms. For Central Europeans now inside the EU, Ukraine's mass protest movement recaptured the spirit of their own civic movements of the 1980s. Lech Walesa had traveled to Kyiv to speak in Independence Square at the height of the protests, as did leading politicians from Germany, France, the Netherlands, Slovakia, and the Czech Republic. European institutions were voicing their support as well. On January 13, 2005, the European Parliament voted 467 in favor, 19 against, for a resolution calling for Ukraine to be given "a clear European perspective, possibly leading to EU membership."

Ukraine's low level of economic development, however, stood in the way of entry into Europe's common market. But some voices offered hope. Poland's president Aleksandr Kwasniewski believed Ukraine would be a part of the EU in fifteen years. Some analysts contended that Ukraine could be invited to begin the accession process within seven years. Yushchenko was intent on moving more rapidly. He entrusted to one of his closest aides, Oleh Rybachuk, responsibility for heading the Ministry of European Integration. With the rank of deputy prime minister, Rybachuk was to supervise every ministry's introduction of European standards and practices. Those early days were heady. In time it would become clear that such optimism and the accompanying public expectations could not be sustained.

U.S.-Ukraine relations were heavily influenced by the contingencies of the Iraq War. Washington had welcomed the Kuchma regime's commitment of troops to the effort as a form of expiation for the Kolchuga scandal. Yushchenko's government underscored its desire to honor this commitment and viewed Washington as a key ally. The Yushchenko team, moreover, expressed its gratitude for the long-term efforts of the U.S. Agency for International Development to support free media, the rule of law, civil society, and civic election monitoring.

Economically, Ukraine's leaders looked to the United States to recognize Ukraine as a market economy and push for the country's integration into the World Trade Organization and to lend its support to Ukraine's EU and NATO aspirations. Diplomatically, Ukraine sought Washington's backing whenever Russia flexed its economic and military muscles or made menacing noises.

Yushchenko's presidential inauguration was a major international event that signaled the rising importance of Ukraine. U.S. secretary of state Colin Powell attended, offering public promises of assistance. The show of Western solidarity included the presence of NATO chief Jaap de Hoop Scheffer, Polish president Kwaśniewski, and Czech president Václav Havel as well as the presidents of Austria, Romania, Hungary, Lithuania, Estonia, Slovakia, and Moldova. Yushchenko's inaugural address reiterated his aim of "Ukraine in a united Europe." He declared: "Our road into the future is the road on which a united Europe is headed."

From the outset, President Yushchenko devoted the bulk of his attention to foreign affairs. Important visits occurred to Russia, Brussels, Washington, and the World Economic Forum in Davos, where Yushchenko drew crowds as large and adulatory as Bono or Angelina Jolie. He hoped to translate Ukraine's short-term allure into geopolitical and economic advantage. On April 6, 2005, Yushchenko addressed a joint meeting of the Congress. Before a packed audience, Yushchenko delivered a strong message concerning the new Ukraine's democratic, civic, and free market values as well as its geopolitical choice of integration into the West. Yushchenko, moreover, enjoyed the advantage of a strong international lobby for Ukraine. He was the first president of Ukraine who was on the same wavelength on cultural, linguistic, and faith issues as the Ukrainian diaspora. His first visits to the United States and Europe had the atmospherics of victory laps by a triumphant athlete.

Emerging Problems

Strong international support characterized the first two years of Yushchenko's presidency. But support both at home and abroad would soon wane amid internecine quarrels and the collapse of the Orange coalition. While Yushchenko personified the Orange Revolution, he was a moderate and pragmatic establishmentarian reformer, not a revolutionary. If he was an idealistic dreamer, it was in the spheres of national identity and culture. When it came to practical matters, he was a budget-balancing accountant at heart. Soon the clash between his socioeconomic pragmatism and the rising expectations of society began to erode domestic support in his administration and to heighten tensions with his populist prime minister Yulia Tymoshenko.

In the summer of 2005, a minor scandal testified to the rising animus of civil society and independent media. A story entitled "The Son of God" revealed that President Yushchenko's nineteen-year-old son Andriy made regular use of an expensive BMW with a foreign registration and partied at some of Kyiv's priciest venues. The article appeared in *Ukrainska Pravda*, an online tribune of the Orange Revolution. It contained no allegations that the president was corrupted through the favors bestowed on his son, but the damage to Yushchenko's image had been done.

Unquestionably the teenage Yushchenko behaved badly. But the relentless attack on the teenaged Andriy persisted for days, enraging the president. An angry and emotional Yushchenko confronted and scolded the journalist who wrote the story, instructing him to not "act like a hitman." The criticism evoked an uproar among reporters, hundreds of whom signed an open letter to Yushchenko denouncing his remarks as an "attack on all journalists in Ukraine" and asserting that his "vocabulary" was "unworthy of a leader of a democratic European country." For days the story echoed in oligarch-controlled media, whose owners wanted to weaken a leader with reformist impulses.

The minor dust-up was nevertheless an early sign that the president was beginning to alienate his maximalist supporters, whose resentments were magnified by a belief that the country was moving too slowly on reforms. The episode was a harbinger of emerging problems for Yushchenko that would plague the rest of his presidency.

Civic and public discontent grew as Yushchenko and his government eschewed radical change, a consequence both of the president's gradualist approach and of the resistance he faced from the establishment-dominated majority in Parliament. Reforms also lagged because Yushchenko's personal energy was sapped by international travel undertaken in the national interest and by the debilitating effects of his poisoning. As a result of these many factors, the window for reforms was narrowing. Yushchenko had made a fateful compromise to resolve the electoral fraud deadlock by consenting to a reduction of presidential powers after one year. And as the end of that year approached, representatives of the corrupt old order sought to run out the clock. Moreover, as time passed and the fervor of the Orange Revolution waned, Ukraine's Parliament—still dominated by the Kuchma-era legislative majority—became less concerned about the power of civic protest and began to revert to previous attitudes and behavior.

The reform agenda was also undermined by internal dissension in the broad coalition that had brought Yushchenko to power. Yushchenko had promised the firebrand populist Yulia Tymoshenko the post of prime minister in return for her support. In the intervening period, Yushchenko had been put off by her will to power, her left-leaning populist economic policies, and her endless conflicts with core members of the Yushchenko team, in particular multimillionaire Petro Poroshenko, a politician who would remain a political force for the next decades.

To honor promises made during the presidential campaign, Yushchenko had reluctantly nominated Tymoshenko as prime minister, all the while seeking to curb her power. He named her key rival, Poroshenko, as secretary of an enhanced presidential body—the National Security and Defense Council. Yushchenko envisioned the council as the central institution charged with shaping the direction of the government's policies and checking the power of a future prime minister and saw Poroshenko, a deal-making pragmatist, as an optimal check on Tymoshenko's populist promises.

Amid a persistent mood of radicalism on the streets of Kyiv and anxiety within the former ruling elite, the first Tymoshenko government had come into office with near-unanimous support, save from fifty-nine Communist legislators. In all, 357 deputies, a constitutional

Prime Minister Yulia Tymoshenko (*left*) presents her government's platform to the Parliament as President Victor Yushchenko (*right*) looks on, February 4, 2005. The two would soon become bitter political rivals. (Mykola Lazarenko / press pool of the President of Ukraine / UNIAN)

majority, supported the new Orange government, including most of Yanukovych's deeply divided Party of Regions, which fragmented into several smaller groupings. Indeed, most of the former Kuchma majority voted compliantly for the Orange team, fearful of the public square.

Apart from Anatoly Kinakh, a former prime minister who had broken with the Kuchma regime to support Yushchenko, most of the new government consisted of longtime Yushchenko loyalists as well as those who had been active in support of the anti-Kuchma and Orange Revolution protests. The government team included Maidan "commander" Yuri Lutsenko, who became interior minister; liberal reformer Viktor Pynzenyk, who returned as finance minister; and

Russia hawk Borys Tarasyuk, who became minister of foreign affairs. Anatoly Hrystenko, an air force colonel and head of an important opposition think tank, was named defense minister. Yulia Tymoshenko got the top post, but she appeared to have few loyalists in the cabinet.

Over time, however, Tymoshenko's personality and willfulness overwhelmed the balance of forces in the cabinet as she frequently arrogated key decisions to herself. She also skillfully began to erode unity inside Yushchenko's inner circle, establishing a close relationship with Yushchenko's chief of staff, Oleksandr Zinchenko, a former media executive, who took over the running of the president's office, while Yushchenko's former right hand, Oleh Rybachuk, became deputy prime minister for European integration.

Endless intrigues and suspicions flared within the governing team. In time Yushchenko began to question Tymoshenko's loyalty, concluding she was building a power base ahead of the next parliamentary elections.

The largest conflict between Tymoshenko and Yushchenko erupted over privatizations. Tymoshenko wished to nationalize and reprivatize hundreds of major factories and enterprises that had been taken over by oligarchs in the first decade of Ukraine's independence. Under intense pressure from the international donor community and Western economists, Yushchenko opposed the plan, as did international financial institutions. Yushchenko argued that Tymoshenko's proposal would place the very solvency of these companies in question, as they would become subject to protracted litigation in local and international courts. In the meantime, such dubious confiscations would scare off new investors and creditors, who would worry that any asset they purchased or financed could be at risk. Instead, the president supported a single reprivatization, that of Kryvorizhstal, which in June 2004 had been sold off in what many believe was a rigged tender, netting a tiny fraction of its market value. The winners of the bid had been Viktor Pinchuk, the son-in-law of President Kuchma, and the main financial backer of the Party of Regions, Rinat Akhmetov. Their partnership won control of the plant with a bid of $800 million, a bargain price for a company whose revenues amounted to nearly $2 billion annually with a net profit of $378 million, and cash on hand of $413 million.

Despite Yushchenko's opposition to wide-ranging reprivatizations, Tymoshenko plowed forward. A court ruling overturned the 2003 privatization of the Nikopol ferroalloy plant, which also belonged to billionaire Pinchuk, who appealed the decision. Pinchuk's representatives accused Tymoshenko of trying to help the Privat group wrest control of the metals plant. Privat, a minority stakeholder in Nikopol, was owned by Pinchuk's rival Ihor Kolomoysky. After the minority shareholders voted in a new management team, Pinchuk's team organized the physical takeover of the facility with the support of some of the plant's workers.

I happened to be in Tymoshenko's office the week of the controversy and was with her when she took an urgent phone call. It was not possible to specify what asset she was discussing. But it was clear that she was directly exercising complete control over a new privatization. "Let's put it up for privatization and sell it off immediately," she said. Then, realizing that she was in the company of an American observer, she hastily added, "Of course in accordance with proper procedures and due process." Whether she was specifically discussing Nikopol was not clear. What was clear was that this was vintage Tymoshenko: a will to power, a desire to move quickly and decisively, a command of detail, and a commitment to results, not due process.

A couple days later, September 1, 2005, I visited President Yushchenko's presidential suburban home in Koncha Zaspa to celebrate First Lady Kateryna's birthday with family friends. As dusk turned to night, we repaired into the mansion, although President Yushchenko had still not arrived. Before the main course, near 11 p.m., he entered, looking harried, and took the seat opposite his wife and next to me. We exchanged pleasantries and there were a few birthday songs. My colleague, Freedom House board member Peter Ackerman, sought to engage the president in a discussion of the Orange Revolution and civic nonviolent action, a topic of one of his books and later of several of his documentary films. "I don't want to talk about politics tonight," Yushchenko replied brusquely.

Unknown to us, the night of the soirée, Prime Minister Tymoshenko had directly challenged Yushchenko on the controversial corporate takeover of the Nikopol ferroalloy plant, siding with Dnipropetrovsk oligarch Ihor Kolomoysky against Pinchuk. Tymoshenko would not relent, setting off a bitter war inside the Yushchenko coalition. On September 7, the president's chief of staff Oleksandr Zinchenko joined Tymoshenko's palace intrigue, accusing Yushchenko loyalist Petro Poroshenko of corruption and empire-building.

A *New York Times* photo from the following day captures what happened next. It shows a shocked Tymoshenko, her jaw literally dropped, as she watches Yushchenko on a TV set announcing her dismissal and that of her government. For the president, the time had come to crack the whip and assert primacy. With Tymoshenko out, security service chief Oleksandr Turchynov, a Tymoshenko stalwart and evangelical pastor, left the government team, while Tymoshenko allies in the Rada entered into opposition. Frustrated by the sniping and infighting, Yushchenko also fired Poroshenko as secretary of the National Security and Defense Council.

While the new government would be more loyal to Yushchenko, without Tymoshenko's bloc of votes, the president would now be even more reliant on parties affiliated with the oligarchs. On September 22, after negotiations between Yushchenko and various political groups, Yuri Yekhanurov was voted in as prime minister with the backing of nearly two-thirds of the legislature.

Yushchenko at last had a prime minister of his choice and a cooperative government team. But the disarray was costing him support, and now he faced a Tymoshenko unconstrained by the exigencies of office. Her omnipresence in the media and her attempts to claim the mantle of the leader of the Orange Revolution—and with it the support of the public square—dealt a severe blow to the president's popularity and political base. The case she made was simplistic: Yushchenko is now in league with the oligarchs. He refuses to seize their stolen wealth and has betrayed us.

Government infighting behind him, Yushchenko tried to stabilize the country and promote growth-oriented policies. He found a cooperative partner in the new prime minister, Yuri Yekhanurov, an architect by training, with technocratic experience as a government administrator. Like Yushchenko, the soft-spoken Yekhanurov espoused moderate liberal values but had no political base of his own. He shared the president's view that at most there should be a handful of "reprivatizations" of companies questionably privatized under President Kuchma. The centerpiece of this reprivatization was to be the Kryvorizhstal steelworks.

At its peak in 2002, Yushchenko's party held 119 seats in the Rada. By the time of his election, that number had dropped dramatically, the losses attributable to a combination of pressures from government agencies and the influence of corruption. Yushchenko understood that support for his agenda required winning over recalcitrant legislators, including defectors from his own party—and that meant entering into a dialogue with the country's oligarchs. On October 15, 2005, Yushchenko invited the country's most powerful business leaders to meet: Rinat Akhmetov, Ihor Kolomoysky, Viktor Pinchuk, and the Surkis brothers were among those who attended. A steady stream of Mercedes and Maybachs arrived at the president's office on Bankova Street. With the moderate Yekhanurov in place and the agenda focused on growth and investment, not retribution, Yushchenko felt there was a basis for greater cooperation. He would be proven wrong.

In typical Yushchenko fashion, the meeting dragged on. He spoke for nearly an hour and a half. His appeal to the oligarchs was rudimentary. Let's find a compromise and agree to work together for the good of the country. Invest in the country, pay your taxes, don't engage in corruption, and all will be well. "The Orange Revolution is over," Yushchenko declared. "We now have the opportunity to show the entire world how successful our country can be." The tone was as conciliatory as it was naïve. Many of the assembled were tough, battle-hardened practitioners of power politics, and an appeal to conscience fell on deaf ears. The aftermath of the meeting led to no dramatic breakthroughs, nor did it build sustained support for Yushchenko among the business elite, who knew that in a matter of a few months the president's powers would be significantly curtailed.

It reminded me of an encounter with one of Ukraine's richest men, Serhiy Tihipko, at Kyiv's Boryspil airport. Tihipko had headed Yanukovych's election campaign but resigned after evidence of widespread fraud. After the election, I was heading home to the United States and he to Italy to visit his daughter. On the bus to our airplane, I asked Tihipko what he thought of Yushchenko's prospects. "All he has to do is to put one of them in jail," said Tihipko. "One

Khodorkovsky, and they'll all fall into line," he said, alluding to the Russian oligarch Putin had jailed. Tihipko wasn't suggesting that Yushchenko become Putin, but that Ukraine's president had to demonstrate strength to keep his own oligarchs at bay. Yushchenko chose not to pursue that path.

The Orange Revolution did not tame oligarchic appetites. The billionaires and super-rich controlled vast assets, employed hundreds of thousands of workers, influenced political parties and individual parliamentarians, and held sway over the country's most popular television networks and newspapers. Sensing they were free of the peril of arrests, prosecutions, and asset seizure, the oligarchs took succor and advantage from the divisions inside the Orange camp. Though they detested and mistrusted Tymoshenko, they saw in her an instrument for weakening Yushchenko, thus strengthening their bargaining power and ability to extract rents. This was a familiar pattern that had been discernible through much of the young state's history.

With a new government in place, Yushchenko garnered his first big win: the transparent privatization of Kryvorizhstal. On October 24, an open tender conducted live before a national television audience saw significant competitive bidding for the asset. Mittal Steel Germany GMBH, part of the world's largest steel company, won the steel mill with a bid of $4.8 billion—$4 billion more than a partnership that included President Kuchma's son-in-law had paid only sixteen months earlier. This sale reversed that abomination and provided enough resources to cover a fifth of the state's annual budget. Mittal had made the largest single foreign investment in Ukraine's history, signaling to the world that Ukraine was worthy of investor attention.

For President Yushchenko, who stood accused of abandoning the Orange Revolution, this was a strong answer to his doubters. Not only had he ensured a transparent and lucrative privatization, he had taken the Kryvorizhstal mill from two major oligarchs—Pinchuk and Akhmetov. Now he had something to show the public and activists.

As important, his new government team was peppered with many stalwarts of the Orange Revolution, including Foreign Minister Borys Tarasyuk; protest leader Yuri Lutsenko as interior minister; Justice Minister Serhiy Holovaty, who had fought corruption and crime in the Kuchma era; and advisor Oleh Rybachuk and Vyacheslav Kyrylenko, the latter a former student activist, as deputy prime ministers.

Yushchenko had used the government reshuffle to signal that the populist policies of Tymoshenko would be replaced by business-friendly approaches. He rejected Western advice to turn the page on the rigged and corrupted privatization of Kryvorizhstal, but he also declared that thousands of past privatizations would not be reopened and the durability of ownership rights would be protected. His approach aimed to redress egregious excesses of the past, but not in a way that hurt foreign investment. He pushed deregulation to spur economic activity and unilaterally lifted Soviet-era visa requirements for European Union and North American travelers.

Such policies piqued investor interest. In August 2005 Austria's Raiffeisen Bank purchased Ukraine's Aval Bank for over $1 billion. Venture capitalist Tim Draper, who had reaped hundreds of millions in profits from an investment in the internet phone service Skype, announced he had created a new fund, DFJ Nexus, to invest in Ukraine's high-tech sector. Ending the disputes over who owned what was good for foreign investors as well as for Ukrainian big business. Oligarchs like Rinat Akhmetov, whose System Capital Management lost its profitable stake in Kryvorizhstal, were now certain they would hold onto their other major enterprises. Akhmetov began to take advantage of the new transparency to prepare his business accounting practices to meet Western standards, enabling his companies to raise billions of dollars on international credit markets for modernization and expansion at home. Several other oligarchs followed suit.

Russia's Energy Blackmail

The Yekhanurov government, however, stood on fragile ground. It survived a major destabilization effort on January 1, 2006, when Russia shut off gas to Ukraine and through Ukraine into Europe. Russia's Gazprom claimed Ukraine had fallen behind in payments for natural gas based on a calculation of a price far higher than the $50 per thousand cubic meters fixed in an agreement meant to last through 2009. Gazprom asserted that this price had expired because Ukraine had failed to sign an annual interstate understanding between the two governments, thus nullifying the long-term pricing agreement. On this basis, Russia claimed Ukraine had accumulated a massive debt calculated at the price of $160–230 per thousand cubic meters—the price Gazprom charged its European consumers. As Ukraine was importing between 50 and 60 billion cubic meters, this amounted to approximately $5 billion.

By January 4, the crisis had abated. Under pressure, Ukraine renounced its existing gas treaty with Russia, receiving in return significant debt forgiveness, but it agreed to a repricing that raised the cost of gas from $50 to $95. The agreement specified Ukraine would be allowed to import gas from Turkmenistan via a nontransparent company, RosUkrEnergo, jointly owned by Dmytro Firtash's Centragas Holding and Russia's Gazprom. Analysts indicated that Gazprom's participation in the highly profitable intermediary scheme was nontransparent and likely a conduit to the enrichment of the Putin clan. Ukrainian gas trader Firtash, who was at the center of the deal, had been close to the Party of Regions, but he rapidly built strong relationships with the Yushchenko team, and numerous reports and sources documented that Firtash was a frequent presence at the presidential office.

Firtash developed a close relationship with Oleksiy Ivchenko, CEO of the state oil and gas company Naftogaz. Through Ivchenko, Firtash lobbied for his interests within Yushchenko's leadership team. Yushchenko had appointed Ivchenko to the Naftogaz post believing him to be a convinced patriot, as he was a legislator from the Congress of Ukrainian Nationalists, a constituent party in Yushchenko's political bloc. In reality, Ivchenko was above all a businessman and wheeler-dealer. He became a nationalist leader in April 2003, a month before the death of Yaroslava Stetsko, the legendary émigré who had returned to Ukraine from exile after the USSR collapsed. Leadership of the nationalists was Ivchenko's ticket to a lucrative state post and control of the country's largest company by revenue.

Ivchenko loved the high life, expensive bespoke suits, and crisp made-to-measure shirts. As chair of Naftogaz, the state oil and gas company that extracted, distributed, and sold natural gas in Ukraine, Ivchenko drove a company-purchased Mercedes S-500 with a 5.5-liter engine, AMG tuning, a refrigerator, television, and vibrating massage chairs. Together with registration, taxes, transport, and insurance fees, the car cost Naftogaz over a quarter of a million dollars. Such high living in a poor country by this and other Yushchenko appointees eroded confidence in the president.

After the Orange Revolution, Russia pursued its traditional approach to Ukraine: to tempt and entrap Ukrainian officials and businesses into lucrative but ultimately corrupt schemes with ruinous consequences for the economy. The relationship with Firtash and Ivchenko epitomized Russia's "soft-power" approach. And it would remain a major factor in Ukrainian politics and geopolitics for another decade.

The factors that motivated the government to compromise with Moscow on pricing remain in dispute. But what cannot be disputed is that the renunciation of the $50-per-thousand-cubic-meter deal and the refusal to litigate Gazprom's unilateral renunciation of its long-term contract cost Ukraine billions of dollars over the next few years.

It would be far from the only costly decision made by Ukrainian authorities in gas negotiations with Russia. Indeed, questionable deals between Russia, Ukraine, and shady intermediaries in the gas sector would continue until the Russian occupation of the Donbas and its illegal annexation of Crimea in 2014. After this, Ukraine suspended gas purchases from Russia, litigated losses caused by questionable deals, and ended its reliance on Russian gas.

Artificially low gas prices also came at high cost—energy efficiency and self-sufficiency. Inexpensive Russian gas served the narrow domestic interests of oligarchs, for whom it was an important source of profits. But overall it was a disincentive to invest in more efficient production.

On January 10, 2006, just days after the gas crisis and after only four months in office, the Rada voted no confidence in the Yekhanurov government, thanks to the votes of Tymoshenko's party and oligarch-controlled legislators. The vote meant that Yekhanurov's team would soldier on as a weak caretaker until legislative elections two months later.

On March 26 Ukrainians again went to the polls and voted for another fragmented Parliament, though with one important difference: Yulia Tymoshenko's bloc and Viktor Yanukovych's Party of Regions registered strong support, while Yushchenko's Our Ukraine saw its support drop from 24 percent to 14 percent.

The Party of Regions claimed 186 seats, Tymoshenko's bloc won 129, Our Ukraine garnered 81, and the Communists won 21 with less than 4 percent support, a drop of over 12.6 percent from the previous election and a harbinger of their final political demise. The election results were insufficient to guarantee the Regions a majority, but theirs was a remarkable comeback from the political abyss. In the end, however, it was the leftist Socialist Party, led by Kuchma opponent and Rada speaker Oleksandr Moroz, that would be the king- or queen-maker, holding the balance of power with 33 seats.

With the Orange forces divided and the Regions Party anathema, the shaping of a new coalition government was delayed by protracted discussions about the division of government posts and regarding the new coalition's priorities. Only on June 22, 2006, was an agreement signed between the Tymoshenko bloc, Our Ukraine, and the Socialist Party to create the Coalition of Democratic Forces. But Yushchenko delayed holding a vote on the new government.

A Fateful Choice

On a hot day in early July 2006, I walked through an archway and across an interior courtyard into a café in Kyiv's Museum Alley, near the National Museum of Art. I came at the invitation of Roman Zvarych, an American expatriate friend who had been the justice minister. Zvarych was worried about the delay in forming a government and had invited me to give his Our Ukraine colleagues a "pep talk." Despite a signed coalition agreement, Yushchenko remained reluctant to appoint Yulia Tymoshenko as prime minister. Waiting to meet me were Mykola Martynenko, a deputy in the Rada and wealthy funder of Our Ukraine, and Petro Poroshenko, former head of the National Security Council and a multimillionaire chocolate baron, in line to be speaker of the Parliament.

Yushchenko's resentment and suspicion of Tymoshenko was enormous. His colleague Prime Minister Yekhanurov and other key advisors also had misgivings based on the poisonous relations that had developed during her earlier turn as head of government. They favored including the Party of Regions in a grand coalition, in part to reduce Tymoshenko's influence and dilute the number of ministerial posts to be assigned to her quota. Others in Yushchenko's inner circle, however, could not countenance an alliance that included their hated enemy from the Orange Revolution, and the president was frozen with indecision.

With three Our Ukraine heavyweights at the table, I offered my own view. Given the pro-Russian views of Yanukovych and his complicity in falsifying the country's presidential elections, there could be no other option than to ally with Tymoshenko, despite her assertive style, demagogy, and populism. That meant no alternative to a government headed by Tymoshenko. "What is the president waiting for?" I asked them. "Yulia has deep flaws and is a populist, but she is subject to pressure from the U.S. and Europe. Yanukovych simply cannot be trusted."

Despite their—and Yushchenko's—deep doubts about Tymoshenko, I urged them to press the president to break the Gordian knot and act. The coalition agreement was a signal of Tymoshenko's willingness to compromise and represented a detailed consensus blueprint to guide the agenda of the government and Parliament.

With a copy of the coalition document in hand, I headed for Poland, where the defense minister Radoslaw Sikorski had invited me to brief his ministry team, the General Staff, and senior Foreign Ministry officials at a country estate belonging to the Ministry of Defense. Over aperitifs, dinner, and after-dinner drinks, I summarized the document's key postulates. Based on signals emanating from Ukraine, I predicted that Ukraine would soon have a new Orange government led again by Tymoshenko. Within days my presentation and the coalition agreement could be thrown in the trash can. Yushchenko's indecision meant he'd lost control of the political process.

On July 7 Orange Revolution firebrand Oleksandr Moroz stunned the political world by announcing that his Socialist Party had withdrawn its signature from the coalition agreement and would support a coalition with the Party of Regions and Communist Party of Ukraine. Moroz asserted he was fed up with Yushchenko's endless delays and was switching sides. In truth, he was unhappy that he would have to relinquish his post as parliamentary speaker to Poroshenko. As a result, in return for the speakership and patronage positions in the government, he facilitated the political rebirth of Yanukovych, the villain of the Orange Revolution who had fled to Russia in fear of prosecution. This turn of events was nothing short of spectacular.

Yushchenko now had no choice but to install the new coalition. A minority of his party even agreed to back Yanukovych, and five Our Ukraine ministers joined the new government in the hope of taming and constraining Yanukovych. The government won a majority with the support of the Party of Regions, the Socialists, the Communists, thirty-four of eighty-one deputies from Our Ukraine, and five defectors from Tymoshenko's bloc. Despite Our Ukraine's participation in the government, the bonhomie of a broad coalition rapidly disintegrated. Yanukovych had come into office with a clear agenda: to sideline Yushchenko, garner as much power as possible, and keep Ukraine from moving toward Europe and NATO.

Ukraine was about to enter territory familiar to the French: cohabitation—a situation in which a powerful president is from one party and the ruling majority and government are from his opposition. If the appointment of Tymoshenko would again have challenged the patience of Yushchenko, cohabitation with his sworn Orange Revolution enemy Yanukovych would quickly morph into a bitter struggle for power, with Ukraine's democracy, national sovereignty, and geopolitical orientation at stake.

The Yanukovych-Yushchenko War

By November 2006, five Our Ukraine ministers had been removed or resigned. Yushchenko's influence in the cabinet was confined to his defense and foreign affairs ministers. In the space of less than three months, Yanukovych had consolidated dominance in the government, although at the price of narrowing the governing majority in the Rada to three.

From the outset, Yanukovych aimed to take most powers from the president to make him, as one ally told me, like "the Queen of England." Several months into the new government, I visited Kyiv and met with Oleksandr Lavrynovych, Yanukovych's justice minister. He and I had a long association stretching from his days in the Rukh movement to his role in the Central Election Commission to his service as secretary of a parliamentary commission examining the death

Prime Minister Viktor Yanukovych (*right*) confers with First Vice Prime Minister Mykola Azarov (*center*) and Vice Prime Minister Andriy Klyuev (*left*) during a session of the Verkhovna Rada of Ukraine on January 12, 2007. Yanukovych's return to government quickly morphed into a power struggle with President Viktor Yushchenko. (Oleksandr Synytsia / UNIAN)

of Heorhiy Gongadze. In 2000 Lavrynovych had even asked me to look into the authenticity of the tapes related to President Kuchma and the kidnapping of Gongadze. Lavrynovych's evolution from democratic reformer to a trusted member of the Yanukovych team was emblematic of the migrations of many other Ukrainian politicians.

The conversation with my old acquaintance was friendly but distinctly chilling. Lavrynovych spoke openly and matter-of-factly of the intention of the Yanukovych government to systematically strip the functions of the president to a minimum. In his view, even constitutionally guaranteed appointments of the ministers of defense, foreign affairs, and the head of state security would eventually be the primary prerogative of the Parliament.

In the months that followed, tensions between president and government escalated. President Yushchenko unsuccessfully sought to use the National Security and Defense Council to check Yanukovych's power grab. To break the stalemate at the apex of power, on April 2, 2007, Yushchenko announced he was dissolving Parliament and calling new elections. The president justified disbanding Parliament because Yanukovych had recruited individual members of that body to join his coalition in violation of the Constitution, which said a parliamentary coalition could be formed by political parties.

Initially, Yanukovych agreed with the decision, but soon reneged and the Rada voted to declare the president's action unconstitutional. More significantly, without legislation that authorized funding for the elections, Yushchenko's decree, although constitutionally valid, could not be implemented.

For weeks the conflict between president and prime minister was in limbo. On May 24 hostilities escalated as President Yushchenko sacked the prosecutor general Svyatoslav Piskun, whom Yushchenko had nominated. Piskun was a Party of Regions member, but the president's nomination came with the stipulation that the chief prosecutor would remain politically neutral. However, Piskun had begun selectively targeting allies of Yushchenko and opposition politicians and refusing to prosecute lawbreakers with links to the ruling coalition.

Initially, Piskun accepted the president's constitutional authority to dismiss him and vacated his office. Then, bolstered by the support of the prime minister, he made an about-face and forced his way back in to the Prosecutor's Office, setting off scuffles between his security detail and officers of the State Protection Directorate, which operated under presidential authority.

As tensions rose, the Socialists' interior minister Vasyl Sushko arrived at the Prosecutor General's Office with heavily armed Berkut riot police. That day, Ukraine teetered on the verge of a violent struggle between the pro-presidential military, security services, and State Protection forces on one side and the Ministry of Interior forces loyal to and answerable to the prime minister and government on the other. While the Ministry of Interior commands a vast number of police and heavily armed riot forces, it did not have sufficient power to force Yushchenko's hand. Importantly, he had the backing of the military (albeit it was legally barred from using force domestically), the General Staff, and the security services. He also enjoyed public support in the patriotically oriented capital Kyiv.

As the crisis threatened to spill into uncontrolled violence, Ukraine's oligarchs began worrying that the standoff posed a threat to stability. At this point, according to then U.S. ambassador John Herbst,

Ukraine's richest man, Rinat Akhmetov, at the Donbas Arena stadium in 2010. Part of a cohort of powerful oligarchs who enriched themselves in the 1990s through the privatization of former state assets, Akhmetov played a key role in ending a standoff between Prime Minister Yanukovych and President Yushchenko by backing new elections. (Andriy Babeshko / FC Shakhtar Donetsk Media Department)

billionaire Rinat Akhmetov stepped in to insist on new parliamentary elections as the only way to break the political deadlock.

Akhmetov, a close associate and financial backer of Yanukovych, had been elected to the Rada from the Regions Party. Nevertheless, he recognized the danger to his economic interests of a violent confrontation inside the Ukrainian state. As he told me in a conversation nearly a decade later, "I have always respected the office of the president. Yushchenko and I had a respectful relationship, and I sought to intercede in a way that preserved the dignity of his office and that of the prime minister. In my view, only an election could hope to break the existing deadlock." Soon other business leaders signaled support for a new ballot. Support also came from dozens of Party of Regions deputies allied with Akhmetov and other business interests. Prime Minister Yanukovych had no choice but to relent and agree to a new election. The announcement was made before thousands of pro-government demonstrators, who had been bused in from Eastern Ukraine to Kyiv's Independence Square in a simulacrum of real civic protests. Echoing Akhmetov's view as his own, Yanukovych declared, "There is no other way to solve this crisis except by holding democratic and fair elections."

Election Day, September 27, 2007, showed modest shifts in support among the parties. The Party of Regions lost 11 seats but remained the largest bloc with 175. The Tymoshenko bloc grew by 27 and held 156 seats. Yushchenko's Our Ukraine won 14 percent support and generated 72 seats (a drop of 9). Voters punished the Socialists for having joined in a coalition with the Party of Regions, voting them out of Parliament, never to return. Their place was taken by a new party representing old politics; the party of Volodymyr Lytvyn, once Kuchma's chief of staff, squeaked through and garnered 30 seats. The Communists won 27, a further sign they were a fading force.

The Tymoshenko and Yushchenko forces alone could now muster a majority of 228. Still, haggling over government posts continued for over two months until in December a new government headed by Tymoshenko was agreed with Arseniy Yatsenyuk, a Yushchenko ally, as speaker of the Parliament.

Tymoshenko's Resurrection

Tymoshenko returned to power with greater influence in both the Rada and the government than she'd had in her earlier turn in office. Her bloc's 156 seats were more than double that of Our Ukraine. In this configuration, the coalition was fragile, possessing like its immediate predecessor a majority of merely 3. Indeed, because two Our Ukraine faithful abstained, Tymoshenko took office with just 226 votes—the minimum needed for a majority, thanks to the vote of an independent deputy.

Tymoshenko named most of the key ministers, including longtime ally and campaign manager Oleksandr Turchynov as first deputy prime minister; the minister of social policy; the minister of transport and communications; the environment minister (responsible for subcontracting the exploitation of natural resources); and Bohdan Danylyshyn, the economy minister.

Viktor Pynzenyk, a fiscal hawk, returned to government as finance minister in a move that was especially well received by the IMF. This support for Ukraine was an important signal to the international business community and a key reason why Ukraine began to see an uptick in foreign direct investment. As a compromise between Yushchenko and Tymoshenko, many of the remaining ministerial appointments went to nonpartisan experts.

In 2008, nearly two decades after independence, Ukraine at last joined the World Trade Organization, an important factor on the path to greater diversification of exports and imports, which had heretofore been excessively connected to Russia and the other former Soviet republics.

This positive momentum quickly dissipated. Less than a year into the second Tymoshenko government, tensions between president and prime minister once again spilled into the open, resulting in a shakeup in the leadership in the legislature. Acting in concert with the Party of Regions opposition, Tymoshenko's bloc introduced legislation that would have severely curtailed Yushchenko's powers, transferring many of them to the prime minister. Yushchenko fiercely denounced and sought to undermine these measures.

Significantly, Tymoshenko sought to erode Yushchenko's presidential powers in the security sphere at a time when Ukraine and Yushchenko were expressing strong solidarity with Georgia, then under attack and partial occupation by Russian forces. In a tumultuous political career, this was perhaps Tymoshenko's worst political moment and one that put in question her patriotism. Tymoshenko may well have thought Yushchenko was wrong to involve Ukraine directly in the Russo-Georgian conflict by trying to restrict Russia's Black Sea Fleet from leaving the Ukrainian port in Sevastopol. But a frontal attack on the power of Ukraine's president was a dangerous signal to a warlike Kremlin that Ukraine's leadership was disunited and the authority of the commander in chief was under attack.

On September 17, as the conflict between president and prime minister intensified, Parliament speaker Areniy Yatsenyuk offered his resignation, voicing frustrations with the infighting of the coalition partners. Instead of picking sides, he announced the launch of his own political party. In October, Yushchenko again threatened to dissolve Parliament. This time it was Tymoshenko's turn to announce there would be no funds for the exercise.

On November 12, 233 deputies voted to dismiss Yatsenyuk as speaker. In the interim, rumors circulated that Tymoshenko was in serious negotiations with Yanukovych and the Regions about a new coalition. Such rumors very likely had been launched primarily to gain leverage over Yushchenko, but they didn't gain traction. Amid threats from Yushchenko to again call elections, the Our Ukraine–Tymoshenko coalition instead was rescued and bolstered by the addition of the small Lytvyn bloc. The creation of the wider coalition was strongly supported by the active diplomacy of Polish president Aleksandr Kwasniewski, who had helped calm the warring coalition partners with the backing of the European Union and the United States. In return for his support, Lytvyn took over the speakership on December 18, 2008.

From Reform to Populism

Although the economy showed impressive growth in the initial stages of Yushchenko's presidency, growth slowed from 12 percent in 2004 to 3 percent the following year. In 2006 the economy again grew a robust 7.6 percent but slowed again to 2.3 percent in 2007. Foreign direct investment also grew, especially in the first three years, over the full five years of Yushchenko's presidency totaling $32 billion, a figure that is more than double any other presidential term and more than was invested in Ukraine over the next decade of independence. These accomplishments were largely due to the centrist market-friendly influence of Yushchenko and Our Ukraine, who successfully muted both Tymoshenko and Yanukovych's statist and populist big-spending impulses.

In 2008, amid the global financial crisis sparked by the collapse of Lehman Brothers and Bear Stearns, Ukraine's modest growth reversed. While the U.S. economy fell by some 2 percent in 2009, Ukraine fell into deep recession as GDP declined 14.8 percent. The hryvnia, Ukraine's currency, weakened from five to the dollar to over eight. In the Yushchenko years, many Ukrainians had taken out hard currency loans, which were offered at significantly lower interest rates than loans in the national currency. Now borrowers were required to continue to make good on those hard currency payments while their hryvnia-based incomes were down by 60 percent vis-à-vis the dollar.

In these dire circumstances, the public blamed the president, not the prime minister—Yushchenko, not the free-spending Tymoshenko—for the hryvnia's decline. His popularity toppled to new lows and his political fate was sealed. In October 2008 Tymoshenko's government signed an agreement with the International Monetary Fund that offered hope for sensible long-term pro-growth policies, including state enterprise privatization, banking reforms, investment incentives, and the taming of large social welfare outlays. The program gave Ukraine a loan of $16.4 billion dependent on adhering to a balanced budget and reform of the corrupt banking sector. In all, the government received $10.6 billion of the entire aid package. However, in late 2009, further tranches of assistance ceased after Tymoshenko, preparing for her own presidential run, reneged on the agreement and busted the budget with large minimum wage and pension increases. Her populist actions led to the resignation of Finance Minister Pynzenyk, who refused to implement what he saw as ruinous policies.

Tymoshenko again reverted to populist rhetoric: opposing further privatization, favoring top-down economic administration, and backing state support of one set of industries over another, often with little rhyme or reason. Together with the decision to bust the budget in favor of large social welfare and pension increases, the pumping of money into the economy led to a modest recovery after the disastrous decline of 2009, and in 2010 Ukraine's GDP grew 3.8 percent.

As she coped with the global economic crisis, Tymoshenko focused with steely determination on the 2010 presidential race. But Tymoshenko did far more than alienate IMF and Western donors by pivoting to statist policies and social welfare programs—to increase her chances for victory, she also slowly tilted toward cooperation with Vladimir Putin.

Tymoshenko and Russia

Sensing Ukraine's economic vulnerability amid the Lehman crisis, on January 7, 2009, Russia once again shut all gas flow to and through

Ukraine. Russia claimed this was a necessary response to alleged nonpayment of debts for past purchases. The stoppage came several months after negotiations between Gazprom and Ukraine's Naftogaz had failed to find a resolution. This cutoff lasted thirteen days, entirely stopping the flow of gas to Europe at the height of an unusually cold winter. The stoppage created an energy crisis in large swaths of southeastern Europe and raised anxiety in the EU. This was an early test of Putin's weaponization of energy and European energy dependence. In response the EU organized a mission to solve the crisis and exert pressure on both parties to settle a deal. On January 18 Prime Minister Putin (who had swapped posts with his political partner President Dmitry Medvedev) and Prime Minister Tymoshenko declared the dispute resolved and announced a new contract that provided a pricing formula to ensure gas deliveries to and through Ukraine for the next decade.

At their press conference in Moscow, Tymoshenko giggled as Putin mocked President Yushchenko and Georgia's President Saakashvili. Alluding to an incident in which Saakashvili was caught on video inadvertently chewing on his tie during the height of Russia's recent invasion of Georgia, Putin joked: "What can I recommend [to the two presidents]? It would be best if they don't wear ties to their dinner. . . . I think you understand . . . Yushchenko's guest would also eat his tie." Andriy Parubiy, a conservative politician from Our Ukraine who in 2015 would become speaker of Ukraine's Parliament, denounced the servile and solicitous demeanor of Tymoshenko: "You get the impression that the head of the Russian government is meeting with one of his own deputies."

Tymoshenko's deal was negotiated without the participation of Ukraine's president. It offered debt relief and was modestly advantageous to Ukraine in its first year, the year before Ukraine's presidential election. But the formula was ruinous to Ukraine in the out years. In making the deal with Putin, Tymoshenko advantaged her short-term political interests and demonstrated to Putin her willingness to bend to the Kremlin's will. As the electoral campaign unfolded, it appeared she also secured the Kremlin's neutrality in the presidential race. Tymoshenko's shift toward the Kremlin was dramatic. Just a few years earlier, in the May/June 2007 issue of *Foreign Affairs*, she had written about "containing Russia" and had called for a Western policy focused on stifling Russia's "neoimperial" intentions.

Within weeks of the gas agreement, Tymoshenko took another step that pleased the Kremlin. She and Yanukovych's Party of Regions launched secret negotiations to create a Russia-friendly coalition government that intended to govern for twenty years. Ukraine's media were filled with reports speculating about the nature of the negotiations. But the full details and scale of the negotiations became public only in the aftermath of the Maidan Revolution of 2014, when civic activists found key documents about the negotiations at Viktor Yanukovych's abandoned estate.

Within the treasure trove of documents was a paper that outlined a power-sharing plan that was to last two decades. Dated April 14, 2009, the "Agreement on Political Partnership" detailed a precise division of government authority between "Party 1, Viktor Yanukovych, the head of the Party of Regions, and Party 2, Yulia Tymoshenko, the head of the Yulia Tymoshenko Bloc." The two parties were to agree on common principles for the "reform of state institutions and the implementation of socio-economic reforms." The specifics of these reforms were vague. What was not vague was the division of power and the alternation of key government and state posts between the two political forces over the next twenty years. Incredibly, the leaders of two fiercely antagonistic parties were seriously planning a permanent government that they expected would rule over Ukraine in perpetuity.

The plan envisaged constitutional changes that would facilitate long-term power sharing, including the election of the president and the prime minister by the Parliament. In this scheme, Yulia Tymoshenko and Viktor Yanukovych were to alternate the posts of president and prime minister every four years. The plan also detailed how every ministerial post, key government agency post, and top parliamentary office would alternate between the two parties over two decades. The agreement committed the two parties to work against the "illegal actions" of President Yushchenko, described plans to organize cooperative mass actions against the sitting president, and in the event of his opposition to their agreement, to open an impeachment process.

In the end the Party of Regions got cold feet and rejected the proposed coalition plan, in large measure due to the vigorous lobbying of Serhiy Lovochkin and Yuri Boyko, allies of gas trader Dmytro Firtash, one of Tymoshenko's mortal enemies. The group was apoplectic about giving power to Tymoshenko, who had squeezed Firtash out of a lucrative role as gas trade intermediary between Ukraine and Russia. The group's resistance won the day, aided by the growing doubts about the plan by Viktor Yanukovych, who was then riding high in the polls and concluded that no deal was necessary to secure his path to power.

After the document was made public by civic activists, it was repudiated by Tymoshenko as a falsification. But there was significant anecdotal evidence, as well as confirmation from some of the parties in the negotiations, that the plan was indeed all too real.

A Failed Presidency?

As Yushchenko's presidential term was running out in the late fall of 2009, the president's popularity plummeted to its lowest level on record and his support in a crowded field of candidates stood at well below 10 percent. For one who had enjoyed majority public support upon his election, his story was one of gradual but inexorable decline in public approval. There is a consensus among Ukraine analysts that the Yushchenko presidency was one of noble intentions and lost opportunities, especially in the effort to tame corruption and prevent the theft of Ukrainian state assets and resources.

Missing in these harsh assessments is an honest evaluation of the domestic and external forces that opposed and sought to undermine Yushchenko throughout his term of office. Indeed, except for the brief interregnum of the Yekhanurov government, Yushchenko never had effective control of the policy agenda. Despite the fact that his party and its ministers participated in all four governments during his tenure, he became a record setter in the number of vetoes he applied to legislation. Nor do critics take into account the physical difficulties of his first year in office, when the obligations to strengthen Ukraine's diplomatic support in the West and the endless focus on internecine conflict within his coalition sapped a body that had been severely poisoned with dioxin during the presidential campaign. Missing too in the critical assessments is the effect of Russia's unending efforts to weaken the Ukrainian economy and disrupt the Ukrainian state, often through economic blackmail, graft, and the use of agents of influence in politics and the mass media. Additionally, Yushchenko's popularity suffered from the relentless blistering personal attacks from Tymoshenko, who was widely covered in oligarchic media whenever she attacked the president.

In the economic sphere, the first three years of Yushchenko's presidency registered modest, steady GDP growth and a big uptick in foreign direct investment. But this progress was undone by the global financial crisis of 2008, which hit Ukraine very hard and triggered a recession. This was largely because Yushchenko never succumbed to profligate economic policies. Instead, he used his influence to promote fiscally responsible policies and jettisoned revolutionary ideas of mass nationalization and reprivatization, which would have wreaked havoc on Ukraine. He also strove—through his use and threat of vetoes—to block budget-busting spending.

Yushchenko, moreover, worked intelligently and consistently to expand Ukraine's trade horizons, overseeing the country's entry into the World Trade Organization and working to deepen Ukraine's links to NATO and the European Union. President Dmitry Medvedev denounced him as anti-Russian because of his pursuit of NATO membership and his consistent efforts to expunge the Soviet and Russian imperial past in favor of a Ukrainian patriotic narrative. These policies so irritated the Russian president that Medvedev declared midway through Yushchenko's years in office that he would no longer do business with the Ukrainian president.

In the security sphere, Yushchenko dismantled some of Ukraine's inefficient military industrial sector and shrank the size of Ukraine's military, based on the idea that Ukraine needed a smaller, more mobile, and better-equipped military. In part this was done on the advice and at the urging of Western donors. But the deep reduction in forces did not dramatically enhance Ukraine's combat readiness and over time contributed to the weakening of Ukraine's military posture.

To his credit, in an environment of endless brinksmanship, internecine conflict, and backroom plots, Yushchenko never used his influence in the security services to threaten, repress, or punish his political opponents. While he often bristled at criticism in the media, unlike his predecessors and immediate successor, he never sought to repress journalists and civic activists, control media content through intimidation, imprison political opponents, or manipulate election returns. In this way he helped habituate the democratic and pluralistic values of the Orange Revolution.

That said, Yushchenko bears some responsibility for his failures. Bracing from criticism, as president he became insular, aloof, and short-tempered. Nor did he effectively manage the decline in his popularity, losing the direct connection he had made with people during his election campaign and the Orange Revolution. Yushchenko had not changed. He was a loving father, a passionate defender of Ukrainian culture, and a deeply patriotic leader. But he ceased being a politician, in part because he understood that his chances for reelection were nil.

Yushchenko's election continued the pattern of alternating presidencies between the country's Russian-speaking east and the Ukrainian-speaking center and west. President Kravchuk, a resident of Volhynia, abutting the Polish border, was the son of a Ukrainian nationalist partisan. President Kuchma, though born in a rural north Ukrainian setting, spent his formative years in Dnipropetrovsk and had lived in the Russified environment of the Ukrainian technological sector. A child of the Soviet Union, he was Russophone and had come to office with a scant idea of what constitutes Ukrainian national identity and had been elected with the heavy support of the Russophone east and south. It was only in the face of unremitting Russian pressure that Kuchma committed to a more distinctly Ukrainian state identity.

Yushchenko and Ukrainian Identity

By contrast, Yushchenko represented a distinctly ethno-national current in Ukrainian political life. More clearly than any of his predecessors, Yushchenko articulated the raison d'être for Ukraine: that it was not just a geographic entity but a homeland state of the Ukrainian people, anchored in Ukrainian language and culture but open to all minorities through its inclusive civic-based identity. Yushchenko also connected Ukrainian statehood to its antecedents, the Ukrainian National Republic of the early twentieth century and the Cossack Hetmanate.

Yushchenko also made unparalleled strides in his support for Ukrainian culture and the arts, in his love for and promotion of Ukrainian history, in the development of a shared patriotic national narrative, and in his commitment to the heroization of Ukraine's fighters for independence.

A central element in Yushchenko's ceremonial, cultural, and educational policies was the memorialization of the man-made Stalin famine—the Holodomor—in which approximately 4 million Ukrainians perished. As part of this effort, recognition of the Holodomor became an important feature in secondary schools and annual national state commemorations. A large memorial complex and museum about the famine was built in central Kyiv. Holodomor research was supported, as were documentary films about the tragedy. Diplomatic efforts to acknowledge the event as genocide were pursued vigorously, and visiting heads of state were asked to lay wreaths at the memorial site as a routine part of their working visits.

Yushchenko opened KGB archives to scholars, and in 2006 he backed the creation of the Ukrainian Institute of National Memory as a special state institution dedicated to the restoration and preservation of national memory. In 2010 the institute would be transformed into a research center under the supervision of the minister of culture. Over time the institute played a key role supporting public exhibitions, devising major state commemorations, and financing historical research and monographs that focused primarily on the period of totalitarian rule and on the history of the centuries-long struggle of Ukrainians for national sovereignty and statehood, themes that were suppressed during the Soviet period.

President Yushchenko's fascination with Cossack history and the Hetmanate, an independent Ukrainian proto-state of the seventeenth and eighteenth centuries, also became the locus of significant state-supported research, museum exhibits, and education. Yushchenko backed the rebuilding of the Cossack settlement of Baturyn, which had been sacked and razed by the imperial armies of Tsar Peter the Great in his conflict with the Ukrainian hetman Ivan Mazepa. Yushchenko also approved the financing of the preservation of numerous important historical sites and monuments. Additionally, Yushchenko strongly supported folk art and high art. His major contribution in this sphere was the development of the Arsenal in Kyiv, a former tsarist and Soviet-era armaments base, which he transformed (in accordance with the hope of its original architect) into a museum and major cultural center—the Arts Arsenal.

While there was much for which Yushchenko deserved praise, the verdict of voters was harsh. Yushchenko received just 5.6 percent of the vote in the first round of the 2010 presidential race, coming fifth in a crowded field that saw Yanukovych and Tymoshenko advance to the runoff. Although he himself did not partake in the illicit division of spoils in the country, Yushchenko had failed to address the public's desire for an attack on systemic grand corruption and was unfairly blamed for the country's economic problems.

Despite the people's verdict, the Yushchenko years were a clear step forward in Ukraine's march toward Europe. Ever larger portions of the public were beginning gradually to shed their Soviet identity. Democratic pluralism—along with its bitter, seemingly endless political contestation—made gains. Some Ukrainians continued to cling to local and regional pride, but many large numbers began to embrace the centrality of their Ukrainian national identity as the use of the Ukrainian language made gains in education and in the life of the state. While publishing, television, and radio remained predominantly Russophone, the identification of citizens with the Ukrainian state was deepening. Though the public scorned elites for their corruption, was angered by huge income inequalities, and resented omnipresent poverty and slow progress toward prosperity, the citizens of Ukraine were increasingly comfortable in expressing their own views, in protesting, in mobilizing, and in exercising their democratic rights.

The twin pillars of national and democratic identity became Yushchenko's main presidential legacy. And in the coming years, these factors would be crucial in the effort to defend Ukraine's sovereignty from the challenges posed by an unscrupulous new Ukrainian president and by a relentless enemy of Ukrainian statehood—Vladimir Putin. Scorned by much of the public while in office, Yushchenko was vindicated in March 2023, when a poll taken at the height of Russia's war against Ukraine showed that the majority of Ukrainians now held a positive view of his presidency.

CHAPTER FOUR

A Thug in Power

The Yanukovych Years

"Everything valuable that could be carved up, has already been carved up. Our challenge, now, is to grow the pie." These words were uttered by Serhiy Lovochkin in mid-January 2010 on the eve of Ukraine's presidential elections at a dinner in Greenwich, Connecticut. Then aged thirty-eight and already a seasoned political operative, Lovochkin was a key campaign strategist and advisor to presidential front-runner Viktor Yanukovych. He had come to the United States as part of an Atlantic Council program that brought key politicians from Ukraine's leading political parties to meet U.S. policymakers. Lovochkin's frank comment, made at the sprawling Connecticut estate of an exiled Russian businessman, came with one proviso: "We won't let the Vikings [that is, foreigners] into our energy sector," Lovochkin declared. "Everything else will be open."

Such a message, made privately by Lovochkin to government and private sector leaders during his U.S. visit, was designed to offer reassurances about the implications of a Yanukovych presidency. So too was Lovochkin's message about Yanukovych's geopolitical orientation and his desire to deepen cooperation with the democratic West.

Reassurances were essential for a U.S. and European audience. After all, Yanukovych carried a lot of baggage. A convicted criminal with close links to Donetsk's criminal underworld, Yanukovych was viewed in the 2004 presidential campaign as Putin's man in Kyiv—anti-American and anti-Western. As the ex-governor of Donetsk and two-time prime minister, he had been closely allied with a small group of business leaders—some with murky origins—whose fortunes climbed in the 1990s and early 2000s, making several of them super-rich. As prime minister, Yanukovych had tried to steal the 2004 presidential election through massive voter fraud, which drove him temporarily into the political wilderness. Later he had knocked heads with President Yushchenko.

The Donbas in Power

Yanukovych's entry into national Ukrainian politics had signaled the ascendance of the Donbas industrial elite and their growing wealth and influence. In the early 1990s, power in Ukraine was held primarily by the Kyiv-based elite of former Communists: later in the 1990s, under President Leonid Kuchma, the leadership morphed into an amalgam of the Kyiv establishment and the business and political elite of Dnipropetrovsk, which had been a Soviet center of high-end industrial and arms production. The Donbas oligarchs and their political agents had accumulated wealth in the coal, iron ore, and steel industries, expanding and diversifying by investing their profits into banking, media, energy, and consumer goods. Members of the Donbas elite had been shaped by the cutthroat competition over control of assets and natural resources. By the early 2000s, they were clamoring for their share of national political power and Yanukovych was their vehicle.

This elite's entry into Kyiv politics was somewhat jarring at first. Over time the relocation to Kyiv helped reshape and broaden the worldview of this regional political-financial elite, giving them a bigger stake in identifying their destinies with the Ukrainian state. The Donbas had long been a preserve of a Sovietized and Russified culture. It had seen small, inchoate separatist movements, many with Russian backing. Successive Ukrainian leaders had long ignored the project of inculcating in the Donbas a sense of Ukrainian patriotism and national identity, not to speak of language, culture, and national heroes.

Yanukovych and Ukrainian Identity

In the absence of a clear national identity, in a region with large numbers of Russian speakers and intermarried, multi-ethnic families, the post-Soviet Donbas electorate was shaped by a political discourse that exploited regional pride. Oligarch-controlled local media trumpeted the idea that the "Donbas feeds Ukraine" and argued that the coal, steel, and other commodities produced by the Donbas were sustaining the rest of the country. The heroism of miners and steelworkers, a relic of Soviet times, was extolled, and the region's political propaganda fed local resentment toward lazy workers in other parts of Ukraine who were said to be riding on the coattails of the Donbas working class. This strong sense of local identity prevented the region from integrating into the gradually emerging national narrative of the young Ukrainian state. To a significant extent, the Donbas's regional identity was reinforced by Soviet-era myths, including that of the unshakable friendship and consanguinity of the Ukrainian, Belarusian, and Russian peoples, and an emphasis on the economic interrelatedness of the Donbas and Russia. These tropes opened a door for Russia to exploit.

In some sense, in the first years of independence, the Donbas represented the key cultural-political cleavage inside independent Ukraine. On one side was a Ukrainophone population dominant in Western and Central Ukraine, which in the first two decades of independence became steeped in the traditions of state independence and democratic nationalism. Ukrainophone politicians celebrated past separatist strivings of the Ukrainian people, honoring heroes who had opposed the Soviet Union, Russia, and Poland, including the Cossack hetman Ivan Mazepa; Simon Petlyura, the social democratic journalist who briefly led an independent state in 1919; the resistance fighters of the Ukrainian Insurgent Army (UPA); and the Soviet-era Ukrainian human rights dissidents. These adepts of the Ukrainian national narrative also backed the autonomous and autocephalous Ukrainian Orthodox and the Eastern Rite Catholic Churches, advocated the status of Ukrainian as the sole state language, supported the gradual Ukrainization of culture, and declared Ukraine's place as a part of the European Union—all policies that were promoted during the Yushchenko presidency. By contrast, with the exception of smaller Ukrainophone rural communities, the citizens of the Donbas were steeped in Soviet-era and Russian pop culture, were open to the Russian narrative that there is a single Russian people, adhered to the Moscow Patriarchate of the Orthodox Church, and saw their economic future as inextricably linked to Russia and Eurasia.

Yanukovych advanced some of these theses in his presidential campaign. In part this strategy was advocated by American political advisor Paul Manafort, who knew little about the details of Ukrainian politics but from U.S. experience understood one big thing: that cultural identity and cultural issues are a powerful force in electoral politics, and often they can overcome and overwhelm cleavages over social and economic issues. In the United States, it was so with immigration, the place of God and faith in the national discourse, and abortion rights. Manafort transplanted and translated this basic framework into a Ukrainian political vernacular and urged a campaign centered on defending the place of the Russian language, Russian culture, and their nostalgic Soviet remnants in the Ukrainian state. Yanukovych's campaign, moreover, sought to play to the fears of a Russophone population that was deeply influenced by Russian media, suspicious of the West, and opposed to joining NATO or the European Union.

Ironically, the Reagan disciple Manafort reinforced many of the same tropes that Yanukovych—aided by Russian political technologists—had employed in his failed electoral campaign five years before.

The ascendancy of Yanukovych in 2010 meant that these Russophone cultural and political narratives, which were pronounced in the first round, seeped into the national electoral discourse. However, when it came to the runoff, Yanukovych understood that to win a national election legitimately, he would need to move beyond the traditional base of the south and east by moderating his political message to appeal to voters in the center of Ukraine. His messages were in part assisted by the presence of voices from the Kyiv establishment inside his electoral campaign, including former Radio Liberty reporter Hanna Herman.

As a result, the 2010 Yanukovych campaign was not as overtly pro-Russian in its second round as in his 2004 run for office. He promised simply to protect the rights of Russian speakers and to keep them in their comfort zone—that is, to forgo a thorough Ukrainization of culture and media and to give Russian an equal standing in the state, in commerce, and in culture. He equally made clear his respect for the place of the Ukrainian language, which he diligently, if in labored fashion, often employed in his campaign. Such a balanced stance allowed him to make inroads into the Ukrainophone electorate that had formerly shunned him.

In the second-round presidential runoff against Prime Minister Yulia Tymoshenko, Yanukovych pivoted decisively toward a more centrist and less pro-Russian message. He secured an alliance with Serhiy Tihipko, the former head of the National Bank and an oligarch with origins in the industrial city of Dnipropetrovsk. Tihipko had shown unexpected strength in the first round, capturing 13 percent of the vote and running a strong third. Tihipko became an important voice for Yanukovych in the center and south of Ukraine, appealing to younger, reform-minded, Russian-speaking voters as well as Ukrainians favoring market-oriented solutions. Tihipko, moreover, reflected a measure of skepticism regarding Russia and had campaigned with warnings about the extensive Russian security service penetration of Ukraine, thus establishing credibility with some patriotic voters. Tihipko's endorsement of Yanukovych was a significant blow to Tymoshenko's chances and an important boost to Yanukovych.

In the first round, held on January 17, 2010, Yanukovych's base had given him 35 percent of the vote compared to 25 percent for Tymoshenko, whose support was battered by her custody of the government during the 2008 global economic meltdown. That global shock had led to a 15 percent decline of the country's GDP and a sharp currency devaluation.

Despite a spirited—at times strident—campaign waged by the charismatic Tymoshenko, Yanukovych prevailed, capturing 49 percent of the vote as opposed to 45.5 for his rival. If not for the animosity between Tymoshenko and Yushchenko—who urged his electorate in Central and Western Ukraine to stay at home or vote for none of the above—Tymoshenko might well have prevailed.

Maneuvering between East and West

In the early days of Yanukovych's presidency, his camp sent strong signals that reinforced the private assurances top aide Lovochkin had made during his preelection U.S. visit. Yanukovych would not tilt toward Russia but instead would pursue a path toward Europe and the West. Importantly, there were some indications that many of Yanukovych's powerful business backers were interested in modernizing and partly opening up the corruption-riddled Ukrainian economy, whose dysfunction and weak growth stood at the heart of Western concerns about the new president and the stability of the country. A maturing generation of super-rich, the argument went, now needed access to Western financing and Western markets and craved legitimacy, which only reforms could satisfy. Moreover, guarded optimism about the Yanukovych presidency in the West, including this author's, rested on the case that the current version of Yanukovych differed from the old. Many in the West thought the new president had been chastised by the events of 2004 and feared the power of civic mobilization such as he witnessed during the Orange Revolution. Yanukovych could not be so stupid as to repeat his catastrophic mistakes of the past and tempt political fate again, this optimistic argument went.

Despite campaigning as a defender of the rights of the Russian language, Yanukovych never supported granting it equal status as the second state language. His administration's attitude toward Russian was based on constant balancing between his Russophone base in Eastern Ukraine and the Ukrainophone electorate on which he was partly reliant. As a result, in 2012 Yanukovych and his majority in the Rada enacted a law that granted official local status for Russian and other minority languages in regions where over 10 percent of the population spoke that language. That law was recognized as unconstitutional in 2018.

Under the new president, the Ukrainian national narrative did not demonstrate a clear pro-Russian tilt. For example, Yanukovych rigorously honored the victims of the Holodomor, requesting visiting international leaders to pay homage to the millions of peasant victims, though he did stop referring to the mass killing of millions of Ukrainians as genocide. While the rhetoric of friendship with

Russia was retained, Ukraine continued to maneuver between Europe and Russia in an effort to protect its sovereignty.

Equally promising in Western eyes was the early announcement of the creation of a center to propel economic reform under the aegis of the new president. The body was financed by Ukraine's richest man, Yanukovych confidant, and Regions Party stalwart Rinat Akhmetov, who craved legitimacy for his business empire and wanted macroeconomic stability and predictable property relations as a basis for his business to prosper.

In the summer of 2010, President Yanukovych launched the Coordination Center for the Implementation of Economic Reforms, which operated under the Presidential Administration. The council recruited a well-regarded group of senior staff headed by former McKinsey analyst Oleksandr Danylyuk (who in 2014 would become a key reformer in the post-Yanukovych government and later would briefly run Volodymyr Zelensky's National Security and Defense Council); Yulia Kovaliv (who would join the Poroshenko administration in a range of senior capacities and also served as economic policy advisor to Zelensky); and Oleh Sayenko, who in 2017 became the minister of the cabinet of ministers. Together with the appointment of Iryna Akimova to the number-two post in the Presidential Administration, the economic advisory team offered hope that the country would move forward with serious structural reforms and intelligent social and health-care reforms.

To replace Tymoshenko as prime minister, on February 21, 2011, Yanukovych proposed three candidates: Arseniy Yatsenyuk, who was the candidate of Our Ukraine; Serhiy Tihipko, who had endorsed Yanukovych in the second round but who had little parliamentary political support; and Mykola Azarov, who had built a close relationship with both Yanukovych and the country's eastern Donbas establishment and from 2002 to 2004 had served as first deputy prime minister under Yanukovych.

Immediately upon Yanukovych's victory, even in the absence of a new legislative election, a number of deputies from Tymoshenko's coalition, mainly businesspersons, defected to the new president to give him a majority needed to elect Mykola Azarov as prime minister. They did so largely to protect their economic interests in a pattern that was a familiar feature of Ukraine's political life.

The Azarov Government

Surprisingly, the Azarov government was not dominated by representatives of the Donbas. Multimillionaire banker Serhiy Tihipko from Dnipropetrovsk became deputy prime minister, and Kostyantin Gryshchenko, Kuchma's foreign minister, former Ukraine ambassador to both the United States and Russia, and a realist concerned about Russia's hegemonic aims became foreign minister. During the Ukrainian-Russian Tuzla crisis in 2003 Gryshchenko had diligently countered the Kremlin's attempts to encroach on Ukraine's territorial integrity. Additionally, the nominations of Kyivites Volodymyr Lavrynovych as justice minister; Dmytro Tabachnyk as education minister; and multimillionaire Lovochkin as the president's chief of staff were signs that the government and administration encompassed far more than the Ukraine's "Eastern establishment." In addition, Kyivite Valery Khoroshkovsky, whose net worth was in the hundreds of millions of dollars, became head of the SBU security service, having been the former deputy head of the service in the Yushchenko administration.

The Donbas was not ignored. Andriy Klyuyev, a multimillionaire with a ball-bearing business and long-standing relationships with coal-mining interests, became first deputy prime minister; chocolate and confectionery magnate Borys Kolesnikov, closely allied with Rinat Akhmetov, became deputy prime minister; Yuriy Boyko, the political partner of gas trader Dmytro Firtash, became energy minister; and Vitaliy Zakharchenko, also from Donetsk, became interior minister. Donbas loyalists assumed most posts that controlled key cash flows in raw materials, energy, and finance—a harbinger of Yanukovych's priorities.

Yanukovych the candidate had promised generous social spending and relief for workers suffering from a recession. His government, however, was dominated by big business and included some of Ukraine's richest individuals and their surrogates. Many of Yanukovych's wealthy backers believed he would be a pro-business president intent on modernizing the country. Optimism among the oligarchs was high. East Ukrainian oligarchs knew Yanukovych as a reliable ally who had facilitated their acquisition of wealth and further enrichment. Now, having attained vast wealth, many of the new rich were eager to legitimate their holdings. They expected Yanukovych to support the creation of an environment where property rights were reliably protected and policies focused on facilitating rapid growth—something desperately needed in one of Europe's poorest countries.

As a prelude to this power shift, Rinat Akhmetov had supported a major McKinsey study that was intended to carve out the path forward. It was written by a team of experts, including Oleksandr Danylyuk, who now were recruited to run Yanukovych's Coordination Center for the Implementation of Economic Reforms. The center was envisioned as a presidential think tank for the elaboration of strong macroeconomic policies, budgetary discipline, needed structural reforms, modernization of health care, taxation policy, trade policy, and the reduction of stifling overregulation. The oligarchs saw the center as the vehicle to develop and push an economic reform agenda.

That the new government and president were opening up to competent young technocrats and experts was reinforced by a series of early appointments to the Yanukovych presidential office. A then highly regarded lawyer, Andriy Portnov, formerly a close ally of Yulia Tymoshenko, joined the new president's camp to serve as his chief in-house attorney. Portnov would become the architect of the legal strategy by which Yanukovych restored presidential paramountcy in Ukraine's mixed parliamentary-presidential system. As a gesture to a hostile civil society, Vladyslav Kaskiv, an ambitious former civic activist who led protests during the Orange Revolution, stayed on as head of the National Investment Agency. Iryna Akimova's role as second in command to Presidential Administration head Lovochkin reinforced the message that economic reform would be a top priority. She had served co-director of the UN Development Programme Blue Ribbon Commission for Ukraine reform in 2004–5. This, the presidential team kept asserting, is a new Yanukovych, committed to strong relations with the West and to making Ukraine a modern, economically productive economy open to investment.

The public relations spin of Yanukovych spokespersons notwithstanding, it was not unreasonable to conclude that the new team represented a glass half full as much as a glass half empty. It was equally clear that powerful old-school statist and pro-Russia forces were also present in the new government and Parliament and were in competition with those who appeared to support a multi-vector approach to trade and foreign policy as offering the best opportunity for economic growth.

Yanukovych's personal experiences in the aftermath of the Orange Revolution had distanced him from Putin, who saw his Ukrainian counterpart as weak and vacillating. Yanukovych had fled Ukraine for Moscow in the aftermath of his electoral defeat in 2004; fearing prosecution at home, he stayed there for several months. During that time, it was reported, he endured a bitter harangue from Putin for squandering his chance at power. Yanukovych was largely shunned by the Kremlin elite, who concluded he was a spent force.

This humiliation stuck with the willful and egotistical Yanukovych. His unlikely political comeback as prime minister in August 2006 did not win him the respect of the Russian leadership. Yanukovych also was unhappy that Putin found common ground with his main rival Tymoshenko when the two leaders signed a major gas deal in 2009. Yanukovych's team had denounced the deal as "unconscionable" and deeply damaging to Ukraine's interests. But they were especially angry because that deal removed Yanukovych's key backers, intermediaries in the gas trade. Yanukovych was further irritated that during Ukraine's presidential election campaign, Russian media stayed neutral and refrained from attacking Tymoshenko. Based on the behavior of Moscow, Russia was not backing any horse (or was fine with either horse) in the race.

Wooing Obama

In the first weeks of his presidency, Yanukovych signaled his desire to deepen cooperation with the United States and Europe. To woo the Obama administration, Yanukovych agreed to a deal to remove nearly 250 kilograms of highly enriched uranium from Ukraine under the supervision of the International Atomic Energy Agency. The agreement—announced during a bilateral meeting in Washington, DC, on April 12, 2010—was a major feather in President Barack Obama's cap and a signal of Ukraine's sensitivity to U.S. policy priorities.

Such initial signals were important to the United States and

Europe, where skepticism about Yanukovych was legion. I recall a conversation with one U.S. intelligence analyst during the heated days of the Orange Revolution. The United States, he told me, feared that Yanukovych had long ago been recruited and groomed by Russian intelligence, and now was assuming the pinnacle of power in Ukraine. In the view of Langley, Yanukovych very likely had been an asset if not an agent of the KGB, likely scouted when he served two sentences for assault between 1967 and 1970. Unusually for a Soviet citizen with a criminal record, he was permitted to travel abroad to attend international motor rallies. Despite two convictions for violent crimes, Yanukovych also was also received into the Communist Party, an exception to standard practice.

Despite this background, Western attitudes to Yanukovych softened after his election. While his links to the Soviet-era and Russian intelligence communities remained a concern, the issue of his ultimate loyalty was now less clear to policymakers. There was little choice but to hope for the best: Yanukovych was now the duly elected president of Ukraine. Throwing in the towel on Ukraine and deciding all was lost was hardly an option. As if in answer to Western hopes, Yanukovych started sending positive signals. His first trip abroad, on March 1, 2010, was to Brussels. It was an important indicator of Yanukovych's desire to strengthen relations with the European Union. After meeting European Commission president José Manuel Barroso, Yanukovych emphasized European integration as a "key priority." But also made clear that Ukraine would seek to "enhance" its relations with Russia.

The meeting in Brussels was followed by a visit to Moscow on March 5, where Yanukovych met President Dmitry Medvedev and Vladimir Putin, then the Russian prime minister. At the summit, Yanukovych sent clear signals that Ukraine would pursue a multivector policy of strategic neutrality but was also open to a quick resolution of the issue of an expiring lease on Russia's naval presence in the Ukrainian port of Sevastopol in Crimea.

The decision to agree to the extension of a long-term lease of Russia's naval base in Sevastopol came in the form of a treaty known as the "Agreement between Ukraine and Russia on the Black Sea Fleet in Ukraine." Better known more colloquially as the Kharkiv Accords, the treaty was signed on April 21. The controversial treaty extended Russia's lease on facilities in Sevastopol from 2017 to 2042, with an option for a further five-year extension. Under the agreement Russia was allowed to maintain up to twenty-five thousand military personnel in Crimea. That large military presence would prove a decisive factor in Crimea's future.

As an inducement to Ukraine, in addition to fees paid for the lease of property used by its Black Sea Fleet, Russia agreed to drop prices for natural gas exported to Ukraine by 30 percent. The price reduction dampened the effect of an unfavorable formula for gas pricing negotiated by former prime minister Tymoshenko. If unaltered, that formula would have seen prices spike to over $400 per thousand cubic meters—a debilitating burden on Ukraine's then energy-inefficient economy.

Because the agreement extended Russia's naval lease and perpetuated and enhanced its military presence in Sevastopol, the treaty led to an explosion of criticism by opposition parties and patriotic groupings, which accused the new president of capitulation and of violating Ukraine's constitutionally enshrined nonbloc status, which forbade the presence of foreign forces on Ukrainian soil. Tymoshenko as well as hard-line nationalists bitterly opposed the deal but failed to disrupt the parliamentary ratification despite storming and blocking the podium of the Parliament and throwing smoke bombs into the great hall of the legislature.

Russia's Growing Presence

Yanukovych's backers countered that the treaty was economically essential and pragmatic. Once the lease expired, they asserted, Russia would hardly have moved out. Leaving the issue unresolved would have been an irritant in relations, exacerbated political tensions between the two countries, and intensified Russian economic pressure on Ukraine's vulnerable economy. Naturally, the pro-Russian intimates of Yanukovych and the numerous Russian agents in his inner circle strongly endorsed the deal. But so too did pragmatists in his inner circle, who believed Ukraine's economic hole must not be allowed to deepen and saw the Kremlin's offer of relief on exorbitant energy pricing as essential to growth. Better to regulate and limit Russia's presence in Crimea now, attain secure rental income, and avoid lethargic economic performance that would scare off foreign investors.

In time, the opposition's fears about the implications of a large Russian military force on Ukraine's soil were proven right. The enlarged presence was accompanied by Russian efforts to deepen its soft-power cultural influence on the peninsula with numerous commemorative events, exhibits, and concerts. In 2014 the aggressive actions of the significant cohort of Russian forces in Crimea territory—the legacy of Yanukovych's treaty—ensured that Moscow's illegal annexation of Crimea would meet little resistance, given its overwhelming on-the-ground military presence.

While the Crimea agreement was seen by many as a tilt toward Russia, other diplomatic steps reinforced the idea that Yanukovych was continuing the Kuchma-era policy of balancing between East and West. The new regime's initial domestic initiatives offered both positive and negative signals about the intentions of the new president. On one level, the new government began to show greater capacity than its predecessor, whose tenure in office had been accompanied by constant internecine tensions. This endless contestation had created policy paralysis between president and prime minister, sapping the Ukrainian state of a great deal of energy and impeding significantly the forward movement of reforms.

Despite a nominally *parliamentary*-presidential system, Ukrainian presidents as a rule have proven able to shape governments by organizing a strong parliamentary base in cooperation with business lobbies in the Rada. President Yushchenko was an exception to this trend. He agreed to relinquish some of his constitutional executive powers, lacked a dominant political faction in Parliament, and generally nominated prime ministers and their governments based on the distribution of forces in the ruling coalition.

With the advent of Yanukovych's presidency and its strong backing in the Rada, Ukraine returned to a presidentially dominated system characteristic of the early Kuchma years. Yanukovych's concentration of power was aided by top lawyer Andriy Portnov, a former Tymoshenko advisor known for his jurisprudence as much as his backdoor relationships with judges and prosecutors. Under Portnov's guidance, Yanukovych made an early appeal to the Constitutional

Court to examine the legality and constitutionality of changes made in 2004 by President Yushchenko, who had agreed to limit presidential prerogatives in national security, foreign policy, internal security, and veto powers, with most government appointments in the purview of the Parliament.

The Constitutional Court ruled on the changes on procedural grounds. Inasmuch as the court itself had not been involved in the review of the revised legislation, the entire amendment process "was unconstitutional due to constitutional violations in their examination and adoption." With this decision of October 1, 2010, the pendulum of power shifted back to the president in the now predominantly presidential republic. This move toward greater executive authority initially was welcomed by the oligarchs. Although their influence was more significant in circumstances of divided power when they exacted favors from a weak executive through their strong parliamentary lobbies, big business now agreed that a strong president was required for growth and stability.

The business elite, however, failed to calculate what this concentration of power would mean in the hands of an egotistical and larcenous president. The Constitutional Court's decision reinforced the worst instincts in Yanukovych and launched him headlong onto a course that over time would propel his massive personal and family enrichment. This greed, in turn, would alienate and anger much of his former political base and eventually plunge Ukraine into economic stagnation and eventually protest, violence, and political crisis.

Nevertheless, in the early stages of the Yanukovych administration, the strengthening of presidential powers was interpreted as a promising development. A new deal with the International Monetary Fund was agreed to in July 2010 that promised Ukraine access over twenty-nine months to over $15 billion in loans if it moved forward with structural reforms and agreed to a 50 percent price hike in domestic gas prices. The agreement renewed the prospect of close cooperation with the IMF, which had lapsed under the Tymoshenko government. This, coupled with the signals emanating from the president's Coordination Center for the Implementation of Economic Reforms, led Western donors to expect that the new government would deliver on needed reforms.

Authoritarian Drift

The positive signals of the early months of the Yanukovych presidency soon began to dissipate. In 2010 and 2011, I met with a mid-level Yanukovych operative charged with facilitating economic reform projects in the new administration. This Ukraine-born operative had the experience of a Western education, life abroad, and service in highly regarded Western businesses and consulting groups. Yet by the second year of the Yanukovych reign, she, like some of her colleagues, began to speak in a chillingly different tone. Yanukovych, she told me earnestly, "is our father and the father of the country." This line reflected the gradual emergence of a cult of worship of the great leader and of a new paternalistic ideology.

As the cult of the great leader was growing, Yanukovych made his first major mistake: the pursuit of retribution against his most fierce opponents, former prime minister and presidential rival Yulia Tymoshenko and President Yuschenko's interior minister Yuri Lutsenko. Both were prosecuted on flimsy, politically motivated charges in 2010–11. The criminal cases and convictions of these prominent leaders isolated Yanukovych from Western support, making him more vulnerable to Russian pressure. To be sure, the West wanted Yanukovych to enter into closer economic and political relations with the EU through an economic and trade deal. But critical diplomatic support and reserves of goodwill toward the president and Ukraine were eroded by his petty attempt to neutralize political enemies as well as by reports of his growing corruption.

The criminal cases against his opponents were dubious. In the case of Lutsenko, the charge involved promoting his chauffeur to the rank of sergeant, allowing him a modest pay raise and access to a one-bedroom apartment. This minor administrative decision was transformed into charges of grand corruption.

The case against Yulia Tymoshenko, while more plausible, was undermined by the politically motivated application of a questionable law that criminalizes state losses or damages resulting from decisions by government officials. That law, if applied broadly, would criminalize and punish miscalculations by government officials even in the absence of corruption. For example, a reduction in taxes could be judged as bringing losses to the treasury, even if it stimulated economic growth. Tymoshenko was charged for her role in the 2009 gas agreement between Ukraine and Russia, which created a disadvantageous price formula for Ukraine's gas purchases. Ironically, Yanukovych and his Regions Party government, which had traditionally campaigned as Russia-friendly, was charging Russia with foisting a deeply unfair and economically ruinous gas agreement on Ukraine.

I was in Kyiv in the concluding days of the Tymoshenko trial and secured a background briefing with Presidential Administration chief of staff Serhiy Lovochkin, whom I had known since his years as a top aide to President Kuchma. After Yanukovych's election, I would meet with him (as well as with a broad range of government officials, opposition and civic leaders, and policy analysts) on my frequent visits to Kyiv. My meeting with Lovochkin on October 11, 2011, occurred in a surreal setting. I was instructed to arrive at the Presidential Administration by way of a side entrance accessible through an arch in an adjacent private building. The main entrances to the presidential offices were heavily patrolled by militia and the State Protection Service for fear of a major opposition protest. In Lovochkin's commodious office, the television was on with a live feed in the precise moment the Tymoshenko verdict was being read. I told Lovochkin this was a terrible political mistake that would be deeply damaging to Ukraine and to Yanukovych internationally. Lovochkin did not respond out loud. Instead, he gazed at me impassively and pointed upward from his second-floor office in the direction of the fourth floor, where Yanukovych sat. The message was clear: he was both aware that his meetings were monitored and wanted it known he had nothing to do with this decision. It was all on Yanukovych.

Amid authoritarian drift Yanukovych and Azarov failed to live up to the IMF's array of reform recommendations, freezing a critical lifeline of financial support. The economic performance of the country began to weaken, augmented by Russian economic pressure and sabotage. In 2011 Ukraine's economy, recovering from deep decline amid the 2008–9 global recession, recovered partially with a 5.5 percent bounce back. In 2012, however, growth declined to a meager quarter percent. By 2013 the GDP dropped by a quarter percent. In large measure, this poor record was due to the effects of the Yanukovych clan's grand corruption, his reluctance to implement needed reforms, and growing efforts by the Putin regime to punish Yanukovych for his negotiation of a free trade agreement with the EU.

Mezhyhirya and Rampant Corruption

On Ukrainian Independence Day, August 24, 2012, came a stark confirmation of a growing problem for Ukraine's president. Intrepid journalist and anti-corruption activist Tetyana Chornovol climbed over the fence of a large estate north of Kyiv located on wooded ground near the Kyiv Sea, a reservoir of the Dnipro River north of the Kyiv Hydro Electric Station dam. The territory the journalist trespassed was known as Mezhyhirya, "a place between the mountains." During her three-hour-long gambol on the grounds, Chornovol obtained visible proof that something was rotten in the Ukrainian state.

What she found—augmented by subsequent videos and photos taken by journalists operating drones—caused a sensation in Ukraine and the international community. Her investigation revealed a lavish hidden estate with vast buildings; a moored galleon with a ballroom used for entertainment; a gigantic wooden main residence of over one thousand square meters called the Honka after the Finnish construction company that had built it; luxuriant gardens; a sprawling garage housing a vast collection of rare automobiles; a small farm; tennis courts; a gym; a private zoo; and ostriches strolling the grounds.

Chornovol began her investigation of the financial machinations around the sealed-off complex in 2006 during Yanukovych's second term as prime minister. Now she had proof of an estate valued in the hundreds of millions of dollars belonging to someone who had been in government service most of his adult life. Her photos and follow-on reports went viral over independent internet news sites and social media. In a country where half the population now had regular access to online sources of information, the story spread quickly, even though it was not reported by major TV channels. Thereafter, Mezhyhirya and Yanukovych's grand corruption would be a constant theme in the country's political discourse. Widespread public knowledge of Yanukovych's lavish wealth—and the anger it generated in the citizens of one of Europe's poorest countries—foreshadowed the president's eventual fate.

The first steps toward the development of Yanukovych's own Xanadu in Mezhyhirya began when he was prime minister during the Yushchenko presidency. The site had formerly been a sleepy, bucolic territory that had served as a nature preserve for the recreation of Soviet-era leaders, including Ukrainian Communist Party first secretary Volodymyr Shcherbytsky, who entertained and sometimes housed visiting international VIPs there. By the time of Yanukovych's presidency, a stately pleasure dome had arisen, dwarfing the older buildings and metastasizing into a temple of corrupt excess. Formally, Yanukovych claimed ownership of a home of approximately 250 square meters just inside the exterior wall of the main campus of Mezhyhirya. This modest residence was trotted out for interviews with journalists, but his real home was an enormous fenced-off complex of 350 acres, almost half the size of New York City's Central Park.

Formally, Mezhyhirya was leased to the private company Tantalit by the State Office of Affairs, a vast agglomeration of resources and real estate controlled by the president. Nominally, the complex was said to be under the administration of an exclusive hunting and sports club. In fact, there was but one real member of this elite club—Yanukovych.

The complex employed hundreds of personnel: maids, manservants, gardeners, cooks, farmers, cleaners, mechanics, plumbers, and medical personnel. They were augmented by a security service of several hundred equipped with radar and anti-aircraft weapons as well as patrol boats deployed on the adjoining Kyiv Sea. Yanukovych clearly was possessed of a healthy dose of paranoia.

Prior to activist Chornovol's exposé there were rumors but few details about the president's wealth. The uncovering of the secret of the Mezhyhirya complex meant that the extent of Yanukovych's corruption and greed was not only confirmed but had become something tangible. In the words of opposition politician and campaign strategist Ihor Hryniv: "For the average Ukrainian earning $200 per month, a billion dollars is as abstract as a million. But when he sees this, it makes concrete the scale of Yanukovych's wealth and the scope of his corruption."

Press revelations of Yanukovych's corruption, made concrete in his vast estate outside Kyiv, fueled public anger and eroded support for the president. Here is the main hall of the Honka house on his Mezhyhirya estate, photographed in February 2019. (Oleksandr Kovalenko)

Ukrainian big business had initially been a cheerleader for Yanukovych. During his years as governor of the Donetsk region, they had known him to be a loyal partner in the expansion of their businesses. Now that he had state power, Yanukovych surprised them. He acquired grandiose ambitions for wealth and power, aspiring to be far more than a mere public servant allied with powerful business interests. In this sense Yanukovych differed fundamentally from his predecessors, none of whom directly used their time in office to build huge fortunes. To be sure, President Kuchma had promoted the economic interests of his son-in-law Viktor Pinchuk, whose already considerable fortune grew quickly after his marriage to the president's daughter Elena in 2002. But Kuchma was not an active direct participant in the struggle for resources, assets, and wealth in Ukraine; rather, he served as an arbiter balancing oligarchic interests. By contrast, Yanukovych had changed the informal rules of the game, directly using his political dominance in a bid to become the country's top oligarch. Yanukovych's personal enrichment did not come through traditional business activity; it came largely through cash transfers from the profits of oligarchic businesses as well as the raiding of state tax and customs coffers. What made the Yanukovych system unique was that it operated to a significant degree on a cash basis. Simply put, Yanukovych demanded tributes in the form of a high percentage of profits.

Throughout Ukraine's post-Communist history, government officials had conspired to assist their families and allies in winning state service tenders, receiving lucrative licenses for the extraction of state-owned natural resources, and winning bids in the privatizations of state enterprises. But Yanukovych showed little interest in building businesses and then systematically expanding or optimizing them. Although his oldest son Oleksandr ("Sasha the Dentist") ran a bank and dabbled in a series of investment funds, these were small when compared to the takings that Yanukovych extorted in cash.

The system by which the thievery worked depended on a network of close associates in crucial government posts with influence on cash flows and resources. These appointees typically headed departments at ministries responsible for budgetary matters, procurements, and resources. Yanukovych seemed less interested in placing loyalists in top ministerial positions unconnected with money and resources. Instead, his cronies took control of key positions that regulated income and expenditure. Typical was the case of the National Investment Bureau, headed by Vladyslav Kaskiv, a former civic activist who rose to prominence as a Yanukovych opponent during the Orange Revolution. The Investment Bureau became a funnel through which tens of millions of dollars were allegedly misdirected at the instruction of Kaskiv's top deputy, a loyal Yanukovych minion from the Donbas. In the Internal Affairs Ministry, Pavlo Zinov was responsible for material supplies and expenses. A business associate of Oleksandr Yanukovych, Zinov had roots in Kostyatynivka, a city in the Donetsk region, where he had worked with the revenue and duties minister Oleksandr Klymenko, another family intimate. In his post, Zinov decided on lucrative contracts for weapons, cars, and technologies for the ministry that housed the police and massive National Guard. Loyalists from the Regions Party and the Donbas elite were also installed in key posts at the energy and coal ministry and in the environment and natural resources ministry, which doled out lucrative extraction and exploration rights and approved production-sharing contracts.

Yanukovych and his clan's corrupt enrichment was not restricted to simple thievery. It included intimidation, corporate raids, and protection rackets that preyed upon successful business. The Prosecutor General's Office also became an instrument of economic coercion as well as of the destruction of opposition politicians.

A widespread and elaborate system of "conversion centers" was developed around the tax administration. Tax service employees at such centers colluded with businesses to help them evade taxes in return for large cash kickbacks. The conversion centers rapidly expanded and served to support tax evasion and money laundering. As a rule, the tax police received fees ranging from 5 to 12 percent to facilitate these schemes, and the bulk of this cash was paid up the chain of command to the Yanukovych clan. According to a report from the country's chief military prosecutor, conversion platforms were under the full control of the minister of revenues and duties, Klymenko, a young associate of the president's elder son. These corrupt machinations resulted in 43.8 billion hryvnia (UAH) in documented nonpayments to the state budget (at the exchange rate of 8 UAH to the dollar), and grew to total treasury losses of over $5 billion during Yanukovych's presidency. In addition, over 50 billion UAH was alleged to have been lost to the Ukrainian treasury because of nonpayments, underpayments, and unjustified refunds of VAT, amounting to another $6 billion in stolen revenues. There were additional losses of 12 billion UAH annually from various credit schemes generated by the conversion platforms over four years, adding up to another $6 billion. These vast revenues were divided among cronies, with a large portion of the proceeds going directly into the hands of the president.

In the first year after the collapse of the Yanukovych presidency, authorities closed sixty such conversion centers, acknowledging they were but scratching the surface of the corruption that had expanded under the Yanukovych clan.

Clandestinely, through a variety of complex schemes and payments, Yanukovych, a man of impressive height and girth and with a huge appetite for the good life, had acquired immense wealth for himself, his family, and his closest allies. Such wealth could not stay entirely hidden. After media revelations about his lavish residence, Yanukovych quickly needed to create a cover for extravagant lifestyle and try to deflect attention from his rapid accumulation of wealth. Yet even the fake residence he represented to the public as his own was priced somewhere in the neighborhood of half a million dollars. How could a public servant with a nearly uninterrupted record of service in government and no known business activity account for even the modest wealth he put on display?

To deflect questions about his lavish living, in 2012 Yanukovych's public income declaration for 2011 contained a suspicious entry that indicated the president had received over $2 million in "author's royalties." The payment was made by New World publishers for four books by the president, consisting mostly of speeches and articles penned for the Party of Regions' political press. Nowhere had the books appeared on any best-seller list. They could not be found on the shelves of Ukraine's bookshops. There was no evidence the books had been released in more than a tiny print run. The "royalties" were a transparent exercise aimed at ending speculation about the true sources of his exponentially rising wealth.

Tensions with the Oligarchs

Yanukovych's greed and that of his family led to tensions with some of his oligarch backers. These differences were exposed during a contretemps between the president and Ukraine's richest man, Rinat Akhmetov, on July 9, 2012, at Yanukovych's sixty-second birthday party. According to former deputy prime minister Raisa Bohatyryova, a Party of Regions leader who attended the celebration, Yanukovych raised a toast: "It's time for us to take it easy. We should begin transferring power to the young." Yanukovych's remarks were accompanied by an approving look in the direction of his thirty-eight-year-old son, Oleksandr, and his young business partners. Akhmetov offered his own toast in a firm rebuttal that challenged Yanukovych before an audience of Ukraine's oligarchs and top officials: "I can't agree with you. It is too early for these youth. They need time to learn."

On October 16, 2012, while waiting to board a delayed flight from Kyiv to Dnipropetrovsk to attend the opening of the Menorah Center, a two-square-block Jewish community facility funded mainly by oligarchs, I ran into the U.S. ambassador to Ukraine John Tefft, who had recently dined with several of Ukraine's richest men. His readout from the meeting confirmed the growing anger of oligarchs at the massive sums Yanukovych was extracting from them. Tefft's wealthy unimpeachable sources confirmed that Yanukovych was taking a huge share of their profits.

How much wealth did Yanukovych extract? In the aftermath of his presidency, there were many estimates of his illicit takings, some reaching as high as $10 billion, of which the Prosecutor General's Office recovered over $1 billion in 2017. One high-ranking former member of the Yanukovych government told me in confidence that when Yanukovych traveled to a major Asian power late in his term, the presidential Boeing aircraft was loaded with two pallets of cash. This eyewitness source estimated that the pallets contained $1 billion, which was to be laundered in the form of investments or deposited in foreign accounts.

The discontent among Ukraine's oligarchs found further confirmation in the weeks before Ukraine's October 28, 2012, parliamentary elections. In the run-up to the vote, oligarch-dominated broadcast media suddenly and surprisingly began to exhibit unusual balance and neutrality in reporting on the policies and campaigns of opposition parties. To be sure, oligarch-owned media were broadcasting the messages emanating from Yanukovych's Party of Regions campaign, but opposition leaders were suddenly getting near-equal access.

Most dramatic was the behavior of Inter-TV, then the country's most popular channel. Inter, owned by First Deputy Prime Minister Valery Khoroshkovsky, was then home to an array of comedy and variety programs produced by an emerging young comic talent, Volodymyr Zelensky. Khoroshkovsky was then part of the government team, as was the man believed to be his minority partner, Serhiy Lovochkin, the president's chief of staff. Yet, in this election cycle, Inter was far from a pillar of the Party of Regions. In fact, the TV station did more than offer a large platform for opposition parties. To insulate itself from pressure, Inter's ownership established a civic advisory council to ensure the channel's political neutrality and objectivity in reporting the election campaign. The council included noted Ukrainian dissident intellectual Ivan Dzyuba; Oleksandr Sushko, executive director of the Institute for Euro-Atlantic Cooperation and chairman of George Soros's International Renaissance Foundation; Valery Chalyy, deputy head of the opposition-linked Razumkov think tank; and Viktoria Syumar, head of the Institute of Mass Information—a respected media monitor.

Other oligarchs behaved in similar fashion. Viktor Pinchuk's STB and ICTV channels and Ihor Kolomoysky's 1+1 offered opposition parties generous airtime and provided neutral news coverage in which opposition politicians could make their case to voters at a time when Yanukovych's unpopularity was growing.

The oligarchs were quietly rebelling for good reasons: they feared that in the absence of equal media access for the opposition, Yanukovych and the Party of Regions would attain a constitutional majority in Parliament, removing remaining checks and balances on the president and opening the door to his consolidation of absolute power on the model of Putin in Russia.

Instead of achieving a constitutional majority, the Regions Party received barely 30 percent support in the party-preference vote that elected half the Parliament. The main opposition parties, Fatherland, the party of imprisoned opposition leader Yulia Tymoshenko headed by Arseniy Yatsenyuk, garnered nearly 26 percent, while the opposition party of former world heavyweight boxing champion Vitaly Klitschko captured 14 percent. The far-right Freedom Party of Oleh Tyanhybok received 9.7 percent, amid rumors that he was being heavily financed by Party of Regions oligarchs to take votes away from Tymoshenko's Fatherland. Despite the vast resources of the state, the opposition received 20 percent more support than the party of power, with the balance going to the Communists with 14 percent in what would prove their electoral last hurrah.

Although he failed to secure a constitutional majority of two-thirds, Yanukovych was able to cobble together a near majority by virtue of the support of deputies who ran as independents but represented major business interests that benefited from a close alliance with those in power. These locally elected legislators helped the Regions scrape together 208 seats in the 450-seat Rada. With the support of independents and 32 votes from the Communists, Yanukovych ushered in a government dominated by his inner circle and Kremlin-linked security sector ministers, but one that would be unable to concentrate all power in the presidency.

Descent into Misrule

The new government—the second Azarov cabinet—was an alarming signal of Ukraine's descent into misrule and corruption, a sign that power had decisively shifted toward the personalistic rule of Yanukovych, abetted by his family and corrupt clan. Key appointments signaled a major power shift benefiting close associates of President Yanukovych and his increasingly influential son Oleksandr. Gone were several independent-minded ministers, including businessmen Serhiy Tihipko, Petro Poroshenko (minister of economic development), and Valery Khoroshkovsky (first deputy prime minister for European integration). Gone too was Deputy Prime Minister Borys Kolesnikov, a close associate of billionaire Rinat Akhmetov.

Mykola Azarov, who had proven his loyalty to the clan, retained the post of prime minister. Cronies of Yanukovych's elder son were put in charge of the key income and asset-related structures of the state. The post of first deputy prime minister went to Serhiy Arbuzov, formerly CEO of UkrBiznes Bank, when it was initially believed to be co-owned by Eduard Prutnik and Yanukovych. By 2010 the bank was the property of the president's son Oleksandr (Sasha). Arbuzov had already run another key cash cow, the National Bank of Ukraine, which was responsible for offering lines of credit to Ukraine's banking system.

Oleksandr Klymenko, another associate of Sasha Yanukovych, was named to head the tax administration in November 2011, replacing Vitaliy Zakharchenko, who in turn was appointed interior minister. Zakharchenko would emerge in 2014 as a notorious figure in the suppression of protests on the Maidan, reconfirming his role as a trusted insider in the Yanukovych clan.

Eduard Stavytsky, who had briefly held the post of minister of the environment and national resources, took over the energy and coal portfolio, eroding the influence of oligarch Dmytro Firtash and his gas-trading group. Stavytsky was associated with Serhiy Kurchenko, a twenty-something gas trader who implemented transactions for businesses that were fronts of the Yanukovych family. Kurchenko operated with the sanction of Yanukovych to expand his family's influence in the energy sector. Kurchenko's rapid enrichment enabled him to purchase a large number of news and broadcast media that in turn were used to promote the positive image of the president, the clan, and the government. These media assets—including the Ukrainian editions of *Forbes* and *Vogue* and the country's then most respected news magazine *Korespondent*—quickly exited the ranks of Ukraine's independent media.

To be sure, the entire government was not exclusively in the hands of the Yanukovych clan. It encompassed a remnant of other centers of influence in the Party of Regions, including Rinat Akhmetov, who was represented by Oleksander Vilkul, a deputy prime minister. Yuri Boyko, an ally of Dmytro Firtash, became deputy prime minister for the energy sector.

Russian Penetration

Trusted representatives of Russian interests held key posts. Dmytro Tabachnyk, a staunch opponent of Ukrainization, stayed on as education minister (he would support Russia's all-out invasion of Ukraine in 2022); Pavel Lebedev, Russian-born businessman and former leader of the Russian Union of Industrialists and Entrepreneurs in Crimea, stayed as defense minister; and Ihor Kalinin, a Russian-born official with links to the Soviet KGB and Russian security services, incredibly was named head of the security service of Ukraine. President Yanukovych's personal security team was headed by yet another Russian, Oleksandr Zanevsky, a right hand of Oleksandr Yanukovych and an important advisor to the president. Lebedev and Kalinin also had close links to the Yanukovych family: Lebedev had gained his post as defense minister to facilitate the family's arms-trading business operating out of the Crimean port of Sevastopol, while Kalinin got his post after having ferried the Yanukovych family around for years on its Crimean-based yacht.

Power had shifted from a government of officials answerable to interest groups throughout Ukraine to one dominated by loyal yes men from the Donbas linked to the Yanukovych family. The new government also saw the significant penetration of Russian interests, especially in the defense and security sectors, setting off alarm bells among patriotic Ukrainians and in the West.

From his beginnings in a hardscrabble life of extreme poverty, Yanukovych had at last reached the apex of power. A man who alternated between jollity and menace was now equipped with all the trappings of legitimacy, including a fake PhD, books and research articles he had not written presented under his name, a no-show professorship, and an extra-legally expunged criminal record. After decades of nearly exclusive devotion to politics and administration, Yanukovych now enjoyed wealth rivaling that of Ukraine's richest. Like Putin, he was now both paramount ruler and major oligarch, having amassed billions in the first three years of his presidency. At last he had achieved the pinnacle, the full privatization of the most valuable asset of all, the Ukrainian state.

Paradoxically, in consolidating power, Yanukovych was building the foundations for his political demise. His grab for wealth and unchecked power alarmed and alienated the oligarchs, enraged the public, and sapped the economy. In a bid to ensure his political longevity, Yanukovych had also become more reliant than ever on Russia-linked officials, especially in the defense and security sectors, increasing his dependency and making Ukraine vulnerable to Kremlin manipulations.

While Yanukovych had authoritarian intentions and despotic inclinations, he failed to build an effective police state. During most of his tenure, few comprehensive measures were taken to effectively restrict civic organizations, reformist groupings, and opposition political parties. Despite his reputation for thuggish behavior and authoritarianism, under Yanukovych most opposition websites, news stations, and democracy and human rights organizations operated with little or no impediment. When on rare occasions a civic activist, university president (Bishop Borys Gudziak, rector of Ukrainian Catholic University), or representative of the many international organizations working in Kyiv (the Konrad Adenauer Foundation's Nico Lange) was harassed, the intimidation was usually mild, was walked back very quickly, and sometimes was followed by apologies. As important, democracy programs, grants to independent media, training of opposition political parties and other democracy-building initiatives supported by the U.S. Agency for International Development, the National Endowment for Democracy, and EU democracy and reform-assistance programs functioned largely without harassment or impediment.

Opposition political parties also operated largely unhindered. The main opposition party, Fatherland, led by Arseniy Yatsenyuk, even held its national convention and a rally on the square outside Saint Michael's Church in central Kyiv while the party's founder Yulia Tymoshenko was under arrest. The Lutsenko and Tymoshenko cases apart, with the exception of a few trials of ultranationalists accused of terrorism, Yanukovych's repression of political opponents was not widespread.

This state of affairs remained in place until the weeks of civic strife that began in November 2013 and presaged Yanukovych's eventual flight from power.

The opposition's greatest obstacle was represented by media, especially the oligarch-owned popular television channels, that had initially excluded them from the airwaves. Yet as coverage in the run-up to the 2012 parliamentary elections had shown, the opposition often had opportunities to put its case to the public. Major internet media outlets such as *Ukrainska Pravda*, Censor.net, lb.ua, and *Novoye Vremya*, and opposition television like Channel 5 and the short-lived independent channel TVI all operated freely. These media offered extensive coverage of opposition politicians, exposed corruption, and provided critical assessments of economic and social policy. Ironically, despite acquiring a great deal of personal wealth, in the first years of his presidency, Yanukovych and his family did not achieve oligarchic status in one area—media ownership. Though Yanukovych threatened to seize TV channel Inter from Valery Khoroshkovsky (who left the country immediately after the fall 2012 legislative elections), and an agent for his clan, Serhiy Kurchenko, purchased a group of periodicals, small-circulation news and business journals, and several websites, the president and his family never achieved ownership or control of substantial broadcast media assets. Instead, they were reliant on support from oligarch-owned media. When it was forthcoming, this support generally offered neutral coverage rather than lavish praise. Though Yanukovych's champions were omnipresent on Ukraine's popular weekly prime-time news talk shows, they were often balanced by the significant presence of voices from the opposition. And Inter, the most popular channel, often satirized the president, the prime minister, and the Yanukovych clan on the popular comedy program the *95th Kvartal*—the product of the satirical imagination of the comedian Volodymyr Zelensky.

Given the complex array of oligarchic attitudes toward Yanukovych's avarice and because of the role played by powerful media, there was far less positive propaganda for the government than in neighboring post-Communist states such as Russia and Belarus. Nor was there anything resembling the well-articulated, state-directed propaganda messaging system that had emerged in Russia. The main advantage Yanukovych could rely on within Ukraine's "mainstream" broadcast media was a strict taboo on covering corruption scandals and investigations of high-level corruption.

A Weak Autocracy

Yanukovych may well have favored an authoritarian model and admired what Putin had accomplished in his own consolidation of power. He may well have pined for a permanent place at Ukraine's political apex, but he was not a hands-on manager, nor did he try to build or prove capable of building a police state until his grasp on power was threatened in the late fall–winter of 2013–14.

Instead of focusing on the details of governance and the formulation of policy, most of Yanukovych's time was concentrated on wealth accumulation and lavish living. Yanukovych delegated running the country to his subordinates and surrounded himself with sycophants who stroked his ego and were reluctant to bring him unwelcome news. He was out of touch with shifting public sentiments, including the steady decline in his personal popularity that followed public revelations of his corruption. Yanukovych's political advisors, including Chief of Staff Lovochkin and political scientist Yuri Levenets, regularly conducted polls and interpreted sophisticated polling data. However, Lovochkin, who was linked to gas traders who benefited from access to power, did not wish to anger an unreceptive Yanukovych. Thus, the president was rarely presented with stark assessments of his failures and of the public's discontents. External campaign advisors like American Paul Manafort conducted polling but also tended to surround the president with positive messages to ensure the continuity of their lucrative contracts. As a result, Yanukovych believed he was safe from a serious political challenge and felt no need to tighten control over the media and society.

A further reason for Yanukovych's unwillingness to countenance mass repression was fear of losing the limited support of the West. Despite strong pro-Russian lobbies and Russian agents of influence inside his government, throughout all but the last months of his administration, Yanukovych pursued a multi-vector foreign policy. He emphasized friendship and trade relations with Russia while negotiating toward an association agreement with the European Union, which Europe pursued despite mounting evidence of Yanukovych's corruption. The aim of European integration was endorsed by most Ukrainian business and political leaders, including oligarch-linked officials from the Party of Regions, who believed such integration could serve as a check on the president's avarice for wealth and power.

The tactics of Western leaders were understandable. Were Ukraine integrally linked to Europe via a free trade and association agreement, it could stimulate the reform of Ukrainian laws and procedures to make them consonant with European best practices. By binding Yanukovych to the West, the theory went, Ukraine would move more consistently in the direction of the rule of law and democracy. European leaders, including European Commission president José Manuel Barroso, Poland's president Bronisław Komorowski, and Poland's hawkish foreign minister Radosław Sikorski, all were convinced that Yanukovych was genuinely interested in securing Ukraine's place in the Western economic world and spent a great deal of time wooing and coddling him. German chancellor Angela Merkel and her foreign ministers Guido Westerwelle and Frank-Walter Steinmeier strongly supported the integration of Ukraine into European institutions, believing this a realistic objective. The German ministers regularly traveled to Kyiv (often in the company of Poland's Sikorski) in a long-term effort to nudge Yanukovych and Kyiv toward Brussels.

Europe's leaders also relaxed their rule-of-law standards to coax Ukraine into closer engagement. Their pressure secured the release of political prisoner Yuri Lutsenko; but later they compromised in agreeing that Yulia Tymoshenko's ongoing imprisonment should not stand as an obstacle to a free trade agreement, a position the political prisoner herself endorsed. After protracted negotiations, Tymoshenko was able to serve much of her sentence in a Ukrainian Railways hospital rather than in a prison camp.

Europe Integration and Russian Retaliation

Did Yanukovych's interest in European integration represent serious intent or was it a ploy? Was he strengthening Ukraine's neutrality by stringing along the West? Many in his inner circle themselves were uncertain. Some genuinely believed—or hoped—Ukraine would sign the agreement with the EU and break free of its excessive dependency on a hegemonic Russia. In early November 2013, I met Hanna Herman, Yanukovych's press flack, at the convention of the Canadian Ukrainian Congress in Winnipeg. We spoke just weeks before Yanukovych was to make his final decision. "What have you heard?" she asked me. "Will he do it?" I was shocked by the question. Surely Herman, an inhabitant of the corridors of power, would have some inkling. Surely it was I who should be asking these questions.

The decision was clearly up in the air. Over two decades, Russia had pursued hegemonic interests in its "near abroad," had corrupted segments of Ukraine's elite, and under Yanukovych had successfully lobbied for the appointment of its agents to key government posts. Russia also had created a strong ideological fifth column in Ukraine. Russia had many agents inside the Party of Regions, the government, and in the oligarchic elite, the latter corrupted with sweetheart deals and financing from Russia. All worked actively to derail an agreement that would accelerate Ukraine's integration into the democratic West.

Russia's all-out effort to stop Ukraine from signing the association agreement included a range of de jure tariffs and de facto customs maneuvers that drastically cut Ukrainian exports to Russia. At the beginning of 2013 nearly a quarter of Ukraine's trade was with Russia. But by July Russia had begun to squeeze the distressed Ukrainian economy by imposing intrusive, thoroughgoing inspections of Ukrainian goods entering the country. Transports laden with perishable foods spoiled at the border or were turned away. Dozens of Ukrainian companies were categorized as representing "risk." Hard hit were exporters of beer, fruits and vegetables, poultry, confectionery, wines, and steel. Customs blocked thousands of transport vehicles and trains, sometimes using the pretext of violations of food safety standards or contaminated or defective goods. The economic screws were tightened on specific products such as steel pipes, with the intent of squeezing influential Ukrainian producers such as businessman Viktor Pinchuk. Russian officials sent a clear signal that if Ukraine signed an association agreement and deepened trade relations with the EU, blockages and restrictions at the border would become permanent.

This message Ukrainian officials received from the Kremlin was clear: the longer your dalliance with the European Union continues, the greater will be the pain for Ukraine. In bilateral discussions, the Kremlin consistently pressed Yanukovych and his top officials to back down from a deal with Brussels and opt for the Russia-dominated Eurasian Customs Union. Over time, as Ukrainian state revenues continued to decline, Russia found a reliable ally in the Russian-born prime minister Mykola Azarov, a budgetary hawk who understood that Ukraine's economy was on an unsustainable path. Although Ukraine's poor economic performance could be traced to high levels of corruption and the absence of the rule of law, a long-term Russia trade embargo, Azarov argued, would be ruinous.

Prime Minister Mykola Azarov was above all a revenue man who had cut his teeth in tax administration, which he had headed under President Kuchma. Azarov was an old-school post-Soviet administrator who believed in a state-directed economy and in state capitalist policies. He governed based on the view that government should disburse financial support, privileges, and loans to crucial industries—de facto, to those with the greatest access to the president, his inner circle, and the ruling Party of Regions. In the late summer and early fall of 2013, Azarov began warning Yanukovych that Ukraine's state budget deficit was rising while its hard currency reserves were rapidly depleting. Indeed, they had dropped from a high of $37 billion in 2011 to $13 billion by 2013. Azarov also understood that neither the IMF nor other lenders in the West would come to Ukraine's aid unless their strict terms, including pension reforms, anti-corruption initiatives, and a balanced budget, were met. First internally and then publicly, Azarov argued that the introduction of European production standards would be highly expensive and ruinous to Ukraine in the short- to midterm. Azarov also asserted that Ukraine would be flooded with European goods—further contributing to the country's economic difficulties. Meanwhile, old-school post-Soviet economists, lobbyists for Ukrainian oligarchs with businesses dependent on Russia, and Russian agents of influence operating in Ukraine joined in a feverish propaganda campaign against the EU pact. Russian media, influential among many Yanukovych voters, also were activated in the effort. Free trade with Europe, it was asserted, would lead to Ukraine's economic ruin.

Ukrainian officials who had run afoul of Yanukovych increasingly sounded the alarm to Western diplomats that Ukraine was preparing to abandon the agreement with Europe. One such voice was former first deputy prime minister Valery Khoroshkovsky, who abruptly left Ukraine in December 2012 after his removal from the number-two government post. In January and February 2013, in discussions with U.S. State Department and National Security Council officials and think tank experts in Washington and New York, Khoroshkovsky asserted that Yanukovych had no intention of signing. Despite such warnings, U.S. and European leaders believed that in the end Ukraine would seal the deal, encouraged in part by the serious progress made in negotiations and the extensive EU-required legislation passed by the Rada. Even inside the Yanukovych team, moreover, some remained hopeful that Ukraine would at last move toward Europe.

Throughout the summer and early fall, Ukraine sought rapprochement with Moscow even as it negotiated with the EU. That rapprochement did not come. In the late fall the situation moved in a decisive direction. Following a secret meeting between Presidents Putin and Yanukovych, Prime Minister Azarov traveled to St. Petersburg on November 21 for discussions with his counterpart, Dmitry Medvedev. Azarov described the dialogue as "one of the most productive meetings" he had held. In the hours that followed, President Yanukovych sent shockwaves throughout Ukraine and the West by declaring that preparations for the upcoming EU summit where a trade deal was to be sealed were being frozen "in the national interest."

In his years in power Yanukovych had sought to preserve room for maneuver between East and West. For a long time he presented himself as a sincere advocate of an agreement with the EU. But the president's true intentions were hidden from much of his inner circle. Indeed, Yanukovych himself may not have had a clear idea of what decision he would take. However, with Ukraine's budget suffering from growing shortfalls exacerbated by Russia's trade embargo, the die was cast. Yanukovych's team had long sought to balance its international relations, pursuing a long-standing multi-vector foreign policy, seeking accommodations with the United States and the European Union. It also sought to deepen trade relationships with Asia, especially China. This path was pursued with serious purpose and was aimed at increasing Yanukovych's and his country's room to maneuver between East and West. The aim was to establish clear limits on both the West's and Russia's influence on Ukraine's domestic policy, but never at the risk of completely alienating the Kremlin, Brussels, or Washington.

Such a policy could no longer be sustained. Yanukovych's massive corruption, the absence of real reforms, and mismanagement had greatly depleted state resources and eroded the country's hard currency reserves. European integration would mean a stronger rule of law, a demand for budgetary discipline, and checks on Yanukovych's inclinations toward aggrandizement and impunity. Russia, by contrast, offered a far more comfortable haven, as well as the prospect of easy cash. By opting for reliance on Russia and the Eurasian trade space, however, Yanukovych now was risking Ukraine's state sovereignty and angering a mobilized public that was eagerly awaiting news of the conclusion of an association agreement that would open the doors of the country to Europe.

Valery Khoroshkovsky, the former insider who had warned that Yanukovych would reject a deal with the EU, had made another accurate prediction about the impact of Ukraine's fateful geopolitical choice. On September 15, 2012, addressing the YES Conference, an annual international gathering in Crimea of world leaders sponsored by Ukrainian billionaire Viktor Pinchuk, Khoroshkovsky asserted: "To avoid any doubts as to where we should go, we must hear our people, who, in their majority, support movement towards the EU. . . . Any politicians who decide to oppose this choice won't be able to have a long-term and effective life in the political arena."

Many Western—and Ukrainian—experts disagreed. Protests had been infrequent in the previous months, while polls showed little appetite for activism in the fall and winter of 2013. Most experts believed Ukraine's 2015 presidential elections—and not EU integration—

could be the next potential trigger for political mobilization and nonviolent mass civic action.

A Facebook Revolution: The Rebirth of the Maidan

The turmoil that was to rock Ukraine for over three months began slowly and unexpectedly. On November 21, 2013, came news that Ukraine had suspended preparations to sign the association agreement with the European Union. In response, investigative journalist Mustafa Nayyem wrote a Facebook post: "Well, let's get serious. Who today is ready to gather at the Maidan before midnight? 'Likes' don't count. Only comments under this post with the words, 'I am ready.' As soon as we have more than a thousand, we will organize ourselves." Fatherland party leader and former speaker of the Parliament Arseniy Yatsenyuk used Twitter to call for a "Euromaidan" to assemble in opposition to Yanukovych's decision. In the end, fewer than two thousand people gathered, a promising beginning, but hardly a harbinger of things to come. Indeed, that night there were few signals that the Maidan protests would become another pivotal event in independent Ukraine's modern history.

Initially, students and civic activists took to the public square. By Saturday, November 24, some one hundred thousand had answered the call of opposition parties and civic leaders to express support for Ukraine's European future and denounce the government's tilt toward Russia. The large number of protestors without doubt surprised the Yanukovych team and set off alarm bells. To dampen the impetus, Prime Minister Azarov asserted several days later that the "negotiating process over the Association Agreement is ongoing." But no one was buying it.

On November 29, at the Vilnius summit of the European Union's Eastern Partnership, Ukraine reneged on signing the association agreement, definitively caving in to Russian pressure. At the same time, egged on by the Kremlin as well as by hard-liners inside his government, Yanukovych decided to violently suppress the emerging protests and arrest protestors. Over time, this decision would be seen as a terrible misjudgment of the public mood and of the staying power and energy of the protestors.

On November 30 at 4:00 a.m. the Berkut (Golden Eagle) special police unit swooped down on hundreds of protestors who occupied Kyiv's central Independence Square (*Maidan Nezalezhnosti*), the site of mass gatherings during the Orange Revolution. Dozens of protestors, mainly young civic activists and college students, were beaten mercilessly and many more were arrested. Hundreds fled to sanctuary offered by clerics from the Ukrainian Orthodox Church of the Kyiv Patriarchate (the wing of the Orthodox Christian Church that had split from the Moscow Church after Ukraine's independence). Protestors huddled at St. Michael of the Golden Domes, up the hill from Independence Square. There, in the early morning, police continued their fierce attacks on anyone in their path, injuring dozens more while workers were heading to their offices and workplaces.

All this occurred under the glare of independent media and, more importantly, television. Significantly, images of extreme police brutality were widely broadcast on several oligarch-owned TV channels as well as on opposition television and on popular news websites. The bloody attack against young people resulted in widespread public opprobrium. Even apolitical parents and grandparents were outraged. That evening, thousands turned out, some of them angered and radicalized by the state's violence. The tactics of what was beginning to be known as the Euromaidan began to slowly evolve.

On Sunday, December 1, the day of the week when protests typically swelled to their largest size, tens of thousands expressed their disapproval of Ukraine's move away from Europe and the state's extreme brutality. The huge crowd that streamed into the Maidan quickly transformed into a major rally against the regime.

By December 2 the early contours of an organized protest city were emerging on the territory of Independence Square. Barriers were put up, a tent city was established, and buildings in areas adjacent to the square were taken over by protestors intent on holding the central space by establishing an infrastructure for prolonged protests.

Disaffection and disapproval began to emerge inside Yanukovych's team. After the violence of the morning of November 30, Serhiy Lovochkin, the president's chief of staff, resigned his post (though he remained an advisor). His wife, meanwhile, took to posting photos from protest sites, siding with the Maidan oppositionists. Andriy Klyuyev, a multimillionaire and Regions Party stalwart who

A mass rally in Kyiv on December 8, 2013: hundreds of thousands of Ukrainians rose up in the Maidan Revolution to challenge the country's president Viktor Yanukovych's decision to reject European integration and to protest brutal beatings of student protestors. (Andrew Kravchenko)

had long mixed business and government service, moved from his post as secretary of the National Security and Defense Council to be the president's chief of staff. Klyuyev advocated a hard line against the protestors, coordinating efforts to disperse them and to suppress Maidan. Concerned that media coverage was feeding the demonstrations, Klyuyev met with TV executives, pressing them to suppress coverage of the protests and block coverage of state violence. Prime Minister Azarov went public with lamentations about "media bias" and lack of coverage of the far smaller pro-government rallies, whose participants were bused in from the Donbas or recruited from government offices.

The following week, further violence and widespread arrests of activists only hardened the determined efforts by protestors to build secure lines of defense at the center of the protest movement—the Maidan. Anger at state violence fueled public mobilization, which reached its apex on December 8. As many as half a million people filled the Maidan, spilling over into the adjacent European Square and filling much of Khreshchatyk, Kyiv's main shopping thoroughfare. If there had been any question before about the staying power of the opposition movement, doubts were now shattered. Not only was the protest movement a massive affair in the capital, large protests were sprouting up in many Central and West Ukrainian cities, serving notice that the government faced more than the resistance of students and civic activists. This was a national movement and it was growing rapidly.

In time the protests spilled onto Hrushevsky Street, which leads from the Maidan to the government quarter. Protestors occupied key buildings near the center of the protest, where an elaborate system of support emerged, including food canteens, an open "Maidan university," cultural events, emergency medical services for victims of attacks, working groups focused on policy demands, a team to deal with domestic and international media, a "diplomatic" team, and logistics coordination.

An Epic Battle

What followed was an epic battle between the authorities and civil society that lasted months, with protestors and activists arrested, abducted, murdered, or severely beaten. Violence by the state and by thugs employed by the Party of Regions was legion, with scores of beatings, a handful of shootings, and thousands of arrests and detentions of demonstrators. Despite the onslaughts, protestors held their ground, sustained by support from the merchants and citizens of Kyiv, who continued to turn out to swell the protestors' ranks after work on weekdays and came by the hundreds of thousands on Sundays. Week after week, the same phenomenon of protests and smaller long-term maidans was replicated in other settings throughout much of the country.

On January 16, 2014, with no sign of protests letting up, the Ukrainian Parliament adopted emergency legislation, dubbed the "dictatorial laws," that criminalized almost all the techniques of protest used by the Maidan. Occupation of government buildings was to be punished with ten years' imprisonment; those wearing helmets, balaclavas, or face masks as well as those setting up unauthorized food and medical facilities were subject to imprisonment and fines.

On January 22 the first deaths occurred in the proximity of the Maidan. Armenian-Ukrainian activist Serhiy Nigoyan died from multiple gunshots at the hands of the Berkut special police. Belarusian-

Ukrainian radical nationalist Mykhailo Zkyzhnevsky was also killed that day, the second victim of a sniper. Pitched battles continued near the barricades that protestors had erected on Hrushevsky Street on the periphery of the government quarter, resulting in several more deaths in January. The rapid escalation of state violence triggered the emergence of self-defense units on the Maidan. These self-defense contingents were overrepresented by activists from marginal far-right groupings, but also included a large number of radicalized middle-class civic activists. Still, the predominant ethos even among the hard-core self-defense units remained liberal and democratic. As rage mounted at state violence among protestors and the broader public alike, demands escalated to include the resignation of the government, the resignation of the president, and new elections of Parliament.

The government answered with more repression. Armored personnel carriers, water cannon, tear gas, and improvised grenades reinforced with nails were part of the government's arsenal. The authorities attempted to block and arrest those seeking to enter Kyiv's central square and so interrupt the Maidan's supply chain of food and medicines. A major effort was made to interdict tires that were burned around the perimeter of the tent city to provide a ring of fire when the security services advanced.

By late January, cracks in Yanukovych's hard-line approach appeared. State violence was showing little effect other than inflaming passions and making the protestors all the more determined. After significant outreach by Western diplomats, including U.S. assistant secretary of state Victoria Nuland, EU foreign affairs commissioner Catherine Ashton, Polish foreign minister Radosław Sikorski, and his German counterpart, Frank-Walter Steinmeier, there were small signals of the possibility for a negotiated solution. I visited Kyiv during those weeks of intense diplomacy and negotiations, which reflected the growing self-confidence of the protest movement. I saw the vibrancy of the living embodiment of civic life that prospered on the Maidan: lectures, film screenings, legal aid clinics, art exhibits, even geopolitical discussions at gatherings of dissident diplomats who had sided with the protest movement and resigned their government posts. At the same time, even as momentum was tilting in the protestors' favor, and amid the bravado of protest leaders, there was a clear sense of how brittle was their hold on the central square.

On January 25 at a meeting with the main political opposition leaders, President Yanukovych offered the post of prime minister to Fatherland Party leader Arseniy Yatsenyuk and agreed that Vitaly Klitschko would take the post of deputy prime minister. The opposition leaders did not accept the offer, instead demanding new presidential as well as parliamentary elections. Despite some concessions from Yanukovych, pitched battles continued near the Maidan and on Hrushevsky Street.

Efforts to reach a negotiated settlement proved elusive, largely because opposition politicians understood they wouldn't be allowed to shape their own government. Real power, especially over the military, the courts, the procuracy, and the security services, would remain with Yanukovych. At the same time, hard-liners around Yanukovych were encouraged by the backing of Russia. As the violence and mayhem escalated, a delegation of Russian Federal Security Bureau officials headed by General Sergiy Beseda quietly came to Kyiv formally to "secure [Russian] diplomatic facilities." In truth, they came to offer significant logistical support to the state security and police forces. Putin aide Vladyslav Surkov, who would later emerge as a major strategist in Russia's effort to carve Crimea and the Donbas out of Ukraine, was also in Kyiv to press for the crushing of the protests and to offer strategic advice. The Russians also had a separate agenda: to heighten tensions for reasons that soon would become clear.

Between February 18 and 21, state violence reached its apogee in a concerted effort to break the back of the protest movement. Over eighty protestors, unarmed and protected only with wooden shields, were butchered. A dozen members of the militia also died, some the victims of gunshots that appear to have come from a sniper or snipers shooting at both sides in an apparent bid to provoke mass violence.

Yanukovych Flees

On February 21, the country reeling, and amid furious efforts to dampen public anger with political concessions to the protestors, Yanukovych declared two days of national mourning to be observed on the 22nd and 23rd. On the afternoon of February 21, the Rada

Snipers (believed to be from the Berkut riot police unit) shoot at Euromaidan protestors on February 20, 2014. (Radio Free Europe / Radio Liberty)

voted to remove Interior Minister Zakharchenko, with 326 in favor, a sign that large portions of Yanukovych's own party were breaking with his leadership team. Then came a shocking development. On the morning of Saturday the 22nd, protestors found the government quarter empty and security forces nowhere to be seen. Thugs who had been recruited by the authorities to attack demonstrators also had vanished. There followed the sensational news that President Yanukovych had fled Kyiv for Kharkiv, where he hoped to convene the political leaders of Eastern Ukraine in a stand against the "usurpers" in the capital. Encouraged by Russia but spurned by local leaders in the east, Yanukovych traveled on to Crimea, from where he was spirited out to the Russian city of Rostov, where eventually he gave a press conference denouncing the "coup" that he claimed had forced him from office.

What made Yanukovych's flight enigmatic was that it had not been triggered by a spontaneous collapse of the security services nor by their defection to the opposition. Rather, there had been an orderly but largely unexplained withdrawal of support for Yanukovych's regime by security forces. Such a comprehensive withdrawal could have been precipitated only by an order from Ukrainian offi-

Public outrage at scenes like these fueled protests that led to the flight and removal of President Yanukovych. Here Ivan Panteleyev pulls the mortally wounded Bohdan Vayda down Instytutska Street at 9:01 a.m. on February 20, 2014. An hour after this photo was taken, Panteleyev himself was killed. (Evgeniy Maloletka)

cials or, possibly, by a signal from Russia to its agents inside Ukraine's leadership. Interior Minister Zakharchenko, whose forces disappeared from central Kyiv, had been dismissed by the Rada and fled to Russia, but his loyal deputies were still in place. In Moscow, he soon after took on an important and sensitive post at Rostec, Russia's state technology development agency, confirming that he was a trusted Russian interlocutor.

Video from CCTVs at Mezhyhirya showed Yanukovych's minions packing his art and valuables beginning on the 20th, just as the dead on the Maidan were being prepared for burial. The packing of truckfuls of huge crates occurred methodically over several days in preparation for an escape on the night of the 22nd, which meant it had started two days before his flight from Kyiv and before a Parliament vote that showed he had lost the legislature's support. More telling was the later official revelation that the Russian operation to annex Crimea had commenced on February 20—that is, while Yanukovych was still in power and Maidan protestors were being decimated. A medal issued by the Russian Ministry of Defense "for the return of Crimea" bears the date for the start of the operation as February 20, 2014. This suggests that, most likely, the Kremlin had decided to use and later ditch Yanukovych in an effort to precipitate the fracturing of the country into east and west and to facilitate the takeover and annexation of Ukrainian territory.

Yanukovych never fully explained the circumstances of the retreat of his forces. But his taskmaster Vladimir Putin did so on October 24, eight months after the Ukrainian president's flight, asserting that it was Yanukovych who "gave the order to withdraw all security forces from Kyiv." This version of events is at odds with reality and may have been part of Putin's effort to hide Russia's hand in the effort to split Ukraine's south and east from the center and west and precipitate its integration into Russia, something Russia began with the illegal annexation of Crimea in 2014 and of portions of four Ukrainian regions in 2022.

As Moscow unleashed its effort to splinter Ukraine, Ukraine's oligarchs would have none of it. Most wished to preserve a unitary state. Rinat Akhmetov, formerly a Yanukovych associate, expressed the view of the powerful Donbas business elite in clear terms: "My position remains unchanged: I am for a strong, independent and united Ukraine." "Today," Akhmetov added in a rebuke of Yanukovych's designs, "I place a special focus on the word 'united' as this has never been more important." In the hours that followed Yanukovych's flight on February 22, Parliament assembled and elected a new speaker, Oleksandr Turchynov, a longtime ally of former prime minister Yulia Tymoshenko, who was released from imprisonment that day. Upon Turchynov's election, a constitutional majority of deputies—328 lawmakers in the 450-seat Parliament—voted to remove Yanukovych from power, basing their action on his abandonment of office. In accordance with Ukraine's Constitution, Turchynov assumed the post of acting president until new elections could be held within ninety days.

Without the support of oligarch-linked parliamentarians, the decision to replace Yanukovych would not have reached a constitutional majority of votes and could have raised questions about the legitimacy of his removal. The much-maligned oligarchs not only supported the preservation of national unity, they played a crucial role in ensuring a legitimate transfer of power.

There were several reasons why many Party of Regions deputies joined in the decision to remove Yanukovych from office: they feared a radicalized, angry protest movement, realizing that the order they had long supported was collapsing. The decision to confer constitutional legitimacy on the new leadership was also motivated by the business elite's interest in the stability of the state and the continuity of leadership. Backdoor negotiations between oligarchs, their middlemen, and leaders of the major opposition political parties had contributed to the legitimacy and rapidity of the transition. So too had naked self-interest.

After Yanukovych's flight, the influence of oligarchs waned for a time as the ethos of the Maidan became the predominant force in shaping public values and expectations. That ethos was pro-democratic, pro-European, deeply intolerant of corruption, skeptical of Russia, and oriented around the values of civic patriotism, not ethnic nationalism. With Yanukovych's exit, an amorphous Russo-Ukrainian identity was losing its political potency. In its place a modern patriotic, pro-European ethos was becoming an important factor in the politics of Ukraine—just as a serious Russian threat was emerging.

The Yanukovych presidency had collapsed. Its epitaph was violence, ruin, and chaos. Yanukovych's tenure ended in utter failure and shook the stability of the young country, opening the door to a new set of aggressive actions by Putin's Russia. In the ensuing months and years, Ukrainians and their state would be challenged by war, foreign occupation, and thousands of deaths. These events would create challenges to Ukraine's next wave of leaders, but also would contribute to the consolidation of a nation that had long been divided between East and West and Soviet/Russo-centric and Euro-centric orientations.

After the collapse of his presidency and government, the media labeled Yanukovych in shorthand as "pro-Russian." The reality of his four years in office was more complex. For most of his presidency, Yanukovych had been, like most of the population of Eastern

Ukraine, neither "pro-Russian" nor "pro-Ukrainian." Like them, he had only a vague sense of being Ukrainian, but he also had a very clear sense of the power of the Ukrainian state.

Yanukovych: A Political Autopsy

In practice, his presidency had been exclusively "pro-Yanukovych," with tragic consequences. Larcenous and corrupt, he became increasingly addicted to wealth and power. The Yanukovych government had been populated by a cabal of Russian agents and pro-Russian politicians. Yet even in the Yanukovych years this pro-Kremlin lobby was in equal if not greater measure offset by advocates of Ukraine's sovereignty, most of them for reasons of self-aggrandizement. Ukraine's oligarchic elite, too, was in the main opposed to the idea of Russian domination or of Ukraine's entry into the Russian sphere of influence. The important presence of an oligarchic lobby inside the government, Presidential Administration, and Parliament proved to be more than a source of rent-seeking; it was also a countervailing factor checking the influence of pro-Russian networks and Russian agents.

Despite a lurch toward Russia in the waning months of his presidency, during most of Yanukovych's tenure in office, Russian business failed to expand its foothold in the Ukrainian economy. Like the Hetmans of the Cossack era who entered into alternating alliances with the Ottomans, Russia, and Poland, until late 2013 Yanukovych had pursued the modern-day equivalent: a multivector foreign policy that sought to balance external relations for as long as a mismanaged and cannibalized economy made this possible.

Through his choices and actions, Yanukovych alienated both the Ukrainian public square and the oligarchs. And he became unreliable in the eyes of the West. Ironically, Putin likewise did not view him as loyal. The compelling proof of this is that Putin launched an operation aimed at annexing Crimea and fragmenting and disintegrating Ukraine before Yanukovych's flight from Kyiv. Putin was not interested in keeping in power a president who had become highly dependent on Russia and would resist European and NATO integration. Instead, Putin's preference was to launch a bold attempt to fragment and destroy Ukraine as a state, or at the very least to ensure it became a "failed state."

In the end, Yanukovych fell from power because he lost the support of each of the four fundamental forces that had contested and determined Ukraine's development since 1991: pro-reform civil society and the public square; the oligarchic business elite; the democratic West; and, at the very end, revanchist Russia.

The courage and perseverance of the Maidan notwithstanding, Yanukovych could well have withstood the protests with Russia's help. But Putin pulled the plug on Yanukovych because he saw him as an unreliable and weak ally in the effort to return Ukraine to Russia's sphere of influence, whether through a customs union, federation, or even annexation into a unitary Russian state. Putin pursued these aims with persistence through hybrid conflict until in February 2022 his imperial ambitions led him to launch an all-out war on Ukraine.

Russian Aggression and Resistance

Yanukovych's undoing was the consequence of his greed, disregard for national solidarity and national unity, and dismissal of the interests of the public and of the powerful economic forces inside Ukrainian society. But Ukraine's descent into violence and its emergence as an inviting target for Russian aggression equally revealed the failure of the first quarter century of Ukrainian nation-building. The nation-building project failed in particular in Yanukovych's former home base, the Donbas. There, successive national governments had done little to instill a sense of Ukrainian identity, nor had they pursued a policy of developing a national narrative that could inure Donbas citizens to Russian influence.

Ukraine's post-Communist leaders had permitted Russian saturation of the media and culture markets, Russian books and periodicals, Russian social media, Russian websites, and Russian propaganda. They had done nothing to countermand the recruitment and training of violent militants by Russian state agents led by Russian parliamentarian Konstantin Zatulin, a major purveyor of the ideas of *Russkiy mir* (the Russian world). These were the means by which Moscow made significant inroads into Ukrainian life and was able to use these compensated recruits to undermine loyalty to the Ukrainian state, spread disinformation, stir up fear, promote ethnic hatred, and descend into violence.

Polls showed that more than half the people in Eastern Ukraine received their information from Russian sources. News and commentary programs as well as Russian popular culture spread imperial themes; Russian crime series and espionage thrillers extolled Russian security structures, including the FSB and its predecessor the KGB. All this distracted Ukrainians in the east and south from a Ukrainian national narrative and made them ambivalent about statehood. Though this did not make these regions welcoming to Putin's efforts to stimulate the fragmentation of Ukraine in what was styled the "Russian spring," it did lead to indifference about Ukraine's independence.

The failure to instill the Ukrainian language was another important reason for the weak sense of Ukrainian identity and patriotism in the east. An additional factor was the absence of a cohesive national narrative that could unify the country. Instead, successive Ukrainian politicians and political parties traded on competing historical narratives and pursued culture wars that stood in the way of shaping a cohesive Ukrainian polis. This flawed inheritance, as much as Yanukovych's policies, was a prelude to Russia's military offensive, invasion, and long-term occupation of large swaths of Eastern Ukraine and Crimea.

In contrast to the inchoate national legacies of a quarter century of Ukrainian statehood, Yanukovych had twice precipitated an unintended legacy—one of resistance in the public square—the Maidan, which in the coming years would fuel the rise of a new sense of Ukrainian patriotism and of a unified national identity.

CHAPTER FIVE

The Poroshenko Presidency and the Foundations of the Patriotic State

AMID DEADLY VIOLENCE AGAINST protestors, the Maidan movement toppled the Yanukovych regime in late February 2014, unleashing a wave of patriotism and radicalism in the country. The loss of nearly one hundred lives in a single day (including fifteen from the security services) fed public anger, coupled with a desire to wipe the slate clean of the corrupt semi-authoritarian system. But what this meant in specific policies was hardly clear.

The Maidan Agenda

An active minority of several thousand nationalists had borne the brunt of the deaths on the Maidan. They had been motivated by the aim of building a distinctly Ukrainian state rooted in patriotic values. What united most nationalists was the rejection of Russia and all things Russian. They sought to secure the reversal of the centuries-long erosion of Ukrainian culture and society and defend Ukrainian sovereignty and statehood. A further priority for these activists was the rebuilding of the state's defense and national security capacities, deliberately weakened by the Yanukovych regime.

By contrast, for most of the middle-class patriotic Ukrainians who in the hundreds of thousands filled Kyiv's central square for months at the height of winter, the agenda was broader. They envisaged a radical attack against rampant corruption, the introduction of liberal market reforms to spur economic growth and protect the middle class from state interference, and legal changes to speed integration into European political and economic structures, thus enhancing the rule of law and national security.

Under the influence of these currents, an agenda reflecting the aims of national patriotic revival, Ukrainization, the rapid transformation of the country through radical reforms, and the fight against corruption became the common denominators of public sentiment in the next years.

As had been proved in the display of people power during the Orange Revolution of 2004–5, Ukrainians again believed fundamental change was possible. But rising expectations were tempered by a serious challenge to the state's very existence.

After President Yanukovych fled Kyiv on February 21, 2014, he was removed from office by a constitutional majority and replaced by the newly installed speaker of the Rada, Oleksandr Turchynov. An evangelical pastor and close ally of Yulia Tymoshenko, Turchynov remained acting president until elections set for May 2014. On February 27 a new government was voted in, headed by Arseniy Yatsenyuk, seasoned politician and protest leader. The new government represented a coalition of the three largest opposition parties in the Rada: Tymoshenko's Fatherland Party, the UDAR Party of former world heavyweight boxing champion Vitaly Klitschko, and Svoboda (Freedom), a smaller ultra-nationalist political party.

Although the coalition was augmented by scores of nonpartisan independent deputies as well as by members of the Economic Rebirth faction and the Sovereign European Ukraine group, both populated by defectors from the Party of Regions, all ministerial posts were divided among the representatives of the three groups. Svoboda, which held thirty-five seats (8 percent of the Rada) was given three ministerial posts—deputy prime minister for humanitarian affairs, minister of agriculture, and ecology minister—and the important post of prosecutor general. Though Svoboda's influence on the government was slight, the presence of the far-right party in the new leadership inspired Russian propagandists to wage a disinformation campaign, both in Ukraine and outside, with the aim of eroding support for the new government by labeling it the product of a "fascist coup." Such language was a precursor to the rhetoric of Ukraine's "Nazi regime" that Russia would use in 2022 to justify its war on Ukraine.

Yatsenyuk's government faced a daunting series of challenges: consolidation of power; an economic downturn precipitated by Yanukovych's misrule and corruption; a major cash-flow crisis resulting from a depleted treasury and hard currency reserve; Russia-directed and Russia-financed uprisings in Southern and Eastern Ukraine; and Russia's annexation of Ukraine's Crimean peninsula, which was implemented in February–March 2014—the first weeks after the victory of the Maidan movement.

Crimea was annexed with lightning speed. It took a month and six days from February 20, 2014, to move from the first deployment of armed Russian "green men" to a quick vote by the Crimean Parliament to a referendum to approval by the Russian Parliament and on to a signing ceremony that annexed Crimea to Russia. With Western officials urging restraint, Ukraine's leaders concluded that their depleted armed forces would be overmatched by Russia and did not intercede militarily.

Putin's "Russian Spring"

Under Putin, Russia's intent to assert a sphere of influence in Ukraine had morphed into revisionism—the changing of existing state borders. Ukraine now confronted an illegal annexation of Ukraine's Crimea, a violent "Russian Spring" in Ukraine's south and east, and the onset of Russia's occupation of parts of Donetsk and Luhansk oblasts (including Ukraine's fifth and twelfth largest cities, respectively). The accompanying escalation of Russia's hybrid war, including the deployment of ready Russian military assets, financial resources, and weapons, as well as the mobilization of well-funded fifth columns in Ukraine's east and south, suggest that this hostile operation had been prepared well before President Yanukovych fled Kyiv. Importantly, the small "separatist" insurgent movements that had sprung up in Ukraine consisted of thugs groomed and trained by Russia. These "militants" were recruited among the poorly educated and underemployed and provided training and education in camps organized in Ukraine and Russia by the Institute of the CIS, the organization Russkiy mir, Aleksandr Dugin's Eurasian Youth Movement, and the Russian security services. Russia's curators of the separatist networks in Ukraine included parliamentarian Konstantin Zatulin and Putin aide Vladislav Surkov. Funds empowered marginal Russian nationalist, neo-Communist, and Crimean separatist political groupings, augmented by remnants of the Yanukovych regime. Notwithstanding the significant media and financial resources Russia deployed, there was no mass support behind the pro-Russian or "separatist" cause, which was never able to muster more than a few thousand protestors anywhere in the country.

As Russia launched its war against Ukraine, it began to expand its effort to destabilize Ukraine by infiltrating its state institutions. For this purpose, the Fifth Directorate of Russia's FSB engaged prominent officials from the Yanukovych team. Senior FSB personnel—including Sergey Beseda, the head of the Fifth Directorate—had in February 2014 traveled to Kyiv, where they worked alongside Andriy Klyuyev, Yanukovych's last chief of staff, and Volodymyr Sivkovych, former deputy prime minister of Ukraine, to suppress the Maidan protests. Sivkovych had long-standing links to Russian intelligence originating in his service in the Soviet KGB, and Klyuyev may have had a long-standing relationship as well.

After Klyuyev and Sivkovych fled to Russia with President Yanukovych, according to Ukraine's security services, they were assisted by the FSB's Fifth Directorate in creating a "Political Office" whose purpose was to infiltrate key intelligence and government institutions for the purpose of intelligence gathering and destabilization. Over time that "office" would have significant successes in creating an internal network of agents inside Ukraine's security services and beyond. Some of these agents would play a destabilizing role in support of Russia's all-out invasion in 2022.

Russia's hybrid war helped cut off 7 percent of Ukraine's territory in Crimea and the Donbas by the end of 2015. But Russia failed in its aim of provoking a massive uprising in Ukraine's south and east that was intended to result in the partition of the country. Although the broader insurgency failed, it was accompanied by deadly incidents that tested the new government team from its first days in power. The most violent clashes outside the Donbas occurred in Odesa, resulting on May 2, 2014, in the deaths of forty-six pro-Russian (anti-Maidan) and two patriotic Ukrainian activists as well as over two hundred injuries incurred during bloody street battles in the city center and at the House of Trade Unions, where a fire claimed most of the lives lost.

The protests spread to several cities, posing the first serious threat to the sovereignty of Ukraine since independence in 1991. Evidence made clear that these uprisings were coordinated and supported by the Russian state to provoke a "Russian Spring" aimed at splitting Ukraine. The ideology of the Russian Spring was supported by numerous Russian websites and information resources that sprang into coordinated action. The Russian Spring was spurred on by major coverage on Russian state-controlled television, then popular in Ukraine's south and east. In the end, the Russian Spring operation succeeded only in the eastern parts of Donetsk and Luhansk oblasts, which were adjacent to the Russian border, allowing for the rapid movement of Russian manpower, resources, and military and paramilitary assets to give muscle to what was a simulation of a mass uprising.

In areas of the Donbas bordering Russia, it was possible to reinforce small, staged uprisings with the sudden emergence of well-armed and well-drilled paramilitaries, which soon were found to be significantly populated by Russian fighters from the private Wagner Group, far-right Russian volunteers, and Cossacks, some of them led by Igor Girkin, a retired Russian State Security colonel. In the initial stages, these insurgent fighters were much better armed and better provisioned than Ukrainian forces, which had been eviscerated under Yanukovych. This was hardly a surprise, given that Yanukovych's two defense ministers were Russians. One, Dmitry Salamatin, was the son-in-law of a former Russian deputy prime minister. His successor, Pavel Lebedev, also held a Russian passport. Similarly, Russia could rely on networks and agents nurtured by the head of Ukraine's security service Igor Kalinin, another Russian national with deep connections to the Russian political and security establishment.

The loss of Crimea and large swaths of the Donbas, as well as efforts to foment violent mass unrest in Southern and Eastern Ukraine, disrupted the economy and required the diversion of significant resources to rebuild and strengthen the country's military and security forces. Additionally, the new government faced an empty treasury. A quick audit revealed that under Yanukovych billions of dollars had been raided from the treasury. The loss of heavily industrial territories and ongoing kinetic conflict sapped productivity, as did the physical loss of port facilities, factories, farms, and banks. Over time a steady flow of refugees from occupied and war-ravaged territories climbed to over 1.5 million. The loss of revenues generated by several million workers in the Donbas and Crimea (both those internally displaced and those under Russian control) accelerated the steep economic decline. All this came on top of Russia's selective trade embargoes on Ukrainian goods. As a result, in 2014 the economy declined by 6.8 percent and in 2015 by 10.4 percent. Ukraine's currency also weakened. At the time of Yanukovych's flight, the exchange rate stood at roughly 8 hryvnia to the dollar; by August 2014 the currency had weakened to 15 per dollar.

Poroshenko Takes Office

The country was in the midst of an acute economic crisis and fighting for its survival as a unitary state on June 7, 2014, when in the assembly room of the Ukrainian Parliament, businessman Petro Poroshenko held aloft the mace, a symbol of Cossack leadership and of his accession to the country's highest office. Poroshenko had just taken the country's oath of office, hand on the sixteenth-century Ostroh Bible, as Ukraine's fifth president. It was the pinnacle of his career, and a post for which the ambitious Poroshenko believed he was eminently well prepared. His presidential aspirations and his Westward orientation were even embodied in his mansion outside Kyiv, whose portico is a direct copy of that of the White House.

Having scored a remarkable first-round victory in which he outpaced his second-place challenger, Yulia Tymoshenko, by a margin of 54.7 to 12.8 percent, Poroshenko was at the height of his influence and basking in public approval. One of Ukraine's wealthiest people, Poroshenko had been a key leader in the Maidan Revolution,

The newly elected president of Ukraine, Petro Poroshenko, holds the ceremonial mace (*bulava*) at the Verkhovna Rada on the date of his inauguration, June 7, 2014. Poroshenko's presidency would see the implementation of serious economic and anti-corruption reforms and the rebuilding of Ukraine's military capabilities, but he was constantly dogged by allegations of deal-making and corruption within his inner circle. (Anastasiya Sirotkina / POOL / UNIAN)

having supported it financially, organizationally, and through personal physical courage. In one famous incident, he and his entourage had held back a column of advancing militia who were preparing to violently clear Independence Square of protestors. Though he was a leader of the Maidan, Poroshenko shied away from publicity during the months of protest, eschewing frequent appearances on the Maidan stage, preferring to contribute to the cause with hard work rather than the hunt for public attention. The Ukrainian people appreciated this circumspection and recognized Poroshenko's contribution to the democratic movement. Voters also were equally impressed by his significant government, management, and entrepreneurial experience.

A key figure in both the Orange and Maidan Revolutions, Poroshenko was a billionaire who had twice risked all his assets to stand with Ukraine's movements for a European and democratic future. His businesses included the country's major confectionary company, Roshen, which bore the core of his surname, major auto and bus manufacturing holdings, and TV news station Channel 5, an important source of information about the Maidan and Orange Revolution movements. Despite his more recent iterations as a political hero, Poroshenko had deep, ongoing connections to the old, discredited political and oligarchic elites. Although he had boldly opposed Yanukovych when the latter sought to steal the 2004 election and again in 2014, Poroshenko had also worked for him as a loyal member of the Azarov government. These polarities, over time, would embody his style of governing, an attempt to reconcile the new emerging Ukraine with its entrenched interests.

After the turmoil of the winter of 2013–14, voters were looking for competence and stability. They chose Poroshenko because he had served as a legislator, as the secretary of the National Security Council, as foreign minister, and as economy minister, giving him a diverse résumé ideally suited to leading a country in crisis. The public saw him as eminently capable of calming down a ship of state reeling from simultaneous and interrelated economic, political, and national security challenges. Voters also chose Poroshenko because he was seen as someone wealthy enough not to be tempted to steal from the public coffers.

Poroshenko ran on the slogan "To Live in a New Way." His inaugural speech echoed this theme and introduced his vision of the country's future and policy priorities. His remarks conveyed a vision of a confident Ukraine with a strong military, a Ukraine that would restore its occupied territories, and a Ukraine that would implement significant decentralization of power to local government and local legislatures. Poroshenko underscored Ukraine's irrevocable European choice and promised that those guilty of terrorism and murder against Ukraine's citizens would be brought to justice. The speech called for a tough-minded and firm response to the takeover of Ukraine's territories. Amid soaring rhetoric about peace, justice, economic reform, and the reclamation of territories from Russian occupation, one word was missing in his speech: *Maidan.* Poroshenko was clearly asserting his personal legitimacy based on the democratic will of the people expressed at the ballot box. He was also signaling that the time for revolutionary activism was over. It was time for professionals to take the reins.

The temporary government in place at the time of Poroshenko's inauguration reflected the political forces present at the Maidan. The new president was signaling that a new leadership had come to power that would be populated by senior business leaders, competent managers, and technocrats, whose task was to lead the country out of instability toward growth and security.

Poroshenko—assisted by detailed monthly private polling from the SOCIS company—understood that amid economic setbacks and Russian aggression, the country craved stability and professionalism. This accurate reading of the public mood had an unintended consequence of reinforcing his inherent cautiousness. As a result, his five-year rule would be marked by the avoidance policies that could alienate some of Ukraine's formal and informal power centers, including oligarchs and the Russophone minority.

Amid steep economic decline, Vladimir Putin saw an opportunity to turn Ukraine into a bankrupt "failed state." For a few days after Poroshenko's victory, the Kremlin and Putin danced around the legitimacy of Poroshenko's election. But by June 4, responding to a French reporter, Putin admitted that "we will respect the choice of the Ukrainian people and we will cooperate with Ukrainian authorities." By June 6, Putin responded positively to plans put forward by Poroshenko to put an end to the conflict in the Donbas, calling them the "right approach." And by the middle of June, the Russian president, officials, and media all referred to Poroshenko as the unquestioned president of Ukraine, dropping their idea that former president Yanukovych still had legitimate claim to the office.

Poroshenko hoped that acceptance of his legitimacy would open the door to constructive relations in the aftermath of Russia's takeover of Crimea and its support for "separatist" violence in Eastern and Southern Ukraine. After all, Poroshenko had campaigned as the candidate of peace, eschewing the belligerent language of his rivals and promising he knew how to deal pragmatically with Russia. He had even promised to resolve the conflict in the Donbas within two weeks of his inauguration.

Yet after a few weeks in office, with Russia unwilling to seriously discuss a settlement, Poroshenko veered from the path of negotiation, believing that the Russia-backed insurgency in the Donbas was not strong enough to withstand a full-on military assault by what was now a better-prepared Ukrainian military.

Poroshenko badly miscalculated. While rhetorically he derided Russia for invading his country and annexing Crimea, Poroshenko acted as if his adversary was not Russia but a ragtag band of irregular forces whose hold on the Donbas could easily be reversed by rapid military action.

The War in the Donbas

Initially, Poroshenko's plan was working. In July 2014 a Ukrainian military offensive made major gains as it recaptured significant swaths of territory of the self-declared Luhansk People's Republic (LNR) and the Donetsk People's Republic (DNR), including the retaking of the southern border with Russia. At one point Ukrainian troops entered the outskirts of Donetsk and its airport, and maintained control, albeit under heavy fire and counterattack. On July 17, 2014, amid Ukraine's effort to reestablish control over eastern Donbas, the conflict in Ukraine reached into the heart of Western Europe. Malaysia Airlines flight MH-17, traveling from Amsterdam to Kuala Lumpur, was shot down some thirty miles from the Ukraine-Russia border in territory under the control of Russia and its surrogates. The passengers were mainly Dutch and Malaysian nationals. Social media posts by fighters from Eastern Ukraine, including Russian operative Igor Girkin, initially took credit for shooting down what they thought was a Ukrainian military plane. Over the months and years that followed, international investigators, Dutch authorities, and the independent British-based open-source investigative group Bellingcat used geolocation from social network postings by Russian fighters and satellite images to prove incontrovertibly that Russian forces had entered Ukraine from Russian territory with the Buk anti-aircraft system that shot down MH-17.

The deaths on MH-17 and Russia's hand in the attack provoked huge media attention in the West and caused an uproar as great as that of the ongoing aggression. The incident strengthened Western consensus for sanctions against Russia and drove home the fact that Putin's revisionism carried serious security consequences for the West as well as for Ukraine itself. Russia's pattern of assassinations and attempted assassinations in Western countries and revelations of massive Russian state-sponsored electoral interference in European and U.S. elections contributed to a broad consensus that Putin was a major threat to the international order.

As MH-17 attracted front-page attention, Ukraine's offensive had reached Debaltseve, a railway center crucial for logistics and economic viability for the breakaway statelet. On July 29, after five days of pitched battles, Ukrainian Ministry of Interior troops took full control of the city. It was to remain under Ukrainian control until February 2015. But after as much as a quarter of the territory formerly held by Russia's LNR and DNR was retaken, Ukraine's gains suffered equally rapid reversals amid evidence Russia had augmented its on-the-ground forces. These formerly consisted of Kremlin-linked private armies, Chechen fighters, local guns for hire, and out-of-uniform Russian military advisors. Now, Russia quietly added cohesive regular units, including tank forces of the Russia military operating in uniforms without identifying markings. These were backed by Russian artillery units that pounded Ukrainian positions from Russian territory.

A clear signal that the war was morphing into direct combat with regular Russian military units came in the battle of Ilovaisk, which lasted nearly four weeks in August–September 2014. That battle saw some four hundred Ukrainian fighters killed, over four hundred wounded, and nearly three hundred missing or captured; Russian losses were estimated at half those Ukraine suffered. Ilovaisk effectively put an end to the Ukrainian advance as Russian forces counterattacked and recovered some lost territories. The setbacks suffered by Ukrainian forces led to the hasty signing on September 5 of the Minsk agreements, in which Poroshenko's Ukraine made major concessions and accepted the framework of a peace plan that, if implemented, would result in the de facto establishment of two Russian-dominated, constitutionally protected enclaves inside Ukraine.

The agreement, made under duress, meant the surrender of significant sovereignty. But it was never implemented under Poroshenko or his successor as Russia never showed serious interest in fully resolving the conflict. The deep concessions offered by Ukraine had been made at a time when Ukraine's military was suffering hundreds of deaths and casualties. Despite huge losses in the battle of Ilovaisk, Ukraine had demonstrated its will to fight and its fighting capabilities. The Ilovaisk battle made clear that an expanded Russian counteroffensive would result in massive loss of Russian soldiers—who, the Kremlin insisted to its own people and the world, were not at all involved in the conflict.

MH-17 and Russia's attack on Ukrainian forces as they made an orderly and agreed-upon retreat from Ilovaisk represented a brutal violation of the laws of war by Russian forces and their proxies. In the aftermath of these events, President Poroshenko came to Washington, DC. There, on September 16, 2014, with international concern about Russia on the rise, he made an impassioned plea for comprehensive support at an address to a joint meeting of Congress. Poroshenko called on the United States to provide lethal defensive weapons, including antitank Javelin missiles, and for an array of serious economic sanctions against the Kremlin and the Russian economy. Poroshenko's reception in Congress was warm, but President Obama was reluctant to commit to arming Ukraine during their meeting at the White House, even though the weapons Ukraine requested were of a defensive nature. It would take several years—and a change of U.S. administrations—to reverse the Obama policy.

As Western sympathy for Ukraine grew, support for the embattled country needed to be structured and made concrete to have significant impact on Russia. Here, Poroshenko and his team demonstrated considerable diplomatic skills. Not only did they press for financial assistance and weapons support for the country, they began to articulate a strategy aimed at imposing economic sanctions on Russia and developed a strategy of litigation—dubbed lawfare—aimed at securing both compensation and penalties for Russia's actions in Crimea and Eastern Ukraine. The Foreign Ministry under Pavlo Klimkin and his deputy Oksana Zerkal was at the center of articulating Ukraine's strategy to counter Russia militarily and economically. This strategy was soon augmented on a new front, through litigation for damages launched by Naftogaz, the state oil and gas giant; Oshchadbank, the state-owned savings bank; and numerous other state and private entities against Russia and Russian companies. Over time, this litigation resulted in rulings in favor of significant compensation. Economic sanctions imposed by Europe, the United States, and Canada began to have an impact, costing Russia between 1 and 1.5 percent in annual growth and contributing to stagnating Russian economic performance from 2015 forward.

The international community rallied to bolster Ukraine, with German chancellor Angela Merkel and French president François Hollande taking the lead. The United States played an important role in assisting Ukraine, but preferred—as President Obama observed—to "lead from behind," deferring to his European partners on diplomacy with regard to Russia.

Alongside a diplomatic response to the challenges posed by a deadly military aggression, occupation, and annexation of territories by Russia, the imperative of building an effective military, rejuvenating Ukraine's defense production, and modernizing and refurbishing weapons systems became an existential priority. At the same time, the president focused on reforming institutions, ensuring fiscal discipline, and combatting corruption. These domestic challenges were expected by civil society and were echoed by the international community, whose financial support a Ukraine under Russian attack would require.

Parliamentary Elections and the Rise of the People's Front

Four months after taking office, on October 26, 2014, Poroshenko faced his first big domestic political test. Nationwide parliamentary elections were held for 423 seats under a system in which 225 seats were selected based on party preference, with the balance of 198 deputies elected from districts under Ukrainian state control (27 unfilled seats represented Crimea and Russian-controlled Donbas).

The results were a surprise. The People's Front (NF), a center-right patriotic party headed by Prime Minister Arseniy Yatsenyuk, captured 22.14 percent of support, besting the Poroshenko bloc (BPP), which came in second with 21.82 percent. A party of conservative reformers with roots in Western Ukraine led by Lviv mayor Andriy Sadovyy, Self-Reliance, ran third, with nearly 11 percent, while the remnant of the Party of Regions received 9.43 percent. The populist Radical Party and Yulia Tymoshenko's Fatherland also captured more than 5 percent. The vote reflected the impact of both

Russia's aggression and the Maidan, which contributed to an erosion of support for Russia-friendly politicians and also meant that several million Russophone Ukrainian voters were no longer living in territory controlled by Ukraine and did not have the opportunity to vote.

Poroshenko and the People's Front immediately began coalition talks, with Yatsenyuk's party carrying significant clout as it had finished first in the party-preference vote. The Front's strong showing was an early sign that support for the new president was beginning to erode. While Poroshenko's party came in second on the party-preference vote, Poroshenko-backed candidates won the plurality of single-mandate seats, helped by the support of local business interests and of regional officials appointed by the president.

The two leading parties held a slim one-vote majority in the Rada but, in a sign of national unity, they agreed to create a coalition with Self-Reliance, the populist Radical Party, and Fatherland. On November 27 a grand coalition of parties associated with the Maidan was created under the name European Ukraine. It controlled a constitutional majority of more than 300 votes and consisted of the BPP (143 seats), People's Front (83 seats), Self-Reliance (32 seats), Tymoshenko's Fatherland Party (19 seats), and Oleh Lyashko's Radical Party (22 seats), which had enjoyed support from a floating array of oligarchs. Gone from the coalition was the far-right Svoboda party, which failed to cross the 5 percent threshold.

Yatsenyuk was approved as prime minister with 341 votes. His government team received 288 votes. Yatsenyuk's new turn as prime minister came with a strong majority largely free of associations with the Yanukovych regime. At age forty, Yatsenyuk was a seasoned government veteran, having served as the acting head of the National Bank of Ukraine, foreign minister, finance minister, speaker of the Rada, and interim prime minister.

The old Yanukovych forces rebranded as the Opposition Bloc. But they were a vastly diminished cohort of forty-six, in part due to the loss of territories now under Russian control. Much of their electorate was disgusted by Yanukovych's mega-corruption and angered by his cowardly escape from Kyiv. Two other parliamentary groups, the People's Will and Economic Development, were created by deputies from single-mandate districts and included several MPs who had backed Yanukovych. These latter groupings represented wealthy local and national business interests and had no distinct ideological cast.

To balance Yatsenyuk's appointment, Volodymyr Groysman, the young mayor from Poroshenko's home base in Vinnitsya, was elected the Speaker of the Rada.

A New Government Tackles an Economic Crisis

The core of the new government consisted of technocratic ministers with impressive credentials. It included Natalie Jaresko, a former U.S. diplomat and fund manager, as minister of finance; Alexander Kvitashvili, former Georgian minister of health, took the same portfolio; and Aivaras Abromavicius, an investment banker, was named minister for economic development. The three were joined by the former head of one of Ukraine's elite universities, historian Serhiy Kvit, who took over the education portfolio. Career diplomat and ambassador to Germany Pavlo Klimkin became foreign minister. The Interior Ministry went to Kharkiv millionaire Arsen Avakov, who over time would become a nemesis of President Poroshenko. Avakov was assisted by his deputy, Eka Zguladze, former acting interior minister in Georgia, who handled the task of reforming the notoriously corrupt national police and traffic police.

The president appointed the CEO of IBM in Ukraine, Dmytro Shymkiv, to head up his Economic Reform Council. International advisors included Leszek Balcerowicz, the former Polish deputy prime minister credited with Poland's economic revival; Slovakia's former finance minister Ivan Miklos; and Georgia's former president Mikheil Saakashvili. Oleksandr Danylyuk, the former McKinsey consultant who developed an unrealized reform program for Yanukovych, joined the Poroshenko administration armed with the same impressive economic blueprint. He initially served as the president's representative to government and in 2016 would replace Jaresko as finance minister. The National Bank of Ukraine received a new governor, Valeria Gontareva, formerly wealth manager for the Poroshenko family. Vasyl Hrytsak, a longtime security service official who also had served as security chief of Poroshenko's private businesses, was named head of the security service of Ukraine, playing a crucial role in Ukraine's efforts to resist Russian aggression.

Many of the appointees had stellar credentials: Western educations and/or the experience of work in Western financial institutions, as well as reputations for integrity. Their appointments signaled that Poroshenko was committed to thoroughgoing change.

The appointment of two investment bankers, Andriy Kobolyev and Yuri Vitrenko, to run Naftogaz, Ukraine's state-owned oil and gas giant and one of Europe's twenty largest companies by revenue, reflected this turn to business professionals. The two, who had worked together in the private sector, undertook one of the most successful reforms of the Poroshenko years, removing Ukraine's greatest source of corruption by introducing market prices for gas and saving taxpayers several billion U.S. dollars per year in corrupt takings. Kobolyev had started his business career at Price Waterhouse Coopers in Ukraine, worked as a private investment banker at AYA Capital alongside Vitrenko, and later at Naftogaz, as both an advisor to the chairman and the head of several departments focused on corporate finance and price policy. He and Vitrenko rapidly transformed Naftogaz from a huge drain on the state budget into a profit-making state enterprise, generating by 2018 as much as $3 billion in dividends annually.

To be sure, there was a cohort of appointees with links to oligarchic and business interests, party loyalists, and old-school politicians. The former head of the National Guard, Stepan Poltorak, was named defense minister. None of the president's appointments raised more alarm than that of prosecutor general Viktor Shokin, a sixty-two-year-old representative of the procuratorial establishment. Shokin had demonstrated independence in 2001 when he refused to press a criminal case against Yulia Tymoshenko. Despite this one instance of integrity, Shokin's appointment was attacked by anti-corruption activists. Still, the nomination of several reformers to the prosecutorial leadership, including attorney Vitaliy Kasko, offered hope for progress on corruption.

While Borys Lozhkin, a young multimillionaire businessman who headed the president's office, advocated a government of professionals, a large portion of the Presidential Administration was populated by Poroshenko's friends, business partners, and longtime political loyalists. Over time, this cohort would add to the friction between the president and prime minister through squabbles over patronage and the disposition of lucrative licenses and contracts.

Western governments, international financial institutions, the international development community, and civil society were pleased with the new team. They believed the new government had the will and competence to maintain budgetary discipline and advance Ukraine on the path of serious reforms. On paper, the government had a comfortable—indeed, a constitutional—majority. In reality, each of these parties was itself an amalgam of different business, oligarchic, and ideological interests. Over time, these competing groups made legislating far more difficult, as loyalty to business donors and patrons as well as corruption fragmented party loyalty and weakened the coalition.

Poroshenko's strong national security background meant he understood that he faced a paramount challenge beyond domestic reforms: to secure the country's territorial integrity and provide for its effective defense in the face of widening Russian aggression. For this he needed national consensus and political stability. As Prime Minister Yatsenyuk would note in 2019, "Ukraine was on the precipice of default in 2014. The state treasury held all of 108,000 hryvnia [several thousand dollars] and US$73 billion in debt, none of which I had borrowed." When he eventually left office, he reported, "there would be 90 billion UAH [nearly $4 billion] in the treasury and the debt would be reduced to US$67 billion."

Lifted by the tide of reform momentum of the Maidan protests, the early days of the political marriage of Poroshenko and Yatsenyuk ran smoothly. Reforms proceeded at a prodigious pace amid the prosecution of a bloody war in Ukraine's Donbas. A short-term IMF agreement, designed to cope with the new government's inherited economic crisis, provided an early disbursement of over $3 billion in urgently needed financing to stabilize the currency and surmount default. A climate of optimism prevailed over the prospects for deep change. However, the evidence of obstacles to change was no less clear.

Big-business and oligarchic interests were well represented in the new Parliament. In early 2014, I met with Andriy Parubiy, a leader of the Maidan recently elected to the Rada. A former far-right nationalist who had evolved into a pragmatic patriot, Parubiy would soon be named secretary of Ukraine's National Security and Defense Council and later became Parliament speaker. On that winter day, over a coffee in the Hotel Kyiv, a home for out-of-town deputies of modest means, Parubiy informed me that several of his former allies from the Maidan were now swept up in a web of corruption. The amounts being offered for their votes were staggering for a poor country: tens of thousands of dollars per month. Sadly, Parubiy reported, among the handful of quickly corrupted legislators were activists who had risked their lives on the Maidan. Corruption was planting roots in the new Rada, weakening the ruling coalition and making the passage of reform legislation far more cumbersome in an alliance in which there were ambitious populists, liberals, and conservatives all pushing their own, sometimes conflicting, agendas.

Tensions between President and Prime Minister

With a public mandate and significant influence on the government, President Poroshenko was full of confidence. A successful businessman with government experience in economic, national security, and foreign affairs, Poroshenko could not be faulted for seeing himself as much or more of a policy expert than many of his appointees. His drive, energy, and management style meant he was hands-on. Very quickly, egged on by his inner circle, this approach would set him on a collision course with his equally expert, self-confident, and politically strong prime minister, Arseniy Yatsenyuk.

Despite tension at the top, the new government team was impressive and competent. But this competence came with a sense of professional pride and the expectation of autonomy. Here Poroshenko's and his inner circle's direct intrusions into the day-to-day functioning of government—sometimes outside the constitutionally delineated separation of authority—created rifts with the talented reform team. Amid criticism over Poroshenko's initial appointment of a retrograde prosecutor general and several business partners in his inner circle, a view began to form that the president was impeding the battle against corruption and restoring the practices of cronyism.

This view, shared by some Western embassies and anti-corruption monitors, was not entirely justified by the facts. Poroshenko's first year proved to be the most ambitious and dynamic of his five-year presidency. But as 2015 began, the war in the east again intensified. This time the battleground was Debaltseve, a city of twenty-five thousand Ukraine had captured from the Russians and their proxies in the summer of 2014. Debaltseve was strategically wedged between the Donetsk and Luhansk "people's republics." In January 2015, with the support of regular Russian military units, tanks, and artillery, the city was retaken amid huge casualties. In all, 185 Ukrainian fighters were killed, well over 500 wounded, and more than 1,000 taken prisoner. The rout forced Ukraine into ever deeper compromise in a ceasefire agreement known as Minsk 2. The second Minsk agreement ended the fighting, but it imposed a detailed formula of the measures required for the restoration of Ukraine's control over its eastern border. Unlike the first Minsk agreement, this one explicitly stated that such control would come only after elections in the Russian-controlled areas of Luhansk and Donetsk.

Though fighting diminished significantly after Minsk 2, with the annual death rate dropping from thousands per year to hundreds, the additional concessions extorted by Russia and the massive military setback in Debaltseve eroded support for Poroshenko at home. He and his military leadership stood accused by some fighters and activists of having blundered in the battle and then shown weakness in accepting Russia's terms in Minsk 2.

The persistence of Russia's hybrid and kinetic war and major losses on the battlefield saw the president's poll numbers slip in his second year. Another factor fed public disappointment. In a rush to pass crucial legislation demanded by international donors as a condition of aid, Ukraine's careful post-Maidan balance between the public square and the boardroom, between civil society and oligarchic interests, was disrupted. Passing laws in a Parliament where big business had huge influence meant backroom deals and the exchange of special favors for votes, further alienating the reform-oriented public. Anger at oligarchic rent-seeking and alleged government indifference to corrupt schemes also awakened anger among Ukraine's newest rich, the generation of technology entrepreneurs, investors, and venture capitalists who were building fortunes from the ground up and needed strong rule-of-law and property rights.

Tangible Reforms

On balance, despite a high degree of lobbying, rent-seeking, and civic-oligarchic conflict, Ukraine was moving in the right direction. David Lipton, the International Monetary Fund's first deputy managing director, summarized the state of play: "Notwithstanding a strong policy-led adjustment effort in 2014, the Ukrainian economy continues to be affected by the conflict in the East and the attendant loss of confidence. The deep recession and sharp exchange rate depreciation aggravated existing vulnerabilities, weakened bank balance sheets, and raised public debt." Lipton also expressed the IMF's confidence in the new Ukrainian leadership team: "Demonstrating strong resolve, Ukraine's authorities have developed a new program to restore macroeconomic stability and address long-standing structural obstacles to growth, including weak governance."

A large and comprehensive IMF agreement was established in March 2015. It included a framework for reforming the country and reducing corruption. In return, Ukraine received access to $17.5 billion in credits over the course of four years, an essential boost to an economy now spending 5 percent of GDP on security.

Western pressure and aid were working. So too was Poroshenko's ability to strike deals. The measures taken by the Parliament and government reversed an economic recession and led to a modest and sustained turnaround, which at the end of Poroshenko's term in office yielded annual growth of nearly 5 percent. As a result of prudent fiscal policies during Poroshenko's presidency, Ukraine had a strong economy that international financial institutions projected would grow between 4 and 5 percent in both in 2020 and 2021. This growth was a major accomplishment as it came even as Ukraine upped its defense spending to 5 percent of GDP—a several-fold increase from the Yanukovych years.

VOX Ukraine, an international nonpartisan analytic group created and populated by respected Western and Ukrainian scholars, concluded three years into the post-Maidan government that significant progress and achievements could be observed in gas-sector reform, reform of the banking system and of the central bank, transparent public procurement, decentralization, an improved business environment, and the reform of the police. At the same time, according to VOX, progress lagged in effective prosecutions and punishment of corruption, judicial system reform, law enforcement, land market and land privatization reform, privatization of state assets, and civil service reform.

A comprehensive study by the Institute of Economic Research (IER), a well-regarded Kyiv think tank, quantified the financial benefits of the early wave of reforms undertaken by the Ukrainian government after 2014. The report, produced by a team of Ukrainian economists and refereed by a panel of distinguished Western economists, calculated the revenue consequences of key reforms. The report showed that reforms had reduced grand corruption by $6 billion per year. At the time this represented nearly 6 percent of Ukraine's official GDP. The increased effectiveness of state tax and revenue authorities also pared the size of the shadow economy, which dropped from 43 percent in 2014 to 33 percent at the end of 2017.

Four reforms contributed significantly to the tangible progress.

Gas market reform significantly reduced the gap between the price of imported gas and artificially lower domestic prices, which had led to price arbitrage resulting in billions of dollars in corrupt profits at the expense of the state treasury. This price gap also created a strong and influential domestic lobby for dependence on Russian gas (which, after 2016, Ukraine ceased importing). Significantly, the Naftogaz reforms fed the government's budget by generating well over $1 billion in profits annually. Cumulatively, under Poroshenko, gas-sector reforms added approximately $3 billion to the state budget as dividends.

Tax administration reform eliminated vast "tax holes" amounting to at least $1 billion per year. Such reforms include electronic filing for VAT, which curbed graft. Under Yanukovych, the revenue system was controlled though a widespread network of money laundering "conversion platforms," which implemented an elaborate system of cash payments to tax inspectors, who for a fee of 6 to 12 percent would approve them, helping to create false documentation of incomes and expenses.

Another reform source came from Prozorro, the electronic system of public procurements introduced in April 2016. Prozorro drastically reduced corruption in government contracts and contributed over $1 billion annual income to the state.

Open-data reform eliminated many rent-seeking schemes and brought in $700 million in new income.

In all, by IER's calculations, the reforms brought $6 billion to the economy. Even this number was conservative as it didn't include the savings that resulted from banking system reform and the elimination of "zombie" banks, so called they took citizens' savings and financed owner-related businesses and shell companies. The economic effect noted in IER's calculation also excluded the economic benefits of health-care reform, which ushered in increased transparency in payments for medical services. An additional revenue source was asset recovery. Through coordinated action by the Prosecutor General's Office, $1.5 billion in assets belonging to the "organized crime group led by Yanukovych" was confiscated and returned to the state treasury.

As the effects of these reforms were kicking in, Finance Minister Natalie Jaresko created budgetary equilibrium, renewed IMF financial support to buttress an economy in freefall, and renegotiated in August 2015 the restructuring of Ukraine's debt with private sector creditors.

Major progress was made on decentralization to democratically accountable local authorities. These reforms gave local authorities and communities direct ownership over funds, significant rights with respect to revenue sharing from tax collection, and included the direct allocation of central government funds to implement local construction and infrastructure projects.

Government decentralization deepened the public's connection with and support for part of the state. By placing funds for local needs and public works directly under the control of local governments, expenditures became more transparent and directly accountable to the community. After the decentralization reforms were introduced, polling data showed that support for local officials, especially mayors, was high; local leaders enjoyed a much higher degree of trust than central government officials. In addition, the reforms made local governments and communities more resilient in times of crisis, when local conditions can differ radically by allowing for rapid local responses to emerging problems. These characteristics, as well as a strong sense of local ownership of government, made the country more resilient for the existential challenges Ukraine would face in 2022.

Tensions with Civil Society

Despite these effective measures, Western officials and the Ukrainian public wanted more: punishment of former and current corrupt officials, a policy Poroshenko appeared to resist. Overall, Poroshenko's programs and initiatives to help reduce the scope of corruption were succeeding. But Western-funded programs and reform priorities were primarily focused on prosecuting corruption and there Ukraine showed poor results. Instead of acknowledging significant positive changes, however, Western-financed civil society groups stepped up their attacks on the Poroshenko reforms as inadequate. In so doing, they discredited the achievements of the reforms, fed left- and right-wing populism, and spurred protests that weakened Ukraine and contributed to instability. The frontal attack on the authorities made them reluctant to cooperate with civic groups. The unrelenting focus by NGOs on failures in the anti-corruption agenda also inadvertently undermined these groups in the eyes of the public, which came to view them as impotent.

The absence of serious progress on convictions in cases of high-level corruption raised tensions between Poroshenko, the government, and donors. Civic groups and Western diplomats saw the locus of the problem in the lack of action by the Prosecutor General's Office, which in May 2016 was placed under the leadership of Maidan leader and former political prisoner Yuri Lutsenko. Lutsenko was a controversial appointee. He was not a lawyer and was seen as too close to Poroshenko. While Lutsenko made significant efforts to press prosecutions on corruption charges, he met with the persistent resistance of the insular court system, which itself was deformed by wide-scale corruption. Amendments to the Constitution removed the procuracy's universal oversight function, a Soviet remnant. Unfortunately, despite this reform, prosecutions remained opaque. In addition, according to Bohdan Vitvitsky, a former U.S. Justice Department prosecutor who worked with Ukrainian leaders on reforms, both the main Prosecutor General's Office and the new Special Anti-Corruption Prosecutor suffered from a weak knowledge of business law and commercial transactions, which constituted the bulk of anti-corruption prosecutions.

Tensions grew between traditional law enforcement entities and the new better-funded and better-compensated anti-corruption bodies. Poroshenko's foot-dragging on creating an anti-corruption court didn't help. For the West, prosecuting and punishing wrongdoers increasingly became the true measure of change. Western governments increased pressure and Western-funded NGOs put out a steady drumbeat of criticism. As a result, large numbers of Ukrainians believed "nothing has changed in the Poroshenko years." In May 2018, a poll by the Democratic Initiatives Foundation showed that 80 percent of people felt that the war on corruption in Ukraine had failed.

Throughout the Poroshenko years Western aid groups pressed for punitive measures to root out corruption. At the same time, comprehensive reform of the courts was put on the back burner. The main investigative body the West sought to empower was the National Anti-Corruption Bureau of Ukraine (NABU), founded in October 2014 with significant Western financial support and technical assistance. Although the organization struck a position of independence from state officials, its senior personnel consisted mainly of the talented members of the old prosecutorial and police establishment. As a result, some bureau practices were decidedly questionable, including the alleged use of illegal means to gain evidence, reliance on pliant judges who were under investigative pressure by the bureau, wiretapping without court orders, use of unregistered eavesdropping devices, and the sharing of confidential case materials with favored journalists. Despite such flaws, NABU showed dynamism. By contrast, the ancillary National Agency on Corruption Prevention operated at a snail's pace, bringing very few charges against politicians whose asset declarations showed unexplained storehouses of money and property.

When government asset declarations became public, they opened a Pandora's box that led to widespread loss of confidence in Ukraine's elites. A large portion of Ukraine's parliamentarians and government officials, many of whom came from business, held multimillion-dollar assets, including multiple homes, fine artwork, and expensive cars. In a country where pensions and wages outside the major cities then averaged $200 to $300 per month, the evidence of upper-middle-class and rich lifestyles among government officials, legislators, and eventually NGO activists heightened public anger that in turn fed the politics of resentment.

Amid the launching of numerous criminal indictments that documented wrongdoings, the failure to address court reform kicked in. Judges were overwhelmed with mounting caseloads and began a de facto slowdown that enabled them to put off taking decisions in sensitive anti-corruption cases involving the rich and powerful. And when cases did make it to trial, prosecutors faced a court system that itself was rife with corruption.

While prosecutors and anti-corruption agencies faced resistance in the courts, a proliferation of Western-funded investigative journalism projects provided a steady and rich diet of TV and print stories about corrupt schemes and unexplained riches, feeding public anger at impunity.

The root cause of the failure of the West's anti-corruption effort of the Poroshenko years was depressingly familiar: the flawed belief that the key to change was individual politicians at the top and not institutions. As civic leaders, analysts, and some policymakers soured on Poroshenko, they focused on creating and empowering adversarial structures and approaches rather than on building cooperative relationships with the Poroshenko team. Though opportunities for corruption narrowed significantly under Poroshenko, a steady Western-funded diet of reports on corrupt practices was cynically amplified by oligarchic media interested in eroding the government's and president's popularity. Poor sequencing of reforms also resulted in a steady stream of charges of corruption, but inaction by unreformed courts only heightened the public's anger.

When limited reform efforts were attempted in the courts, the system fought back. One of the first major legal reforms, "on renewal of trust to judicial system," was approved in April 2014. It introduced lustration of judges. Yet over time, 75 percent of court chairpersons fired by this law were reinstated by their peers. Judicial reforms focused on gradual upgrades to achieve greater trust and independence in the system. New legislation granted an imperative power to Supreme Court decisions, introduced open competition for all positions in the court system, dramatically raised salaries of judges, and set up a self-governing body for the judicial branch—the Higher

Council of Justice—empowered to make all decisions regarding the appointment, promotion, and punishment of judges. To minimize corruption, judges were required to submit annual e-declarations, which are public and available online. Nevertheless, the inherent conservatism and resistance of the judicial branch was on full display as the Higher Council of Justice refused to reject or dismiss judges shown to be corrupt or dishonest by an integrity commission comprising civic activists and think tank experts. And in time, it would become clear that the ostensibly reformed Supreme Court itself suffered from corruption.

The dysfunction of the criminal justice system and a judiciary often unwilling to fulfill its duties or mired in corruption led to a backlog of 5 million criminal cases in the country. The net result was a steady and growing public anger at elite impunity and the absence of elementary justice. Nor was the system's resistance limited to the judiciary and procuracy. While Deputy Interior Minister Eka Zguladze's creation of a reconstituted patrol police was a success, the other police services (namely, the investigative police) remained unreformed. During 2016 all eighty thousand police officers were screened for integrity, but only 6 percent were dismissed (and many of that number were reinstated in their jobs on the basis of court rulings).

In this environment, the Ukrainian public's growing alienation from those in power was understandable. But the focus of anger on the Poroshenko team was misplaced. Poroshenko legitimately felt he had made significant progress in eliminating major corruption schemes and had taken great political risks in challenging part of the oligarchic establishment, including taking on billionaires Dmytro Firtash and Ihor Kolomoysky, who wielded tremendous influence through their major national TV channels and lobbies in Parliament.

Russia's kinetic war against Ukraine was hardly an excuse to ignore fundamental domestic reforms; nevertheless, the conflict and the desire for stability deepened Poroshenko's inherent caution, slowing down a reform process that had achieved significant momentum under the government of technocratic reformers of 2014–16. The years that followed, regrettably, were characterized more by stasis and disappointments than breakthroughs.

Poroshenko's Inner Circle

By early 2016 tensions between Poroshenko and Yatsenyuk were boiling over amid signs that the president aimed to force the prime minister from office. Rather than reach a modus vivendi with his People's Front coalition partner and embrace dialogue with civic forces, Poroshenko increasingly relied on a narrow group of long-time associates installed in key institutions. Some associates—mainly his junior business partners—justly or not developed reputations for rent-seeking and were accused of corruption inside the government, in state-run enterprises, and in the military industrial sector and would become an important factor in the public's loss of trust in Poroshenko.

Three businessmen were central to Poroshenko's rule: Boris Lozhkin, Ihor Kononenko, and Oleh Hladkovsky. All held key leadership positions, and their presence in the state sector contributed to rising public unease about Poroshenko.

Lozhkin, formerly a business partner of Poroshenko's in a small, influential newsmagazine, *Korespondent*, had made his fortune building a radio and magazine business, selling it in 2013 under pressure to the clan of President Yanukovych. Lozhkin was a competent administrator who successfully advocated for the inclusion of reformers and technical experts in the government. He resigned after two years in August 2016, sending an important signal that it was time for business-linked servants to exit the government. Other businessmen in the inner circle did not take the cue.

Ihor Kononenko, another insider, had been a close friend of Poroshenko since their military service in the mid-1980s as well as a business partner: he had served as a member of the supervisory board of Poroshenko's holding company and worked in executive positions at several Poroshenko-owned companies. In a public asset declaration in 2015, Kononenko revealed he was the head investor in the Leninska Kuznya plant in Kyiv and co-owner with Poroshenko of a glass-manufacturing plant, a sports and recreational complex, the truck manufacturer Bogdan Motors, the International Investment Bank, and an investment fund. Kononenko also was a leader inside the Petro Poroshenko bloc, serving as first deputy head of the parliamentary group and as an influential member of the Rada's Energy and Fuel Committee. Anti-corruption activists claimed Kononenko used political access to win a large stake in an energy company, was involved in the sale of petroleum and propane imported from Russia, and indirectly acquired extraction rights for lithium.

Oleh Hladkovsky, another Poroshenko business partner and manager, was widely criticized for his influence on the military industrial complex. Hladkovsky had worked for Poroshenko in the Bohdan bus-manufacturing holding and was a 10 percent partner in the concern, where he served at various times both as board chairman and CEO. His appointment to the National Security and Defense Council with special responsibility for military production, and later to the leadership of the massive UkrOboronProm state defense industry conglomerate raised concerns about a conflict of interest and generated a wave of media speculation about corruption in the Poroshenko camp.

Hladkovsky became the focal point of regular accusations of illicit profits from transactions between his companies and state defense companies. He notoriously was attached to a damaging scandal involving price gouging by his son in the provision of spare parts to refurbish Ukraine's weapons. The scandal, made public weeks before the April 2019 presidential election, resulted in Hladkovsky's dismissal as head of UkrOboronProm and contributed significantly to weakening public support for Poroshenko's reelection.

Poroshenko tried to deflect criticism of these appointments by arguing he needed competent managers in key positions to help him lift the country out of crisis and rebuild the country's defense production after years of neglect and underinvestment. While these justifications may have been credible in his first months in office, the long-term presence of business partners in official posts eroded trust in the president.

Occasionally the lobbying and activities of Poroshenko's friends met pushback from reformers in the government. Hladkovsky and Kononenko may well have been operating in their own name and interests, but the public saw them as part of a system of war profiteering that operated with Poroshenko's approval. One such case, pressure to appoint a Kononenko associate as deputy economy minister, led to the very public resignation in February 2016 of Minister Aivaras Abromavicius and came at a time of rising tensions between the government and the president. While there was no evidence that Poroshenko and his companies directly benefited from such machinations (although what some regard as politically motivated criminal cases alleging just that were launched in the fall of 2019 under President Volodymyr Zelensky), the public reaction was harsh.

A Selective War against Oligarchs

The pace of reforms during Prime Minister Yatsenyuk's tenure had been impressive. Over time, powerful business lobbies began to reassert their influence over the policymaking process. Reformers lamented that President Poroshenko failed to stifle these lobbies and resented that some were associated with his longtime associates. Poroshenko's inconsistent behavior was morally unacceptable to many who had risked their lives on the Maidan. Nevertheless, his decisions were comprehensible given the challenges he faced. The Parliament, whose cooperation was essential, was riddled with representatives of business interests and legislators beholden to oligarchs. Many deputies had entered Parliament backed by the resources of oligarchs and powerful local businessmen. Paradoxically, reform legislation could not be passed without their support. Their votes were also needed to pass tough economic policies required by the International Monetary Fund. Big business's support was also needed in the effort to combat Russian influence in the south and east of the country. This reality meant that Poroshenko and his political allies frequently made concessions to special interests that were required to get things done.

Since independence, oligarchic business had emerged as a major force in the economy, in the media, and in politics. Faced with a Russian invasion, Poroshenko chose to rely on some of these plutocrats. He initially engaged steel magnate Serhiy Taruta as the governor of his home base in Donetsk oblast in a bid to win over the loyalty of the local elite. He bargained with steel, energy, and coal magnate Rinat Akhmetov, who over time helped stabilize Mariupol and other population centers of the Donbas under threat of a Russian takeover. Poroshenko also appointed billionaire Ihor Kolomoysky, who would become one of his most determined enemies, governor of his business base—the Dnipropetrovsk region. Kolomoysky's business associate Ihor Palytsia was installed as governor of the Odesa region.

Many such alliances did not last. An ineffective Taruta seethed quietly at his dismissal and allied with Yulia Tymoshenko. Ihor Kolomoysky, who was dismissed as governor after a tense midnight meeting with Poroshenko at the Presidential Administration on March 25, 2015, left office in anger. Kolomoysky had earned plaudits for stabilizing Dnipropetrovsk, a region close to the conflict zone further east. The litigious and tough-talking oligarch had even helped finance armed detachments of volunteers who stymied territorial advances by Russians and their proxies. He also had effectively coped with the flow of hundreds of thousands of refugees who were fleeing the battleground of Eastern Ukraine. But even one of his closest associates admitted that the oligarch saw access to government office as an opportunity for personal gain.

At issue was Kolomoysky's stake in a state oil company, UkrNafta. Kolomoysky had maneuvered to gain control over management of the company, allegedly using it to milk the company for cash, while withholding the payment of billions of hryvnias in dividends to the state. Ukrainian law had required 60 percent of shares for a quorum at meetings of state-owned firms, allowing Kolomoysky and his business partners, who held a 42 percent stake, the ability to block management's removal and giving him de facto control. But on March 19, 2015, Parliament passed a law reducing the quorum requirement at state firms to a simple majority, denying Kolomoysky a veto. Days later a group of armed men, apparently loyal to Kolomoysky, arrived in a military vehicle and built metal barricades around UkrNafta's headquarters in Kyiv. Kolomoysky had earlier appeared with a phalanx of guards at another state-owned oil company, UkrTransNafta, after the government tried to replace a manager loyal to him. At both companies, Kolomoysky ultimately backed down but soon after was removed as governor of Dnipropetrovsk.

The clash was the biggest in an unfolding confrontation between Poroshenko and segments of the oligarchy. Serhiy Leshchenko, formerly an investigative journalist and then a reformist member of Parliament, who eventually turned against President Poroshenko, referred to the Kolomoysky affair as the second phase of the revolution: "The Maidan removed former president, Yanukovych, but not

Ihor Kolomoysky, March 19, 2015. One of Ukraine's most controversial oligarchs, a bitter enemy of President Poroshenko, and a backer of President Zelensky, Kolomoysky came to be accused by Ukrainian officials of stealing billions of dollars from his bank's deposits. He would be arrested in September 2023. (Radio Free Europe/Radio Liberty)

the oligarchic system." For Leshchenko and civic activists this was the logical next step on the path to reform. But for Poroshenko such an attack threatened to ignite an all-out war with the oligarchs at a time when Ukraine could ill afford instability. Instead, Poroshenko chose the path of tactical alliances with some oligarchs while challenging others he regarded as the most dangerous. One such was Kolomoysky, whose dismissal as governor and a government challenge to his economic interests angered the oligarch and turned him against the president. Just six months later, his television channel, 1+1, launched a satirical TV program, *Servant of the People*, in which a fictional president fights corruption and an obdurate bureaucracy. The program would be the unofficial start of the political career of a comedian, Volodymyr Zelensky, who in 2019 would defeat Poroshenko for the presidency.

In the end, Poroshenko's balancing act of pressures on and incentives for the oligarchs failed. Intimations of nontransparent government-business understandings caused significant political and reputational damage to Poroshenko and his team. Over time, his frequent zigzags and temporary alliances, all designed to preserve his independence, alienated most of the powerful oligarchs and corporate stakeholders. Poroshenko's willingness to compromise with some to achieve gains against others also was never accepted by most of the civil society, investigative media, or Western policymakers, who pressed him, heedless of the resistance he faced and uninterested in his calculations about a second term in power. Still, it was clear that by the third year of his presidency, reform momentum had slowed dramatically.

Reform Momentum Slows

As reforms slowed, conflicts over turf deepened between the president and Prime Minister Yatsenyuk. In mid-2016 Poroshenko appointed former Georgian president Mikheil Saakashvili, his friend from university days, as governor of Odesa. The strategic Odesa region was dominated by the port city of the same name, and had a reputation for notoriously corrupt local government. Saakashvili replaced Ihor Palytsia, a political ally of oligarch Kolomoysky, now a sworn Poroshenko enemy. As president of Georgia, Saakashvili had won a reputation for successful market reforms, self-promotion, and authoritarian shortcuts to defeat corruption. Now in local office, he spent much of his time in self-promotion and little in actual implementation of reforms. His penchant for public staff dismissals, theatrical confrontations with local representatives of corrupt interests, and public browbeatings of ineffective bureaucrats smacked of populism but brought little concrete progress to Odesa. In short measure, with the encouragement of Poroshenko, Saakashvili turned on Prime Minister Yatsenyuk, blaming him for ineffective leadership of the reform effort and tarring the government with his own failures in Odesa. As attack dog, Saakashvili was efficient, and along with unrelenting pressure from Poroshenko and his allies, the campaign against the effective Yatsenyuk succeeded. In mid-April 2016 Yatsenyuk resigned following a February no-confidence vote in Parliament that came along with the defections from the governing coalition of Self-Reliance and the Fatherland Party.

With Yatsenyuk waylaid and the coalition weakened by defections, but with a majority intact, Poroshenko further alienated Western donors, reformers, and technocrats through a disingenuous, half-hearted effort to install reformer Natalie Jaresko as prime minister. The U.S.-born Jaresko had won plaudits as finance minister, and was supported by civic activists, investors, Western governments, and international financial institutions. But she was strongly opposed for the post by oligarchic groups, business lobbies, and professional party activists from the Poroshenko bloc, who felt they deserved the spoils of electoral success. After a vote for Jaresko failed in the absence of strong support from the president, Poroshenko asked his longtime mentee, Volodymyr Groysman, the parliamentary speaker and former mayor of Poroshenko's home base of Vinnytsia, to take the post of prime minister and form a government.

The president was basking in renewed confidence: "We will not have a president's team or the prime minister's team. . . . We will have one team to reform the country." To bolster the reform credentials of the new government, then under intense criticism after the growing exodus of reformers, Poroshenko reenlisted Balcerowicz and Ivan Miklos, the architects of Poland's and Slovakia's deep reforms, to advance the reform process in the new post-Yatsenyuk government.

Despite tensions between Poroshenko and Yatsenyuk, the bulk of them generated by the president, the government had accomplished a great deal. Indeed, the appointment of Groysman would not push the country toward a new phase of rapid reforms, and Groysman's tenure in power quickly saw the return of tensions between prime minister and president. The last two years of the Poroshenko presidency saw glacial reforms that occurred less as part of Ukrainian initiatives and more as a consequence of intense Western pressure. These included unpopular but necessary gas price increases and the establishment of an independent Anti-Corruption Court, both of which came as a condition for the release of desperately needed IMF financing.

The decision to topple Yatsenyuk and replace him with Groysman came at a high political price. First, it angered many that Poroshenko was not content to limit himself to his presidential powers but aspired to dominate government decision-making. Second, it signaled to the population that the president was now fully responsible for all dimensions of Ukrainian life, including the slowly recovering economy.

Additional dissension was brewing. In November 2016 Odesa governor Saakashvili tendered his resignation, accompanied by a jeremiad against the current political leadership and government, which he charged with grand corruption. From that moment forward, Saakashvili went on the political offensive against his college classmate Poroshenko. The winter of 2016–17 was replete with a national "anti-corruption" tour and protests against Poroshenko's rule. These Saakashvili-led rallies usually attracted only a few thousand protestors, some of whom pitched a tent city outside the Ukrainian Parliament. Oligarch media, intent on weakening Poroshenko, gave the protests wider publicity. Over time, the protest movement sputtered. In July 2017 Saakashvili would be stripped of his rapidly acquired Ukrainian citizenship on the basis of irregularities in his application. He was the subject of a manhunt and, after two ineffectual attempts, was successfully expelled from the country for a while.

Russia's War

Throughout Poroshenko's tenure his central concern was Russia's war against Ukraine. From 2014 to 2019, it would cumulatively claim some thirteen thousand lives. The war was economically devastating and hugely disruptive, resulting in over 2 million people displaced. But it also had a significant effect on deepening Ukrainian national consciousness and shaping national identity and cohesion. Patriotic sentiment—heretofore weaker in Eastern and Southern Ukraine—was solidifying amid Moscow's aggression and diminishing the impact of Russian soft power. The net result was the public's growing aspiration to integrate into the economic and security structures of the West. In addition to precipitating a shift in views of Putin and Russia among Ukrainians in the east and south, Putin's annexation of Crimea and de facto occupation of the eastern Donbas removed several million Russian speakers from participation in Ukrainian political life, further Ukrainianizing the national discourse.

On November 25, 2018, after months of low-intensity warfare in Eastern Ukraine, which was now claiming scores of lives per month, a new military crisis arose. The Russian Coast Guard attacked and seized three Ukrainian vessels in the Kerch Strait. A day later, President Poroshenko introduced martial law for thirty days in ten regions. Poroshenko's instinct had been to declare a more extensive and lengthier martial law, but he met firm resistance and criticism in Parliament, within the media, and from civil society. Critics felt the level of crisis did not warrant this drastic step and feared Poroshenko was seeking an advantageous political environment prior to elections in March–April 2019.

While Putin propagated the idea that Ukrainians and Russians were one nation, not only were Ukrainians increasingly begging to differ, they were drifting ever further away from Russia's cultural and political influence. Use of the Ukrainian language was increasing, and identification of Ukrainian as the mother tongue was also on the rise in the period 2014–19. The proportion of inhabitants of Ukraine who self-described themselves as ethnic Ukrainians was climbing. Most citizens indicated strong support for Ukraine's statehood, sovereignty, and territorial integrity. Pride in the country, too, was on the rise, even as statistics showed a general distrust of the ruling elite. At the same time, confidence in Ukraine's military was climbing.

A poll taken in August 2019 on the anniversary of Ukraine's declaration of independence found that 89.5 percent of Ukrainians would vote for Ukraine's independence were a referendum held today. Such results led many analysts to conclude that Russia's territorial expansion was the crucial factor in the consolidation of Ukraine's national identity. More accurately, it was an additional catalyst for a process that had been taking shape since independence.

Despite the war and rising Ukrainian patriotism, the public temperament remained tolerant. For a country at war, jingoism and hatred of the aggressor remained fringe phenomena. Nor did the war result in the rise of militarism or the growth of authoritarian political values, as the healthy political and public reaction to Poroshenko's invocation of a state of emergency had shown. Ukrainians remained even-keeled and were open to eventual reconciliation and cooperation with Russia, though on the basis of respect for their sovereignty. While a number of former volunteer fighters and military officers entered Parliament and government service, their proportional representation was no more than a handful. Nor were there signs of a surge in support for far-right parties, which had virtually no presence in the Rada.

Perhaps the most important contribution that Poroshenko made, albeit with deep caution and occasional reluctance, was the shaping of a more focused Ukrainian national identity. Initially, Poroshenko resisted suggestions to introduce legislation protecting and promoting the Ukrainian language. As had been the case with his reluctance to implement de-Communization laws, Poroshenko worried that language legislation could exacerbate the internal rift between the pro-European Western and Central regions and the traditionally Russia-friendly attitudes that had prevailed in the east and south.

However, many of his political partners and advisors understood that society had moved on, and a national consensus on Ukrainian identity had developed around both the importance of a national language and a total rejection of the Communist and imperial past. As the brilliant Ukrainophone novelist, poet, and Maidan activist Serhiy Zhadan, a native of the eastern city of Kharkiv, told me during a conversation in New York City in mid-April 2016, "People may not yet be speaking Ukrainian [in Kharkiv], and the older generations never will. But they now see Ukrainian as something progressive . . . a sign of modernity. Their children, who are learning Ukrainian in schools, will speak it." In his view, the country had turned the corner on language and the momentum needed to be maintained.

Ukrainization: Limiting Russian Influence

In his last two years in office, Poroshenko came to better understand the necessity for determined steps to block Russian soft-power penetration of and disinformation in Ukraine. In 2017 the Rada introduced laws that effectively banned many popular Russian social media and internet platforms from access to Ukrainians without VPNs (virtual private networks). This was done because of heavy Russian state penetration of such social media platforms as Odnoklassniki and Vkontakte as well as the search engine Yandex. But policymakers also worried that Russia was gathering metadata on Ukrainians and using bots and trolls in a major effort to spread disinformation in order to demoralize the populace. Russian television and most Russian-produced television and film content were also banned. All this was intended to remove Russian propaganda as well as disinformation masquerading as news. The ban reduced the heroization of the Soviet era and the glorification of the antecedents of the very military and security services that were waging war against the Ukrainian population.

At times Ukraine's control over Russian content was severe. For example, the Russian liberal democratic channel Dozhd (TV Rain), itself under Russian state pressure, was removed from Ukraine's airwaves and cable TV for having shown maps of occupied Crimea as part of Russia, something that as a Russia-registered entity Dozhd was required to do by law.

Legislation was also passed to accelerate the de-Communization of society through the removal of Soviet murals and statues and the renaming of regions, cities, towns, public squares, boulevards, streets, and institutions that bore the names of Soviet-era personages. In many localities, a similar process occurred with Russian imperial personages, a process that would gain pace in 2022.

An important contribution to the Ukrainization of institutions was made in the president's diplomatic efforts to secure the canonicity of Ukraine's independent Orthodox Church. The establishment of a distinctly Ukrainian Orthodox church had been the fruit of the early years of state independence, but the indigenous church had made few inroads in recruiting the faithful from Ukraine's Moscow-affiliated Orthodox Church, many of whose clergy were sympathetic to an increasingly hostile Russia. Poroshenko and his aide Rostyslav Pavlenko played a major role in this effort on October 11, 2018, by helping to secure the recognition of the Orthodox Church of Ukraine by the ecumenical patriarch of Constantinople, the Greek Orthodox Church, and the patriarch of Alexandria. This meant the Ukrainian national church could now compete on a canonically legitimate basis for the loyalty of the faithful.

During the Poroshenko years the population of Southern and Eastern Ukraine began to show a higher degree of identification with Kyiv and the Ukrainian state. While this trend had accelerated due to Russian aggression, it was also advanced by the state's Ukrainization and de-Communization policies. Another factor in the east's shift was economic. Russia historically had sought to corrupt and to win over Ukraine's powerful business elite, seeing in it a potential ally inside Ukrainian society. But the occupation of Crimea and the invasion and occupation of the Donbas attacked these oligarchs' business interests and drove them further toward identification with the Ukrainian state.

One telling example was the shifting worldview of Ukraine's richest man—Rinat Akhmetov. In the first months of the Donbas conflict, Akhmetov had been ambivalent, balancing his loyalty to a unitary Ukraine with what he understood to be local discontent within the Donbas population. Some experts believed that as an associate of the disgraced Yanukovych, Akhmetov was in a vulnerable position after the Maidan and might well have seen the conflict as an opportunity to strengthen his hand by emerging as power broker/arbiter with the recalcitrant Donbas. Whatever his motives, Akhmetov clearly had adopted a wait-and-see neutrality in the local upheaval.

Very soon it became clear to Akhmetov that beyond a small group of marginal separatist activists, far more powerful forces were at work in his bailiwick. The small insurgent movement against Kyiv was not only being augmented by resources and fighters from Russia, it also was becoming a force controlled, directed, financed, and animated by the Kremlin.

Far from becoming a broker, Akhmetov was being marginalized by Putin's ploy to dismember Ukraine. Once he understood the threat, Akhmetov acted with purpose and effectiveness to secure Ukraine's control over parts of the Donbas. With the city of Donetsk in Russian hands, Akhmetov used his resources and employees to defend the port city of Mariupol, the second largest in the Donetsk oblast and, effectively, an Akhmetov company town. Fighters from the far-right Azov battalion made a bold move to take back Mariupol from local Russian-backed fighters in May 2014. By June 14 they had prevailed. Azov had the strength to retake but not hold the city of nearly half a million. Someone had to win the hearts and minds of the people and offer stability and security. As Interior Minister Arsen Avakov, under whose aegis Azov operated, told me months after the event (in an interview in Kyiv on March 25, 2016), here Akhmetov stepped in. In Avakov's telling, Akhmetov stabilized Mariupol by directing his employees and the security personnel from his large workplaces to secure the city by serving in the city's formal and informal security structures as an armed presence loyal to Kyiv. Akhmetov's employees were mainly well-respected locals, not outside fighters with wacky and dangerous ideas. Their intervention ensured that the recapture of Mariupol would stick. Akhmetov's local and national media helped reinforce the liberation of the city with firmly patriotic messaging.

This intervention made Akhmetov an enemy of the Kremlin, and payback would soon come. On March 20, 2016, a group of radical activists shut down railway traffic between Ukraine and the occupied Donbas. In retaliation, the Luhansk (LNR) and Donetsk (DNR) People's Republics nationalized scores of Ukrainian companies. Foremost among these were the assets of Akhmetov, making his political allies, and his powerful mass media, more determined enemies of the Kremlin and its proxies.

Not only Akhmetov had moved from the belief that an independent Ukraine could find a modus vivendi with Russia—so too had many Ukrainians from Eastern and Southern Ukraine. A comprehensive poll in 2014 by the respected in *Zerkalo Nedeli* showed high levels of alienation from Russia and the absence of support for secession from Ukraine in its eastern and southern Russian-speaking populations.

As elections neared, Poroshenko at last backed the major language reform he had been reluctant to implement. The law passed on April 25, 2019, just days after Poroshenko's defeat in a bid for reelection. It required all newspapers, magazines, and websites other than those publishing in Crimean Tatar and the languages of the European Union to provide a Ukrainian equivalent of their content. Equally far-reaching were the requirements for cinema. Only 10 percent of films would now be allowed to be screened without being dubbed into Ukrainian in each cinema. A broadcast law adopted earlier had introduced similar strictures for television. In education too, legislation protected teaching in the languages of the EU and in Crimean Tatar in specialized settings, but Russian would now be taught in preschool or in primary education only if requested by parents.

While government measures to strengthen Ukrainian language media, Ukrainian culture, and Ukrainian arts contributed to greater national unity, they and Russia's aggression also sparked a flowering of the arts. Much of the creative dynamism was fed by a sense of national purpose that was a response to Russia's challenge to Ukraine as a nation and a state. A range of artists confronted the war in the Donbas. Others engaged Ukraine's rich, complex, and painful history of foreign occupation. Still others, inspired by the Maidan protests, focused on social issues such as crime, corruption, and poverty.

A Cultural Revival

Notable writers who attracted significant reader interest included Yuriy Andrukhovych, whose *Lovers of Justice*, a fragmentary novel that offers a series of nine vignettes, presenting portraits of assassins and criminals resonant in Ukrainian history. His daughter Sofia Andrukhovych's novel *Felix Austria*, published in 2014, takes place in 1900 in Stanyslaviv (now Ivano Frankivsk), then part of the Austro-Hungarian Empire, and tells the story of a Ukrainian maid in the employ of a family of an Austrian physician. The year 2016 also saw the publication of Oksana Zabuzhko's *And Again I Climb into a Tank*, a collection of essays and journalism focused on Russian's war of aggression and its imperialism. Serhiy Zhadan, a poet, novelist, and rock musician from the Eastern city of Kharkiv and an important voice in the Maidan protests, published his collection of stories and verse, *Mesopotamia*, as well as *Internat* (The Orphanage), a powerful novel that evokes the squalor and destruction of wartime Donbas and tells the story of a schoolteacher crossing enemy lines to rescue a relative from an orphanage on the Russian-controlled side.

Dozens of small publishing houses proliferated, producing vast numbers of books in Ukrainian translation and original works by Ukrainian authors. Kyiv's Art Arsenal attracted tens of thousands of bibliophiles, hundreds of authors, and over 150 publishers each year to a week of well-attended panel discussions, author interviews, and displays of the latest books. A large book fair in Lviv and Meridian Czernowitz in Chernivtsi testified to the dynamism of Ukraine's literary reawakening.

Major films produced in this period included the powerful *The Tribe* by Myroslav Slaboshpytsky, a chronicle of the life of impoverished teens from a school for the deaf, some of whom fall into a gang involved in theft and prostitution. The quirky *Ukrainian Sheriffs*, directed by Roman Bodnachyuk, depicts daily life in a village near the Crimean Peninsula, annexed by Russia in 2014, interweaving geopolitics and local life and exploring the complex cultural interaction of Russian-speaking and Ukrainian-speaking Ukraine. A distinctly neorealist, stripped-down aesthetic—the product of low budgets but also of the social and political issues arising from the country's development and from Russia's aggression—became a feature of Ukrainian film.

Laws requiring the dubbing and subtitling of Russian and foreign films ensured that Ukrainian was now omnipresent in films and TV programs, contributing to the growing re-Ukrainization of society. Ukrainian musicians in genres ranging from hip-hop to post-punk also witnessed a huge shift to Ukrainian, as Ukrainian-language quotas became obligatory over the airwaves. In these years, Ukrainian music's greatest international impact was generated by the victory of the Crimean Tatar Ukrainian singer Jamala, whose song about the deportation of the Crimean Tatars from Crimea, "1944," won the Eurovision song contest in 2016. The song is a powerful multicultural evocation of the suffering of Ukraine's largest Muslim minority group.

The period saw the cresting of the popularity of Okean Elzy, a lyrical and anthemic rock band fronted by Svyatoslav Vakarchuk. As President Poroshenko prepared for a second run for office, Vakarchuk was touted as a potential rival. In the end, despite strong poll numbers he chose not to run, a decision, he told me, dictated by his fear of splitting the patriotic vote with Poroshenko and allowing a pro-Russian candidate into the second round. Though Vakarchuk eventually helped build a small but important liberal patriotic political party, appropriately called Holos (the Voice), his decision not to run was fateful: it inspired another entertainer, comedian Volodymyr Zelensky, to throw his hat in the ring.

The Poroshenko Balance Sheet

On balance, the Poroshenko years saw tangible accomplishments in the cultural, economic, and security spheres, although some of these were extracted through civic action and Western pressure. He and his coalition stabilized the state; rebuilt the army; skillfully worked diplomacy to maintain strong Euro-Atlantic sanctions against Russia; strengthened international support for Ukraine; enhanced Ukrainian culture, language, and identity; reoriented trade away from Russia toward Europe and Asia; and created a basis for economic growth.

Ukraine's export economy also was radically transformed under Poroshenko, with fully 36 percent of exports flowing to the European Union. Trade with Russia drastically fell, dropping to a little over 10 percent of all trade turnover, down from one-third a decade before. By 2019 Poland had replaced Russia as the single country with the most trade with Ukraine. Significantly, in the last three years of Poroshenko's presidency, Ukraine completely ceased to import Russian gas.

At the end his of term, Western leaders declared Ukraine had implemented more reforms under Poroshenko than in its previous twenty-four years. Despite this record, Poroshenko was deeply unpopular with most Ukrainians, although he retained the loyalty of a cohort of deeply committed followers numbering in the millions. Despite Poroshenko's effective efforts to defend Ukraine against aggression and despite significant reform progress, the public came to perceive the president as a wheeler-dealer surrounded by disreputable cronies who was resistant to reform. A contributing factor to his unpopularity was the economic effect of Russia's war and occupation of Crimea and the Donbas, which kept Ukraine in the ranks of Europe's poorest states.

As elections approached, Poroshenko believed Ukrainians would embrace his wartime focus on patriotism, Ukrainization, religious faith, and a renewed military. But this emphasis was not enough to overcome the effects of conflicts with his allies, unhappiness with a dysfunctional justice system, continuing corruption, and the alienation of civil society, especially the activists of the Maidan. Oligarch-run media, whose owners perennially sought to erode the authority of the state to enhance their own influence, attacked Poroshenko and amplified the criticisms of civic activists and anti-corruption investigators. Coupled with the growing power of anti-corruption activists, activist websites, and social media, the echo chamber of negative reporting became the dominant trope, overwhelming Poroshenko's own messaging. By the third year of his presidency, the effect of these trends was profound. His poll ratings had fallen into negative territory and would spiral further downward as elections neared.

Despite ushering in reforms and pushing inexorably for his country's entry into a united Europe, Poroshenko, the billionaire businessman turned political leader, was, like his predecessors, shaped by the early post-Soviet years, when politics was transactional. Although his accomplishments were more impressive than his predecessors' he did not—possibly could not—overcome the post-Soviet-era culture that had shaped him.

For civil society, whose young activists had lived in a world in which Communism had disappeared and who had been radicalized in the Orange Revolution and Maidan protests, Poroshenko was part of a different generation and world. The rising influence of civil society had been spurred by civic protests. But its influence grew even more as a consequence of the mass volunteer movement that emerged in the form of fighters who rallied to the defense of their country. Their heroism temporarily compensated for Ukraine's hollowed-out military in 2014 and stemmed the tide of Russia's aggression until a regular professional military force could be reconstituted. Together with the influence of oligarchs and the rising new rich from the technology, services, and agriculture sectors, these forces underscored that Ukraine was fast becoming a heterarchy: a society in which the influence of nongovernmental, big-business, and state forces ebbed and flowed, a tableau that at times looked chaotic but was a source of Ukraine's democracy and pluralism.

Just weeks before the 2019 presidential election, a scandal rocked the Poroshenko administration, sounding the death knell for his reelection. Bigus.info, a Western-supported investigative news project, revealed that the son of Poroshenko's close associate Ihor Hladkovsky was price gouging and engaging in corrupt practices in the clandestine procurement of Russian spare parts for the refurbishment of weapons for the war in the east. The scale of the alleged corruption—tens of thousands of dollars—was small. But because the revelation involved the war effort and was linked to Hladkovsky senior, the head of Ukraine's state arms-manufacturing conglomerate, it reinforced the view that the president and his inner circle were war profiteers.

In the end, despite major reform accomplishments, a stronger military, and an economy growing at over 4 percent per year, Poroshenko lost to an outsider—a political neophyte with no links to the existing political establishment. Notwithstanding his defeat and the low regard in which he was held by the vast majority of the country, Poroshenko left office with a strong and loyal following, representing a quarter of the country. He also left a legacy that would serve Ukraine well in the coming years: decentralized rule, significant erosion of corrupt financial schemes, a strong military and military industrial complex, and significant strides in reinforcing the country's Ukrainian national identity. Poroshenko's was the most reformist tenure in office of any president in modern Ukraine's history. It is likely to be judged so from the vantage point of future generations.

CHAPTER SIX

Volodymyr Zelensky

The Unlikely President

IN 2019, AS THE third decade of independence approached, Ukrainians were discontented. Despite years of strong budgetary discipline, three years of decent economic growth, the introduction of reforms that resulted in a reduction in corruption, and the stymying of Russia's advance in Eastern Ukraine, most Ukrainians remained unhappy, disheartened by widespread poverty and economic inequity. It was tempting for them to see their country as a failing state in the thrall of kleptocratic oligarchs, a cohort that many came to believe included their president, Petro Poroshenko.

In this difficult political environment, Poroshenko chose to fight his 2019 reelection campaign as a war president and the conservative standard-bearer of patriotic values. This strategy proved risky as Russia's war on Ukraine had shifted from a deadly kinetic conflict to one with a small number of victims. Far from the front lines, there was little reminder of war, apart from daily reports dutifully but sparingly recorded in the news media about a soldier or two shot by a sniper or felled by a land mine or mortar salvo. In Kyiv, Odesa, Dnipro, and other major cities, cafés were buzzing, restaurants were filled to the rafters, and discotheques were crowded with nighttime revelers. With the military draft replaced by volunteer service, the only reminder of war was the occasional sight of a soldier on home leave or an amputee on the streets.

Ukrainians were fatigued by the war in the Donbas and in increasing numbers were ready to repair relations with Russia. Some of those who resented or feared Russia also believed a new president, unencumbered by animosity to Putin, could find a pathway to peace. In this setting, President Poroshenko doubled down on a campaign that focused on his foreign policy acumen and hard line against the Kremlin. "Faith, Language, and the Army," became his slogan and central campaign message.

The Search for a "Fresh Face"

This gap between public sentiments and Poroshenko's message created a political market for an alternative. Polls throughout 2017 and 2018 revealed a public looking for a fresh face to lead the country: someone honest, self-sufficient, and unburdened by ties to the despised elites. Two prominent celebrities fit the bill. One was Svyatoslav Vakarchuk, a brainy Ukrainophone rock idol with a doctorate in theoretical physics and fellowships at Yale and Stanford. The other was a Russophone comedian, Volodymyr Zelensky, who specialized in broad political satire, pratfalls, and making impudent and irreverent fun of the country's leaders—a Ukrainian version of Benny Hill.

Vakarchuk spoke about politics in a theoretical and conceptual fashion. While his anthemic, inspirational ballads made an instant connection with Ukrainians, when it came to politics, he lacked the common touch. As important, he vacillated on the question of running for office. Amid the indecision, his ratings quickly plummeted and he unequivocally opted out of the presidential campaign on January 28, 2019, less than two months before the vote.

Vakarchuk's decision cleared the way for the other outsider, Volodymyr Zelensky, and gave him a significant boost. Like Vakarchuk, Zelensky was a well-known celebrity who had built a vast national audience. Zelensky's TV production company had been co-owned with multimillionaire Valery Khoroshkovsky, former first deputy prime minister, and was broadcast on Inter, a popular channel supportive of President Yanukovych. Zelensky's parodies and satires were lacerating—one cartoon series mercilessly lampooning Yanukovych was pulled from the channel. Zelensky eventually ended his relationship with Inter and switched to 1+1, the television company owned by another oligarch, Ihor Kolomoysky, who replaced Khoroshkovsky as co-owner of Zelensky's company.

In 2016 Petro Poroshenko and the Ukrainian state had nationalized PrivatBank after an audit found billions in allegedly dodgy lending to shell companies related to Kolomoysky and partner Gennadiy Bogolyubov. An assessment for the National Bank of Ukraine by Kroll, Inc., alleged that Privat had been subjected to "a large-scale and coordinated fraud over at least a ten-year period . . . which resulted in the Bank suffering a loss of at least USD 5.5 billion." Fully 95 percent of the lending had been made to "parties related to [former] shareholders and their affiliates."

Kolomoysky had long burnished a reputation as a bad boy known for hardball tactics. Kolomoysky's political acumen was in evidence within weeks of his dismissal as governor of Dnipro. Poroshenko had won the first round of his battle with the oligarch, but he had awakened the ire not only of Kolomoysky but of Ukraine's most highly rated TV channel.

Kolomoysky's media soon went on the attack against the government and president. Most important, business partner Zelensky began planning a comedy series that would attack the political establishment and, indirectly, the incumbent president. In the new series Zelensky played the role of Vasyl Holoborodko, a regular-guy high-school history teacher who is accidentally elected president following a viral video of his rant about how everything is wrong in Ukraine. The program, *Servant of the People*, struck a nerve and became the name and basis of a political party that launched in early 2019 and became the base for political neophyte Zelensky's presidential campaign.

At his birthday party in 2017, Kolomoysky was already trotting out Zelensky and presenting him to Ukraine's assembled rich and powerful as "our president." Zelensky did not make it to Kolomoysky's birthday celebration in Tel Aviv on February 13, 2019, but according to one attendee, the tables were festooned with signs that declared "Zelensky+1," signaling the partnership between oligarch and entertainer turned politician.

Zelensky Emerges

Zelensky's electoral campaign was the world's first successful presidential run that was entirely virtual. Not only did the new politician trade on the image of a complete outsider, he also avoided face-to-face campaigning, made no speeches, held no rallies, eschewed travel across the country, gave no press conferences, avoided in-depth interviews with independent journalists, and until the last day of campaigning, did not debate. His main instruments were social media and his omnipresence on Ukraine's most popular TV channel. The channel filled hours of weekly programming with his variety shows, comedy talent contests, and above all with reruns and new episodes of *Servant of the People*.

When Zelensky announced his candidacy in a New Year's 2019 video greeting on oligarch Kolomoysky's TV channel 1+1, preempting Poroshenko's address, many assumed he would run a typical celebrity campaign—full of public appearances and stump speeches. He didn't. Unlike Donald Trump, who staged regular rallies and appeared in town halls and in televised debates, Zelensky avoided human contact with his electorate. He addressed voters through short YouTube and Instagram posts and appearances on TV. (One online video garnered 14 million views.) Instead of preparing for the presidency by holding substantive public meetings, he occasionally traveled with his comedy troupe and performed in variety shows.

After winning first place in round one of the election with 30 percent and triggering a runoff—Zelensky played table tennis at his campaign headquarters with a reporter, made a vague one-minute statement laced with platitudes, and allowed just three minutes for questions. As the campaign continued, there was a fifteen-minute interview for his TV base, 1+1, and a softball interview with him and his wife at home. That was it. This was all the detailed press scrutiny he faced. Meanwhile, Kolomoysky's 1+1 news programs aired reports claiming Poroshenko had murdered his brother, a canard that had originated in Russian disinformation.

Zelensky's virtual campaign allowed him to run for office on general themes and vague promises. His political messaging focused on discontent with the way things were—and lambasting Ukraine's business and political elites for making them that way. Those searching for serious policy positions did so in vain. Zelensky's online platform contained only a few anodyne sentences each on key issues of security, the economy, health care, education, and fighting corruption. Instead, he solicited advice from voters on a campaign website, calling on the public to help him devise his platform virtually. Moreover, scarily, he preached plebiscitary, direct democracy. Throughout the presidential campaign, short video blogs showed Zelensky interacting with a range of informal advisors, usually well-regarded reformers or NGO leaders who explained to the public what they *thought* the candidate believed. But his real inner circle was mainly made up of longtime colleagues from show business, members of his comedy troupe, and corporate lawyers linked to his company and his main backer Kolomoysky.

Typically when outsider celebrities, sports heroes, or entertainers run for office, they try to allay fears about their inexperience by showing a command of the issues. Zelensky did the exact opposite, instead embracing his inexperience, suggesting this meant he was open to fundamentally new approaches to reforming the country and brokering a peace deal with Russia.

As one of Ukraine's preeminent intellectuals, the writer Oksana Zabuzhko, observed, in many ways Zelensky's campaign eerily resembled an episode from the Netflix series *Black Mirror* titled "The Waldo Moment"—in which an animated blue bear satirizes and degrades politicians competing in a British by-election, and eventually joins them in the quest for office, campaigning semi-virtually from a video display on a truck that interacts with voters on the hustings.

The big difference is that in the fictional story, the bear came in second. In the real world, Zelensky won. Voters rejected an experienced incumbent—President Petro Poroshenko, who had rebuilt Ukraine's military and competently marshaled international aid—and took a chance on a political novice.

Ironically, Zelensky's vague and laconic platform allowed him to appeal to both the Ukrainian-speaking west and center and the Russophone east and south, to both rural and urban voters, to both rich and poor. His billboards boldly predicted, "The Epoch of Poverty Is Over" and pledged that corrupt officials would be in jail by the coming spring. This promise of economic improvements was targeted at Ukrainian workers and the poor, and it was reinforced by

Zelensky's garrulous, combative speaking style, which—despite his high income and legal degree—was a carryover of his beginnings in a working-class district of Kryvyy Rih, home to Ukraine's largest steel mill.

The Zelensky Landslide

On April 21, 2019, Zelensky was elected president in a landslide (73 percent to 25 percent for Petro Poroshenko). He assumed office on May 20 as one of the least prepared individuals to head a democracy in world history.

Ukrainians, one of Europe's poorest peoples, could not be faulted for falling for the blandishments of someone who seemed a populist candidate, albeit one who was more charmer than demagogue. Nor could one fault Ukrainians for succumbing to the appeal of a new face promising peace, prosperity, the eradication of corruption, and unsparing justice.

Zelensky won with a vast majority, but he lacked support in three active and significant segments of Ukrainian society: the patriotic protestors who had fueled the Maidan protests of 2014, the volunteers who had fought in the Donbas, and the critical intelligentsia who animated civil society. The latter in particular regarded Zelensky as a rank amateur, unschooled in public policy and woefully unqualified to implement reforms. As one of Ukraine's most prominent liberal journalists told me: "His election is a profanity."

Zelensky's assumption of power was full of potential peril. The entire architecture of Europe's defense and security rested on a stable Ukraine. An unsteady and inexperienced leader at the helm in Ukraine had the potential to tempt Russia to escalate military actions to restore Ukraine to its sphere of influence, to establish outright control, or to induce a novice leader to make concessions that would erode sovereignty and provoke internal cleavages. A weak Ukraine would give new impetus to Russia's imperial ambitions and enhance the Kremlin's capacity to project power regionally, including through the disruption of U.S. and European politics.

Despite Zelensky's inexperience, there were two upsides to his election. First, as a novice politician, especially one willing to shed some of his oligarch patrons, his leadership opened the possibility for fundamental reforms that could accelerate Ukraine's transition. As a leader from outside the existing political system, Zelensky might be able to assemble a capable team of reformers unconnected to the ruling elite. Second, as an entertainer, Zelensky knew how to read and connect with his audience, allowing for more durable support for his agenda.

Zelensky chose Andriy Bohdan to head his office. Because he was a lawyer with a close working relationship with the oligarch Kolomoysky, Bohdan's appointment was met with suspicion. Surprisingly, the abrasive Bohdan successfully pressed for the appointment of well-regarded reformers to top government posts. Bohdan had experience in government service, having worked in the Yanukovych administration, and he had even dabbled in electoral politics. Most others who staffed the President's Office were without political and government experience. These included entertainment lawyer and film producer Andriy Yermak, who became the first deputy in the new executive team, and Serhiy Shefir, co-founder of Zelensky's entertainment company, who became the president's chief assistant.

A Stunning Parliamentary Victory

To capitalize on President Zelensky's popularity, his team quickly set about building a political party, Servant of the People, and prepared for a snap election. In a fashion characteristic of Ukraine's politically attuned top judges, Zelensky secured a Constitutional Court decision that the president was within his powers to call for a new vote. The court agreed with the president's assertion that there was no longer a majority coalition in the Parliament. Public optimism surrounding Zelensky carried over into the legislative election. In the national proportional vote, by which 225 seats are allocated, Servant of the People received 43 percent; the Opposition Bloc, a Russophone and Russia-friendly party, captured 13 percent; the party of defeated Poroshenko, European Solidarity, suffered a severe setback, winning just 8.1 percent (down from 22 percent); Tymoshenko's Fatherland won 8.2 percent; and Holos (Voice), a liberal patriotic party, received 5.2 percent. No other party passed the 5 percent threshold.

The Servant Party did even better in the case of legislators in their local districts in a first-past-the-post vote. Here Zelensky's forces captured 130 of the 199 seats (26 seats in Crimea and parts of the Donbas remained unfilled due to their occupation by Russian forces). As a result, Servant of the People entered Parliament with 254 out of 424 seats. The Opposition Platform had 43 seats, Fatherland 26, European Solidarity 25, Holos 20, and the Opposition Bloc took 6. United Center, the right-wing Svoboda, and Self-Reliance each captured 1 seat each, while 46 seats were won by candidates generally representing business interests who ran without party affiliation.

By design, no Servant deputies had heretofore served as national legislators or held government office. Most had never taken part in electoral politics, even at the local level. In a populist pledge to the people, Zelensky had promised to populate the Parliament exclusively with new faces, arguing that all established politicians were corrupt.

Political Boot Camp

In the first week of August 2019, around two hundred Servant deputies attended a week-long policy boot camp at the Truskavets spa in the Carpathian Mountains in Western Ukraine organized by Tymofiy Mylovanov, president of the Kyiv School of Economics (a longtime friend of mine who would soon be named economy minister). For many it was their first encounter with systematic policy discussions. In attendance were comedians from Zelensky's TV empire, champion athletes, restaurateurs, small-business owners, a wedding photographer, and a slew of journalists, mainly from oligarch Kolomoysky's 1+1 channel. Scattered among the new legislators was a handful of NGO activists and policy analysts. The most politically savvy and experienced new Rada legislators had served as campaign consultants, lawyers, or staff to former parliamentarians. But the new faction's cumulative level of policy expertise was appallingly low. The policy school in Truskavets was a four-day crash course in economics, legal reform, corruption, and foreign and security policy.

At one session, Nikita Poturayev, a political consultant and newly elected legislator, told the deputies, "You are nobodies." He reminded them they—and he—were there solely because of Zelensky's popularity. Voters, he said, "cared nothing about what name was on the list." Poturayev made clear that the president was after a parliamentary majority wholly dependent on him, one that would rubber-stamp policies generated by his inner circle—an inner circle equally unprepared to map out a clear path for Ukraine.

In time it became clear that some Servant legislators had hidden their relationships with financial interests, while others were soon co-opted by these interests. Moreover, neophyte deputies represented a range of attitudes to the market, the war in Eastern Ukraine, and Ukraine's European path. This heterogeneity would soon generate problems of political cohesion.

The root problem for Zelensky, his party, and eventually even his government was the absence of shared political values. While Zelensky himself had no coherent political worldview, his new legislators represented disparate sets of ideas. Some were socialists, some social liberals, others libertarians. Some were patriotic and nationalist; some saw Ukraine as a multiethnic, bilingually Ukrainian-Russian state. Ruslan Stefanchuk, the party's chief ideologist, pushed the party in the direction of libertarian approaches, but soon the party jettisoned liberalism, saying its ideology represented "elements of libertarianism and social democracy."

Initially, the new political formation displayed discipline. On August 29, 2019, Parliament elected as speaker Dmytro Razumkov, a thirty-five-year-old campaign manager and economist by training, who had advised Zelensky during the presidential race. The young Razumkov came from an illustrious Ukrainian family. His father had been a key advisor to former president Leonid Kuchma. His mother, Natalia Kudrya, was a famous Ukrainian actress, while his stepmother, Yulia Mostova, was the editor of Ukraine's most respected political newsweekly, the *Mirror of the Week*. Razumkov *fils* had briefly been associated with the Party of Regions. That association and his insistence on speaking Russian rather than Ukrainian throughout Zelensky's campaign raised alarm bells among patriotic forces. However, upon assuming office, Razumkov strictly adhered to the use of the Ukrainian (state) language and articulated and pursued policies that supported Ukraine's sovereignty and territorial independence.

On August 29 the Rada voted in a new government headed by Oleksiy Honcharuk with a tally of 283 votes "for" out of 395 deputies in attendance. Of those votes, 238 came from Zelensky's party. A parliamentary group, For the Future, composed of independents, added 22 votes to the tally. The new group was headed by Ihor Palytsia, a longtime business associate of Ihor Kolomoysky. Unaffiliated, nonpartisan deputies cast 21 votes for the new team.

Zelensky named his childhood friend Ivan Bakanov to head the security service of Ukraine. Like other crucial appointees, Bakanov was a lawyer who worked for Zelensky's entertainment company, LLC Kvartal 95 Studio. He had no previous experience in national security or intelligence gathering. NGOs soon criticized him for dragging his feet on reforming the security service and decoupling it from Section K, a notoriously corrupt division that dealt with economic crimes. Over time Bakanov's lack of experience opened the door to major Russian infiltration of the Ukrainian security service.

A New Government

Zelensky's selection of his economic advisor, Oleksiy Honcharuk, as prime minister was something of a surprise. Thirty-five when he took office, Honcharuk had never held a government post. His government experience was as an outside advisor to several ministers in the Groysman government. His sole executive experience consisted of running BRDO, a small, nongovernmental policy group with a staff of several dozen who advised the government on business deregulation and assisted businesses in their interactions with government. Several BRDO staff had been elected to the Parliament on the Servant ticket.

Despite Honcharuk's parlous résumé, the new government met with approval from the international community and reform advocates as it was populated with well-regarded reformers. The post of deputy prime minister for European integration went to longtime Foreign Ministry operative Dmytro Kuleba, a hawk on Russia who had served as Ukraine's representative to the Council of Europe. Vadym Prystaiko, the new foreign minister, was a seasoned diplomat who had served as first deputy foreign minister, ambassador to Canada, and Zelensky's top foreign policy advisor.

Tymofiy Mylovanov, who had headed up Servant's week of policy training, was named minister of the economy, agriculture, and trade, a new hydra-headed ministry created as part of Zelensky's commitment to streamlining government. A University of Pittsburgh professor who headed the Kyiv Economic School, a small university, Mylovanov had a strong grounding in macroeconomics, clear ideas on reform priorities, and a large network of policy experts from Ukraine and the West. Mylovanov assembled a team of competent professionals to serve as deputy ministers and rapidly developed a list of clear policy objectives and draft reform legislation. Finance Minister Oksana Markarova, a well-regarded technocrat, was retained from the previous government in a sign to the public, international financial institutions, and investors that fiscal discipline would remain a central aim of the government.

Andriy Zahorodnyuk, the young entrepreneur who took over the Defense Ministry, had built an international business that manufactured rigs for the oil and gas industry. He had also served as an unpaid advisor to the Defense Ministry on reforms and procurement. Zahorodnyuk became independent Ukraine's first defense minister without a military background. He made significant progress in implementing NATO standards and began to reshape the country's force structure, training, and weapons procurement priorities. His strategic perspectives won strong admirers at the Pentagon and at NATO, and his openness to the views of the senior military leadership won plaudits from the armed forces. Zahorodnyuk deepened trends in the military that had developed during the Poroshenko presidency, including an emphasis on modern means of warfare and extensive training for military personnel by Western militaries. This training and Zahorodnyuk's reforms would assume an important role when Russia's full-scale war began in early 2022.

Most of Zelensky's key appointments were welcomed as a sign of his reliance on qualified experts with strong reform credentials. There was little evidence of oligarchic influence in the new government team. In his first address to the nation, Prime Minister Honcharuk echoed Zelensky's message and promised that "in the new government there will be no thievery." He pledged major investments "in science, education, and culture" and to create conditions for the delivery of "quality and accessible services to people."

The new Zelensky team proclaimed the start of the self-styled "turbo regime," promising Ukrainians rapid progress on electoral reform, an end to parliamentary immunity from prosecution, land privatization, the sale of state-owned enterprises, and strong anti-corruption measures. At the same time, President Zelensky intensified his search for a settlement to the war in Eastern Donbas.

Honcharuk's political inexperience sometimes became a liability. The new prime minister declared he intended the economy to grow by 40 percent over five years, a target serious economists regarded as impossible. Nevertheless, a public in the thrall of Zelensky euphoria believed such promises as it had the president's earlier declarations that he would successfully negotiate a peace in Eastern Ukraine, eradicate corruption, sentence corrupt politicians, and create a new era of prosperity.

Nearly thirty years after independence, Ukraine remained one of a handful of countries on the globe where land ownership was not possible, a consequence of strong populist opposition in Parliament coupled with an agricultural lobby that preferred the advantage of low-priced long-term leases. In opposition to these interests, Economy Minister Mylovanov pressed for land privatization and for the first time compiled a comprehensive digital database of land. His team assisted legislators and the Presidential Administration in developing draft laws that by March 31, 2020, resulted in the passage of a land privatization law, the first in three decades of independence. Mylovanov also drove the process of the privatization of state enterprises, many of which had been managed ineffectively. In all, the government transferred over a thousand enterprises to the State Property Fund, making inevitable their eventual transfer to the private sector.

Another major success was the replacement of ineffective managers at state companies, including some suspected of corruption. Among the companies were EnergoAtom, the Odesa Port Factory, and the Centrenergo utility. Several tenders for private management of the important port facilities of Olivia in the Mykolaiv region and in Kherson were achieved through transparent public procedures. Although the Honcharuk government and Minister Mylovanov laid the groundwork for the privatization of most remaining state assets, after their dismissal, the impetus to sell off assets slowed. A major government-led initiative to lower the cost of borrowing for small and midsize business established affordable credits at 5, 7, and 9 percent.

Ukraine's state oil and gas monopoly Naftogaz also underwent reforms, including the unbundling of its downstream exploration and extraction assets from its distribution entities, mainly its pipeline and storage systems, in accordance with EU regulations and best practices. Despite Russia's aggression in Eastern Ukraine, a gas transportation agreement was negotiated with Russia in December 2019, ensuring a measure of stability in that sector and allaying European anxiety over new gas wars.

In October 2019, reforms were introduced to the underperforming Western-supported agency the National Bureau to Prevent Corruption (NAZK), and a new director was appointed. The bureau was established to monitor the assets of government personnel and compare them with their declared assets, reporting discrepancies to criminal authorities. But despite a large staff, under the prior leadership it had brought forward a paltry number of cases.

Prisoner exchanges with Russia and the Russian-controlled Donbas were restarted, and progress was made in negotiations toward a cease-fire in the Donbas. These negotiations were accompanied by controversies surrounding concessions Zelensky appeared ready to make, including steps that seemed to suggest direct negotiations with the self-styled Donetsk and Luhansk "People's Republics" as well the withdrawal of Ukrainian forces from key strategic posts near the line of contact. These negotiations triggered a number of protests in Kyiv, although they never drew more than a few thousand participants.

Zelensky Adrift

Zelensky's January 1, 2020, New Year's address to the nation was a great disappointment to those who saw him as a master of communication. It represented a confused jumble of mawkish sentiments, his "Why can't we all just get along?" moment. Instead of projecting a unified sense of identity rooted in Ukrainian culture, language, and history, Zelensky suggested that national identity and attitudes to the past didn't matter. It didn't matter, he intoned, whether one spoke or refused to learn Ukrainian, whether one warmed to the

Soviet era or to contemporary Ukrainian culture, whether one celebrated Soviet-era holidays or not, whether one was for or against NATO. Instead, Zelensky appeared to suggest that Ukrainian citizens should unite solely because they lived in a common territory and all sought better lives. Some experts argued that Zelensky's obfuscation of the core issue of identity contributed to the unification of the Ukrainian people, a view not shared by this author. Indeed, in the years to come, Zelensky would recognize that attitudes toward the past, toward language and culture, not only matter, they are central to the country's survival, and that a nation and its state are more than a territory and the desire for the good life.

Zelensky's evasion of a distinct ethno-linguistic Ukrainian identity was hardly surprising. He had grown up in a Russophone family, and despite studying Ukrainian in school, his cultural orientation, the books he read, the films he watched, and the music he enjoyed were mainly Russian in language and origin. In May 2019, soon after his election, he had visited the Book Arsenal, Ukraine's major book fair in which hundreds of publishers exhibited Ukrainian-language fiction, nonfiction, and poetry, representing a dynamic Ukrainian cultural awakening. Yet when asked what books he had purchased, the novice president demonstrated no familiarity with Ukraine's celebrity authors and feebly answered he'd acquired a book by the Kobzar of Ukraine's nineteenth-century national bard, Taras Shevchenko. His purchase was a sign of the superficiality of his connection to Ukrainian literary discourse, a confirmation of how out of touch he was with the dynamic Ukrainian literary awakening that was occurring in his country.

Soon after Zelensky's confused plea for national unity, Ukraine's government was rocked by a crisis. In mid-January 2020 an audio recording surfaced of Prime Minister Honcharuk making disparaging comments about President Zelensky. He is "a layman" with "a primitive understanding of economic processes," Honcharuk was recorded as saying. In fairness, the prime minister also called himself as "an economic illiterate," despite having served as Zelensky's economic advisor during the campaign. On the clandestinely recorded conversations, Honcharuk also discussed how to respond to a "president [who] feels the situation is out of control, that we lack an understanding, that we [the government] have no plans."

Honcharuk called the leaks a deceptive montage of fragments of recorded government meetings and blamed unspecified "influential groups." But the damage had been done. A few days later, on January 17, Zelensky met with and agreed to let his prime minister continue to govern. Despite the public display of trust in the prime minister, a bond of confidence had been broken, and this would soon have consequences for the entire government. On February 11, 2020, President Zelensky dismissed Chief of Staff Andriy Bohdan, a strong advocate of the Honcharuk government, replacing him with lawyer Andriy Yermak, whom the president had tasked as his emissary to key Western countries. Yermak's responsibilities included managing Ukraine's troubled relations with Donald Trump, which had included the famously controversial "perfect" phone call with Zelensky, in which the U.S. president inferred a linkage between the opening of a criminal investigation of Joe Biden and his family and the release of U.S. aid to Ukraine.

Leaks of secretly recorded sensitive government conversations were a long-standing feature of Ukraine's cutthroat politics. Oligarchs, politicians, and foreign intelligence services made regular use of such eavesdropping in their political battles. Although there was no conclusive evidence as to who clandestinely made the Honcharuk recordings, journalists determined their release came from Servant of the People legislators linked to oligarch Kolomoysky's media empire. Suspicion as to the motives of making the recordings was heightened because Kateryna Rozhkova, the National Bank deputy director responsible for pursuing alleged fraud by Kolomoysky's bank, appeared to be the real target in the damaging recorded conversation with Honcharuk. At that time, Kolomoysky's media and allies pressed an attack on the monetary policy of the National Bank, which had played the central role in the confiscation of his PrivatBank holding. Kolomoysky and his acolytes asserted that Ukraine would benefit from a major currency devaluation and urged the rejection of terms international financial institutions had set, one of which was the return of assets transferred offshore by Kolomoysky's PrivatBank. Kolomoysky, who was discussing a settlement of his dispute with the Ukrainian government, had become interested in a weaker currency, as Ukraine's claims against him were denominated in hryvnia.

While Honcharuk's government made considerable progress on reforms, serious problems also emerged. Courts frustrated efforts to prosecute corrupt officials. Frivolous, politically motivated criminal investigations were launched against former president Poroshenko (including a charge of treason). Foreign direct investment stagnated. Factions linked to oligarchs and subgroups with worldviews ranging from statist to libertarian emerged in Zelensky's hastily assembled and poorly vetted parliamentary group, with some analysts speculating that many of the new "uncorrupted" deputies were now on the take. The economy—which had grown at 4 percent annually in the last two years of the Poroshenko presidency—slowed dramatically. Machine building and steel production dropped by nearly 10 percent. Overall, in the last quarter of 2019 GDP growth slowed to 1.5 percent annually, and in the first two months of 2020 declined by 0.2 percent. Particularly troubling was the steep decline in industrial production, which in March 2020 continued its freefall, dropping 7.7 percent. All this began to manifest itself well before COVID-19 led to a deeper economic downturn.

Cleaving to an unrealistic set of campaign promises, Zelensky and his inner circle were ill prepared for the difficulties of real governance, which requires time for the effects of policy changes to be felt. With the economy in decline and his own popularity registering a steep deterioration, Zelensky pushed the panic button. Instead of fine-tuning a competent reformist government and searching for a more experienced prime minister, Zelensky fired nearly the entire Honcharuk cabinet in March 2020. Ironically, the government he fired had set in motion a series of genuine reforms and had performed quite competently, receiving good marks from the investment community.

Controversial Russia Negotiations

Just days after the dismissal of the Honcharuk government, Chief of Staff Yermak approved the formation of a controversial consultative council that would include representatives of the occupied territories in Eastern Ukraine. In doing so, he effectively recognized their legitimacy, suggested that the war with Russia was a civil war within the Donbas, and made Russia a neutral third-party peacemaker. Recognizing the self-styled rulers of the occupied territories, however, did not open the door to a peace settlement. Instead, for over a year, it would entangle Zelensky and Ukraine in a complex, time-consuming, and politically destabilizing web of intrigues involving the Kremlin and its puppets.

Zelensky's initial willingness to make concessions to Russia was controversial but understandable. He was operating with a very weak hand. Europe's support for Ukraine in its conflict with Russia was limited. And Donald Trump's mercurial foreign policy and his friendly relationship with Vladimir Putin meant Ukraine had little certitude of consistent U.S. backing. Indeed, Zelensky had seen how Trump viewed Ukraine as a mere instrument in his hunger for power, having withheld Ukrainian military aid in 2019 as he pressed Ukraine's president to launch a criminal inquiry into Joe Biden's son Hunter.

Whatever the motives, Zelensky's concessions to Moscow provoked angry, large-scale demonstrations and dissent inside Zelensky's own parliamentary faction, with nearly a quarter of his deputies expressing opposition. The outrage would only grow, as many politically active Ukrainians concluded that Zelensky was selling out their country amid a nationwide quarantine. Demonstrations involving thousands of people in the streets of Kyiv and other cities raised alarm within the presidential team, which tried to argue that the president's effort to mollify Russia with a limited set of concessions was an effort to test Russia's interest in peace and that the offer would expire by the end of 2020. National Security experts worried that the inexperienced Yermak was taking his own counsel, ignoring the warnings of Western diplomats and marginalizing Ukraine's foreign minister, who was shut out of talks that Yermak held with Dmitry Kozak, Putin's deputy chief of staff.

The president compounded his problems by replacing a young, reformist team with a new government of timeservers, some of whose careers had been forged during the corrupt regime of former president Yanukovych. Some new appointees were former employees of the very oligarchs whose influence Zelensky denounced. Zelensky also dismissed his well-regarded prosecutor general, displeased that he was not moving forward with politically motivated but juridically weak cases. A lawyer for disgraced President Yanukovych became the deputy head of the State Bureau of Investigations.

A New Government Team

On March 4 the Parliament elected as prime minister Denys Shmyhal, a senior manager in Rinat Akhmetov's energy empire. The new prime minister received 291 votes, the bulk of them—242—from the Servant faction. The government ministers were approved *en bloc* with the support of 277 parliamentarians. Just four ministers were held over from the Honcharuk government, most significantly the justice minister Denys Malyuska and the veteran interior minister Arseniy Avakov, who had served throughout the Poroshenko years but backed Zelensky in his presidential bid.

If the Honcharuk government was mainly dominated by thirty- and forty-somethings, the Shmyhal government added a dose of people in their fifties and sixties, several with service in the discredited Yanukovych government. Only a few had links to the Maidan or the Orange Revolution. As defense minister, Zelensky appointed Andriy Taran, a sixty-five-year-old former lieutenant general who had served in military intelligence and was appointed on the strength of service at the Ukraine embassy in the United States and at the Ukraine Mission to the United Nations.

The health minister Ilya Yemets, an old-school official, was dismissed within three weeks for shunning the press amid the COVID outbreak. The following weeks saw the dismissal of the new finance minister and energy minister. The rushed dismissal of the previous government meant that it took months to find a new culture minister, and the new government went through three acting education ministers in a few months. Another old-school politician, the former head of the National Space Agency Oleh Urusky, became deputy prime minister for strategic industrial policy. The only appointments that were well received were those of prominent attorney Oleksiy Reznikov as deputy prime minister for the reintegration of occupied territories, Dmytro Kuleba as foreign minister, and Serhiy Marchenko, an investment banker who had served in the Poroshenko administration, as the government's second finance minister.

In April Zelensky and his inner circle compounded their personnel mistakes, dismissing well-regarded reformers at the Customs and Tax Inspection Offices and conducting a one-day search for candidates to replace them. Having driven out most of the government and replaced young reformers with timeservers, Zelensky faced the challenge of leading a country in the throes of an economic downturn. Repopulating the government was of some help in reviving public opinion ratings. But trust in the Shmyhal government quickly began to plummet, as did the support for the Servant of the People Party, which fared poorly in the October 2020 local elections.

Having fired the Honcharuk cabinet, Zelensky risked underscoring his incompetence should he jettison the new Shmyhal team. But Zelensky was unfazed, declaring he would keep firing ministers "until we create the ideal government." Such bravado notwithstanding, Zelensky had backed himself into a corner while accentuating doubts about his sure-handedness. The only silver lining was polling that showed the public continued to see Zelensky as personally honest and free of corruption, even as the public now disapproved of his performance by a margin of 51 to 35 percent.

A Deepening Crisis

In the spring of 2020 Ukraine's novice president faced a new crisis—COVID-19. Initially, Zelensky had handled the challenges well, shutting down the country briefly and keeping infection rates and fatalities far lower than in Central and Western Europe. But the nearly complete shutdown of the economy and society had long-standing negative effects that were aggravated by the global recession. In the fall and winter of 2020, the COVID-19 crisis spiked again, with fatalities rising above one hundred per day and daily recorded cases beginning to climb toward ten thousand. Early vigorous preventative steps to reduce social contact, including the short-term closure of metros and schools, helped, but Ukraine's underfunded health system was hard-pressed to meet the population's needs.

A run on hard currency in the spring of 2020 forced the central bank to spend over $2 billion to protect the national currency, which moved from 23 hryvnia to the dollar to nearly 28. Pressure on the currency and the COVID-linked economic decline of nearly minus

4 percent necessitated a new agreement with the IMF. This meant pressing ahead vigorously with land privatization and banking reform as well as ensuring that public spending was kept in check and would not ignite a spurt of inflation. Under international pressure, Zelensky lobbied his increasingly fractious legislature to vote for legislation that made the return of PrivatBank to its former owner impossible. In August 2020, U.S. authorities initiated a money-laundering case against oligarch Kolomoysky, something Presidents Poroshenko and Zelensky had failed to achieve at home.

Amid complex economic and health challenges, in his first two years in office, President Zelensky pursued his internally divisive peacemaking effort with Russia. He and his team believed progress was possible even as Vladimir Putin intensified his hostile rhetoric against the Ukrainian state. As Putin and his Ukraine advisor, Vladislav Surkov, repeatedly and ominously asserted, there was no "real" Ukraine and Ukrainians were merely members of the greater Russian people temporarily in the thrall of Western-supported propaganda.

Despite Russia's menacing rhetoric, Zelensky refrained from public criticism of President Putin and avoided blaming the conflict in the Donbas on Russia. This unwillingness risked damage to international support by reinforcing a Russian narrative that the Donbas conflict was a civil war rather than Russian aggression and occupation. Zelensky's foreign policy approach to Russia as executed by aide Yermak confused Western diplomats. It also was roundly condemned by nationalist and patriotic political forces and, increasingly, by some of his own party's legislators. At the same time, Zelensky's administration began to further alienate civil society and pro-reform activists as a series of corruption scandals took the sheen off the image of the president and his colleagues.

The case Zelensky had made for his presidency was threefold: he would bring in a new team of honest professionals to grow the economy, secure a peace with Russia, and reduce corruption and the influence of the oligarchy. In the second year of his presidency, the first aim had evaporated amid economic decline; the second was stalled with little sign of a breakthrough. What was left was the fight against corruption. And here too problems began to multiply for Zelensky, his team, and his political party. Serious prosecutions and convictions for corruption yielded no more results than under the

Poroshenko administration. No big fish were enmeshed in criminal cases, most notably the biggest fish of all, Ihor Kolomoysky, whose bank was alleged to have defrauded the country of $5.5 billion. Moreover, a series of corruption scandals began to implicate members of the Servant of the People as well as the periphery of the president's core team.

Controversy erupted in March 2020 when clandestinely recorded videos showed Denys Yermak, brother of the president's chief of staff, discussing payments in return for help in securing appointments to key posts in the government and state-owned companies. Though the chief of staff was not implicated in the alleged corruption scandal, there were no legal consequences for Yermak's brother. The scandal eroded confidence in the president and focused attention on the large presence of Zelensky's school chums and relatives in his inner circle and in the government.

Problems also emerged inside the rule-of-law structures. Ruslan Ryaboshapka, Zelensky's first prosecutor general, had endorsed his presidential run, but was seen as politically independent. Widely respected in the international diplomatic community as a diligent and competent professional, in his brief time in office, Ryaboshapka dismissed thousands of prosecutors of dubious reputation while raising the wages of the more honest and capable prosecutors who remained. Yet he quickly ran afoul of the president, in part due to his independence. Deeply critical of corruption during the Poroshenko years, Ryaboshapka refused to bring forward cases against the former president that were politically motivated and lacking an evidentiary base.

By contrast, his successor, former Servant of the People parliamentarian and head of the State Bureau of Investigation Iryna Venediktova, quickly gained a reputation for partisanship and selective justice. Her office opened or pursued dozens of cases against Poroshenko. Some of the cases were frivolous or even preposterous. One involved the "usurpation of state power" because the president named two first deputy heads to the Foreign Intelligence Service rather than one, as provided for in the statutes. Another case involved the seizure of Poroshenko's Ukrainian art collection, which had been scrupulously assembled and was backed up by detailed records of customs excise payments. A third case posited that Poroshenko had put Ukrainian naval personnel at risk by ordering them to cross Ukrainian and neutral territorial waters on the Kerch Strait, where they were attacked and seized illegally by Russian naval forces. As these cases advanced, Ryaboshapka voiced dismay at the judicial incompetence of his successor and her team.

Venediktova also launched a controversial new approach to the violence that had occurred during the Euromaidan of 2014 and during the Kremlin-backed Russian Spring separatist uprising. Her office opened criminal cases against Maidan activists, including a case in which patriotic protestors defending Ukrainian state sovereignty and territorial integrity engaged in a deadly clash with pro-Russian separatist activists in Odesa.

In October 2020 the National Bank of Ukraine Council, an advisory body, reprimanded two bank directors, ostensibly for a frank press interview in which they spoke about threats to the National Bank's independence. Zelensky's newly appointed central bank governor, Kyrylo Shevchenko, joined in the reprimand of Kateryna Rozhkova, first deputy governor of the bank, in charge of bank supervision, and Dmytro Solohub, responsible for the bank's monetary policy. It was reported that the effort to express no confidence in the well-regarded directors was spearheaded by a recent appointee to the bank's board, Vitaly Shapran, who came from President Zelensky's hometown of Kryvyy Rih. Shapran was also a vocal proponent of the bank adopting a more relaxed monetary policy, reflecting a widely held view that the president was being advised by intimates to weaken Ukraine's currency, the hryvnia, as part of a strategy to resuscitate the economy—albeit at the risk of high inflation. Furthermore, Rozhkova, one of the censured officials, had led efforts to seize recovered assets from Ihor Kolomoysky for allegedly fraudulent loans.

Controversial Appointments

Not surprisingly, a survey in late 2020 by the Kyiv International Institute of Sociology found that 83 percent of the public believed Zelensky's fight against corruption had failed. After several years of improvement in the fight against corruption registered during the Poroshenko years, Zelensky's Ukraine dropped in the rankings of Transparency International, falling six places and coming in 126th out of 180 countries. Instead of drawing lessons and revising anti-corruption approaches, Zelensky-linked social networks and legislators began a campaign of calumny against philanthropist George Soros's Ukraine grantees and Western-funded anti-corruption programs.

The campaign against Western-funded anti-corruption initiatives was waged on several fronts. The first consisted of anonymous channels on the Telegram app linked to political technologist Mykhaylo Podolyak, who consulted with presidential chief of staff Yermak on media and public relations. The second was led by politicians and media linked to oligarch Kolomoysky, who saw in the reformers a force pressing the state to seize the his assets. A third, separate front was led by TV stations linked to the man who ran Russia's fifth column in Ukraine, Viktor Medvedchuk.

The drumbeat of attacks on recipients of Western reform assistance was accompanied by Zelensky's arm's-length relationship with Western diplomats. EU and U.S. diplomats worried about more than slippage in the reform agenda; concern mounted over backdoor discussions with Russia about the Donbas, over a growing economic relationship between Ukraine and China, and over closer cooperation between Ukraine and Recep Tayyip Erdoğan's Turkey. Concerned about losing contact with the president and the ability to engage him, Western ambassadors ironically refrained from public criticism, a practice common during the Poroshenko presidency, when diplomats aired policy criticism and crossed the line into micro-management of domestic Ukrainian policies.

As lofty election promises remained unrealized, Zelensky placed the blame on a deficit of cadre that his administration and government faced—a direct result of Zelensky's government purge and alienation of reformers. Ironically, public trust in the new government was now lower than confidence in the Honcharuk team.

In July 2020 the president appointed Leonid Kravchuk, Ukraine's eighty-six-year-old first president, to lead complex peace negotiations with Russia. In announcing the appointment, Zelensky asserted that Kravchuk commanded the respect of all Ukrainians, forgetting that under Kravchuk Ukraine suffered economic collapse and endured hyperinflation. Just as important, in 2006 Kravchuk was discredited when he joined an anti-NATO/anti-EU political alliance with Viktor Medvedchuk, Putin's man in Ukraine.

Soon after his appointment, Kravchuk caused embarrassment by agreeing on Russian television with his propagandist hosts' claim that Russia was not party to the war in Eastern Ukraine. An octogenarian who needed extensive rest breaks, Kravchuk named as his top advisor Vitold Fokin, the eighty-seven-year-old former Ukrainian prime minister best known for resistance to market reforms. Kravchuk explained that Fokin, who had not been in government for nearly three decades, was the best informed about what is going on in the Donbas among his acquaintances. Zelensky went further, asserting, "Kravchuk and Fokin are a pair of modern-day Ukraine's most powerful diplomats." Within weeks Fokin became a one-man wrecking crew as he dismantled Kyiv's claims of Russian aggression. Absurdly, Fokin asserted there was no Russian military participation in the war in the Donbas. In late September 2020 President Zelensky dismissed Fokin from his advisory role.

Prosecutor General Iryna Venediktova appointed another old-school veteran, former prosecutor general Svyatoslav Piskun, as a key advisor. Piskun is a longtime member of the Ukrainian political establishment, whose family reportedly owns a $2 million villa on the French Riviera. In TV and print interviews, Piskun bizarrely stated that he used a "sixth sense" while working as the state prosecutor and claimed that he is a "koldun," a warlock with magical powers, including the ability to diagnose early-stage cancers in dozens of friends and acquaintances. Piskun too was dismissed after a month as advisor, amid reports he was telling business contacts he could resolve their problems with law enforcement.

No appointment aroused more consternation than that of Oleh Tatarov as deputy head of the President's Office with responsibility for internal security, and post he held as this book was sent to print. Tatarov served as deputy head of investigations in the Ministry of Internal Affairs during President Yanukovych's violent suppression of the 2013–14 Euromaidan protests. In this capacity, he processed criminal cases against numerous activists and served as spin doctor for the Interior Ministry at the time of its brutal suppression of mass civic protests. Several years later, Tatarov—an able litigator—defended stalwarts from the Party of Regions and the Yanukovych administration in criminal proceedings. Among them were billionaire parliamentarian Vadim Novinsky, a principal bankroller of the Party of

Regions, and Andriy Portnov, deputy head of Yanukovych's Presidential Administration responsible for legal affairs, who gained a notorious reputation for his influence on the courts. In defense of the controversial appointment, Zelensky asserted that Tatarov did not flee the country with the Yanukovych team. This was a rather low standard for a president who vowed to end politics as usual and promised to populate his administration with a new generation of Ukrainians unblemished by association with the failed or discredited regimes of the past.

While there were few Maidan activists in the Shmyhal government and the President's Office, by the middle of 2020, there was a growing cohort of appointees closely linked to the Yanukovych team. Oleksandr Babikov was Zelensky's choice for first deputy head of the State Investigation Bureau, an agency investigating Yanukovych-era crimes. Incredibly, he served as a lawyer for President Yanukovych's defense during the former Ukrainian leader's treason trial. Serhiy Demchenko, a prominent parliamentarian from Zelensky's Servant of the People Party, also had served as a defense lawyer for top Yanukovych aide Andriy Portnov.

Even the few Maidan activists on the Zelensky team came with an asterisk. Andriy Smirnov, the deputy head of the President's Office for legal affairs, has been a Euromaidan activist. However, like Babikov, for several years, he had defended prominent Party of Regions politicians under prosecution for anti-Maidan crimes and was a bête noire for reformers.

Support in Freefall

Well into the second year of his presidency, his wholesale personnel changes notwithstanding, Zelensky, the government, and his political party saw their support in freefall. Zelensky, who had won 73 percent in his election, now had 22 percent support for reelection. Figures for the Servant Party registered a drop in approval from 43 percent to around 15 percent. Additionally, polling showed that the government's approval rating had fallen to minus 60 percent, with 73 percent of the public dissatisfied with government performance. Only 35 percent of Ukrainians were happy with Zelensky's performance; 57 percent were unhappy.

In an effort to reverse flagging fortunes and demonstrate that his presidency was bringing positive tangible results, Zelensky launched a nationwide effort to build and repair Ukraine's decrepit road system. Although highway construction was not a presidential function (this was in the purview of the government), Zelensky crisscrossed the country from the late summer to the early autumn to inspect progress on the major infrastructure project. Such visits were accompanied by public meetings and local media appearances.

Even this initiative suffered from criticism amid charges of favoritism in the awarding of contracts, price gouging, excessive profits, and because funds initially allocated for the fight against COVID-19 had been diverted to the initiative. As important, in 2022–23 critics retroactively asked if highway construction funds could not have been spent on national defense in the face of a massive Russian troop buildup that began in March–April 2021.

Another initiative to revive Zelensky's flagging popularity was an ill-considered "plebiscite." The hasty introduction of a vote on the day of nationwide local and regional elections, October 25, was roundly condemned as being both extralegal and surrounded by procedural questions. No one could explain clearly how the effort was being financed, who was collecting the votes and where (the vote could not be held at the polling places, nor proximate to them), nor who would be monitoring the counting of votes and ballot security. Yet Zelensky said the controversial vote would guide his administration's priorities in the coming years. The questions were both populist and vague: asking voters about life imprisonment for grand corruption, a free economic zone for the Donbas, the reduction of the size of the Parliament, legalization of cannabis, and new security guarantees for Ukraine.

Despite these initiatives, local government elections in October 2020 confirmed what polling over the summer and fall had shown. Not a single mayoral candidate of the Servant of the People Party won in any of Ukraine's largest cities—including Kyiv, Odesa, Kharkiv, Mariupol, and Lviv. Nationwide, the party performed poorly and was shut out of power-sharing in many municipalities.

In the late summer and early fall of 2020, sources inside the president's office suggested that Zelensky was despondent, if not depressed, about the turn in his political fortunes. One source told me that the president feared that mass protests against his rule were in the offing. “He isn't going to fight them,” my source said. “If . . . people rise up against him, he will walk away from the presidency.”

With the decline in the president's popularity, his haphazardly assembled parliamentary group was adrift as different interest groups and factions emerged. One small group of deputies oriented itself around fundamental reforms, liberal market–oriented economic policies, and a hard line in negotiations with Russia. Other groupings reflected the growing influence of their oligarchic patrons. Still others sought to trade political support for personal enrichment or advantage.

Ukrainska Pravda, a well-informed and well-regarded investigative news site, estimated in September 2020 that oligarch Kolomoysky could count on the support of as many as fifty to seventy deputies inside the Parliament. *Pravda* suggested that deputies strongly allied with billionaire Rinat Akhmetov numbered between twenty and thirty.

The fragmentation of the Servant Party was solely a function of the president's declining popularity. It had its origins in the haphazard construction of a politically inexperienced legislative faction and a degree of naïveté about “new faces” who quickly established “old connections.” Political fragmentation also was the consequence of an absent governing philosophy and President Zelensky's predisposition to win the approval of widely divergent electoral segments of the population.

Zelensky Regains the Initiative

In the second half of 2021, Zelensky appeared to find his political sea legs as his support stabilized. The year saw the economy recover modestly, rising nearly 3.5 percent. In reality, given previous losses, this meant there had been no growth over the first two years of Zelensky's presidency. Slowly Zelensky began to make adjustments in his inner circle and to replace ineffective ministers. The most notable change was at the Defense Ministry, which saw the appointment of Deputy Prime Minister Oleksiy Reznikov to a post that in 2022 would become a focal point of Ukraine's existential struggle in the face of Russian invasion.

Moreover, the public generally gave high marks to a major roadworks infrastructure initiative, whose progress and impact could be seen and tangibly experienced. "Big Construction," which was budgeted at over $7 billion in a two-year period, had resulted in the rebuilding, renovation, and expansion of over 40 percent of the country's roads by October 2021, a total of some eight thousand miles of roadworks and six hundred bridges. The Big Construction project came with a huge price tag, but as its results were easy to see, it reinvigorated support for the president.

Zelensky's presidency also benefited from a legacy of his predecessor. Just weeks before leaving office, under international pressure, Petro Poroshenko launched the High Anti-Corruption Court. Composed of justices vetted by a joint Ukrainian-international screening group, the court started work at the onset of the Zelensky presidency. Over time, working in tandem with a special anti-corruption prosecutor, the court would make significant headway in prosecuting high- and mid-level government corruption. After two years of work, it had convicted thirty-nine officials, mainly mid-level functionaries.

The Rising Russian Threat

Zelensky's promise to secure peace with Russia stalled in February 2021, as Russia began a buildup of troops near Ukraine's borders that eventually rose to well over one hundred thousand. The threatening troop buildup came soon after the arrest of parliamentarian and Putin friend Viktor Medvedchuk, who headed Russia's fifth column in Ukraine. As Russian troops massed, the rogue Donetsk People's Republic withdrew from earlier agreements, announcing a policy of "preemptive fire for destruction" against Ukrainian forces. Simultaneously, Russian propagandists launched a campaign claiming Ukraine was targeting civilians in the occupied east, although the level of cross-border military incidents on both sides of the line of contact was similar to that of the previous two years. Russian rhetoric attacking Ukraine's legitimacy as a state also accelerated. In July 2021 Vladimir Putin's essay "On the Historical Unity of Russians and Ukrainians" was published on the president's website, alleging that Ukrainians and Russians were "one people" whose destiny was to be together. Russia and Ukraine analyst Anders Aslund, my former colleague at the Atlantic Council, described Putin's essay as "one step short of a declaration of war."

Despite menacing Russian rhetoric and a military threat on Ukraine's borders, the United States and its NATO allies pursued business as usual. According to a report in the *Washington Post*, by October 2021, the United States had concluded that Putin was certain to launch a war against Ukraine. That meant that from October 2021 to the start of Russia's invasion in late February 2022, the United States and Western allies had a crucial window in which to provide Ukraine significant weaponry and the training to use it. But instead of howitzers, multiple-launch rocket systems, and heavy ordnance, the United States doled out much more modest assistance.

In the months after the U.S. administration learned of Russian intentions, it sent Ukraine a tiny $60 million allotment of small arms and ammunition. Only in December 2021 did President Biden approve a long-delayed $200 million shipment of weaponry conducive to a partisan resistance, including three hundred Javelin anti-tank missiles that arrived in January—a full three months after the intel assessment that an invasion was certain, and mere weeks before Russian forces began their assault. Even this welcome support was far short of an adequate response to the war drums emanating from Moscow. Ukraine's president Zelensky also acted as if it was business as usual. He made no effort to significantly increase Ukraine's military spending, nor did he redirect spending on his extravagant road and bridge repair initiative. As 2021 drew to a close, Zelensky still appeared to believe that a negotiated peace in the Donbas was attainable.

Even as U.S. intelligence shared information suggesting the likelihood of a Russian invasion, there were few signs of urgency in the President's Office and Zelensky steadfastly refused to believe a Russian attack was imminent. Huge budgetary expenditures financed a massive roadworks program, while the defense budget remained relatively flat. Two days before Russia launched its all-out invasion, Ukraine's leaders briefed key parliamentarians across the political spectrum, suggesting that an invasion was unlikely although there might be an acceleration of conflict in the partially occupied Donbas.

While Zelensky and his team misread Russia's intentions, they had an uncanny skill for reading the Ukrainian public. In the first years of his presidency, Zelensky's agenda was shaped by his keen sense of public opinion as well as by major domestic civic, cultural, and business forces. Though his domestic accomplishments paled when compared to his extravagant promises, he had important advantages that would serve him well as Ukraine faced the existential crisis posed by Russia's all-out invasion: first, he was sensitive to public desire; second, he benefited from the public's trust in him as someone focused on governing rather than on personal enrichment. Yet on the eve of war with Russia, Zelensky—like part of the population he led—remained rudderless and without a clear sense of the nation's identity and national purpose. Events in early 2022 would shake him and the Ukrainian people from their torpor in the greatest test to sovereignty in the three decades of the country's existence.

CHAPTER SEVEN

The War President

Zelensky and Ukraine under Russian Attack

In the third year of his presidency, Volodymyr Zelensky and his country faced an existential threat: a massive attack by Russia aimed at the obliteration of the Ukrainian state and nation. That full-scale war began on February 24 as a multi-front offensive involving some 150,000 Russian forces reinforced by tens of thousands of Russian-armed and Russian-trained fighters of the self-styled Donetsk and Luhansk People's Republics. The attacks came across a wide perimeter of the Ukraine, which is an area the size of Massachusetts, Connecticut, New York, New Jersey, Maryland, Pennsylvania, Indiana, Ohio, and Illinois combined.

Russian forces attacked Ukraine's northeastern border regions of Kharkiv and Sumy; from Belarus Russian forces streamed south toward Chernihiv, the birthplace of Nikolai Gogol (Mykola Hohol), and neared the periphery of the capital Kyiv. In the south, Russian troops mustered in Crimea in advance of an offensive that soon occupied large swaths of Ukrainian territory north of the Azov Sea. These advances were accompanied by missile attacks on military facilities, communications and transportation hubs, and civilian infrastructure.

The precursors of Russia's attack had been present for nearly a year. In March and April 2021, Russia had begun to mass what soon became some 150,000 troops at Ukraine's eastern and northern border. This massive array of Russian forces, armed with tanks, artillery, and armored personnel carriers, ebbed and flowed but never fell below around 100,000 fighters. According to a 2021 estimate by the International Institute of Strategic Studies, they were augmented by 44,000 well-armed fighters from the self-styled Russian People's Republics of Luhansk and Donetsk. While Russia maintained this menacing posture, the United States and its NATO allies paid little attention to the entreaties of Ukraine's leaders for a major increase in military aid. While U.S. aid in the form of anti-tank weapons had first been provided to Ukraine during the Trump administration, under President Biden there was no uptick in weapons supplies amid the growing threat. When a modest $200 million in military aid was voted by the U.S. Congress, the Biden administration dragged its feet in delivering the urgently need assistance. After Russia withdrew an inconsequential few thousand troops from Ukraine's border, the Biden administration further delayed delivery of this modest aid. As *NBC News* reported on December 10, 2021, according to administration sources: "The . . . delay of the smaller shipment of weapons and military equipment was designed to give more time for diplomatic efforts to defuse tensions and to retain leverage in the case of a Russian attack on Ukraine." A well-sourced report from a team of *Washington Post* journalists showed that as early as October 2021, U.S. intelligence concluded that a Russian attack was likely and warned Ukraine's leaders of this impending threat. In the weeks that followed, U.S. diplomats notified their Russian counterparts that an attack would be met with massive sanctions and unified support of Kyiv. Still, no serious transfer of weapons was contemplated and even the small amount of allocated assistance was delayed. This decision would lead to major unnecessary Ukrainian military and civilian losses.

Biden's decision to delay arming Ukraine came after another major concession to Putin. On May 19, 2021, Biden decided to waive the congressionally mandated sanctions against Russia's Nordstream 2 gas pipeline. Washington saw this as a parting gesture to German chancellor Angela Merkel, an integral part of Biden's effort to solidify U.S.-German relations after a tense period under President Trump. Yet, as critics noted, from Putin's perspective the waiver was a sign of the Biden administration's weakness and lack of resolve.

As important, the freezing of weapons and the decision to acquiesce in Europe's gas dependency on Russia came amid growing evidence that the United States was turning inward. The rapid and haphazard withdrawal of U.S. forces from Afghanistan concluded on August 31, 2021, may well have reflected U.S. national interests and good judgment. But to Russia, the actions of the new Biden administration signaled that the United States was abandoning an assertive security policy, focusing on the growing challenges posed by China, and pivoting to domestic priorities. All these administration decisions conveyed Western weakness to Putin.

As 2022 began, the Kremlin launched a ferocious barrage of criticism of the Ukrainian regime. Russia's rhetoric declared the Kyiv regime illegitimate, ignoring that Ukraine's authorities derived their power from two free and fair presidential and parliamentary elections. Russia falsely asserted that a "coup" had removed President Viktor Yanukovych, ignoring that fact that Yanukovych was stripped of his offices by a constitutional majority in Parliament after he had fled the country. Russia further alleged that Nazis had taken over the Ukrainian government, an absurd claim for a country led by a Jew and in which far-right parties had failed to win election to Parliament. An equally preposterous claim was that Ukraine's much smaller military force had been built up as a beachhead for a Western attack on Russia. The Kremlin's propaganda also charged Ukraine with genocide against the people of the Donbas, though in all of 2020 and 2021 international observers from an OSCE Monitoring Mission recorded no more two dozen civilian deaths on both sides each year, many the inadvertent victims of land mines, and annual military fatalities on both sides had dropped to around one hundred.

Putin's Imperial Blueprint

In July 2021 Vladimir Putin had delivered the justification for his eventual invasion in an ominous lengthy essay entitled "On the Historical Unity of Russians and Ukrainians." Putin's missive carried echoes of Russian Nobel Laureate Aleksandr Solzhenitsyn's 1990 essay "How Should We Rebuild Russia." Solzhenitsyn's draft, written before the USSR collapsed, sought to preserve the empire.

Putin admired Solzhenitsyn's neoimperialist views and his call for the re-creation of a "Russian Union" of Russia, Belarus, Ukraine, and the majority Slavic region of northern Kazakhstan. Solzhenitsyn argued that Crimea, the Donbas, and the areas that had been known as Novorossiya should be allowed "self-determination" in the event there was an independent Ukraine. Yet nowhere did Solzhenitsyn call for a military solution, and he appeared to favor negotiations among the Soviet republics. In 2007 Putin visited an elderly and ailing Solzhenitsyn in a display of admiration for the writer and his ideas. But in his 2021 essay, Putin built a case for implementing Solzhenitsyn's agenda without reference to the effects of three decades of independent Ukrainian statehood.

Putin's essay was replete with historical errors and falsifications that denied Ukraine any agency or expression of national will. He contended that a Ukrainian identity separate from Russia was a creation in the historical sequence of Austria, Poland, Germany, Lenin's Soviet Union, and today's West. His rendering of history denied that Ukraine had experienced independence, conveniently appropriating Kyivan Rus, which predated Muscovy by centuries, and explained away long periods of independent rule under Cossack Hetmans as the result of war and chaos. He also dismissed the brief period of Ukrainian statehood during World War I as the creation of Western powers. Above all, Putin ignored the will of the Ukrainian people as expressed over the last three decades of independence.

Finally, he asserted that Ukraine's and Ukrainians' destiny must be as part of the single great Russian nation, and ended his essay with an ominous assertion: "Ukraine was dragged into a dangerous geopolitical game aimed at turning Ukraine into a barrier between Europe and Russia, a springboard against Russia."

The essay became the foundation of Russian state propaganda, which soon would begin making the case for the undoing of the Ukrainian state. That undoing began on February 15, 2022, with an act of subterfuge. Russia declared it was removing troops from the

Ukrainian border in what many saw as a sign of de-escalation. In fact, it was a deception designed to lower Ukraine's guard. Just two days later, the forces of the Luhansk and Donetsk breakaway statelets launched thirty-nine separate artillery attacks on the entire line of contact dividing Ukrainian and Russian-led forces in the Donbas. After an attack hit a school in Ukraine-controlled Stanytsia Luhanska, Ukraine's forces did not respond in kind. Nevertheless, Russian propaganda denounced Ukraine's military escalation. A day later, without any escalation on Ukraine's part, Russian officials declared there had been a drastic increase in the shelling of civilian targets by Ukraine. Denis Pushilin, the rump Donetsk People's Republic's leader, called for the immediate evacuation of women, children, and the elderly from the region. At that point, only one civilian in the Russian-controlled regions had died, and he was shot with ordinary ammunition far from the front lines, which meant the bullet could not have come from distant Ukrainian forces.

On February 22 President Putin convened a gathering of his National Security and Defense Council that was broadcast live across the vast array of Russian media. After hearing high-ranking officials denounce Ukraine's "genocidal" regime, Putin declared Russia's intention to annex the Donetsk and Luhansk regions. He warned belligerently that if Kyiv did not stop its alleged violence, it would bear responsibility for any "ensuing bloodshed." It was clear that Russia was about to move. Less clear was the scope of the planned aggression. In response, President Zelensky gave no signs he was readying the country for a major onslaught. Indeed, in a year in which Russia had massed its forces near Ukraine's border, Zelensky had done little to ramp up Ukraine's military expenditures, and secret briefings to key legislators suggested the president and government did not believe a wide-scale invasion was in the offing. NATO and the United States were worried as they had few details of Ukrainian plans for the defense of the country. Such details were closely held by the commander of the armed forces General Valeriy Zaluzhny, who had made his own contingency plans but did not wish such information to leak and reach enemy hands. Some sources intimate that Zaluzhny, who took U.S. warnings of an imminent Russian attack seriously, did not even inform his president of some of his troop deployments.

Russia's Full-Scale War

On February 24 Russia's onslaught began with missiles raining down on civilian and military targets. Especially hard hit were major cities. Airports, military bases, and air defense batteries were the initial targets. Some Russian forces moved in massive numbers across the border into the Chernhiv, Kharkiv, and Sumy regions, while others marched out of Crimea to threaten Kherson and Southern Ukraine, including Ukraine-controlled portions of the Donetsk region. At the same time, Russian-reinforced forces of the Luhansk and Donetsk statelets began probing attacks on well-entrenched Ukrainian forces along the line of contact. As massive numbers of Russian forces marched from the north, Russian helicopters swooped onto the Ukrainian air base at Hostomel on the outskirts of Kyiv.

Echoing Russian news media, initial Western coverage suggested a dire outcome. On the first day of the war, *Newsweek* reported that U.S. intelligence experts believed Ukraine would fall in a matter of days. The Russians were moving at lightning speed, and Ukraine's response was not yet discernable. With Kyiv surrounded, Western experts conjectured that Ukrainian forces would resort to guerrilla warfare. Russian military briefers declared their forces had struck and destroyed much of Ukraine's military command and control, eliminated Ukraine's air power, and were advancing quickly on a range of fronts in Ukraine's north, east, and south. A palpable mood of anxiety had overtaken many Ukrainians, who by the millions fled westward toward central Europe.

On February 25, as initial Russian efforts to march on Kyiv were being repulsed, it fell upon the man who had once been the Ukrainian voice of Paddington the Bear to inspire the nation. Volodymyr Zelensky, Ukraine's forty-four-year-old president, made a powerful video address to his people in the company of his chief of staff, defense minister, and leader of his political party in Parliament: "We are here!" Zelensky intoned defiantly in answer to disinformation that the government had fled the capital. "Our army is here, our civil society is here. We are all here! . . . We are defending our independence, our state, and we will continue to do so." Amid heroism on the front lines, that night Ukrainians and the world saw a new hero, a resolute man who had risen to the task of being his country's war president and was now stepping onto the world stage.

Amid the chaos and the fog of war, Ukraine's air defenses—heretofore believed to be negligible—were showing remarkable effectiveness. A friend, Tymofiy Mylovanov, formerly Zelensky's economy minister and later board chair of UkrOboronProm, the state weapons manufacturer, had told me just a few days earlier in New York that if Russia attacked from the air, "it would be in for a surprise." Do you mean Ukraine has an Iron Dome? I had asked. "No one knew Israel had an Iron Dome until [she] was attacked," he responded. A few days into the invasion, a clearer and more complex picture began to emerge of the significant firepower, resilience, and creativity of the Ukrainian armed forces and of the effectiveness of Ukraine's air defenses.

The first days of the war also saw the start of a massive flow of internally displaced refugees fleeing cities and towns under attack or the scenes of pitched battles. The war inevitably came to my Ukrainian family. The first night of the attack, my stepdaughters packed in the early morning to depart our apartment in a high-rise located just a few blocks from the Parliament and the Cabinet of Ministers. After an anxious full day's drive through heavy traffic they arrived in Western Ukraine. A few days later, they were spirited out to Warsaw, where they would spend several months in anxious safety. As they fled, my stepdaughters saw heart-rending scenes of thousands upon thousands of women, children, and the elderly crossing the Polish border at Medyka.

Similar scenes played out in Hungary, Slovakia, and Romania, creating an atmosphere of fear, chaos, and flight. Soon it became clear that these heart-rending scenes were only part of the story. On a variety of fronts, Ukrainian resistance was growing. In Hostomel airport, just six miles from Kyiv, two Russian air assault units landed on dozens of helicopters. They were met by lightly armed Ukrainian forces who did just enough to slow the eventual capture of the facility, which was intended as a landing base for a major Russian assault on Kyiv. Ukrainian resistance bought time, which allowed for the mustering of a Ukrainian counterattack that included armed Ukrainian civilians, an international fighting unit called the Georgian Legion, and Ukraine's own air assault forces. MANPADS (man-portable air-defense systems) and other air defenses took down several Russian aircraft, and though the airfield remained in Russian hands, larger landings of Russian forces were prevented. Hostomel was a harbinger.

Pitched battles ensued in neighboring suburbs, including Bucha, which fell under temporary Russian control and later would be revealed to be the scene of major Russian war crimes. A similar picture emerged in the commuter suburb of Irpin. In time both would be scenes of the mass murder of hundreds of civilians. By September 2022 the official body count of civilian dead in the Russian assault on Kyiv stood at 1,356, according to the head of Kyiv's regional police. An additional 1,207 remained missing.

Unable to land large numbers of forces by air, and with some forces pinned down by Ukrainian fire, Russian troops began to march down the narrow highways of Ukraine's north, through Chernihiv and into Kyiv's periphery. But that maneuver was not going well. On March 1 the *Wall Street Journal* cited a U.S. defense official who reported, "The Russian advance on Kyiv and other Ukrainian cities has stalled amid food and fuel shortages, Ukrainian resistance and slower-than-expected troop movements toward the capital." In early March numerous reports and satellite evidence indicated that a long convoy stretching forty miles from the north of Kyiv was stuck and not moving. Social media began to buzz with videos of Ukrainian and Turkish Bayraktar combat drones taking out Russian tanks and armored vehicles, and of Ukrainians using thousands of Javelins and the lighter British-supplied NLAWs to take out Russian armored vehicles and tanks. Most important, no major Ukrainian city had fallen. Kyiv and Kharkiv, in particular, were holding fast. Russian jubilation at imminent victory was premature, and Western fears of a collapse of Ukraine's military were in error.

In the first days of the war, a spontaneous civic movement resulted in the creation of a people's army, the territorial defense. Much as with the nascent volunteer units created in 2014, when the first Russian aggression began, by early March one hundred thousand Ukrainians had volunteered for service in light infantry units. Territorial defense units received some weapons, helmets, and body armor from the state, but many were of low quality. Often these units were equipped through volunteer crowd-funding efforts. Many of these fighters would later sign contracts and move on to serve in regular military units. One such was my fifty-year-old brother-in-law, a professional violinist, who joined the territorial defense, initially patrolling checkpoints in the Kyiv region. Eventually he signed a contract for service in the armed forces, received extensive training, and was deployed in the Mykolaiv and Kherson regions in Southern Ukraine. After a year of combat duty, he was offered the option of a desk job, which he politely refused.

The war inspired an explosion of voluntarism, with soldiers augmented by masses of volunteers who raised funds for the war effort and assisted the internally displaced and homeless. Prodigious amounts of money were donated to purchase drones, body armor, armored personnel carriers, and even a satellite to aid in targeting the enemy. Other efforts organized foodstuffs for soldiers and volunteers near the front. A poll conducted in October 2022 by the Democratic Initiatives Foundation found that 30 percent of Ukrainians had financially supported voluntary efforts or volunteered their time to assist the war effort. Ukraine's Tocquevillian moment—massive engagement by wide swaths of society in volunteer efforts—had deep roots in civic engagement in both the Orange and the Maidan Revolutions. Volunteerism had roots, as well, in the thousands of civic initiatives that Ukrainians had launched over three decades to compensate for the weakness and incapacity of the state. In this instance, as before, Ukrainian citizens mobilized to make their country work when the government was overwhelmed.

Russian Territorial Gains

In the early weeks of the all-out war, Russian forces occupied parts of the Chernihiv and Kyiv regions in the north, and made inroads in Sumy and Kharkiv in the northeast. Most spectacularly, tens of thousands of Russian forces streamed into Kherson, Zaporizhya, and the southern Donbas regions. The motorized forces moved quickly and faced an ill-equipped and small conventional military augmented by recently mobilized fighters from the territorial defense. Ukrainian resistance quickly broke down, and Kherson, an important port city and regional center, fell on March 2. Russia also made rapid gains in the region and in neighboring Zaporizhya, occupying about a third of that region. We later would learn that Russia's spectacular gains in the south were assisted by traitors in the upper regions of Ukraine's state security service, leading to the dismissal of the head of the SBU, Ivan Bakanov, a close friend of President Zelensky who had been appointed despite no background in military affairs or intelligence.

The lack of resistance in the south allowed Russia to launch a pincer movement against Mariupol, located on the Azov Sea. Russian troops moved quickly from all directions against the port city, which had a population of 430,000. By March 2, Russian forces had effectively surrounded Mariupol and begun launching fierce artillery attacks against Ukrainian forces and targeting infrastructure, cultural, and civilian targets. On March 9 Russian missiles landed on a maternity and children's hospital, killing three. Shocking images of the devastation and of a pregnant woman covered with debris and soot made front-page news around the world. By March 14, with reports indicating that Russian attacks had already killed several thousand civilians, Russia permitted a humanitarian corridor allowing tens of thousands to flee. By early April it was believed that fewer than 150,000 residents remained in the city. On March 16 the Donetsk Regional Drama Theater—clearly demarcated as a place of civilian sheltering—was bombed, killing some three hundred. Pitched battles on the streets between Ukrainian and Russian forces continued as the civilian death toll rose. Aerial photos showed that most of the city had been destroyed or severely damaged. Additional fatalities were the consequence of Russia's destruction of the city's water and electricity infrastructure, which led to a major cholera outbreak.

Ukraine had defended the city with approximately twenty thousand troops, but Russia deployed far larger numbers in its attack. By April 18 Ukrainian forces had retreated to the massive Azovstal steel mill complex, built in Soviet times, with deep underground shelters that could house thousands in the event of attack. Soldiers were joined at Azovstal by thousands of frightened civilians. By May 7 most civilians—mainly women, children, and the elderly—were permitted to evacuate the complex. But the fighters defending Azovstal continued their heroic resistance, appearing each day on Ukrainian TV broadcasts, inspiring the nation by their courage. The fighters withstood Russian assault until May 20, when the last of the thousands of defenders surrendered.

Russia's destruction of the city of Mariupol. A city with a population of 430,000 was almost completely destroyed by Russian forces, resulting in its depopulation and the deaths of many thousands of civilians. (Author's screenshot of drone video footage [https://www.youtube.com/watch?v=BSE_vYo4CCM], taken in March 2022. The Azov Brigade, the National Guard of Ukraine, Ministry of Internal Affairs of Ukraine)

After Mariupol fell, open-source intelligence from satellite and drone photography offered growing evidence of Russian war crimes in the city, including summary executions, the alleged use of chemical weapons, wanton and deliberate bombing of civilian targets, and efforts to relocate civilian dead in mass graves outside the city in order to hide the death toll, which Ukrainian officials believed ranged into the tens of thousands. Although Mariupol fell, its resistance over three months had played a crucial role in the war. First, it demonstrated the courage of Ukrainian fighters and their will to resist. Second, the long siege had expended large amounts of Russian military assets and weapons, drawing forces from other battlefronts, where Russian advances slowed, keeping parts of Zaporizhya and Kherson free and stifling Russian advances elsewhere in Donetsk oblast.

By the early spring of 2022, Russian forces were either significantly present or controlled well over 20 percent of the internationally recognized territory of Ukraine. They had captured nearly twice as much territory as had been taken from Ukraine in the period 2014–15. Russian gains in the east, by contrast, were small and stymied by the impressive trench defenses Ukraine had put up near what was known as the line of contact with Russian and Donbas forces under Russian control, and where Ukraine had expected most fighting to occur. Only in the Luhansk region, into which Russia poured huge resources, did Russia succeed in capturing and holding most of the oblast.

The Tide Turns

Russian efforts to encircle Kyiv proved a complete failure. Ukrainian forces launched a major counteroffensive, quickly reclaiming a twenty-mile perimeter of formerly Russian-occupied territory around Kyiv. On March 29, 2022, defeated and exhausted, Russia's forces declared they were making a strategic retreat. By early April all of the Kyiv and Chernihiv oblasts were back under full Ukrainian control.

With Ukrainian forces holding their own and making gains in country's north and northeast, U.S. and European leaders slowly realized that Russia had badly miscalculated. At this point Ukraine belatedly began to receive major infusions of Western precision weapons, tanks, and armored personnel carriers. U.S. aid pivoted from a strategy of support for what officials thought would be an insurgency to one of full-scale combat. Ukraine's heroic resistance and Russia's massive war crimes fueled support for ever deeper economic sanctions against Russia.

Russia's establishment—its cultural, media, business, civic, and political elites—echoed the militaristic rhetoric of Vladimir Putin. Typical of this sentiment were the remarks of Mikhail Piotrovsky, director of St. Petersburg's Hermitage Museum, a powerful center of Russia's culture and its many European echoes, which were on display in a new exhibit of the works of Matisse, Gaugin, Van Gogh, Picasso, and Monet. However, there was no trace of democratic Europe's values to be found in Piotrovsky's interview with *Rossiyskaya Gazeta*. "We understand the historic mission of our country," he declared. "All of us are militarists and imperialists. . . . On the one hand, war is blood and death, on the other it is the self-affirmation of individuals—the self-affirmation of the nation."

Despite Ukrainian gains on the battlefield and despite unity within NATO and the democratic community, on June 9, 2022, Putin doubled down on his monomaniacal dreams. Comparing himself to Peter the Great, who expanded the Russian Empire, Putin used the backdrop of an exhibit entitled *Peter I and the Birth of an Empire* to declare: "It has become our lot to return [territories] and to secure [them]." The exhibit was emblematic of a long-standing propaganda campaign that Putin had launched to highlight imperial themes and imperial grandeur as a means of building domestic support for Russia's war against Ukraine.

In the spring and summer of 2022, amid Russia's relentless attacks on civilians and civilian targets, a wide array of weapons came Kyiv's way, as did weapons from the hardware surpluses of former Warsaw Pact countries that were now part of NATO. In June 2022 Ukraine received its first allotment from the United States of game-changing HIMARS, multiple-launch rocket systems that shoot six two-hundred-pound rockets with deadly accuracy over a distance of some fifty miles. By the fall of 2022, Ukraine was deploying twenty of these systems as well as six M270 rocket systems that fire twelve surface-to-surface precision-guided missiles per minute. In early 2023 Ukraine received sophisticated air-defense systems, including the U.S. Patriot system. Powerful artillery pieces were supplied by the United Kingdom and Poland. Britain also gave Ukraine long-range Storm Shadow missiles. Hundreds of tanks and armored personnel carriers of Western manufacture too began to come Ukraine's way.

While the number of weapons they provided was relatively small, the most assistance to Ukraine per capita came from the Baltic states. What was crucial was not just the quality and accuracy of these new weapons and munitions but their scale. In all, according to a tracking project of the Kiel Institute for the World Economy, well over $150 billion in financial, humanitarian, and military aid was given or committed to Ukraine in the first twelve months of the war, with military assistance accounting for well over $60 billion. By the fall of 2023, the total assistance and commitments of support to Ukraine's self-defense and state budget had climbed to nearly $250 billion.

Western weapons, many of them more mobile and precise than their Russian counterparts, began to change the situation on the ground in the late summer of 2022. As important, these missiles, rockets, ammunition, and other ordnance came just as Ukraine started depleting its Soviet-era weapons and ammunition.

On October 29, 2022, the *New York Times* reported that Ukraine now had artillery superiority over Russian forces. This superiority initially helped to stymie rapid Russian advances. In September it facilitated major Ukrainian gains in a counteroffensive that reclaimed large swaths of the Kharkiv region. In a matter of a few weeks, Ukrainian forces had reclaimed around twenty-five hundred square miles of territory, an area larger than the state of Delaware, as beleaguered Russian forces retreated eastward across their border. The recapture of Russian-held territories in Kharkiv oblast made possible a push by Ukrainian forces east and south, recapturing small areas of Luhansk—a region that President Putin had declared was under Russia's complete control. The momentum shift on the battlefield was also seen in northern Donetsk oblast, as Ukraine recaptured the cities of Siversk and Svyatohirsk while successfully holding off for over half a year major assaults by the private Wagner Group and Russian special forces on the city of Bakhmut, whose siege would continue into the summer of 2023, with Russia taking the razed and depopulated city, but with Ukrainian forces continuing to operate on its periphery. U.S. estimates placed the number of Russian combat dead at twenty thousand from January to May 2023; the Ukrainian military estimated a like number of dead and wounded in the final months of 2022. Ukrainian losses were high, but several times more Russians had died in combat than Ukrainian fighters.

While the impact of Western weapons on the field of battle was a game changer, it would not have been so without Ukrainian-produced armaments and ammunition. The flow of Western weapons was not on the scale that it could supplant and replace the majority of tanks, armored personnel carriers, artillery pieces, missiles, and ammunition that Ukraine's nearly 1 million mobilized forces needed. While the Kremlin had claimed in the early stages of the war to have taken out Ukraine's extensive military industrial capacity, the reality was quite different. Russian attacks disrupted but did not destroy Ukraine's capability to refurbish, renovate, and produce weapons. Most industrial plants that were hit were only partially damaged and accompanied by a surprisingly modest loss of life, according to a source close to the Ukrainian defense establishment. By the beginning of 2023, Ukrainian officials reported that most Ukrainian production had been revived and was operating far closer to its prewar pace, contrary to the insignificant output that Russian propaganda claimed. The combined use of Ukrainian and Western weapons deployed intelligently under a skilled command were the true reason for Ukraine's combat success.

Ukraine's military ingenuity manifested itself in several attacks on Russia's Black Sea Fleet and on Russian military targets in occupied Crimea, sometimes to spectacular effect. On April 13, 2022, a Ukrainian missile assisted by drone technology hit and eventually sank Russia's flagship in the Black Sea, the *Moskva,* a guided missiles cruiser that was intended to provide anti-missile cover for the rest of the Russian fleet. As a result, Russia's naval forces were redeployed to areas distant from Ukraine, making them less capable of launching missiles at Ukrainian land targets. As the war progressed, Ukraine would impose major losses on Russian sea power in the Black Sea.

On August 9, Ukrainians again succeeded in an attack on a Crimean air base, taking out as many as nine Russian bombers and attack aircraft, most likely by domestic long-range missiles.

On October 8, 2022, at around 6:00 a.m., a period of light traffic, the land bridge between Russia's Kerch region and occupied Crimea was severely damaged in a truck explosion in the proximity of seven fuel cars on an adjacent train. The precision explosion on a prominent Putin infrastructure project took two of the lanes on the bridge's highway out of commission and did severe damage to the rail tracks. As a result, the bridge—a crucial means for the shipment of weapons through Crimea to the Ukrainian front—would be under repair until July 2023.

From April 2002 forward, Ukraine began making territorial gains as Russian forces retreated or surrendered. In total, Ukraine recaptured some twenty-five hundred square miles of territory from Russia, primarily in the Kharkiv, Kyiv, Donetsk, and Kherson regions. Significantly, nine months into the invasion, major Ukrainian gains in Kharkiv, in right-bank Kherson, and in parts of Donetsk encouraged Ukraine's Western donors to double down on supporting the

Residents of Kherson greet Ukrainian soldiers on November 11, 2022, after Russian troops were forced to withdraw. (Anton Tatochenko)

country's bid to reclaim occupied territories. After launching its war in February, Russia had wrested control of only one regional capital, Kherson, with a population of nearly three hundred thousand. By November, fearing a rout, Russia announced its withdrawal from Kherson to west of the Dnipro River. Sergei Markov, a political analyst close to the Kremlin, decried this retreat as "the greatest geopolitical setback for Russia since the collapse of the Soviet Union."

Although Russia faced significant challenges on the field of combat, it was learning from Ukrainians how to fight a modern war. In 2023, Russia began to deploy far higher quantities of drones for surveillance and combat. Its electronic warfare systems proved partly effective in disabling Ukraine's drones and Western-made missiles. It also had built a complex, multi-layered system of defenses designed to repel ground attacks on its positions. Most significantly, it was generating massive devastation against civilian targets. As the war went on, Russia's maximalist aims became explicit. Putin's attack had started the first interstate war in modern times where the stakes for the country under attack were its very survival as a state. Russia's attacks on Ukraine's civilians and Russian conduct in areas under occupation conformed to the UN's definition of genocide. In the twentieth and twenty-first centuries, major wars and conflicts often threatened the sovereignty of states as well as the survival of stateless peoples and national minorities. But this war was unprecedented in putting both at risk.

Solidarity and National Consolidation

This dual existential threat explained the vehemence of Ukraine's nationwide resistance, and was a key reason for the massive outpouring of national solidarity that united Ukraine's prosperous and poor, professionals and workers, civil society and oligarchs, and Orthodox Christians, Catholics, evangelicals, Jews, and Muslims—all factors contributing to Ukraine's battlefield successes.

Over the thirty years of Ukraine's modern-day existence, ethnic Ukrainians and national minorities gradually had overcome linguistic and cultural divisions, shaping a powerful civic patriotism that united those who identify as ethnic Ukrainians with those who identify as Ukrainian through civic pride in their imperfect but democratic, free, and tolerant polity. A survey undertaken by a respected Ukrainian polling group in March 2017 had found that some 92 percent of the inhabitants of Ukraine identified as ethnically Ukrainian, up from 79 percent in 2001. Only 6 percent of Ukrainians still described themselves as ethnic Russians.

This diverse yet inclusive sense of Ukrainian identity was personified in President Volodymyr Zelensky, a Jew who grew up in a Russian-speaking community, but whose powerful wartime leadership rests on his uncanny understanding of how to bring together the many currents that make up the modern Ukrainian nation. Before the war, Zelensky's message of national unity was confused and contradictory. He made an unconvincing case for the many cultures and traditions present in Ukraine—whether ethnic Ukrainian, Russian, or even Soviet—to pull together with the aim of building a better life. His appeal for unity ignored Ukraine's traditions of freedom and democratic, contested politics. Lacking in his prewar rhetoric was any sense of deep patriotism. But the war consolidated Ukrainians around their ethno-political core, and Zelensky, with his keen sense of the public mood, embraced powerful narratives: of freedom, of a distinct Ukrainian culture, and of a manifest Ukrainian path. In doing so, Zelensky was transformed from what may had believed was an accidental president into an essential leader, one who not only embodied the desire for freedom in his people but reanimated that noble purpose within the wider community of the world's democracies.

Russia's conduct of its war and occupation made clear that, rhetoric notwithstanding, the Kremlin clearly understood the powerful patriotic political and cultural dynamic within the perception of the Ukrainian people and its capacity to stifle Russian aims. As a rule, conquering forces and powers seek to win hearts and minds, allay public fears, and offer the promise of security and stability. As a means of calming and reassuring local populations, occupiers typically look for collaborators who can give a local face to the new regime and try to win over the vanquished. In the territories of Ukraine captured since February, Russia departed from such tactics. Instead of building a cadre of cooperative local leaders, or even using quislings from the rump Donbas republics and Crimea, top Putin aide and former prime minister Sergei Kiriyenko was appointed the *gauleiter* of a team of Russian administrators recruited to run local governments and implement a policy that combined acts of genocide, terror, repression, filtration camps, torture during interrogations, the uprooting of local traditions, forced deportation to Russia of Ukrainians, especially children, and the supplanting of Ukrainian culture, language, and education with Russian versions.

War Crimes and Genocide

Russian tactics aimed to reeducate Ukrainians in order to rob them of their ethnic identity. This meant far more than the emplacement of Russian texts and curricula in place of Ukrainian. A U.S. State Department report in July 2022 indicated that around 260,000 Ukrainian children had been separated from their parents, uprooted from their communities, and forcibly deported to Russia as part of the process of "de-Ukrainization." In all, by the fall of 2022, as many as 1.6 million Ukrainians under Russian occupation, some of them children orphaned by Russia itself, were forcibly removed to Russia in violation of international law, triggering arrest warrants from the International Criminal Court against President Putin and Russia's

Russian war crimes: bodies are exhumed from a mass grave in the Kyiv suburb of Bucha on April 13, 2022. (Oleksandr Synytsia / UNIAN)

children's rights commissioner. Huge numbers of civilians were subjected to filtration camps, detentions, and interrogations as part of this process.

Another Russian tactic was the deliberate depopulation of Ukraine through bombings of civilian targets and essential infrastructure. Given the strong sense of national identity that developed and given Ukrainian resistance to external rule, Russia pursued military policies intended to drive Ukrainians from their country. By September 2022, according to the UN, Russia's aggression had internally displaced over 8.7 million people, most of them in Central and Western Ukraine. In addition, the UN estimated that the number of externally displaced stood at 6.3 million, of whom 2.5 million are children—some 40 percent of the population.

Depopulation was augmented by the intentional extermination of thousands of Ukrainians by occupying forces, as in Bucha and Irpin, and the murder of tens of thousands more through indiscriminate attacks on apartment buildings, shopping malls, schools, and theaters. Included in these numbers was the toll from the near-total destruction of Mariupol, a city formerly populated by nearly half a million people that became a ghost town inhabited by as few as one hundred thousand. Estimates of the death toll in Mariupol ranged from thirty-five thousand to one hundred thousand, though the real numbers still remain hidden as Russian forces prevented international rights monitors from accessing the city.

In the aftermath of Stalin's and Hitler's regimes, legal scholar Raphael Lemkin coined the term *genocide* in 1941 and was a driving force behind the adoption of the UN Convention on Genocide. Lemkin, a native of Lviv, now a city in Western Ukraine, observed that "genocide does not necessarily mean the immediate destruction of a nation . . . it is intended as a coordinated plan of different actions aiming at the destruction of essential foundations of the lives of national groups." Russia's actions clearly fit Lemkin's definition. Even by the narrower definition in the UN Convention on Genocide, Russian behavior met the criteria of genocide as its attacks deliberately inflicted "on members of the group conditions of life calculated to bring about its physical destruction in whole or in part."

The elimination of the Ukrainian nation and its identity through the destruction of the nation's political, civic, and cultural infrastructure was accompanied by the explicit suppression of its language, history, and educational system and the illegal deportation of Ukrainian children to Russia. All these actions were justified to a Russian domestic audience by the widespread dissemination of propaganda related to ethnic hatred. Russian state and state-controlled television became a direct copy of Radio Mille Collines in Rwanda, spewing a steady diet of hate speech that depicted the idea of a distinct Ukrainian identity and an independent state as a criminal form of ultranationalism and dehumanized Ukrainians, calling them "worms."

Putin had long falsely argued that inasmuch as there was no separate Ukrainian nation, its separation from Russia was artificial. Putin also claimed that there was no authentic historical or ethnopolitical basis for Ukrainian statehood. To make this claim a self-fulfilling prophecy, Russia's war targeted a vast array of cultural targets for destruction. An October 27, 2022, report by Freedom House, the rights-monitoring organization I headed for over a decade, found that by the end of July 2022, "UNESCO had verified damage to 168 cultural sites . . . [including] 73 religious sites, 13 museums, 33 historic buildings, 24 buildings devoted to cultural activities, 17 monuments, and 8 libraries." Freedom House analyst Emily Crouch noted that in addition, there were numerous cases of "Russian forces looting and razing museums to the ground. "In one notable case, Russian forces burned down a museum housing many paintings of Ukraine's renowned—indeed, legendary—naïve artist Maria Pryymachenko. Her granddaughter observed that in the town of Ivankiv, "the museum was the first building . . . the Russians destroyed . . . because they want to destroy our Ukrainian culture."

To convince Russians of the necessity for the destruction of Ukrainian culture, identity, and statehood, Putin and Kremlin propagandists claimed Ukraine was an artificial construction created and groomed as to be "anti-Russia," a long-standing political project of the West designed to threaten Russia's security. Given Russia's vast advantages in military power, nuclear weapons, population, natural resources, and GDP, as well as the fact that Ukraine had never engaged Russian forces outside Ukrainian soil, the idea that Ukraine was a looming threat to Russia was patently absurd. Putin's aim of "denazification" was not focused on the preposterous claim that the Ukrainian state was run by fascists. Russia propagandists instead referred to Ukrainians not as Nazis (Natsisti), but as Natsiki (little Nazis). "Natsiki" was intended as a synonym for nationalists, not Nazis. And nationalism, in turn, became a synonym for seeking to protect a distinct Ukrainian national identity within a Ukrainian state.

This created an existential threat to most of the inhabitants of Ukraine. Thirty years of state independence had resulted in a fundamental cultural and artistic awakening in the country. Thousands of novels, histories, biographies, films, plays, and artworks were produced premised on the idea of Ukrainian statehood and linguistic and ethnic distinctiveness. Putin's aims necessarily meant the near-complete destruction of this vast literary, cultural, and artistic inheritance on a scale not attempted since the Second World War. Life for Ukrainians under occupation offered a glimpse of how all of Ukraine would look were Putin to prevail. Russian victory would mean a devastated and depopulated country whose remaining inhabitants would live under a totalitarian regime of political terror, total media censorship, and tight ideological control aimed at extinguishing the virulent ideology that was Ukrainian identity.

Stateless peoples, like the Uighurs in China and the Kurds in Turkey, have long been subjected to pressures by states to limit or constrain their national identity and will to statehood. These brutal campaigns of repression have been accompanied by significant repression, censorship, reeducation, and indoctrination. But stateless peoples, who preserve their cultures through private and voluntary institutions, are less well resourced than a culture and an identity that have the support of a nation-state. This makes the suppression of the cultures of stateless peoples a simpler matter. By contrast, the cultural and ideological war that Putin unleashed against the generations of Ukrainians who had lived under independence represents a totalitarian undertaking without precedent. For millions of Ukrainians, Russian rule will create the stark choice of cleansing themselves of their ethnicity or being ethnically cleansed.

But Putin's grandiose plan for the destruction of the Ukrainian state and nation did not go according to plan. By the fall of 2023, Russian combat fatalities were estimated by the Ukrainian military as approaching three hundred thousand dead and multiple more severely wounded. Western estimates, though approximately half those of Ukraine's, placed the Russian death count in the neighborhood of one hundred thousand.

Ukraine's forces too had taken significant, though unreported, losses. Ukraine also had destroyed, degraded, or captured massive numbers of Russian weapons, including nearly 50 percent of Russia's entire tank arsenal. As Russia was taking heavy losses, Putin sought to change the subject. Failing to win control over Ukrainian territory on the battlefield, in September 2022, he would pretend he was winning simply by declaring the annexation of Ukrainian lands.

Russia did not fully control all of Luhansk, nor hold sway over wide swaths of Donetsk, not to speak of its weaker footholds in the Kherson and Zaporizhya regions. Yet the military occupation facilitated rushed wartime "referenda" on joining Russia in these four regions in late September. The referenda were far from the expression of the popular will. They took place under a wartime occupation, in conditions of martial law, and under wartime censorship. The vote could not have been the expression of the popular will inasmuch as the majority of the original population was now displaced to other parts of Ukraine or Europe, or forcibly relocated to Russia.

Indeed, much of the population of these very regions had settled in areas under Ukrainian rule. The vote also occurred amid extensive coercion and very likely massive vote fraud. The referenda were not only nonsense, they were criminal, constituting a clear violation of the rules of war. Within days of the exercise, on September 30, Putin rushed the integration of the four Ukrainian regions into Russia in a grandiose Kremlin signing ceremony accompanied by public celebrations and nonstop media coverage.

Targeting Housing and Infrastructure

Putin also pivoted on the conduct of the war. On October 1, 2022, General Sergei Surovikin was named the commander of Russia's war effort. Surovikin, who would be removed as head of Russia's Aerospace Forces for alleged support of an insurgency by the Wagner Group, had led Russia's military campaign in Syria, in which artillery and airpower devastated civilian housing, causing masses of refugees. Under its new commander, Russia began a massive campaign of missile and combat drone attacks on Ukraine's electricity and power generation infrastructure. Most major power plants and substations were damaged, and nationwide some 40 percent of Ukraine's energy system was knocked out, with Kyiv and most large municipalities left without electricity as necessary blackouts often lasted the majority of the day. Amid the attacks on Ukraine's infrastructure, President Zelensky accused Russia of "energy terrorism," as long-term energy blackouts would also disable water supplies, heating in winter, and the disposal of sewage, leading to massive loss of civilian lives.

In the first weeks of October, the ever more frequent Russian attacks on infrastructure had little effect on Ukrainian morale. Citizens stood defiantly and coped with the hardships that winter weather and interruptions in electricity presented. Restaurants remained open by candlelight, serving wine and snacks. Mayors introduced heating stations for people to warm up while traversing the city. In Kyiv, hit hard by rolling blackouts, people gathered around the city's numerous *buvets*, public fresh-water wells located in many neighborhoods. Going out to dine or taking a stroll in the darkened streets became acts of solidarity and defiance against Putin's Russia.

In the fall and winter, after Ukraine's major advances in the Kharkiv and Kherson regions, the war moved into a static, grinding phase of slow advances and bitter positional battles centered on a few key cities and towns in the Donetsk region. Ukraine also made a few probing attacks in Southern Ukraine. The conflict had devolved from a twenty-first-century war to the kind of trench warfare seen in World War I.

Though Russian media reported that President Putin had set a deadline of March 2023 for the capture of the entirety of the Donetsk and Luhansk oblasts, Russian advances over a six-month period amounted to a few tens of kilometers in small patches along the line of contact and the occupation of several smaller towns and cities, most of them depopulated and destroyed by Russian bombing and artillery. The failure of General Surovikin's campaign of civilian destruction to break the will of Ukraine's population and the failure of Russia to make territorial gains in the Donbas led to his dismissal as head of the war effort in January 2023, with General Valery Gerasimov, the chief of the General Staff of the Army, taking over command of the military operations. Gerasimov's was the fourth appointment in eleven months to head the Russian invasion forces.

The pitched battle over the city of Bakhmut became emblematic of the difficulties facing Russia's offensive. In August 2022 Russian forces began a ferocious uninterrupted assault on Bakhmut, which before Russia's war had over seventy-five thousand inhabitants. According to Western and Ukrainian sources Russia sent wave upon wave of fighters in a daily effort to first encircle and later seize the city. In half a year the only significant Russian gain in the part of the Western Donbas where fighting was the most intense was the town of Soledar. A salt-mining center with a population of ten thousand, Soledar fell in January 2023 after five months of intense fighting, including several months of street battles.

Russian forces conducting these attacks were predominantly composed of fighters from the Wagner private army, which largely consisted of felons released from imprisonment backed up by regular Russian forces. The intensity of shelling and ground attacks by Russian forces obliterated the city's basic services and infrastructure as well as most of the housing stock. March came and went and Russia had failed to capture Bakhmut, where four thousand of the city's civilian inhabitants remained. It was only in early April 2023 that Wagner Group fighters entered into the bombed-out residential governmental and commercial areas, raising a Russian flag over the rubble of the municipal government building. By early May Ukrainian forces held the fringes in the western part of the city, with much of the areas they had abandoned reduced to rubble. Ukrainian officials denied the loss of the city as intense fighting continued at a huge cost to Russian fighters, which Ukrainian sources claimed ran as high as two hundred fatalities per day. But as the Institute for the Study of War pointed out on May 20, 2023, because most of Bakhmut had been reduced to rubble, it no longer held any strategic or tactical importance. Indeed, with Ukrainian forces making gains in outflanking the city, Russian forces there were in a highly vulnerable position. In short, Russia had made very meager gains in Bakhmut, but the costs of those gains had sapped Russian strength, helping to stall the broader offensive that Putin had promised.

On September 1, 2022, Oleksiy Hromov, the deputy head of the Main Operational Directorate of Russia's General Staff had announced that Russia aimed to take control of all of the Donetsk and Luhansk regions. However, the broader Russian offensive to retake Ukrainian-controlled Donbas followed the pattern in Bakhmut: huge losses in fighters and weaponry in return for minor territorial advances. Months later, in April 2023, the British Ministry of Defense concluded that General Valery Gerasimov had failed to extend Russian control over the Donbas after he assumed the post of the theater commander of the invasion of Ukraine in January 2023. Most Western and Ukrainian analyses indicated that Russian gains in the much-vaunted campaign were modest. The invasion had turned into a quagmire, and by May 2023 most Western experts expected Ukraine to launch a significant counteroffensive.

Before Russia's invasion, Zelensky's support had dropped dramatically from its high point in 2019 amid public criticisms about his unmet promises, which eroded confidence in him. For a public figure who had basked in approval all his creative and political life, this was a bitter pill. In the months leading up to February 2022, his tone had become combative and he bristled at critics from civil society and the media. This grating image as a streetwise tough guy was losing its luster. Still, even with an increasingly fractious parliamentary majority, Ukraine's government remained fully under the control of the president and his increasingly influential chief of staff, Andriy Yermak. This unchecked political power reinforced Zelensky's decisiveness as well as his desire for quick results.

These leadership traits, so out of sync with Ukrainian public opinion in peacetime, were ideally suited to the new circumstances. Zelensky also benefited from a live performer's keen rapport with his audience, making him acutely sensitive to public needs and expectations. Plainspoken, tough, courageous, and decisive—Zelensky was the ideal leader for a country at war: a tough and determined everyman, embodying and energized by the civic and martial heroism that was deepening the consolidation of his nation.

Zelensky, the Wartime Leader

Amid the remarkable courage of Ukraine's military and the country's ordinary people, Zelensky had emerged as a compelling moral leader of the democratic West, a leader defending democratic values, the primacy of international law, and respect for the rules of war. Virtually every day of the war, via the internet, Zelensky addressed international fora from his redoubt in the presidential complex on Bankova Street, making the case for Ukraine to the UN, to NATO, to the European Union and European Parliament, to the U.S. Congress and many of the world's parliaments. He tirelessly addressed university audiences, made an appearance at the Grammys, spoke at symphony halls and at mass demonstrations, and met with a growing stream of world leaders, writers, artists, intellectuals, and movie stars who ventured to Kyiv in a wave of solidarity. He also regularly made well-timed and cogent appearances on the world's major news networks and in key newspapers. In each appearance he appealed for specific actions, for specific forms of aid, and above all for specific weapons to aid Ukraine's war effort.

What Zelensky accomplished at the top, Ukrainian officials, parliamentarians, writers, musicians, and cultural figures echoed and deepened in their many visits to divergent outposts of the democratic and developing world and on global media. The flood of Ukrainian refugees who streamed into Europe and the United States were articulate spokespersons for the nation, and their tales of suffering

As the Russians attacked, President Volodymyr Zelensky emerged as a confident and inspiring wartime leader. Here he visits the Kharkiv region on September 14, 2022, after it had been liberated from Russian forces. (president.gov.ua, CC BY-NC-ND 4.0)

and resistance built growing sympathy for Ukraine and revulsion for Russia's brutality. Zelensky's own keen sense of the public mood together with his entourage of sophisticated media managers and speechwriters touched hearts and minds at home and abroad. As a result of effective communications, in 2022–23 Ukraine became the country with the greatest soft power in the world.

As the president faced wartime challenge upon challenge, changes occurred in his inner circle as he removed longtime friends and business partners with little political competence. His coterie of former entertainment and business partners, including the Shefir brothers, was shed under the pressure of the war. He also concluded that the head of the Ukrainian security service, his longtime associate and friend Ivan Bakanov, was not up to the task amid revelations that several of the top security officials he appointed were Russian agents. These developments enhanced the influence of his chief of staff Andriy Yermak, who enjoyed Zelensky's complete trust and raised the profile of Yuri Podolyak, a media strategist. Yermak, an entertainment lawyer and film producer by background, emerged as the second most influential person in Ukraine. He had achieved this status not by pushing his own ideas, but by serving as Zelensky's alter ego, virtually inseparable from the president, totally loyal to his instructions and objectives, and highly effective in finding the means to implement them.

Zelensky's Team

In the early stages of the war, Zelensky also came to rely on the work of four highly capable appointees who proved effective and visionary leaders and spokesmen. The cohort consisted of Foreign Minister Dmytro Kuleba, Digital Transformation Minister Mykhaylo Fedorov, Defense Minister Oleksiy Reznikov, and—most important—the chief of staff of the Ukrainian Armed Forces, General Valeriy Zaluzhny.

Kuleba, age forty when the war began, was a scion of the diplomatic service and a veteran of the Maidan protests. He had served as Foreign Ministry spokesman, ambassador to the Council of Europe, and deputy prime minister for European integration before he became foreign minister in March 2020. A media-savvy diplomat known for his well-prepared and brainy presentations, his personal charm was on display for American television viewers on the *Late Show with Stephen Colbert* in September 2022. Under his leadership, a roster of effective ambassadors, many from outside the foreign service, enhanced wartime Ukraine's public outreach. Among the most effective of these were Oksana Markarova, a former finance minister posted in Washington; Yulia Kovaliv, Zelensky's economic advisor posted in Ottawa; Serhiy Kyslytsya, former deputy foreign minister who established a reputation as an acerbic and witty polemicist at the United Nations; and Andriy Melnyk, who lacerated Germany's Russia illusions in assertive media appearances before returning to Kyiv as deputy foreign minister and later moving on as ambassador to Brazil.

No less important was Defense Minister Oleksiy Reznikov, who entered politics after a career as a partner in Ukraine's largest law firm, where he headed its negotiation and mediation practice. These skills prepared him for service as deputy head of Ukraine's delegation to the Trilateral Contact Group where, together with Russian and

OSCE representatives, he aimed to negotiate the implementation of the Minsk agreements. Following service as deputy prime minister and minister for the temporarily occupied territories, he became defense minister in November 2021, as tensions with Russia were rising. After the full-scale Russian aggression began, Reznikov was Ukraine's key contact with NATO and in Ukraine's bilateral defense relations with allies. He established rapport with U.S. secretary of defense Lloyd Austin and UK defense minister Ben Wallace, and was an effective advocate of Ukraine at meetings of the Ramstein process, in which some fifty nations gathered regularly to coordinate large-scale military assistance. As important as Reznikov was to the launching of the war effort, and to the hunt for weapons, ammunition, and financial support in the early stages of the war, his lack of administrative experience would prove his undoing. In the rush to equip and support the armed forces, he neglected—or had little time for—the construction of tight control systems over the vast array of weapons and resources Ukraine's war was consuming. A couple minor scandals erupted in the spring and summer of 2023, the first over overpriced eggs for the armed forces, and the second over winter jackets for frontline troops. While each of these represented a miniscule portion of the wartime budget, growing public intolerance at even a hint of government waste or corruption led to his dismissal in September 2023.

Another crucial cog in the Zelensky team was the digital modernization minister, Mykhaylo Fedorov, age thirty-one as the war began. Fedorov contributed to state resilience by putting most government data online and onto people's apps. The digitalization of COVID certification, registration of foreign residents, financial aid, unemployment insurance, pension applications, tax filings, and a digital passport—the world's first—all made it easier to obtain government services and resources at a time of missile attacks and air raids. At the center of this effort was the Diya ("Action" in Ukrainian) app, which was supplemented by information centers, digital literacy programs, and an IT hub. By transferring government registrations, services, and identity documents to mobile phones, Fedorov precluded chaos in a disruptive wartime environment. As the wartime mayhem expanded, Diya deftly adapted, establishing a system to record and document damage to personal property and creating a mechanism for digitally transferring small grants to over 5 million Ukrainians in need. The Diya system, Fedorov, and his connections among IT entrepreneurs contributed to wide-ranging crowd-funding initiatives that supported the "Army of Drones." Astonishingly, private funding provided around 90 percent of all drones used by the armed forces in the first year and a half of the war. His ministry also engaged in linking the private IT sector and government security agencies in efforts to fend off Russian cyberattacks and launch their own counterattacks on Russian state targets. In the early days of the war, Fedorov appealed to Elon Musk to donate his Starlink stations, enabling Ukraine to maintain internet services through the satellite-based system in places where wireless networks were not operating. Eventually thirty thousand such stations were disbursed in Ukraine, many in zones of intense combat, enabling ordinary Ukrainians to connect to essential information.

Most important in this cohort of leaders was Valeriy Zaluzhny, appointed in July 2021 as commander in chief of the armed forces at age forty-eight. Zaluzhny's promotion reflected his competent and innovative leadership on the Donbas front. According to Aleksandra Klitina of the *Kyiv Post:* "Ukrainian officers describe Zaluzhny as a very open general who understands the problems that can beset soldiers and junior officers and as someone who does not allow a pattern of shiny stars on uniforms to create a sense of arrogance."

While he expected military discipline, Zaluzhny was invested in developing a culture of decentralized responsibility down to the grassroots. This military approach mirrored modern Ukraine's ethos of civic engagement and initiative. By the summer of 2022, he earned plaudits for overseeing what Western military experts deemed a surprisingly effective military and a tactically and strategically brilliant military campaign against Russian forces.

In 2019–20 Zelensky's first defense minister, Andriy Zahorodnyuk, had accelerated reform of Ukraine's formerly hidebound military with the support of officers who had experienced combat in the Donbas. The pressure for reforms had begun in 2014, when commanders were underresourced and began establishing their own direct links with civil society and Ukraine's high-tech sector.

The weakening of the military during the Yanukovych presidency accelerated the process of change. The military had to be built up

Defense Minister Oleksiy Reznikov (*left*) and Commander in Chief of Ukraine's Armed Forces Valeriy Zaluzhny. (Courtesy of the Ministry of Defense of Ukraine / ArmyInform)

from below, and the officers who most rapidly advanced along the ranks were younger veterans of brutal combat in the Donbas, inclined to jettison ineffective Soviet-era military tactics.

In 2014 the chief of the operational staff of the Ukrainian Armed Forces, General Viktor Nazarov, became the subject of a criminal investigation by the Prosecutor General's Office for "negligence" that led to the shooting down of a military transport plane by Russian forces, resulting in the death of forty-nine soldiers and airmen. In March 2017 Nazarov was found guilty of responsibility for the soldiers' deaths. While he had coordinated the entire counterterrorism operation for the armed forces, Nazarov could not possibly have had full awareness of the dangers presented in the flight. In May 2021 he was exonerated by a Supreme Court decision. Ironically, because the case made commanding officers responsible for decisions made down the chain of command, it spurred even Sovietized senior officers to buy into decentralized decision-making, not only as an innovative reform but as a way of avoiding the fate of Nazarov.

At the same time, the military also looked to NATO for answers to its poor performance in 2014–15. Here again, decentralized decision-making and on-the-ground responsibility began to enter into standard military practice. General Zaluzhny earned plaudits for being one of the senior officers who embraced this modern means of warfare, which contrasted markedly to the conventional approach of the Russian and Soviet militaries. Commanders' burgeoning connections at the grassroots with Ukraine's high-tech community also spurred the creation of decentralized systems with locally adapted software that gave Ukraine a net-based system of communication.

After he became commander in chief, Zaluzhny emphasized his reformist inclinations. "The overall course of reforming the armed forces in line with NATO principles and standards remains irreversible. And here the key is the principle: change must take place in the worldview and attitude toward human beings," he told his officer corps. "I would like you to turn your face to the people, to your subordinates." In other words, he was preaching a chain of command based on mutual respect as much as on discipline. This approach allowed lower-ranked, noncommissioned officers and rank-and-file soldiers to develop a strong esprit de corps while empowering small military units to take decentralized battlefield decisions. Such flexibility would prove a crucial advantage in countering Russian forces.

Politico reported on April 8, 2022, that Zaluzhny was part of a group of officers who had both fought in the Donbas after 2014 and trained with NATO. These experiences and the new culture fostered by the Ministry of Defense gradually replaced the Soviet-style authoritarianism that had prevailed in the Ukrainian military. As the *Politico* report noted: "Collaboration with NATO has molded a group

Ukraine's armed forces at war: a 2S7 Pion self-propelled cannon, operated by the Forty-Third Hetman Taras Triasylo Heavy Artillery Brigade of the Armed Forces of Ukraine, fires toward Russian positions on the administrative boundaries of the Donetsk and Kharkiv oblasts on August 27, 2022. (Ihor Tkachov)

of professional-minded officers that aspired to Western standards and helped build a decentralized, empowered, more agile way of warfare than the Russian model, which had floundered in the Ukrainian mud."

Zaluzhny's tactics also allowed for elements of the modern military theory of swarming—that is, the effective mobilization of decentralized smaller military units that at times coalesce to carry out larger tactical operations but often are free to improvise under the leadership at the troop level. This style of warfare allowed for the effective use of Ukraine's limited military resources and ammunition. And it was facilitated by the tech-savvy nature of Ukraine's fighting forces.

In the months before Russia's aggression, amid skepticism by President Zelensky that a multi-front invasion was likely, Zaluzhny quietly took steps in deploying forces to hedge against an all-out war. After it began in February 2022, Zaluzhny demonstrated strong management skills in supervising the complex task of integrating a wide array of new Western weapons systems introduced to replace destroyed or captured Ukrainian weapons, as well as the transition to Western ordnance to replace the dwindling arsenal of Soviet-standard ammunition and missiles. Not only was Ukraine making this transition in the middle of a war, the country's armed forces faced the challenge of mastering and maintaining a dizzying array of weapons that arrived from the Poles, Czechs, Germans, French, and Americans. Each required specific training to operate, maintain, and repair. The introduction of this varied assortment of weapons needed sophisticated coordination and rapid integration within Ukraine's armed forces. That Ukraine coped with this challenge while fending off a multi-front invasion was a tribute to the open environment and intelligent systems Zaluzhny established.

Central to Zaluzhny's success as commander was his relationship with President Zelensky. Aware that Zelensky sought to preempt political rivals, Zaluzhny consistently signaled that he was a military man without political ambition. In the war's first year, Zaluzhny rarely granted media interviews, leaving to press officers the task of explaining military operations. When interviewed, he remained opaque about Ukrainian strategy and specific military operations, all the while exuding a charming informality and frankness.

By contrast, Russia's armed forces operated in a hyper-centralized manner inherited from the Soviet era, a system that relied on top-down approval for actions on the battlefield. A dispatch from Ukraine in March 2022 quoted Andriy Zahorodnyuk on Russia's doctrine: "The Russians don't empower their soldiers. . . . They tell their soldiers to go from Point A to Point B and only when they get to Point B will they be told where to go next, and junior soldiers are rarely told the reason they are performing any task." The former defense minister observed that this approach works well when things go according to plan, but when circumstances change, the "centralized method collapses." This proved a major factor in Ukraine's ability to outperform a better-armed military force.

In the first year of the war, according to Western intelligence estimates, Russia had lost twenty general officers and scores of high-ranking colonels. The stunningly large number of high-ranked officers who died in combat means they were deployed near the battlefield, necessary if they were to issue most of the commands in Russia's highly centralized command system.

Ukraine's battlefield successes were also rooted in the flexible use of a variety of military and private sector technologies and assets. An April 2023 study by T. X. Hammes for the Atlantic Council concluded that Ukraine had outperformed and out-innovated Russia in a number of spheres. Russian cyber-warfare had proved largely impotent against Ukrainian defenses, which were far stronger than Russian attacks.

Hammes pointed to several "game-changers" that significantly augmented Ukraine's twentieth-century weaponry and contributed to military successes. These included the integration of domestic civilian systems into the military's command and control, and Ukraine's quick recovery from Russia's disruption of communications through the deployment of tens of thousands of Starlink terminals connected to more than three thousand Starlink satellites in orbit. This technology provided "small tactical units . . . bandwidth previously reserved for major commands."

Rapid coding by private and state programmers enabled Ukraine to link its digital government portal Diya for use by civilians as well as the military. A government chatbot received hundreds of thousands of reports from Ukrainians on Russian military movements, landmine placements, and collaborators. A new Delta system provided "comprehensive understanding of the battle space in real time, which can be accessed on laptops, tablets and mobile phones." Delta was an outgrowth of nearly a decade of grassroots cooperation between the military and civilian programmers and was augmented by tens of thousands of drones provided by private donations. As Ukrainian analyst Oleh Danylov wrote: "Roughly speaking, Delta is a modern-day real-time map and troop control center." The Delta system, which was linked to NATO data, made use of artificial intelligence to integrate intelligence coming from individuals, open sources, drones, private satellites, and military surveillance systems. Ukrainian technology became so important that coders were assigned to every battalion-size unit, enabling "prioritizing of targets and developing attack options" on the ball field.

A further crucial source of Ukrainian battlefield effectiveness was the creation of the "Army of Drones," which deployed thousands of

Ukrainian special forces gather: Ukraine's decentralized battlefield decision-making and high morale were seen as important factors in major successes against Russia's powerful armed forces in 2022–23. (Courtesy of the Special Operations Forces of the Armed Forces of Ukraine)

attack and surveillance drones as part of the war effort. Ukrainians contributed over $200 million for the purchase of over three thousand drones for the armed forces. Other civic initiatives raised money for additional drones and even purchased a satellite for use by the military. By early 2023 Ukraine began manufacturing massive numbers of drones and deploying them on the battlefield.

There were important generational differences between Ukraine's and Russia's military leadership. Zelensky's national security and foreign policy team was made up of people in their thirties and forties who had grown up after the fall of the USSR. The top Russian leadership, headed by Putin, Defense Minister Sergei Shoigu, and the chief of staff of the Russian Armed Forces General Valery Gerasimov, all were approaching their seventies as the war unfolded and had spent years working inside Soviet institutions. Their attitudes were heavily influenced by the hierarchical authoritarian Soviet model.

Ukrainian Democracy and the "Leviathan"

The contrasts between Ukraine's and Russia's response to war went far beyond innovation and creativity on the battlefield. Putin's Russia tightened its control over society and introduced ever deeper restrictions on freedom of speech and assembly. By contrast, Ukrainians preserved their democratic values, and public support for democracy grew. According to a nationwide poll conducted in January 2023 for the U.S.-based National Democratic Institute, 94 percent of Ukrainians stated that it was important for them that Ukraine be a full-fledged democracy. Just four years earlier that number stood at 76 percent.

Still, Ukraine's wartime policies required the concentration of power and created challenges for the long-term persistence of liberal and democratic values in Ukraine. Mykhaylo Dubinyansky, one of Ukraine's most thoughtful essayists, penned an article for Ukrainian *Pravda* on July 30, 2022, entitled "The Leviathan in Camouflage." Dubinyansky reflected on the Ukrainian public's traditional skepticism, suspicion, scorn, and occasional outright hostility to government. For centuries the state had represented colonial rule. This attitude to the state extended to the young postcolonial state that emerged in 1991, and Ukrainians frequently took to the streets to clip the wings of statist threats to their freedoms. The war had changed all this. "Never before in the modern history of the country has the interference of the Ukrainian state been so evident." This process, wrote Dubinyansky, was clearly both justified and accepted by society. Nevertheless, the author raised questions about the implications of this concentration of power in the event of a long-term conflict, legitimately asking what limits there should be on the wartime exercise of power.

Dubinyansky's essay warned about the long-term effects of a largely voluntary policy of national consolidation around the president. His essay came on the heels of evidence of wartime's limiting effects on Ukraine's mainly freewheeling media and political environment. In the weeks before the essay appeared, Ukraine's richest man announced he was shutting down his news and entertainment media empire, leaving some four thousand television, print, and online journalists and reporters facing the prospect of unemployment.

Rinat Akhmetov had complied with the requirements of anti-oligarch legislation passed in Ukraine in late 2021. That legislation imposed higher taxes and tariffs on wealthy businessmen who finance political parties, exert political influence, and/or own media assets. The legislation left the determination of these conditions and the designation of oligarchs to the National Security and Defense Council, whose composition is solely determined by the president.

The rights of media in wartime represented a major challenge for Ukraine's democracy. President Zelensky and his team successfully asked the main oligarch-controlled TV channels and several state media to voluntarily consolidate into two nationwide channels that could speak in a unified voice. The first channel targeted Ukrainians and offered updates from the front and featured a range of analysts from civic government and political leaders, all mainly friendly to Zelensky and the ruling party. The second channel, named Freedom, was broadcast in Russian to reach Russian speakers in Ukraine-controlled and Russian-occupied regions as well as citizens of Russia. The channel deciphered Russian policy, propaganda, international developments, and the course of the war and explained Ukrainian government actions and policy.

Several channels were not part of the common effort. Two such channels, Pryamyy (Prime) and Espreso, lost their licenses to broadcast over the airwaves, though they maintained a vigorous presence on cable and over the internet. Pryamyy was formerly owned by previous president Poroshenko, who transferred ownership to the channel's journalists to comply with anti-oligarch legislation. The war also saw the proliferation of a series of independent journalistic projects and channels, some populated by newly jobless journalists from billionaire Akhmetov's channel. These mainly operated via YouTube and social media networks. Scores of weblogs and news sources appeared on Telegram and YouTube, ensuring that millions of citizens had access to a wide range of opinions. In the absence of major financing through advertising revenues, these were, however, resource-poor initiatives focused more on opinion than on deep-dive reporting and detailed analysis. Additionally, Telegram, Facebook, and Twitter made it possible for Ukrainians to access a diverse array of opinions by experts and politicians shut out of the national channels.

As the war raged, and respect for the state was enhanced, Ukraine's anti-corruption institutions made inroads and opened criminal cases against several oligarchs, including the notorious gas trader Dmytro Firtash and against Zelensky's former business partner and cheerleader Ihor Kolomoysky, who would be arrested and imprisoned in September 2023. Most spectacularly, the National Anti-Corruption Bureau exposed the head of the country's Supreme Court in a $3 million case of graft in return for a favorable verdict. These tough measures revealed the corruption in the court system and in big business, but they also gave hope to those fighting for Ukraine's existence that Ukraine's flaws could be repaired.

Dubinyansky's "Leviathan in Camouflage" referred to far more than government in combat dress—it meant unchecked government that uses war to camouflage encroachments against independent media and opposition. In the first year of the war, this threat was neither imminent nor widespread, and polls showed Ukrainians retained confidence in the country's leadership. But there was a distinct danger that if encroachments on freedom were not challenged, they could become habits of the heart as society slowly became accustomed to a more authoritarian form of rule during wartime.

Politics in a wartime democracy is largely self-limiting, and opposition is tempered by the public desire for unity. In Ukraine there were two broad political forces in opposition to Zelensky and the Servant of the People. The first represented patriotic parties, including the liberal Holos, the populist Fatherland of Yulia Tymoshenko, and ex-president Petro Poroshenko's European Solidarity. Representatives of these parties complained that they were kept off the two official national wartime channels and were reduced to appearing on smaller independent cable and internet channels, although these outlets' audiences swelled as viewers searched for a variety of voices. Former Zelensky ally and ex-speaker of the Rada Oleksandr Razumkov complained that he was completely blocked from the airwaves.

These patriotic opposition parties mainly supported the president in the war effort and only gingerly criticized domestic policies and priorities. In part this was dictated by the public mood of national unity and in part by the imperative of preserving a broad front in the face of Russian aggression.

A more complicated situation was presented by the Opposition Bloc for Life, composed of politicians who had supported disgraced president Viktor Yanukovych. A wing of the party led by Yuriy Boyko, a former Yanukovych-era minister, half-heartedly but dutifully joined in condemning Putin and expressing support for the military defense of Ukraine. Leaders of part of the party, long known to be Russia's fifth column, openly sided with Russia. Many of these fled Ukraine for Russia or Belarus, including Renat Kuzmin, former deputy prosecutor general, who was in hiding amid charges of treason; Ilya Kiva, who was stripped of his legislative office after he fled to Russia and became a regular on Russian airwaves calling for the total destruction of the Ukrainian "Nazi" regime; and Deputy Oleh Voloshyn, a former Foreign Ministry functionary who was relocated to Belarus, where his Ukrainian wife soon became a pro-Lukashenko and pro-Putin TV talk show host. The group's main leader, Viktor Medvedchuk, was placed under arrest on April 12, 2022, while preparing to flee the country. Held in detention by decision of Ukrainian courts, Medvedchuk was released to Russia in a prisoner exchange of Ukrainian soldiers from Mariupol on September 21.

In March 2022 the Opposition Bloc's activities were suspended by the National Security and Defense Council. Its parliamentary faction dissolved in April, with twenty-three of forty-four deputies reconstituting themselves as the For Life and Peace faction. Critical of Russia's invasion and supportive of Ukraine's territorial integrity, the Life and Peace faction highlighted its desire for a negotiated settlement and future cooperation with Russia.

In the first year and a half of a major war, Ukraine's armed forces and the nation's society demonstrated impressive resilience and effectiveness, maintaining national solidarity and scoring gains on the field of combat. Despite Ukrainian successes, the toll of the Russian attack on the country was immense. Russia had launched the largest and bloodiest war on European soil since the Second World War. By the fall of 2023 the death toll of civilians and military on both sides was well in excess of 200,000 dead, with Ukrainian estimates of over 300,000 Russian combat fatalities (Western intelligence placed the number at less than half that claimed by Ukraine) and many more wounded on the field of combat. On August 1, 2023, the *Wall Street Journal*'s Bojan Pancevski reported that as many as fifty thousand Ukrainians had lost one or more limbs since the start of the war.

The Scale of Destruction

The sheer scale of the destruction of public infrastructure, housing, and cultural and education institutions was equally shocking. At one of Ukraine's most innovative academic institutions, the Kyiv School of Economics (KSE)—a graduate university with several small but important think tanks, professors, researchers, and students—joined in a complex effort to document the devastation. The KSE adopted a strict methodology for the documentation of wartime destruction, recording only those damaged sites for which it received or could find anecdotal eyewitness accounts buttressed by geolocated photographic evidence. This meant, for example, that much of the mayhem in Mariupol, in which most of the housing, infrastructure, museums, theaters, and workplaces in a city of nearly half a million inhabitants was destroyed, was not fully recorded given the lack of access to what became a Russian-occupied city.

"Our records represent a significant underestimate of the scale of the destruction," the coordinator of the project, Natalia Shapoval, who heads KSE's think tank program, told me. She said she believed the toll could be several times greater than recorded by the project. As of the beginning of July 2023, KSE had documented over $150 billion in damages. In all, the toll that KSE scrupulously documented included 150,000 single-family homes, 17,000 apartment buildings of housing space, and some 300 dormitories. After Russia destroyed the Nova Kakhovka dam on June 6, 2023, a further 36,000 homes were flooded or suffered serious damage, creating additional tens of thousands of homeless. The total housing damage in the country amounted to nearly a million square feet of housing, representing between 8 and 9 percent of all the housing stock in Ukraine. By the summer of 2023 the Ukrainian government estimated that 3.4 million people had seen their homes destroyed or seriously damaged.

Losses of $9.7 billion came through the destruction of schools and institutions of higher learning, including the 915 educational facilities destroyed and 2,165 damaged. In all, by March 2023, 1,216 hospitals and clinics were hit in Russian attacks. Some 3,000 stores and shopping centers were damaged or destroyed, as were numerous office buildings. Agricultural losses through fires, the disruption of feed for livestock, the mining of agricultural areas, and the theft and destruction of agricultural equipment amounted to $8.7 billion. Forest fires resulting from hostilities resulted in a fifty-fold increase, claiming 298,000 hectares of land, according to the Zoi Environmental Network. Russian attacks also damaged 126 railway stations and 344 bridges. The rising toll of electrical power and heating stations went well beyond the ten that KSE recorded.

A March 2023 joint assessment by the World Bank, the European Commission, and the government of Ukraine estimated that the costs required for Ukraine's recovery would be $422 billion, with the price tag set to rise significantly with every month of war.

The toll on the economy was massive amid the destruction of workplaces, roads, rail links, airports, schools, museums, and homes, exacerbated by power interruptions, loss of income because of the blockade of Ukrainian ports, and the internal and external displacement of 40 percent of the population. A report prepared by the World Bank indicated that in 2022 the Ukrainian economy had contracted by 29.2 percent. This represented an improvement on Ukraine's performance in the first months of the war, when the economy declined by 45 percent and reflected a major influx of international financial support.

Resilience, State Capacity, Confidence

Remarkably, in most of the country, schools remained open, local government operated, stores and restaurants greeted customers, there were no runs on banks, no panic buying, and no shortages of essential supplies. Ukrainians acted calmly and accepted the harshness and the challenges of life in wartime, often enduring long periods without electricity, hot water, and heat. For a country long described in Russian propaganda as a failed state, Ukraine demonstrated remarkable state capacity, resilience, and coherence. Nevertheless, in significant measure the Ukrainian economy could function only with the infusion of monthly subsidies of around $5 billion from the United States and Europe—roughly 30 percent of its monthly prewar GDP.

On November 3, 2022, the Ukrainian Rada adopted a state budget for the coming year. It projected income of 1.3 trillion and expenses of 2.6 trillion hryvnia. Fully 1 trillion of these funds were allocated for the armed forces in wartime. The drastic decline in state revenues was a product not only of the destruction rained on the private and civilian sector by Russia, but also a result of the Russia-induced depopulation of large parts of Ukraine. The budget deficit amounted to 20 percent of the wartime economy's GDP, with inflation projected at 28 percent in the coming year. The projected budget gap required at a minimum $38 billion in support from Ukraine's partners in Europe, North America, and beyond. By 2023 a large infusion of international financial support was disbursed and the economy not only stabilized but, despite ongoing Russian attacks, was projected to rebound by nearly 3 percent.

While Ukraine's economy continued to chug along defiantly, major changes occurred in the country's cultural and artistic spheres. Artists naturally focused on depicting and documenting the horrors of war, adding to the rich literature on the Donbas and the conflict with Russia that had emerged since 2014. Public anger at Russia's barbarism resulted in the wholesale rejection of Russian culture and symbols that had survived in independent Ukraine. Many Russian-speaking Ukrainians made a deliberate decision to shift to Ukrainian. Others flocked to the internet to watch lectures by historians and political scientists. Books on Ukrainian history saw a jump in sales. Ukrainians debated whether to read Pushkin's imperial narratives or the work of Kyiv-born Mikhail Bulgakov, who scorned Ukrainian separatism. Ukrainian distaste for Russian music and Russian musicians grew, with 40 percent saying they had stopped listening to Russian music since the war began. In Eastern and Southern Ukraine around 70 percent of those polled said they had never watched or had stopped watching Russian TV content.

In Odesa the city council voted for the removal of the monument to Empress Catherine the Great. In Kyiv streets named after Russian historical figures were renamed for Ukrainian civic, cultural, and political leaders. Kyiv's centrally located Lev Tolstoy Place was slated to be renamed in 2023. Some of these acts of "separation" were mainly symbolic. But the net effect of this shift in consciousness was to deepen the sense of national unity between Russophone Ukrainians and the traditionally patriotic Ukrainian-speaking population.

For three decades Ukraine had evolved along two polarities. The first reflected the tension between independent civic society and a slowly emerging middle class versus the largely antagonistic entrenched, rent-seeking oligarchic elite; the second reflected the influence of the West, which competed for influence with Russia.

Putin's invasion of Ukraine in 2014, the annexation of Crimea, and the occupation of parts of the Donbas influenced both, sharply eroding the influence and appeal of integration with Russia. The conflict also weakened Ukraine's oligarchs, who were heavily invested in Eastern Ukraine's industries.

In a poll released in late October 2022, amid some of the worst attacks on civilian infrastructure since the beginning of the war, the Reyting (Rating) Agency reported, surprisingly, that 86 percent of Ukrainians believed their country was moving in the right direction. A poll by the Kyiv International Institute of Sociology (KIIS) showed similar positive sentiment and optimism: 89 percent of Ukrainians believed their country would be a prosperous member of the European Union in ten years' time, with the highest level of confidence in such an outcome demonstrated by those ages eighteen to twenty-nine. When asked whether they would be prepared to endure three to five years of hardship to rebuild the country, 97 percent answered in the affirmative. That same poll found that 89 percent of Ukrainians believed it was important for Ukraine to fight on to regain territories rather than to launch negotiations, even if this resulted in the further bombing of Ukrainian cities. Finally, in a poll conducted by KIIS a month earlier, 68 percent of Ukrainians considered themselves content with their lives. In short, the Ukrainians who remained in Ukraine during wartime were determined to win back occupied portions of their country, and were increasingly united, content with their lives, and optimistic about the future.

National Consolidation

Over thirty years of statehood, the gradual evolution of a consolidated Ukrainian identity had been slow, halting, and sporadic. In part this was because independent Ukraine is not and never has been an ordered, top-down polity in which a small elite freely manipulates and shapes public opinion. Such a narrow elite in fact could not have reshaped a nation with a population whose sense of themselves and their past had been distorted by centuries of Russian rule. Nor could the nation-building process have been achieved solely by the actions of civil society and the Ukrainian-speaking cultural elite. This consolidation happened only in the interplay of state and society. The nationally conscious elite and the masses that flocked to public squares time after time to press first for statehood in 1990, then for democracy in 2004, and finally for European integration and a turn away from Russia in 2013–14, helped infuse the state with the spirit of independence and pressured its indifferent political-financial establishment to embrace the nation-building agenda around Ukrainian ethno-political identity.

From the onset of modern-day independence, Ukraine was a battleground in which people shaped their ethno-political identity. Before it became the literal battleground of a brutal kinetic war, it was a battleground of political and cultural contestation between the values of democratic Europe and authoritarian Russia and Eurasia. It equally was an internal battleground of conflicting ideas of national identity, of conflicting narratives about Ukraine's past, present, and future.

The cultural, political, and now wartime battleground of Ukraine shaped a thirty-year path toward national consolidation. It helped ground contemporary Ukrainian identity in liberal values and reinforced an interpretation of the Ukrainian past that emphasized democratic antecedents. This consolidation of a unified Ukrainian nation proved slower and more difficult to achieve than many advocates of Ukraine's independence thought in 1991. But the pluralism that has emerged from this contestation preserved Ukraine's political openness, ensured democratic contestation, and prevented the consolidation of unchecked authoritarian power. The space for freedom that emerged in Ukraine, in turn, allowed for and was reinforced by the emergence of a dynamic civil society and a private sector. The interplay of forces built a state rooted in civic patriotism and a distinctly Ukrainian cultural and linguistic identity. This inclusive national identity, as well as the freedoms that emerged amid Ukraine's weak, embattled state, became a key reason why Ukrainians have fought so committedly against Russia's military onslaught.

The civic courage and nationwide mobilization of Ukraine's citizenry has generated strong admiration among the publics and leaders of the democratic world. This support has given Ukraine a pipeline of weapons and financial backing that have leveled the field of combat to a degree few military experts anticipated. Amid a historically weak and poorly performing state, Ukraine's heterarchic interplay of political, civic, economic, and state forces allowed the nation's multiplicity of voices to be heard, enhancing its unity and resilience.

A poll by the Kyiv International Institute of Sociology conducted in January 2023 showed that 95 percent of the population now identified as Ukrainian and only 3 percent as Russian. In 1992, one year into independence, a similar poll by KIIS found that just 45.6 percent of Ukrainians identified as citizens of Ukraine, with the balance identifying with their regions or expressing nostalgia for the former USSR. As important, by 2023, 96 percent of the population expressed trust in the armed forces and 84 percent in the president. Such unified trust in institutions represents a remarkable achievement given Moscow's decades-long financing of subversive anti-Western Russophone and Russophile forces in the country and Russia's immense propaganda machine and its diligent efforts to infiltrate Ukrainian society and institutions. Efforts to promote ethnic cleavages flagged when in 2014 Russia occupied or annexed those portions of Ukraine that were the most resistant or indifferent to the Ukrainian ethnic and democratic narrative. National consolidation came at the most perilous moment in Ukraine's modern history, creating the foundation for a state and society capable of meeting the challenge of a powerful and deadly aggressor.

In the spring of 2023, Russia's war on Ukraine was primarily fought out in the Donetsk region, where Russian forces relentlessly attacked Ukrainian positions in a largely ineffective effort to retake the entire oblast. Most military analysts, however, pointed to the likelihood of a major Ukrainian military offensive, most likely in Ukraine's south, in the region above the Azov Sea and in eastern Kherson. As part of the effort to amass resources sufficient for a significant recapture of territory, President Zelensky traveled to Rome, Berlin, Paris, and London, where he received major commitments of billions of dollars in new armaments and munitions, including long-range missiles from the U.K.

On June 6, 2023, Russian forces destroyed a major dam in Southern Ukraine to preclude a Ukrainian counteroffensive near the city of

Nova Kakhovka. That action flooded villages, towns, and cities, leaving homeless tens of thousands of Ukrainians and creating a major ecological catastrophe, resulting in fresh-water shortages affecting 700,000 people. Ukraine was fighting a war of survival against a brutal enemy. But Ukrainians were also fighting for the preservation of the post–World War II order rooted in respect for the territorial integrity of states. Indeed, Russia's annexation of Ukrainian territory was the first such annexation of the territory of an internationally recognized state by an aggressor since the creation of the United Nations.

While the outcome of this war was uncertain, a Ukrainian counteroffensive was launched late the summer of 2023, aimed at taking back major swaths of territory. The costs of the counteroffensive were high. In September 2023, high-ranking military officials confirmed that Ukrainian soldiers were dying at a rate similar to that of Russian forces. A year earlier, in August–September 2022, a Ukrainian counteroffensive had recaptured most of Russian-occupied Kharkiv in the northeast and had liberated the city of Kherson in the south in rapid fashion.

But the picture dramatically changed during Ukraine's second major counteroffensive of the late summer and fall of 2023. By the time of this Ukrainian advance, Russia had constructed multiple lines of defense along a five-hundred-mile perimeter of the territories in the occupied south of Ukraine. The extensive defenses consisted of a sequence of anti-tank ditches followed by trenches, barbed wire, minefields, and concrete "dragon's teeth" designed to block the progress of tanks and armored personnel carriers, all followed by another layer of trenches and barbed wire, backed up by concrete parapets for snipers, machine guns, and tanks, ending finally with concrete bunkers. It took Russia almost a year to complete this defensive array, a fact Ukrainian officials privately lamented was made possible by the slow pace at which needed Western armaments reached their fighters. Such delays, officials told me in September 2023, gave Russia the time to build their prodigious defenses.

The counteroffensive of 2023 proceeded at a grindingly slow pace, with Ukrainian forces moving forward several hundred meters a day. By October 2023, four months into Ukraine's attack, Kyiv claimed to have recaptured just several hundred square kilometers of territory, less than one-half percent of the territory Russia held,

The most significant gains came in a Ukrainian advance on the municipality of Tokmak in the south-central Zaporhizhia oblast and around Bakhmut in the east, where the counteroffensive was poised to surround some ten thousand Russian forces holding the rubble that had formerly been a thriving city of seventy-three thousand.

The winter of 2023 and early spring of 2024 were expected to give stronger indications whether the armed forces of Ukraine can drive Russian forces out of most of occupied Ukraine. But the focal point of the counteroffensive appeared to be south-central and southeastern Ukraine, where success would mean cutting off Russian-occupied Crimea from a land bridge on mainland Ukraine. Were the counteroffensive to succeed, it would make Crimea vulnerable to systematic Ukrainian attacks, deeply demoralize the Russian side, disrupt the flow of weapons and ammunition to Russian fighters in the south, and potentially open the door to a de facto Russian concession. President Zelensky alluded to the aim of the counteroffensive in an August 23 interview for Ukrainian television. He spoke of the need to wage war in a way that produces "fewer victims" and added, "If we are on the administrative . . . border of Crimea, I believe it will be possible to push for the demilitarization of Russia on the territory." Such a statement was an indication both of Ukraine's war aims and of Zelensky's openness to a peaceful way to reassert sovereignty over its occupied regions.

While this book was being finished, the short-term trajectory of the Russian war was far from clear. What was clear was that the war had transformed Volodymyr Zelensky from someone with a vague connection to Ukrainian culture to a leader who now fully embraced a distinct Ukrainian national identity. Ukrainians too had undergone a transformation. Over three decades of Ukrainian independence an interplay of civic, oligarchic, and cultural forces and influences had resulted in the emergence of a capable state inhabited by a determined people united by both ethnic and civic patriotism. Their desire for freedom and independence will be impossible to deny.

CHAPTER EIGHT

The Future of Ukraine

A UNITED PEOPLE, a mobilized society, and a capable, if flawed, state. All were on full display in Ukraine in the first years it fought its war against Russia. All, too, were ready to meet the challenges that ongoing war would offer.

The scale of destruction wreaked upon Ukraine over two years of war was massive, resulting in hundreds of thousands of Ukrainian civilians and military killed or wounded, millions displaced, and hundreds of billions of dollars in housing and infrastructure damaged. Despite this, the will and capacity of Ukrainians to resist remained strong and unwavering. Polls showed Ukrainians ready to sacrifice and unwilling to compromise the territorial integrity of their country.

Still, given the ruthless determination of Putin to wipe out the Ukrainian state from the political map, it is not inappropriate to end this history of modern Ukraine with a discussion of the Ukrainian future. As this volume has argued, three decades of Ukrainian statehood transformed consciousness and moved the vast majority of those who live in Ukraine toward a shared national narrative rooted in Ukrainian identity, democratic practices, and the desire to integrate into Europe and away from Russia.

While that process culminated as Putin launched his full-scale attack, it had already taken decisive form after Putin's annexation of Crimea and his partial takeover of the Donbas in 2014. Eight years before Putin's all-out invasion, his partial invasion had given Ukraine and Ukrainians time to consolidate fully around a culturally Ukrainian civic identity largely shaped by the national democratic civic forces and values that had opened the door to the country's statehood in 1991.

The question nevertheless remained: Was this enough? Was the will of a 45-million-strong nation sufficient to overcome the imperial ambitions of the dictator sitting atop the Kremlin?

In the first stages of Russia's war, Western leaders and policy experts believed not. They underestimated the state and the people. Indeed, there was widespread belief that Ukraine would not survive. Most analysts predicted Kyiv and Kharkiv would fall, and Western governments were preparing to assist Ukrainians in conducting a guerrilla war. But fierce Ukrainian resistance and the rapid collapse and retreat of Russian forces between April and September 2022 changed the mood from deep pessimism to growing confidence in the Ukrainian military, the people, and their leaders. In turn, this loosened the flow of military support and financing, permitting Ukraine to score further major battlefield victories against a military regarded as one of the world's most powerful.

The initial battlefield successes of Ukraine as well as evidence of multiple mass atrocities committed by invading Russian forces facilitated widespread public and elite support for Kyiv in the West and resulted in the massive flow of munitions and weapons to the Ukrainian armed forces. Total financial and military aid provided or committed by the international community approached a quarter billion U.S. dollars by October 2023, according to the Kiel Institute for the World Economy.

Western financial aid and domestic resilience allowed the battered Ukrainian economy and currency to stabilize. Though strained, the state budget, and consequently social services and government functions, remained robust, predominantly funded with Western financing. After a decline of 30 percent in 2022, wartime Ukraine's GDP rebounded to show growth of nearly 4 percent in 2023, with the EU estimating that the economy would grow a further 6 percent in 2024. As importantly, in 2022–23, Ukrainian fighters augmented by military aid were able to retake around a third of the territory Russia had occupied in the first stages of the war.

The survival of much of Ukraine's own arms industry after Russia's initial punishing attacks and the arrival of technologically advanced and precise weapons systems, such as HIMARs and advanced howitzers from the United States and Storm Shadow cruise missiles from the United Kingdom, contributed to Ukrainian gains and ushered in a period of high optimism in the media and among experts that Ukraine could prevail. These trends were reinforced by the Prigozhin/Wagner Group mutiny of June 2023, which pointed to some fragility within the Russian system.

But Russia, too, showed significant resilience. Putin quietly stood down the brief Wagner Group mutiny, and according to a *Wall Street Journal* report from December 22, 2023, Nikolai Patrushev, the head of Russia's Federal Security Service, organized and directed the subsequent assassination of Yevgeniy Prigozhin. Moreover, Russia began to adapt and learn from Ukrainian military tactics. Although in the early stages of the war Russian soldiers on the front had poor command of electronic warfare and low skills in operating drones, these deficiencies were slowly remedied. Significantly, Russia began to produce and employ prodigious numbers of drones and to effectively exploit its state-of-the-art electronic warfare capabilities to partly interdict or neutralize Ukraine's many technological advantages. Russia also constructed elaborate multilayered defenses that impeded and raised the human costs of a Ukrainian counterattack. Throughout the war, Ukraine's military commander General Valery Zaluzhny had been careful never to underestimate or paint the Russian military as a paper tiger, nor to denigrate the military leadership as "idiots." His tactic was proven right.

On November 27, 2023, President Putin signed a three-year budget that envisioned near doubling in military spending, up to 6 percent of the country's GDP, a total of US$115 billion. That number is far higher as it does not include money to rebuild military infrastructure (in Russia and in occupied territories) or to cover the costs of rehabilitation and medical care for wounded soldiers, which are contained in civilian budgetary line items. These planned expenditures followed on the heels of huge increases in Russian military spending in 2022–23.

The effects of Russia's improved tactics and defenses became clear in the late summer and fall of 2023, when Ukraine launched what the country's leaders had promised would be a major multifront counteroffensive. Several months into the operation, it became evident that Ukrainian forces were making only minor territorial inroads in Southern Ukraine, in a slow, grinding advance toward the city of Melitopol. Indeed, according to a September 28, 2023, *New York Times* report, since after months of the counteroffensive, Ukrainian forces had retaken several hundred square miles, a territory the size of New York City, and on balance had suffered a small net loss of territory for the year. More worrying were the immense combat losses, with entire Ukrainian battalions requiring renewal and reconfiguration after just a few days of combat as losses of dead and wounded often claimed the majority of the fighters.

In September 2023, a leading Ukrainian national security official, speaking on background in Kyiv, told me and several other Ukraine analysts that Ukraine was taking as many losses during the counteroffensive as the Russians, which Ukraine estimated at 500 to 1,000 fatalities and serious woundings per day. Civic activists who provide drones and ancillary support to Ukrainian units on the frontline estimated that in nearly two years of war, deaths had at a minimum exceeded 100,000, with the death toll in the fall counteroffensive representing approximately a quarter of that number. These terrible numbers were dwarfed by the nearly 400,000 Russian fighters killed or permanently maimed, according to reports by the Ukrainian military.

By October 2023, having evaluated the durability of Russian defenses and in the absence of air power and adequate numbers of advanced weapons in their arsenal, Ukraine's military commanders abandoned the idea of a concerted multidirectional counteroffensive. Instead, they focused on disrupting Russian military supply lines, attacking military and armaments facilities on Russian territory, building defenses against potential Russian advances, and continuing to degrade Russia's Black Sea fleet.

The most effective of these measures was the effort to eviscerate the Russian navy in the Black Sea. By December 2023, the British Ministry of Defense estimated that 20 percent of the fleet had been destroyed, with the effect that the Russian navy had retreated from operations in the Black Sea. In turn, this had opened the door to the shipment of Ukrainian grain exports along the western Black Sea, with most cargo ships evading Russian attack, interdiction, and mines.

In November 2023, General Valeriy Zaluzhny, commander in

chief of Ukraine's armed forces, whom polls showed to be Ukraine's most trusted leader, gave a forthright interview to the *Economist* about the state of Ukraine's war and Ukraine's military requirements for the battlefield. His sobering picture of a military deadlock contrasted markedly with the high optimism and boastful claims of some of President Zelensky's official spokesmen, including Mykola Podolyak, who had famously claimed he would be drinking a victory shot while sunning in Crimea by the summer of 2023.

In his interview and an accompanying article he penned, General Zaluzhny spelled out Ukraine's military requirements in clear terms. He emphasized that technology was the key to victory in the emerging positional war. Zaluzhny emphasized that air defenses, then operating at 76 percent efficiency, needed strengthening lest they be overwhelmed by massive Russian missile and drone attacks that target infrastructure and threaten the country's energy grids. He indicated Ukraine needed a functioning air force, which in early 2024 was still awaiting the delivery and deployment of F-16s promised by the United States and other allies. Zaluzhny outlined other specific needs: "330 tanks, 600–700 IFVs, and 550 howitzers," if Ukraine was to reclaim the territories Russia captured since its all-out invasion. Moreover, he added that Ukraine needed assistance in overcoming Russia's advanced electronic warfare capabilities and in securing mine-breaching tanks and radar-like anti-mine sensors. Finally, he noted that Ukrainian forces on the front needed replenishment and a new wave of soldiers needed to be mobilized and trained.

In the *Economist* and in other public statements in the fall of 2023, General Zaluzhny articulated a radical rethink of how the war was to be conducted in order to regain captured territory at the lowest possible cost to Ukraine's fighters. Zaluzhny's innovative tactics, his decentralization of battlefield decision-making, and his flexible, nonbureaucratic approach to cooperation with private donors and volunteers provided the technologies and innovations that ensured Ukraine's early successes. But with Russia's capacities improving, Zaluzhny understood that Ukraine's waging of war must also adapt. In this new context, and given the differences between the two societies, Zaluzhny was pivoting to a model of warfare heavily reliant on the newest Western technologies and air power.

In December 2023, President Zelensky agreed to a plan that

would mobilize half a million fighters in the new year, who would be trained in waves and gradually would replace fighters who had been on combat duty for two years. President Zelensky also announced the state was planning to provide a million drones to the armed forces in 2024. But this also meant that after two years of war, and after loud pronouncements about the country's "Army of Drones," Ukraine's government was only beginning to provide large numbers of drones to the front. Ninety percent of all the drones that were used by Ukraine's innovative military in nearly two years of war had been crowdfunded by private donors through domestic and international nongovernmental organizations, such as Dignitas, an initiative that had also trained 60,000 fighters in the use and operation of drones.

At the same time as the war entered a new period of complexity, Ukraine's democracy saw the gradual return of politics, with opposition leaders, still careful to project national unity, increasingly second-guessing President Zelensky. Significantly, Zelensky's trust rating, which had hovered around 90 percent since the beginning of the war, saw erosion in a November 2023 poll that showed two-thirds of Ukrainians trusted the president, while nearly a third did not. General Zaluzhny was now Ukraine's most trusted leader. Such a decline in the rating of a president making hard choices in wartime was hardly unexpected, and his level of support remained high. What was remarkable was the spirit of optimism about the future and the national unity that the polls also continued to register.

While international public and elite support for Ukraine remained high in the democratic community of nations, the uninterrupted flow of weapons and financial aid offered new challenges in early 2024. In the United States, political jockeying between the Republican-controlled House of Representatives and the Democratic-led Senate delayed a major bill to finance Ukraine's war and economy. Still, despite delays, well over three-quarters of the House and a higher proportion in the Senate supported aid to Ukraine.

While European Union aid for Ukraine in early 2024 was delayed by the efforts of Hungary's prime minister, Viktor Orbán, to block assistance, Ukraine benefited from strong support of major European leaders for the preservation of Ukraine's statehood and independence. As this book was nearing completion, most analysts and government leaders believed Ukraine would soon get all its projected funding from both the EU and the United States.

Ukraine's long-term capacity to counter Russia's aggression received another boost as news media reported that U.S. and European leaders were increasingly open to the idea of seizing and using over $300 billion in Russian hard currency reserves now frozen in Western banks. Such a resource, if employed, would provide long-term support to Ukraine's war effort and show Russia that it had no viable path to victory.

The war had awakened the global public to the reality of a rich and diverse Ukrainian culture and identity and to the ingenuity and potential of its capable citizens, reversing stereotypes about a dysfunctional state riddled with corruption. The war reminded the world of Ukraine's imperfect, but persistent democracy, and of Ukraine's remarkable civil society, which has mobilized to protect its basic rights over nearly three and a half decades of post-Soviet Ukrainian statehood. These trends have given Ukraine significant soft power, which is likely to be sustain long-lasting support for the country's renewal.

With the strong backing of the Euro-Atlantic democratic community, as well as of many democracies around the world, Ukraine has been able to fight back effectively against what was once considered one of the world's strongest military powers.

This state of affairs makes a Russian victory and Russian domination over the Ukrainian people an unlikely scenario. Far more likely is that Ukrainians will preserve their statehood and succeed in their aim of integrating into Europe. And this means that, with the help of the world's democracies, Ukraine will eventually have an important opportunity for a postwar recovery that can help correct the legacies of a state once controlled by ex-Communists and get-rich-quick oligarchs, who lacked a clear national identity, a sense of civic mindedness, and an understanding of the country's human potential.

The international democratic community appears committed to assisting Ukraine in fighting back, but is equally ready to give it the tools to build a stronger, more effective society, economy, and polity after the war. The resources for that rebuilding were likely to come not only from the government budgets of the democratic world, but through reparations from Russia and the injection of over $300 billion in Russian hard currency reserves held in European and North American banks. These resources will be crucial to Ukraine's postwar recovery. But Ukraine's most important source of revival and growth resides in its remarkable people, and a new generation of nimble civic, political, and military leaders who have shown the world their capabilities, skills, and commitment to freedom.

In 1990, a study by Deutsche Bank predicted Ukraine was likely to become the fastest-growing post-Soviet republic, in large part because of the country's impressive human capital. Ukraine's promise was not achieved after 1991, and the country suffered from years of misrule, corruption, and economic malaise. Yet while Russia's war has been the source of vast devastation and loss of life, Ukraine's battleground has mobilized Ukrainian citizens as never before, and ironically given Ukraine a second chance to make good on the potential many saw in the country at its modern-day founding.

In 2024, the thirty-fourth year of its existence, Ukraine remains a battleground. The battle for its identity and unity has been won. The battle it now is fighting is a kinetic war against a powerful colonial invader. The fact that Ukrainians have won that crucial first battle has increased the likelihood the country will prevail in the second.

Notes

Chapter One. A New State

"You, as Ukrainians": Adam Michnik, cited in *Kyiv Post*, https://archive.kyivpost.com/article/opinion/op-ed/bohdan-nahaylo-how-rukh-transformed-ukraine.html.

"Chicken Kiev" speech: George H. W. Bush, "Remarks to the Supreme Soviet of the Republic of the Ukraine in Kiev, Soviet Union," August 1, 1991, https://bush41library.tamu.edu/archives/public-papers/3267.

"Without Ukraine": Zbigniew Brzezinski, *The Grand Chessboard* (New York: Basic Books, 1997), 46.

A widely cited study by Deutsche Bank: Jürgen Corbet et al., *The Soviet Union at the Crossroads: Facts and Figures on the Soviet Republics* (Frankfurt: Deutsche Bank, 1990).

"It wasn't until relatively late": Katya Gorchinskaya, "A Brief History of Corruption—The Kravchuk Era," *Kyiv Post*, May 6, 2020, https://archive.kyivpost.com/article/opinion/op-ed/katya-gorchinskaya-a-brief-history-of-corruption-in-ukraine-the-kravchuk-era.html.

John Mearsheimer famously argued: John J. Mearsheimer, "The Case for a Ukrainian Nuclear Deterrent," *Foreign Affairs*, Summer 1993.

"We have to learn": Adrian Karatnycky, "The Ukrainian Factor," *Foreign Affairs*, Summer 1992.

"was parting with the remnants": Ibid.

Chapter Two. Money and Power

"This unit, their methods": Adrian Karatnycky, "Meltdown in Ukraine," *Foreign Affairs*, May–June 2001.

This recording's authentication: Ibid.

"At one point we divided our assets": Serhiy Taruta, conversation with the author, September 2007.

"Disco mafia": Sergei Zhuk, "'The Disco Mafia' and 'Komsomol Capitalism' in Soviet Ukraine during Late Socialism," in *Material Culture in Russia and the USSR* (New York: Routledge, 2016), https://www.taylorfrancis.com/chapters/edit/10.4324/9781003086024-12/disco-mafia-komsomol-capitalism-soviet-ukraine-late-socialism-sergei-zhuk.

"among his greatest mistakes": "Kravchuk, Kuchma and Yushchenko Told about Their Main Mistakes during the Presidency," August 20, 2011, https://vikna.if.ua/news/category/ua/2011/08/20/5953/view.

the CIA published a national intelligence estimate: George Kolt, January 1994, cited in Daniel Williams and R. Jeffrey Smith, "U.S. Intelligence Sees Economic Plight Leading to Breakup of Ukraine," *Washington Post*, January 25, 1994, https://www.washingtonpost.com/archive/politics/1994/01/25/us-intelligence-sees-economic-plight-leading-to-breakup-of-ukraine/48282f8d-0fe9-457f-b252-39d98137c003/.

Ukraine Is Not Russia: Leonid Kuchma, *Ukraina—ne Rossiya* (Kyiv: Vremya, 2003).

Chapter Three. Yushchenko

"keystone in the arch": Sherman Garnett, *Keystone in the Arch: Ukraine in the Emerging Security Environment of Central and Eastern Europe* (Washington, DC: Carnegie Endowment for International Peace, 1997).

"Razom nas bahato!": Sourced from my article "Ukraine's Orange Revolution," *Foreign Affairs*, March–April 2005, https://www.foreignaffairs.com/articles/russia-fsu/2005-03-01/ukraines-orange-revolution.

"the biggest election fraud": Ibid.

"They are going to steal the election": Tymoshenko's discussion about the effort to steal the election is from ibid.

boasted some 6 million distinct users: "Internet Penetration Rate in Ukraine from 2004 to 2023," *Statista*, https://www.statista.com/statistics/1023197/ukraine-internet-penetration/.

Ukraine's military and security services began to fragment: C. J. Chivers, "How Top Spies in Ukraine Changed the Nation's Path," *New York Times*, January 17, 2005, https://www.nytimes.com/2005/01/17/world/europe/how-top-spies-in-ukraine-changed-the-nations-path.html.

"In 2004 . . . Russia and its agents": Volodymyr Horbulin, *Svitova Hibrydna Viyyna, Ukrainskiy Front* (Kharkiv: Folio, 2017), 271.

"Our road into the future": Viktor Yushchenko, quoted in Ian Traynor, "Yushchenko Hails Victory over Tyranny," *Guardian*, January 25, 2005, https://www.theguardian.com/world/2005/jan/24/ukraine.iantraynor.

The criticism evoked an uproar: "Ukrainian Leader under Fire from Journalists," Radio Free Europe/Radio Liberty, July 27, 2005, https://www.rferl.org/a/1060203.html.

"The Orange Revolution is over": Olga Kesarchuk, "The Attitudes and Adap-

tation Strategies of Oligarchs to Ukraine's Democratization" (paper presented to the Canadian Political Science Association, Vancouver, June 4–6, 2008), https://cpsa-acsp.ca/papers-2008/Kesarchuk.pdf.

"What can I recommend": Putin comments, cited at https://ua.korrespondent.net/ukraine/1019807-u-nashij-ukrayini-obureni-hihikannyam-timoshenko-na-repliki-putina-pro-yushchenka.

"Agreement on Political Partnership": reported in Sergiy Pivovarov, "Ten Years Ago, Tymoshenko Planned to Share Power with Yanukovych 20 Years in Advance, but She Lost the Election and Now Denies Everything," February 7, 2019, https://babel.ua/texts/25379-desyat-rokiv-tomu-timoshenko-planuvala-podiliti-z-yanukovichem-vladu-na-20-rokiv-napered-a-potim-prograla-vibori-i-teper-vse-zaperechuye-zgaduyemo-golovne-z-cogo-dogovoru.

Chapter Four. A Thug in Power

"was unconstitutional": Tadeusz A. Olsazański, "Ukraine's Constitutional Court Reinstates Presidential System," OSW: Centre for Eastern Studies, October 6, 2010, https://www.osw.waw.pl/en/publikacje/analyses/2010-10-06/ukraines-constitutional-court-reinstates-presidential-system.

"For the average Ukrainian": Ihor Hryniv, conversation with the author, mid-September 2012.

the tax police received fees: *Ukraine's Fight against Corruption: The Economic Front* (Kyiv: IER, 2018), available on the institute's website (http://www.ier.com.ua/files/publications/Policy_papers/IER/2018/Anticorruption_Report_EN.pdf).

"It's time for us to take it easy": Yanukovych's birthday toast and Akhmetov's response are cited in https://ipress.ua/articles/protyvostoyanye_olygarh_protyv_prezydenta_5872.html.

"To avoid any doubts": "Valeriy Khoroshkovskiy: Moving towards the EU Remains a Priority for Ukraine," Yalta European Strategy, September 15, 2012, https://yes-ukraine.org/en/news/dvizhenie-v-es-ostaetsya-prioritetom-ukrainy-valeriy-horoshkovskiy.

"Now let's get serious": Mustafa Nayyem's Facebook post is quoted in Andrei Soldatov and Irina Borogan, "Here's How Facebook Kicked Off Ukraine's Euromaidan Revolution," *Insider*, September 5, 2015, https://www.businessinsider.com/heres-how-facebook-kicked-off-the-euromaidan-revolution-2015-7.

"negotiating process": Interfax-Ukraine, "Azarov: Ukraine's Talks on Association with EU Continuing," *Kyiv Post*, November 27, 2013, https://archive.kyivpost.com/ukraine-politics/azarov-ukraines-talks-on-association-with-eu-continuing-332511.html.

"secure (Russian) diplomatic facilities": "How Russia's FSB Is Fighting against Ukraine: Murders, Terrorist Attacks, Moles and Cyberattacks," *Ukrainska Pravda*, March 13, 2023, https://www.pravda.com.ua/eng/articles/2023/03/13/7393096/.

"gave the order to withdraw": Anastasia Zanuda, "How Yanukovych Left Ukraine: First-Hand Versions," *BBC News*, February 22, 2017, https://www.bbc.com/ukrainian/features-russian-39049755.

"My position remains unchanged": Rinat Akhmetov, quoted in Andrew Higgins and Andrew E. Kramer, "Archrival Is Freed as Ukraine Leader Flees," *New York Times*, February 22, 2014, https://www.nytimes.com/2014/02/23/world/europe/ukraine.html.

Chapter Five. The Poroshenko Presidency and the Foundations of the Patriotic State

"we will respect the choice of the Ukrainian people": "Vladimir Putin's Interview with Radio Europe 1 and TF1 TV Channel," President of Russia, June 4, 2014, http://en.kremlin.ru/events/president/news/45832.

"right approach": "Putin Says Poroshenko Has 'Right Approach' to Stop Ukraine Violence," France 24, June 6, 2014, https://www.france24.com/en/20140606-putin-poroshenko-meeting-russia-ukraine-d-day.

"Ukraine was on the precipice of default": Prime Minister Arseniy Yatseniuk, cited in "Yatsenyuk Recalled His Premiership, Arguing about the Default," May 27, 2019, https://www.epravda.com.ua/rus/news/2019/05/27/648182/.

"Notwithstanding a strong policy-led adjustment": David Lipton, quoted in "Press Release: IMF Executive Board Approves 4-Year US$17.5 Billion Extended Fund Facility for Ukraine, US$5 Billion for Immediate Disbursement," IMF Press Release no. 15/107, https://www.imf.org/en/News/Articles/2015/09/14/01/49/pr15107.

Institute of Economic Research: Data on anti-corruption measures during the Poroshenko presidency are from the Institute for Economic Research report *Ukraine's Fight against Corruption* (Kyiv: IER, 2018), http://www.ier.com.ua/files/publications/Policy_papers/IER/2018/Anticorruption_Report_EN.pdf.

"nothing has changed in the Poroshenko years": In May 2018 a poll by the Democratic Initiatives Charitable Foundation showed that 80 percent of people felt that the war on corruption in Ukraine had failed. "The Fight against Corruption in Ukraine: Public Opinion," https://dif.org.ua/en/article/the-fight-against-corruption-in-ukraine-public-opinion.

"The Maidan removed": Serhiy Leshchenko, quoted in "President v Oligarch," *Economist*, March 28, 2015, https://www.economist.com/europe/2015/03/28/president-v-oligarch.

"We will not have a president's team": Poroshenko is quoted in "Balcerowicz Became Poroshenko's Representative in the Cabinet," *New Voice*, April 22, 2016, https://nv.ua/ukr/ukraine/politics/baltserovich-stav-predstavnikom-poroshenko-v-kabmini-112265.html.

A comprehensive poll in 2014: https://zn.ua/ukr/internal/pivdenniy-shid-gilka-dereva-nashogo-.html.

Chapter Six. Volodymyr Zelensky

"You are nobodies": Political consultant Nikitia Poturayev, reported in Roman Olearchyk, "Boot-Camp Shakes Ukraine's Parliamentary 'Nobodies,'" *Financial Times*, August 2, 2019, https://www.ft.com/content/875eeb76-b47c-11e9-bec9-fdcab53d6959.

"Ruslan Stefanchuk": "'Servant of the People' Will Change Its Ideology to Something between Liberal and Socialist," *Ukrainska Pravda*, November 10, 2019, https://www.pravda.com.ua/news/2019/11/10/7231552/.

"in the new government": The ambitious promises made by Prime Minister Oleksiy Honcharuk are reported in "Ukraine's New Government Unveils Ambitious Five-Year Development Plan," Radio Free Europe / Radio Liberty, October 1, 2019, https://www.rferl.org/a/ukraine-new-government-unveils-ambitious-five-year-development-plan/30192662.html.

"a layman": Oleksiy Sorokin, "Prime Minister Honcharuk Targeted in Latest Audio Leak," *Kyiv Post*, January 16, 2020, https://archive.kyivpost.com/ukraine-politics/prime-minister-honcharuk-targeted-in-latest-audio-leak.html.

"until we create the ideal government": "We Will Change Ministers until We Create an 'Ideal Government'—Zelensky," *New Voice*, April 22, 2020, https://nv.ua/ukr/ukraine/politics/zelenskiy-hoche-stvoriti-idealna-derzhava-novini-ukrajini-50083705.html.

"Kravchuk and Fokin": "President Assessed the Presence of Kravchuk and Fokin in the Negotiations on Donbas," *Ukrinform*, August 22, 2020, https://www.ukrinform.ua/rubric-polytics/3085884-prezident-dav-ocinku-prisutnosti-kravcuka-i-fokina-u-peremovinah-po-donbasu.html.

"sixth sense": Svyatoslav Piskun, quoted in my essay for the Atlantic Council, "Zelensky's Old New Faces," August 11, 2020, https://www.atlanticcouncil.org/blogs/ukrainealert/zelenskyys-old-new-faces/.

Vladimir Putin, "On the Historical Unity of Russians and Ukrainians," July 12, 2021, http://en.kremlin.ru/events/president/news/66181.

Chapter Seven. The War President

Vladimir Putin, "On the Historical Unity of Russians and Ukrainians," July 12, 2021, http://en.kremlin.ru/events/president/news/66181.

"We are here!": "In Video, a Defiant President Zelinsky Says, 'We Are Here,'" *New York Times*, February 25, 2022, https://www.nytimes.com/2022/02/25/world/europe/zelensky-speech-video.html.

"We understand the historic mission": Mikhail Piotrovsky's interview with *Rossiyskaya Gazeta*, discussed in Sophia Kishkovsky, "'No One Can Interfere with Our Offensive': Hermitage Director Mikail Piotrovsky Compares Russian Export of Culture to Country's 'Operation' in Ukraine," *Art Newspaper*, June 24,

2022, https://www.theartnewspaper.com/2022/06/24/no-one-can-interfere-with-our-offensive-hermitage-director-mikhail-piotrovsky-compares-russian-export-of-culture-to-countrys-operation-in-ukraine.

"It has become our lot": Andrew Roth, "Putin Compares Himself to Peter the Great in Quest to Take Back Russian Lands," *Guardian*, June 10, 2022, https://www.theguardian.com/world/2022/jun/10/putin-compares-himself-to-peter-the-great-in-quest-to-take-back-russian-lands.

"the greatest geopolitical setback": Peter Dickinson, "Putin Suffers Humiliating Defeat as Russia Announces Kherson Retreat," Atlantic Council, November 9, 2022, https://www.atlanticcouncil.org/blogs/ukrainealert/putin-faces-humiliating-defeat-as-russia-announces-kherson-retreat/.

"genocide does not necessarily mean": "Raphael Lemkin Defines Genocide," Genocide Watch, March 14, 2013, http://genocidewatch.net/2013/03/14/raphael-lemkin-defines-genocide-2/.

Freedom House report: Emily Couch, "In Postwar Ukraine, Democratic Development and Cultural Restoration Will Go Hand in Hand," Freedom House, October 27, 2022, https://freedomhouse.org/article/postwar-ukraine-democratic-development-and-cultural-restoration-will-go-hand-hand.

"Ukrainian officers describe": Aleksandra Klitina, "Ukraine Army Commander Valery Zaluzhny: Time to Erase 'Soviet Thinking,'" *Kyiv Post*, May 30, 2022, https://www.kyivpost.com/post/6626.

"The Russians don't empower their soldiers": Former defense minister Andriy Zahorodnyuk, quoted in Elliott Ackerman, "Ukraine's Three-to-One Advantage," *Atlantic*, March 2022, https://www.theatlantic.com/ideas/archive/2022/03/american-volunteer-foreign-fighters-ukraine-russia-war/627604/.

T. X. Hammes, "Game-Changers: Implications of the Russo-Ukraine War for the Future of Ground Warfare," Atlantic Council, April 3, 2023, https://www.atlanticcouncil.org/in-depth-research-reports/issue-brief/game-changers-implications-of-the-russo-ukraine-war-for-the-future-of-ground-warfare/.

"comprehensive understanding of the battle space": Ibid.

Chapter Eight. The Future of Ukraine

a quarter billion US dollars by October 2023, according to the Kiel Institute for the World Economy: Kiel Institute for the World Economy, Ukraine Support Tracker, https://www.ifw-kiel.de/topics/war-against-ukraine/ukraine-support-tracker/.

General Zaluzhny articulated a radical rethink of how the war is to be conducted: "Ukraine's Commander-in-Chief on the Breakthrough He Needs to Beat Russia," *The Economist*, November 1, 2023, https://www.economist.com/europe/2023/11/01/ukraines-commander-in-chief-on-the-breakthrough-he-needs-to-beat-russia.

U.S. and European leaders were increasingly open to the idea of seizing and using *over $300 billion in Russian hard currency reserves:* David E. Sanger and Alan Rappeport, "U.S. and Europe Eye Russian Assets to Aid Ukraine as Funding Dries Up," *New York Times*, December 21, 2023, https://www.nytimes.com/2023/12/21/us/politics/russian-assets-ukraine.html.

Sources and Readings

This is a guide to the sources I relied on in the writing of this volume. It is also a guide to reliable sources for readers who seek a deeper understanding of the history of modern Ukraine and Ukrainians. I have selected the works, some available only in Ukrainian, that were most important in shaping my understanding of Ukraine.

As background to this book, which focuses solely on contemporary Ukraine, readers will benefit from the following works:

Serhiy Plokhy's *Gates of Europe* (New York: Basic Books, 2015) is quite simply the best and most judiciously articulated short history of Ukraine and Ukrainians from their origins to the twenty-first century. It provides a brief but sophisticated explication of the genesis of the Ukrainian nation and of the states and proto-states that were antecedents to the sovereign Ukraine that emerged in 1991.

One of the preeminent historians of the many nations that have lived on Ukrainian soil is Paul Robert Magocsi, whose *A History of Ukraine: The Land and Its Peoples*, 2nd ed. (Toronto: University of Toronto Press, 2010), is an essential guide to the histories of the various nationalities that have coexisted on Ukrainian soil.

Anne Applebaum's *Red Famine: Stalin's War on Ukraine* (New York: Doubleday, 2017) retraces the death of some 4 million Ukrainians in 1932–33 as a result of the Holodomor, Stalin's forced famine. The book is the most thorough study of a horror that is a central component of Ukraine's national identity.

Myroslav Shkahndrij's *Ukrainian Nationalism: Politics, Ideology, and Literature: 1929–1956* (New Haven: Yale University Press, 2015) is a reasoned volume on the phenomenon of the Ukrainian nationalist right, which looms so large in today's Russian deceptive propaganda against Ukraine.

Michael Browne, ed., *Ferment in Ukraine* (Boulder: Praeger, 1971), is a compilation of documents on the persecution of Ukrainian dissidents during the Brezhnev era. It conveys the atmosphere of state persecution through underground dissident chronicles, legal documents, and Soviet prosecutorial documents, offering a picture of the courageous but limited phenomenon of post-Stalin-era dissent in Ukraine.

Paul Robert Magocsi and Yohanan Petrovsky-Shtern's *Jews and Ukrainians: A Millennium of Co-existence* (Toronto: Ukrainian Jewish Encounter, distributed by the University of Toronto Press, 2016), an encyclopedic set of thematic essays about the interrelationship of Jews and Ukrainians, serves as a strong source on the history of two peoples that have left a deep imprint on the emergence and evolution of Ukraine.

Mykhaylo Minakov, Georgiy Kasianov, and Matthew Rojansky are the editors of *From "the Ukraine" to Ukraine: A Contemporary History, 1991–2021* (Stuttgart: Ibidem, 2021), a volume that gathers essays from over twenty leading scholars who examine the country's politics, economics, social trends, and cultural developments in a series of overview essays.

The richest source of granular reporting on Ukraine since the Kuchma presidency is *Ukrainska Pravda* (www.pravda.com.ua), founded by the murdered investigative journalist Heorhiy Gongadze. Its comprehensive digital archive, which reaches back to May 2000, provides access to tens of thousands of articles, and in recent years its daily output yields dozens of detailed news reports and a large number of longer analytic articles, profiles, and interviews that make it a treasure trove of information that was heavily mined in the preparation of this book.

The two best sources in Ukrainian on the evolution of Ukrainian public attitudes are the online archives of two polling companies, the Kyiv International Institute of Sociology and the Democratic Initiatives Foundation. Both provide extensive samplings of public attitudes toward politics, national security, and national identity.

Radio Free Europe Research has produced deep and detailed reporting and analysis on Ukraine in English since 1991 and has been an important source for most of the chapters in this book.

NV.UA, which is under a paywall for much of its Russian- and Ukrainian-language content, offers strong investigative reporting, deep dives, and important profiles of leading figures from politics, finance, culture, and civic life. In 2022 NV launched an English-language service. Some of its reporting is republished by Yahoo News.

The *Kyiv Independent* is a go-to resource for daily reporting and analysis on Ukrainian politics and the war. See www.kyivindependent.com.

Since its launch in 2014, the Atlantic Council's *Ukraine Alert* has been an excellent source of analysis on national security, foreign policy, and domestic reform issues. It has benefited from a sequence of strong editors, Iryna Chalupa, James Rupert, Melinda Haring, and most recently Peter Dickinson. While the *Alert* has occasionally become a place of contestation among Ukrainian political actors—especially on the eve of election cycles—it is strongest when it covers issues of Ukrainian policy, Ukraine-Russia relations, and military and national security issues. The in-depth research papers of the council's Eurasia Center offer insights on the economy and national security.

Freedom House's annual *Survey of Freedom in the World* is a reliable source for understanding civil liberties and political rights trends. Its *Nations in Transit*—a research project I developed in 1995 that is now in its third decade—is invaluable for its detailed annual overview essays and for its evaluation of developments in electoral politics, civil society, the media, and governance. The study is used as an indicator of progress by the U.S. Agency for International Development. Both these annual studies are accessible at www.freedomhouse.org.

The Jamestown Foundation website (www.jamestown.org) is a reliable source for assessments of Ukraine's foreign policy, national security, and energy-related matters. As have I, readers will benefit from the wisdom of their outstanding analysts Margarita Assenova and Vlad Socor.

The Dixi Group (www.dixigroup.org) is the go-to source for Ukraine's energy politics.

Chapter One. A New State

Bohdan Nahaylo's *The Ukrainian Resurgence* (London: C. Hurst, 1999) is an authoritative in-depth study of the movement toward Ukrainian independence and the early years of the state under Presidents Kravchuk and Kuchma.

For an eyewitness sense of the civic, national, and political forces that led to the disintegration of the USSR, in particular the forces and processes behind the emergence of an independent Ukraine, I am perhaps biased in referring readers to *The Hidden Nations: The People Challenge the Soviet Union* (New York: Morrow, 1990), a book I coauthored with Nadia Diuk.

Nadia Diuk and I also cowrote *New Nations Rising* (New York: John Wiley and Sons, 1993), which tells the story of the dissolution of the USSR to the emergence and first years of Ukraine and the other independent states that replaced the Soviet imperial state.

Uri Ra'anan and Kate Martin, eds., *Russia's Return to Imperialism* (New York: St. Martin's, 1997), is a helpful source for Russia's evolving discourse on empire after the breakup of the Soviet Union. It offers important insights into neo-imperial discourse well before the emergence of Vladimir Putin and includes my essay on Russia's relations with the "nearest abroad."

The *Ukrainian Weekly*, an English-language periodical published in the United States, is an important source of information about the emergence of early Ukraine, largely through the eyewitness reporting of its Kyiv correspondent, Marta Kolomayets.

Sherman W. Garnett's *Keystone in the Arch: Ukraine in the Emerging Security Environment in Central and Eastern Europe* (Washington, DC: Carnegie Endowment for International Peace, 1997) offers a concise statement of Ukraine's strategic importance and its early foreign policy with special focus on the Ukraine-Russia relationship.

Alexander Motyl's *Dilemmas of Independence: Ukraine after Totalitarianism* (New York: Council on Foreign Relations Press, 1993) is an important early consideration of Ukraine's foreign and domestic policies.

Taras Kuzio and Andrew Wilson's *Ukraine: Perestroika to Independence* (Edmonton: Canadian Institute of Ukrainian Studies Press, 1994) was a valuable resource for my discussion of the movement of Ukraine's civic forces and elites toward the ideas of statehood and sovereignty.

Chapter Two. Money and Power

Anders Aslund's *How Ukraine Became a Market Economy and Democracy* (Washington, DC: Peterson Institute, 2009) is an invaluable source on the then fragile country's political development as well as a masterful history of the Kuchma presidency and the Yushchenko years from an economist who advised Ukraine's leaders on reforms. It contains a detailed accounting of the emergence of oligarchs in Ukraine's political and economic life and is an authoritative volume on the forces driving the economy and politics in the period 1991 to 2008.

Mykola Ryabchuk's *Zona Vidchuzhennya* (Kyiv: Krytyka, 2004) examines Ukraine's oligarchs' relationships to their country and Russia and includes a detailed assessment of the Kuchma presidency.

I benefited greatly from Serhiy Leshchenko's excellent *Amerykanska Saha Pavla Lazarenka* (Lviv: Yi and Istorychna Pravda, 2013), which covers the former prime minister's criminal case in the United States but is equally an excellent source on his numerous corrupt schemes and role in the Ukrainian political landscape.

Beheaded: The Killing of a Journalist (Reading, UK: Artemia, 2003) by J. V. Koshiw is a deep dive into the abduction and murder of investigative journalist Heorhiy Gongadze. It provides insights into the crusader journalist's life, the circumstances of his disappearance, the evidence implicating Kuchma, the Kuchmagate tape scandal, and a detailed account of numerous efforts by Ukrainian officials to cover up the crime. It contains an invaluable journalistic account of the state of Ukraine's government institutions as well as the resilience of civil society during the Kuchma years.

Discussion of Kuchmagate, the Gongadze case, the Kolchuga scandal, and Kuchma's relations with the oligarchs is informed by my essay "Meltdown in Ukraine," *Foreign Affairs*, May/June 2001.

Leonid Kuchma's apologia *Ukraina—ne Rossiya* [Ukraine Is Not Russia] (Moscow: Vremya, 2003) is an important source of the president's thinking about Ukrainian geopolitics and Ukrainian-Russian relations, written both for his own citizens and for Russian readers.

An important source on Kuchma-era media controls is Vakhtang Kipiani, ed., *Vlada T'my i Temnykiv* (Lviv: Prosvita, 2005). The volume contains detailed documentation of state-generated "theme directives" to the media as well as details about the implementation of media controls by Kuchma's top aide Viktor Medvedchuk.

Chapter Three. Yushchenko

Askold Krushelnycky's *An Orange Revolution* (London: Harvil Secker, 2006) is a deeply personal chronicle of a British journalist's experience of Ukraine before and during the mass democracy protests that made front-page headlines in 2004.

Anders Aslund and Michael McFaul, eds., *Revolution in Orange* (Washington, DC: Carnegie Endowment for International Peace, 2006) consists of essays that help explain the phenomena and forces that brought Viktor Yushchenko to power and protected Ukraine's fragile democracy from electoral fraud and an authoritarian revanche.

Mykola Ryabchuk's *Ulyublenyy Pistolet Pani Simpson* (Kyiv: K.I.S., 2009) is a reliable chronicle of the successes and failures of the Yushchenko years.

The chapter also borrows significantly from my writing on Yushchenko and the Orange Revolution for *Foreign Affairs* and the *Wall Street Journal*.

Chapter Four. A Thug in Power

Serhiy Leshchenko's *Mezhyhirskyy Syndrom: Diahnoz Vladi Viktora Yanukovycha* (Kyiv: Brayt Buks, 2014) offers detailed documentation and understanding of the corruption at the heart of the Yanukovych presidency, with important insights into the history of Ukraine's key oligarchs.

Alexander Motyl's *Ukraine vs. Russia: Selected Articles and Blogs, 2010–2016* (Washington, DC: Westphalia, 2017) is a scabrous laceration of the Yanukovych regime and an insightful set of considerations of Russia's project to annex and fragment Ukraine, written for *Foreign Affairs*, the *Wall Street Journal*, the *World Affairs Journal*, and the Atlantic Council.

Andrew Wilson's *The Ukrainians: The Unexpected Nation*, 4th ed. (New Haven: Yale University Press, 2015) despite its inapt title, is an excellent resource on modern-day Ukraine's history and offers detailed analysis of the Yushchenko presidency and a perceptive chapter on the Yanukovych period.

Sonia Koshkina's oral history *Maidan: Nerozkazana Istoriya* (Kyiv: Brayt Star, 2015) is an important resource on the perspective of participants in the struggle that unseated Ukraine's president Viktor Yanukovych. It is also a valuable compendium on politics, human rights, and society during the Yanukovych presidency.

Chapter Five. The Poroshenko Presidency and the Foundations of the Patriotic State

The Ukrainian Crisis Media Center (www.uacrisis.org), established by Maidan activists and Ukrainian public relations specialists, is an important venue with a rich library of press briefings, panel discussions, and research projects. It has become a major source of independent research on Russia's hybrid war on Ukraine as well as an excellent resource monitoring Russian state propaganda related to Ukraine.

The best coverage of the Poroshenko presidency can be culled from the excellent reporting of *Ukrainska Pravda* (www.pravda.com.ua) and the *Dzerkalo Tyzhnya* (www.dt.ua) and *Novoye Vremya* (www.nv.ua) weeklies and websites.

David Marples, ed., *The War in Ukraine's Donbas* (Prague: Central European University Press, 2022), was a helpful resource in my discussions of Russia's hybrid war. It offers important insights into the human consequences of war in Eastern Ukraine, and on life and governance in the occupied areas of Donetsk and Luhansk.

Lawrence Freedman's *Ukraine and the Art of Strategy* (New York: Oxford University Press, 2019) is incisive on Putin's evolving efforts to assert control over Ukraine and the Western response to the Russian challenge after the seizing of Crimea and the launching of the 2014 war in the Donbas.

The most thoughtful assessment of Russia's hybrid war in Ukraine is *Svitova Hibrydna Viyna: Ukrains'kyy Front* (Kharkiv: Folio, 2017), edited and supervised by Volodymyr Horbulin, one of Ukraine's most important strategic thinkers. The book is especially strong on the economic and national security challenges Ukraine faced during the Poroshenko years. An abbreviated English-language edition was published as *The World Hybrid War: Ukrainian Forefront* (Kharkiv: Folio, 2017).

Mykhaylo Wynnyckyj's *Ukraine's Maidan, Russia's War* (Stuttgart: Ibidem, 2019) focuses primarily on the Poroshenko years and is especially strong in its analysis of Ukraine's civil society and volunteerism. The author's discussion of the phenomenon of heterarchy in a variety of papers and presentations has been invaluable in my own thinking about how the country has been able to preserve its democratic culture despite the ambitions of authoritarian politicians, Russian fifth columns, and a powerful oligarchy.

Vladislav Davidzon's *From Odessa with Love: Political and Literary Essays from Post-Soviet Ukraine* (Washington, DC: Academia, 2021) is an excellent compilation of reporting from Ukraine during the Poroshenko years. The author's writing for *Tablet* and *Foreign Policy* has also been a valuable resource on events in Ukraine from 2015 to Russia's expanded war.

Taras Kuzio's *Putin's War against Ukraine* (Toronto: Chair of Ukrainian Studies, University of Toronto, 2017) is a comprehensive resource on developments from Russia's attack on Ukraine through 2016, and has extensive considerations of the precursors to Russia's aggression during the presidency of Yanukovych, Russian imperialism, and the impact of Putin's military aggression on Ukrainian national identity in the Poroshenko years.

The life of the Maidan and the rise of a dynamic civil society is reflected in Marcy Shore's *The Ukrainian Night: An Intimate History of Revolution* (New Haven: Yale University Press, 2017). The book is a deeply personal account of interactions with Ukrainian civic and political activists and conveys a sense of the turbulent rise of an influential civil society in 2014–15.

The chapter benefited significantly from a seminal study by economist Ihor Burakovsky and the Institute of Economic Research: *Ukraine's Fight against Corruption: The Economic Front* (Kyiv: IER, 2018), available on the Institute's website (http://www.ier.com.ua/files/publications/Policy_papers/IER/2018/Anti corruption_Report_EN.pdf).

In Wartime: Stories from Ukraine by Tim Judah (New York: Tim Duggan Books, 2015) offers compelling journalism on the 2014–15 war in Eastern Ukraine as well as the details of Russia's effort to build a separatist "Novorossiya" from the Donbas across the Ukrainian Black Sea littoral to Bessarabia on the Moldovan border.

David Patrikarakos's *War in 140 Characters: How Social Media Is Reshaping Conflict in the Twenty-First Century* (New York: Basic Books, 2017) includes excellent war reporting from Ukraine, 2014–17, and offers an important perspective on propaganda and social media as a part of hybrid warfare.

Natalia Ryabynski's *Ukraine's Post-Communist Mass Media: Between Capture and Commercialization* (Stuttgart: Ibidem, 2017) was a helpful source for insights into the interplay between oligarchy, the state, and the media.

Alexander Motyl's and my articles for foreignaffairs.com, "Ukraine's Promising Path to Reform," July 16, 2018, and "How Western Anticorruption Policy Is Failing Ukraine," May 29, 2018, summarize and evaluate both the successes and failures of anti-corruption policies during the Poroshenko presidency.

Chapter Six. Volodymyr Zelensky

As this chapter covers less than half of Zelensky's term in office, most of the sources come from the reputable news and analytic sites mentioned among the general sources above.

Helpful analysis of energy politics in the Zelensky years has come from Andrian Prokip's research for the Kennan Institute.

There has been a slew of books on Ukraine's president since the Russian war on Ukraine began, with much of their focus on the early part of the Zelensky presidency. Most are superficial and lack analytic rigor. Two exceptions are the recent *The Zelensky Effect*, by Olga Onuch and Henry Hale (New York: Oxford University Press, 2023), which contains detailed information on evolving Ukrainian attitudes and the emergence of a civic national identity, and Iulia Mendel's *The Fight of Our Lives: My Time with Zelensky, Ukraine's Battle for Democracy, and What It Means for the World* (New York: Simon and Schuster, 2022), which effectively conveys Zelensky's personality and offers a closely observed view of his inner circle.

Chapter Seven. The War President

The excellent daily analysis of the Institute for the Study of War was and remains an essential resource for the ebb and flow of the war (www.isw.org).

Equally important is the work of the Kyiv School of Economics and its think tank, whose assessments of the economic impacts of the war and its tracking of the destruction caused by Russia's aggression were important sources for this chapter. See https://kse.ua/kse-department/kse-institute/.

I have relied on the outstanding front-line reporting of the *Wall Street Journal*, *New York Times*, and *Financial Times*. Especially excellent has been the reporting of Yaroslav Trofimov and James Marson of the *Wall Street Journal* and Roman Olearchyk of the *Financial Times* and war reporting from David Patrikarakos for *Unherd* and Ihor Ponomarenko of the *Kyiv Independent*.

Alexander Motyl's writing on Ukraine for the *Hill*, the website *1945*, and *Politico* offers sophisticated examinations of Russia and Russian propaganda under Putin, Ukrainian resistance to Russia's aggression, and the follies of "realist" responses to Russian aggression.

Luke Harding's *Invasion: The Inside Story of Russia's Bloody War and Ukraine's Fight for Survival* (New York: Vintage, 2022) provides significant details about the first months of the Russian invasion of 2022. It is especially powerful as a source on Russian war crimes and atrocities and on the resistance and resilience of ordinary citizens.

Serhiy Plokhy's *The Russo-Ukrainian War* (New York: Norton: 2023) is an important first attempt at explaining and depicting Russia's aggression, written by the twenty-first century's preeminent historian of Ukraine.

Serhiy Kudelia's essay "The Ukrainian State under Russian Aggression," *Current History*, October 2022, examines the sources of Ukrainian state capacity, resilience, and national unity, important themes in this chapter.

The *Washington Post* has provided detailed coverage of U.S. and Western policy in the run-up to the war through excellent reporting by Karen DeYoung, Isabelle Khurshudyan, Shane Harris, Paul Sonne, and Liz Sly. Khurshudyan and Sonne, in particular, have been exceptional reporters in their coverage of the war.

Chapter Eight. The Future of Ukraine

For a good source on the state of Ukraine's economy in 2023 and projections for 2024, see "Ukraine GDP to Rebound in 2023, Inflation to Fall—EU Commission," Reuters, November 15, 2023, https://www.reuters.com/markets/europe/ukraine-gdp-rebound-2023-inflation-fall-eu-commission-2023-11-15/.

Discussion of battleground shifts amid Ukraine's counteroffensive comes from a range of analytic and news sources, including Josh Holder, "Who's Gaining Ground in Ukraine? This Year, No One," *New York Times*, September 28, 2023, https://www.nytimes.com/interactive/2023/09/28/world/europe/russia-ukraine-war-map-front-line.html.

Acknowledgments

I AM GRATEFUL FOR the advice, counsel, and encouragement of a wide range of colleagues, associates, and family members. This is a long list and it represents discussions, the sharing of insights, and joint travel to and within Ukraine.

It was Harvard historian Serhiy Plokhy who suggested I write a history of Ukraine since 1991 that would give significant weight to each of its periods and would be written not from the perspective of the most recent dramatic events but instead would synthesize all the complex processes that have contributed to the shaping of a new state and nation.

Many thanks to Marin Strmecki and Nadia Schadlow of the Smith Richardson Foundation, whose patience and belief in this project in its several incarnations gave me the resources to support travel, research, and the time to write.

Special thanks to Vladyslav Davidzon, Myroslava Gongadze, and especially Ihor Hryniv and Alexander Motyl for frequent and lengthy discussions that have helped shape my understanding of events in Ukraine. Most of all, I benefited from the wisdom and insights of my late ex-wife Nadia Diuk, with whom I coauthored two books and who throughout her life was an important sounding board and source of knowledge.

The Atlantic Council has been a hospitable home since 2006, when we launched a comprehensive Ukraine program. I have been grateful for the support there of President Fred Kempe, Fran Burwell, Shelby Magid, Peter Dickinson, Ambassador Daniel Fried,

Anders Aslund, Natalie Jaresko, and Damon Wilson (who now heads up the National Endowment for Democracy). Special thanks to Melinda Haring, who helped improve my first drafts and urged me on amid the COVID funk. Above all, an emphatic *gracias* to Ambassador John Herbst, a great colleague and an important sounding board.

Others in North America and Europe who have helped me hone my views on modern-day Ukraine include Ariel Cohen, Andrew Frank, Chrystia Freeland, Paul Grod, Archbishop Borys Gudziak, Lenna Koszarny, Taras Kuzio, Bernard-Henri Levy, Orysia Lutsevych, Andrew Mac, Paul Robert Magocsi, Regina Maryanovskya-Davidzon, Matteo Mecacci, the late Mary Mycio, Arch Puddington, Max Pyziur, Ambassador Bill Taylor, Ambassador Roman Waschuk, Peter Zalmayev, Hilary Zarycky, and Walter Zaryckyj.

During many visits to Ukraine, my guides to developments in domestic politics, national security, and defense have included Taras Berezovets, Valery Chalyy, Anton Drobovych, Alyona Getmanchuk, Katya Gorchinskaya, Serhiy Gusovsky, Anton Herashchenko, Volodyrmyr Horbulin, Ludmila and Vladyslav Hrynevych, General Vasyl Hrytsak, Evgeniy Kiselyov, Ivanna Klympush-Tsintsadze, Danylo Lubkivsky, Oleh Medvedev, Hryhoriy and Ludmila Nemyria, Ihor Novikov, Volodymyr Paniotto, Rostyslav Pavlenko, Viktor Pinchuk, Vitaliy Portnikov, Serhiy Rakhmanin, Natalia Stelmashchuk, Boris Tarasyuk, Volodymyr Viatrovich, Yuri Vitrenko, Jock Mendoza Wilson, Danylo Yanevsky, Arseniy Yatsenyuk, Yaroslaw Yurchyshyn, Kateryna Yushchenko, and Andriy Zahorodnyuk. My ongoing conversations in Ukraine about matters economic have been assisted by the insights and counsel of Tymofiy Mylovanov, Natalia Shapoval, Yulia Kovaliv, and Dmytro Sologub, formerly of the National Bank of Ukraine.

Colleagues at the Ukrainian Jewish Encounter have been an important source of encouragement and support as well as of insights into Ukraine's discourse about its past. They include Alti Rodal, Wolf Moskovich, Natalia Feduschak, Raya Shadursky, and above all my close friend Berel Rodal.

Thanks to my editors, including James Taranto of the *Wall Street Journal*, Stephanie Giry, formerly at the *New York Times*, the late Fred Hiatt and the op-ed team at the *Washington Post*, and *Foreign Policy*'s

Stefan Thiel. Thanks too to a range of editors at *Foreign Affairs*, who commissioned pieces that allowed me to trace the new Ukrainian state's evolution. Over the years these have included James Hoge, Fareed Zakaria, and Gideon Rose. All have been important interlocutors who helped sharpen my thinking on Ukraine.

My work has benefited from the longtime support and encouragement of a good friend, James Temerty, president of the Temerty Family Foundation and one of the principal charitable supporters of a range of civic, educational, and health-care initiatives in Ukraine. My thanks too for conversations with Carl Gershman, the former president of the National Endowment for Democracy, and journalists Neil Buckley, David Frum, Franklin Foer, and Roman Olearchyk. All have been important interlocutors.

Much thanks as well for the team at Yale University Press: especially Jaya Chatterjee, who took on the book, Amanda Gerstenfeld, and Joyce Ippolito.

For the last fifteen years, my colleague and right hand in Kyiv, Myroslava Luzina, a lawyer and MBA by training, has helped build a network of relationships essential to my ability to engage with the broad range of individuals who have shaped modern Ukraine. Her collegiality, deep knowledge, and assistance have been essential in the writing and completion of this book.

Finally, my marriage to Natalia Dobrovolska, a native of Kyiv, has given me a new Ukrainian family, connecting me deeply to the events that are herein described. Amid the stress of daughters who returned to Kyiv under attack and a brother at the front, Natalia has been a source of encouragement for the project and of deep insights into historic events and processes she has experienced firsthand.

Index

Page numbers in italics indicate a figure.